The Editor

PHILIP APPLEMAN is Distinguished Professor Emeritus at Indiana University, where he was a founding editor of *Victorian Studies*, national committee chairman for English Section II of the Modern Language Association, and member of the national council of the American Association of University Professors. He is the author of a book on overpopulation, *The Silent Explosion*; coeditor of *1859: Entering an Age of Crisis*; editor of *Darwin: A Norton Critical Edition*, and of the W. W. Norton abridged edition of Charles Darwin's *The Origin of Species*; and author of several award-winning volumes of poetry, including *Darwin's Ark* and *New and Selected Poems: 1956–1996*, as well as three novels, including *Apes and Angels*.

Norton Critical Editions in the History of Ideas

For a complete list of Norton Critical Editions, visit
www.wwnorton.com/college/english/nce

A NORTON CRITICAL EDITION

Thomas Robert Malthus
AN ESSAY ON THE
PRINCIPLE OF POPULATION

INFLUENCES ON MALTHUS
SELECTIONS FROM MALTHUS' WORK
NINETEENTH-CENTURY COMMENT
MALTHUS IN THE TWENTY-FIRST CENTURY

Second Edition

Edited by

PHILIP APPLEMAN
INDIANA UNIVERSITY

W • W • NORTON & COMPANY • *New York* • *London*

W. W. Norton & Company has been independent since its founding in 1923, when William Warder and Mary D. Herter Norton first published lectures delivered at the People's Institute, the adult education division of New York City's Cooper Union. The Nortons soon expanded their program beyond the Institute, publishing books by celebrated academics from America and abroad. By mid-century, the two major pillars of Norton's publishing program—trade books and college texts—were firmly established. In the 1950s, the Norton family transferred control of the company to its employees, and today—with a staff of four hundred and a comparable number of trade, college, and professional titles published each year—W. W. Norton & Company stands as the largest and oldest publishing house owned wholly by its employees.

Manufacturing by the Courier Companies, Inc.
Book design by Antonina Krass.
Production manager: Ben Reynolds.

Library of Congress Cataloging-in-Publication Data

Malthus, T. R. (Thomas Robert), 1766–1834.
  An essay on the principle of population : text, sources and background,
criticism / Thomas Robert Malthus ; edited by Philip Appleman.—2nd ed.
    p. cm.—(A Norton critical edition)
  Includes bibliographical references and index.

  ISBN 0-393-92410-6 (pbk.)

  1. Population. I. Appleman, Philip, 1926– II. Title.

HB861.M36 2003
304.6—dc21   2003048741

W. W. Norton & Company, Inc., 500 Fifth Avenue, New York, N.Y. 10110
www.wwnorton.com

W. W. Norton & Company Ltd., Castle House, 75/76 Wells Street, London
W1T 3QT
1 2 3 4 5 6 7 8 9 0

TO THE MEMORY OF

Gertrude Appleman
Martha Haberkorn

magnae matres

and with love
to Margie

Contents

Preface to the Second Edition

In the preface to the first edition of this book, I observed that an anthology is always a compromise between the richness of the outside world and the meager insides of a book. This new edition, the first one of the twenty-first century, is no exception: the literature of Malthusianism is vast and various, and to try to represent it in a single volume is a frustrating task. I hope that this collection at least indicates some of the more important influences that Malthus' thinking has had, both on his own world and on ours.

Malthus' *Essay on the Principle of Population* is represented here by the 1798 text, plus additional significant passages from his second edition of 1803. I have taken the editorial liberty of modernizing the antique *s*'s and *c*'s of the original and also of deleting a multitude of commas, colons, and semicolons (and inserting a few of my own) to conform to contemporary usage.

I would like to thank all of those who offered various kinds of advice and assistance in the planning of the first edition, and also those who helped me in this new edition: Ronald Bleier, Lynton K. Caldwell, William R. Catton Jr., Antony Flew, Robert Gillispie, H. Scott Gordon, Garrett Hardin, Jay Keller, James R. Kincaid, J. Kenneth Smail, and Michael Wolff. None of them, of course, bears responsibility for any faults remaining in the volume.

Special thanks are due to my editor at W. W. Norton & Company, Carol Bemis, and also to Brian Baker and to James L. Mairs, editor of the first edition.

And I am happy to record once again my gratitude to my wife, Margie, for her acute and creative criticism.

Philip Appleman

Introduction

At the end of each day, the world has over 225,000 more mouths to feed than it had the day before; at the end of every week, 1.5 million more; at the close of each year, an additional 80 million plus. In the world's poorest countries, where population growth is most rapid, the lives of hundreds of millions of people are constantly plagued by hunger and by diseases aggravated by malnutrition. Humankind, which numbered 4.5 billion in the 1980s, is now well over 6 billion and is caught in an ambush of its own making. Economists call it the "Malthusian trap," after the man—Thomas Robert Malthus—who, in his famous essay of 1798, most forcefully stated our grim biological predicament: population growth tends to outstrip the supply of food.

Malthus was born in 1766, in a country house near the town of Dorking, in England, the son of a gentleman who prided himself on his advanced ideas and was an admirer and friend of both Hume and Rousseau. Young Robert (he was never called Thomas) was at first privately educated; then, in 1784, he went up to Jesus College, Cambridge, where he graduated creditably as Ninth Wrangler (an honors degree in mathematics) in 1788. In that same year he took holy orders and later was appointed to a rectory. In livelihood, however, he was less a "parson" (as his detractors have often chosen to call him) than a college professor, for in 1805 he became the first professor of political economy in the English-speaking world, at the new East India College, in Hertfordshire, a post he held until his death in 1834.

Malthus was amiable, gentle, and good-natured—"one of the most serene and cheerful" of men, the contemporary writer Harriet Martineau called him. He was a devoted family man: he married Harriet Eckersall, one of his "pretty cousins," in 1804, and they had three children, two of whom survived to maturity. He was a faithful friend: his correspondence with the economist David Ricardo covered the last dozen years of Ricardo's life in amicable and generous disagreement ("I should not like you more than I do," Ricardo wrote him, "if you agreed in opinion with me"). And Malthus was a prophet of what might be called long-range benevolence: "My ultimate object," he wrote, "is to diminish vice and misery." When he died, he was remembered fondly by his friends, one of whom wrote for his epitaph at Bath Abbey:

> The spotless integrity of his principles,
> The equity and candour of his nature,
> His sweetness of temper, urbanity of manners,
> And tenderness of heart,
> His benevolence and piety,
> Are the still dearer recollections of his family and friends.

Yet this was the man whose social views were immediately and persistently assailed by humanitarians and social reformers all over Europe: "this abominable tenet" (Coleridge); "the dismal science" (Carlyle); "that black and terrible demon that is always ready to stifle the hopes of humanity" (Godwin); "this vile and infamous doctrine, this repulsive blasphemy against man and nature" (Engels). "Unless Mr. Malthus can contrive to starve someone," Hazlitt fumed, "he thinks he does nothing." James Bonar wrote, "He was the 'best-abused man of the age.' For thirty years it rained refutations."[1] And the chorus of disapproval has continued into our own time (pp. 233–246).[2]

It is not difficult to understand this bitter and sustained hostility toward the genial Malthus and his work, for the basic idea he enunciated—that population tends to increase at a faster rate than its food supplies—is indeed an ominous one, and few people are fond of prophets of doom. How did Malthus arrive at such a bleak view of the human condition?

It helps to recall that Malthus grew up during the Enlightenment, was ten years old when the American Revolution began, and came to maturity at the time of the French Revolution. Hume and Rousseau had visited at his father's house when Robert Malthus was a baby, and the dates of his life also overlap those of Voltaire, Diderot, and d'Alembert, as well as Washington, Jefferson, and Franklin. The late eighteenth century was for European nations what the twentieth century was for much of the developing world: on the one hand, a time of economic hardship and social despair; on the other hand, a time of intellectual ferment, of movements for social and political reform, a time of energetic speculation about the possible improvement of societies and of people. Enthusiasm for science ran high; and hopes that science, applied to society, would transform the

1. James Bonar, *Malthus and His Work* (London, 1885), pp. 1–2.
2. Parenthetical page references are to passages in this volume.

world, were reinforced by the recent discoveries of "paradises"—supposedly "perfect" societies—in the South Seas. "Our hopes for the future condition of the human race," wrote Condorcet, "can be subsumed under three important heads: the abolition of inequality between nations, the progress of equality within each nation, and the true perfection of mankind." To these ideals, European intellectuals were giving their sympathetic attention, and often their loyalty. It may have been the worst of times for some people, but it was the best of times for visionaries.

Then in 1789 came the French Revolution, and in its wake regicide, the Reign of Terror, and the savaging of half of Europe by that imperialistic Jacobin, Napoleon Bonaparte. The Directory then governing France was rumored to be planning an invasion of England. British suspicion of French institutions and French intentions, never at that time far below the surface, boiled up in widespread alarm and hostility. In England it was no longer the best of times for social reformers; and yet the infection of "French philosophy" was still there, and determined social critics like William Godwin went on with their work. Godwin's influential *Enquiry concerning Political Justice* appeared in 1793, and in 1797 he issued a collection of essays called *The Enquirer*, in one of which, "Of Avarice and Profusion," he continued his examinations of the "first principles of morality," "justice between man and man," and "the extensive diffusion of liberty and happiness." Robert Malthus and his father read that essay, with far-reaching results.

As it happened, the two men differed on precisely Godwin's question of whether "the extensive diffusion of liberty and happiness" was possible in human affairs. The elder Malthus, true to his progressive ideas, held that it was. Robert disagreed; the reasons for his pessimism were fundamental. He had been reading Hume and Robert Wallace on the question of whether human populations had grown or declined since ancient times (Hume believed they had grown; Wallace, the reverse) and Adam Smith on how the numbers of laborers affect wages ("The demand for men, like that for any other commodity, necessarily regulates the production of men"); and Robert had arrived at a theory of population that, if "certainly not new" (as he said), had just as certainly never been presented as forcefully as he was now to present it. "I mean to place it in a point of view," he wrote, "in some degree different from any that I have hitherto seen"—a remarkable understatement, as it turned out. In his systematic way, he immediately wrote down his thoughts in a manuscript that he titled *An Essay on the Principle of Population, as It Affects the Future Improvement of Society.* He published it anonymously in London in 1798.

2

Parts of what Malthus had to say on his subject were indeed "not new." He had been anticipated in the book of Ecclesiastes by twenty-five hundred years: "When goods increase, they are increased who eat them"; and by thinkers as diverse as Confucius and Plato, who had explored similar notions. More to the point, contemporary social theorists like Hume, Smith, and Benjamin Franklin had shown an awareness of the tendency of populations to increase very rapidly unless somehow "checked." Eighteenth-century thinkers, however, viewed population growth as a mark of social well-being, not as a threat to the "improvement of society." An increase in people was generally taken to imply an increase in wealth. Hume wrote, "Every wise, just and mild government, by rendering the condition of its subjects easy and secure, will always abound most in people, as well as in commodities and riches" (p. 3).

Malthus saw it differently. He began with the awesome redundancy of nature: "Through the animal and vegetable kingdoms," he wrote, "nature has scattered the seeds of life abroad with the most profuse and liberal hand. . . . The germs of life contained in this spot of earth, with ample food and ample room to expand in, would fill millions of worlds in the course of a few thousand years." That observation may not have been "new" with Malthus; but it always *seems* new, simply because it is always, upon contemplation, staggering. And it always gives rise to the inevitable next question: if all organisms have this potential for rapid multiplication, if any single species could, in a comparatively brief time, overrun the earth—why does it not happen?

In *The Wealth of Nations* (1776), Adam Smith had already implied the question and given the answer: "Every species of animals naturally multiplies in proportion to the means of their subsistence, and no species can ever multiply beyond it." Nature, Malthus asserted, "has been comparatively sparing in the room and the nourishment necessary to rear them." "Room," then, is one of Malthus' two ineluctable limitational factors; but his emphasis in the *Essay* falls on the second one: "nourishment." Malthus could not reasonably anticipate (or, as he put it, "The most enthusiastic speculator cannot suppose") an increase in food supply that was greater than arithmetical, each generation. It follows that the tendency of population to multiply, if unchecked by other means, will be checked by "vice and misery"; people will simply (and of course only temporarily) outrun the supply of food. This is the most brutal and final of "positive" checks to population growth.

For Malthus' contemporaries, the immediate force of his argument derived from the quasi-scientific way he chose to illustrate his premises. The former mathematics student could not resist a mathematical illustration: population can increase *geometrically*, whereas agricultural production can only increase *arithmetically*. He wrote:

> Taking the population of the world at any number, a thousand millions, for instance, the human species would increase in the ratio of—1, 2, 4, 8, 16, 32, 64, 128, 256, 512, &c. and subsistence as—1, 2, 3, 4, 5, 6, 7, 8, 9, 10, &c. In two centuries and a quarter, the population would be to the means of subsistence as 512 to 10, in three centuries as 4096 to 13, and in two thousand years the difference would be almost incalculable [p. 23].

It was a persuasive illustration, partly because of its stark simplicity and partly because the first half of it—the geometric power of population increase—is true on its face: the reproductive potential of any plant or animal species verifies it. (Charles Darwin and Alfred Russel Wallace, impressed with Malthus' argument, found in it the key to the theory of natural selection; see p. 154.) The other half—the arithmetical maximum for agricultural production—was a conjecture rather than an observation, and its history is more complicated. It certainly seemed a safe supposition when Malthus wrote his essay; to imagine agricultural production increasing even by arithmetic progression each generation, given the farming methods of the eighteenth century, seemed generous. Malthus tried always to be empirical, which is why he steadily took issue with the Utopians of his time. The *Essay* persistently appeals to experience:

> —We shall be assisted in our review by what we daily see around us, by actual experience, by facts that come within the scope of every man's observation.
> —Such establishments and calculations may appear very promising upon paper, but when applied to real life they will be found to be absolutely nugatory.
> —How little Mr. Godwin has turned the attention of his penetrating mind to the real state of man on earth will sufficiently appear . . .

And so on, throughout the *Essay*.

Ironically, when he came to the crux of his own argument, Malthus himself had to speculate. No better than others at foreseeing the future, he extrapolated from the best evidence he had, which was the agricultural practice of the late eighteenth century. The steam engine had been invented in that eventful year 1776, but it was not yet apparent in 1798 that the emerging shift from muscle power to machine power would revolutionize agriculture, making possible unprecedented increases in food supplies. (The application of mod-

ern biochemistry and genetics to agriculture was of course still further in the future and even less conceivable in Malthus' time.) When
this began to happen, in the course of the nineteenth century, Malthus' celebrated ratios seemed to be discredited; and by the early
twentieth century (as people of the industrialized countries increasingly chose to have smaller families), when someone spoke of the
"population problem," he was as likely to mean the threat of under-
population ("race suicide," it was often called) as of overpopulation.
Malthus' fears then seemed distant and groundless. But after World
War II, when death rates in many of the developing countries were
abruptly reduced to the levels of the industrialized countries, population growth rates shot up, and Malthus' handwriting once again
appeared, clear and portentous, on the wall.[3]

Today, even in the face of a Malthusian crisis of vast proportions,
people in the West tend to remain the philosophical heirs of the
eighteenth- and nineteenth-century prophets of Progress. Inclined
to be problem solvers, they pattern the future on the success of the
recent past. And yet, the rapidly increasing food production of the
last two centuries may be as misleading a guide as was the relatively
static situation in Malthus' time. Many people are now becoming
uneasy about our reliance on agricultural and industrial technologies, which often have hidden, sometimes devastating costs. Accelerated agricultural productivity has become the norm for a modern
society; however, it may be a splendid but temporary luxury, a historical aberration. For it is increasingly clear that the necessity of
supplying food to very large and rapidly growing populations has pollution and resource-depletion effects that are more imminent and
far more destructive than they would be in a less densely populated
world. For example, the large amounts of pesticides and herbicides
that are required to protect high crop yields in Sri Lanka or Indonesia, so that larger and larger populations can be supported there,
are inevitably being carried down to the sea, with toxic effects, often
widespread and persistent, on the living resources of the ocean. So
the short-range gain in rice will be paid for by a long-range loss of
much of the world's supply of protein-rich sea food. And the spectacular productivity of American agriculture is based on methods

3. Although he did not foresee the great increases in food production of the nineteenth and
twentieth centuries, Malthus believed that his theory allowed for such a possibility without
loss of force. See, e.g., his letter to Nassau Senior, dated March 23, 1829: "The meaning
which I intended to convey . . . was, that population was always ready, and inclined, to
increase faster than food, if the checks which repressed it were removed; and that though
these checks might be such as to prevent population from advancing upon subsistence,
or even to keep it at a greater distance behind; yet, that whether population were *actually*
increasing faster than food, or food faster than population, it was true that, except in new
colonies, favorably circumstanced, population was always pressing against food, and was
always ready to start off at a faster rate than that at which the food was actually increasing."
(See Nassau W. Senior, *Selected Writings on Economics* [New York, 1966], p. 61.)

that demand such massive investments of fossil fuels and machinery that the energy required to produce some foods has long since become greater than the energy obtained from them.[4]

Thus, even with the "green revolution" fresh in our memories, Malthus' speculation about agriculture seems less mistaken these days than it once did. The validity of Malthus' argument depends, after all, not on the mathematical accuracy of his two ratios, but on their long-range relation to each other. And if Malthus was right— if population growth does, in the long run, have a tendency to out-strip food supplies—what, then, could he have hoped for by way of "the future improvement of society"? The answer is that, as of 1798, he saw no real hope for permanent improvement, because he thought of the ratios as representing a law of nature as immutable as Newton's; and he saw no effective way of averting the grim con-sequences of that law. In Malthus' time, after all, there were only the crudest and most barbarous kinds of birth control: undependable methods of contraception or abortion by shockingly dangerous self-induced means or infanticide. To Malthus all of these were unacceptable on moral grounds, and they therefore played no part in his first *Essay*[5]—which means that he was left without any prac-ticable options, any effective way of preventing that excessive growth of population that is decreed by the redundancy of nature. So, he wrote, "This argument appears to be conclusive . . . against any marked and striking change for the better . . . [against] any great and decided amelioration of the condition of the lower classes of man-kind."

That is almost how he left it at the end of his first *Essay* in 1798— but not quite. Despite the relentless logic that drove him to this gloomy judgment, he apparently could not feel comfortable in a con-clusion that seemed to recommend only an inhumane and fatalistic acquiescence in human misery. Malthus therefore recommended policies that would help alleviate human suffering: land reform, the transfer of laborers from luxury manufactures to farming, and a shift of national emphasis from foreign trade to agriculture.

Still, his conclusion was undeniably "melancholy," as he himself called it, and in his preface he apologizes for that, pleading "that he has drawn these dark tints from a conviction that they are really in the picture, and not from a jaundiced eye." He would have been pleased, he says, to believe the optimistic visions of a Godwin or a

4. See, e.g., Eric Hirst, "Food-Related Energy Requirements." *Science*, 184 (1974), 134–38.
5. When in 1822 Francis Place suggested contraception as a remedy for overpopulation, he felt obliged to put it in the most circumspect and defensive terms (p. 139), and for more than a century thereafter, those who publicly advocated birth control risked imprisonment. Ironically, although Malthus himself disapproved of birth control, contraceptives were often called "Malthusian appliances" later in the century; see Peter Fryer, *The Birth Con-trollers* (London, 1965).

Condorcet, but (in an ironic thrust) he "has not acquired that command over his understanding which would enable him to believe what he wishes, without evidence."

3.

That is where the matter rested with Malthus in 1798. Then, for five years, he pondered it further, as he collected new evidence, and in 1803 brought out a revised edition of the *Essay*, which was greatly enlarged (from 50,000 to 250,000 words) and less pessimistic than before. In those five years of reconsideration, Malthus had thought of the possibility of "another check to population which does not come under the head of either vice or misery." He called this check "moral restraint"; by which he simply meant delayed marriage. "It is clearly the duty of each individual," Malthus wrote, "not to marry till he has a prospect of supporting his children."

The importance of recognizing this third potential check to population growth was that it admitted into Malthus' equation for the first time a conscious and potentially benevolent human element, a possibility that undesirable population growth could conceivably be brought under human control. This tended, as Malthus said, to "soften some of the harshest conclusions of the first Essay"; and it prompted Malthus' new way of viewing his grim subject—no longer simply as a sort of biological juggernaut, but rather in terms of a moral imperative:

> If moral restraint be the only virtuous mode of avoiding the evils arising from this principle [of population], our obligation to practise it will evidently rest exactly upon the same foundation as our obligation to practise any of the other virtues (p. 127).[6]

Malthus' first *Essay*, by not accounting for the possibility of effective human intervention, described a real biological tendency without showing all of the possible alternatives. The second *Essay*, by allowing for conscious human intervention, showed the same consequences as before, plus one more possibility, and a far preferable one; but the biological problem represented in the first *Essay*

6. Walter Bagehot later commented acidly, "He does not seem to see that he has cut away the ground of his whole argument . . . In its first form the *Essay on Population* was conclusive as an argument, only it was based on untrue facts; in its second form it was based on true facts, but it was inconclusive as an argument" (*Economic Studies* [London, 1880], p. 179). Bagehot's analysis of Malthus' position, however, is itself defective. It is not the "facts" that are changed in Malthus' second edition; they remain exactly as before and are as true, or untrue, as they had previously been. What Malthus changed was the range of possible alternatives in the face of these facts, now for the first time admitting the possibility of human intervention into a situation he previously considered unalterable.

remained the same in the second *Essay* and remains a problem to this day. Whether or not people will in fact interpose prudential checks to catastrophic population growth seems to have been answered in the affirmative for the industrialized countries, but not for the eight hundred million people of Africa, currently doubling their numbers in twenty-eight years, or for Central America or western Asia, doubling their numbers in thirty-three years, or for other rapidly growing areas of the developing world. There is a vast difference between the abstract possibility of problem solving and the actual achievement of solutions.

For Malthus the human obligations were clear:

> We are not, however, to relax our efforts in increasing the quantity of provisions, but to combine another effort with it; that of keeping the population, when once it has been overtaken, at such a distance behind as to effect the relative proportion which we desire; and thus unite the two grand *desiderata*, a great actual population and a state of society in which abject poverty and dependence are comparatively but little known; two objects which are far from being incompatible [p. 128].

That reasoning and that kind of optimism, cautious and qualified, have never been improved upon.

After two centuries of criticism of the so-called Malthusian gloom, it may seem odd to hear Malthus called optimistic; but the conventional labels have been misleading. It is often the cheery voices of the self-proclaimed optimists of the far right (theologians, businessmen, and technologists who argue that bigger is better, and that unlimited population growth and material growth are not only possible but desirable) that encourage the neglect of pressing social problems, thereby condemning multitudes of unfortunate people to continuing misery; whereas the doomsayers, the so called pessimists, are often the ones to raise an alarm, thus sometimes producing effective social action. (By writing *Silent Spring,* the "pessimistic" Rachel Carson, passionately opposed to the indiscriminate use of DDT, was a more genuine benefactor of humanity and, therefore, a truer optimist than her smooth-spoken antagonists in the pesticide industry.) Similarly, the "optimists" of the far left, by obdurately refusing to recognize rapid population growth as a threat to social improvement, have compromised their own—and others'—attempts to deal with poverty, crime, racial injustice, and other problems.

What Malthus did was to set a tough-minded empiricism against the often woolly-headed Utopianism so popular during his youth. Only after he had done this could Malthus propose a different sort of optimism, a qualified and wary optimism, about a future for humankind that recognizes and accounts for the dangers implicit in our biological nature. Concluding his revised *Essay,* Malthus wrote:

> Though our future prospects . . . may not be so bright as we could wish yet they . . . by no means preclude that gradual and progressive improvement in human society which, before the late wild speculations on this subject, was the object of rational expectation (p. 133).

To call this attitude, this message, a "warning against all attempts to ameliorate the condition of society" or a "gospel of despair" is obviously a misreading.[7] John Maynard Keynes' tribute to Malthus is far more accurate. Commenting in 1933 on the *Essay on Population,* he wrote:

> The book can claim a place amongst those which have had great influence on the progress of thought. It is profoundly in the English tradition of humane science—in that tradition of Scotch and English thought, in which there has been, I think, an extraordinary continuity of *feeling,* if I may so express it, from the eighteenth century to the present time—the tradition which is suggested by the names of Locke, Hume, Adam Smith, Paley, Bentham, Darwin, and Mill, a tradition marked by a love of truth and a most noble lucidity, by a prosaic sanity free from sentiment or metaphysic, and by an immense disinterestedness and public spirit. There is a continuity in these writings, not only of feeling, but of actual matter. It is in this company that Malthus belongs.[8]

Malthus' theory of population originated, as we have seen, in an argument with his father about "the future improvement of society"; significantly, nearly all of the subsequent controversies, still animated after more than two hundred years, ultimately turn on that question. Discussions of "Malthusianism" have always been, and still are, compounded less of economics, narrowly defined, than of social philosophy, and less of demography than of moral exhortation. The early followers of Malthus included classical economists like David Ricardo, Nassau Senior, and James and John Stuart Mill. The long

---

7. About the "willful misrepresentations" of Malthus' ideas that are frequently assigned to the adjective "Malthusian," William Peterson writes: "Is this word ever used to designate, say, the first significant economist to recognize the importance of effective demand and thus the only nineteenth-century figure in the main line of classical economic thought to suggest the serious lacks in laissez-faire policies; or, in social thought, a pioneer advocate of universal education, the initiator of social science as a university discipline: or, specifically with respect to population, the theorist who analyzed both the relation between humans and resources and the effect of social man's rising aspirations on his fertility? Very little of the full and well rounded thought of Professor Thomas Robert Malthus is recalled in the commentary even of professionals" ("The Malthus-Godwin Debate, Then and Now," *Demography,* 8 [1971], 25).

8. John Maynard Keynes, *Essays in Biography* (New York, 1933), p. 120.

correspondence between Ricardo and Malthus, in fact, bears little on the question of population, simply because Ricardo agreed so thoroughly with Malthus on that subject, differing only in certain emphases. Similarly, Senior wrote that Malthus' theory places him "as a benefactor to mankind on a level with Adam Smith" (p. 143); though Senior was more optimistic than Malthus about the effectiveness of "preventive" checks to population growth.

John Stuart Mill published his *Principles of Political Economy* in 1848. By that time he was heir not only to Malthus' original generalizations but also to the subsequent discovery of the law of diminishing returns in agriculture, made almost simultaneously by Malthus, Ricardo, and two other British economists. Malthus' 1814 essay on the Corn Laws had described the operation of diminishing returns. In fact, as early as the second edition of the *Essay on Population* (1803), he had casually anticipated his own later discovery:

> It must be evident to those who have the slightest acquaintance with the agricultural subjects, that in proportion as cultivation extended, the additions that could yearly be made to the former average produce, must be gradually and regularly diminishing.[9]

However, he made only passing reference to diminishing returns in the *Essay on Population*, thinking perhaps that his essay rested on other generalizations that were already sufficiently convincing. When John Stuart Mill published his *Principles of Political Economy*, however, he regarded diminishing returns as fundamental to agricultural production:

> It is vain to say, that all mouths which the increase of mankind calls into existence, bring with them hands. The new mouths require as much food as the old ones, and the hands do not produce as much [p. 148].

Mill's work was so influential that he may be said to have shifted permanently the post-Malthusian emphasis away from Malthus' ratios and onto the law of diminishing returns. In doing so, he gave new force to the Malthusian principle.

Meanwhile, the anti-Malthusians, who were largely well-intentioned social reformers of various persuasions, were rallying against the hated notion that population growth is an inevitable and insuperable "natural" obstacle to human betterment. Malthus, having argued for the retention of the protectionist Corn Laws (and thus for higher food prices) and for the abolition of poor relief, was soon characterized as a "hard-hearted" public enemy of poor people, despite his sincere insistence that these short-range severities were in their long-range best interest. Malthus may have been a "serene

9. Malthus, *An Essay on Population*, Everyman's Library ed., Vol. I, p. 11

and cheerful" man, as Harriet Martineau said, but some of his social
nostrums seemed undeniably hard-hearted in the short run:

> —I should propose a regulation to be made, declaring that no
> child born from any marriage . . . should ever be entitled to par-
> ish assistance.
> —With regard to illegitimate children . . . they should not be
> allowed to have any claim to parish assistance.
> —The infant is, comparatively speaking, of little value to the
> society, as others will immediately supply its place.

Stripped of their context of "long-range benevolence," these
notions have the odor of barbarity about them. At any rate,
nineteenth-century humanitarians refused to accept the inevitability
of Malthus' grim "law" of population and his draconian remedies,
stressing instead the need to reform society itself in order to rescue
humanity from poverty and misery. Godwin (Malthus' original target) responded:

> Man is to a considerable degree the artificer of his own fortune.
> We can apply our reflections and our ingenuity to whatever we
> regret [p. 138].

Moralists throughout the nineteenth century repeatedly voiced
their distaste for Malthus, and some well-known economists joined
the assault. Walter Bagehot's ill-considered criticism, in his *Economic Studies* (1880), has already been noted. In the same year,
Henry George wrote, in *Progress and Poverty*:

> I assert that in any given state of civilization a greater number
> of people can collectively be better provided for than a smaller.
> I assert that the injustice of society, not the niggardliness of
> nature, is the cause of want and misery which the current theory
> attributes to over-population. . . . I assert that, other things
> being equal, the greater the population, the greater the com-
> fort.[1]

It is revealing that many literary people in the nineteenth century
were also anti-Malthusians—revealing, because it demonstrates how
deeply Malthus' message offended humanitarian values. "The voice
of objective reason," Keynes said of Malthus' theory, "had been
raised against a deep instinct which the evolutionary struggle had
been implanting from the commencement of life." That same voice
spoke against the religious command to "increase and multiply"; and,
despite Malthus' protestations from 1803 on, his doctrine was also
held, by socialists and other radical reformers, to be an immovable
obstacle to any human action for social betterment. It was no won-

1. Henry George, *Progress and Poverty* (New York, 1942), pp. 141–42.

der, then, that nineteenth-century writers, characteristically thinking of themselves as humanitarians, resisted the Malthusian
propositions. Shelley (Godwin's son-in-law), Coleridge, Wordsworth,
and Hazlitt all spoke out against them; Carlyle's sarcasm is well
known; Dickens' Scrooge, in his most misanthropic moods, speaks
as a pseudo-Malthusian ("If they would rather die . . . they had better do it, and decrease the surplus population"); and others of Dickens' villains are Malthusian caricatures:

> "A man may live to be as old as Methuselah," said Mr. Filer,
> "and may labour all his life for the benefit of such people as
> those; and may heap up facts on figures, facts on figures, facts
> on figures, mountains high and dry; and he can no more hope
> to persuade 'em that they have no right or business to be mar-
> ried, than he can hope to persuade 'em that they have no earthly
> right or business to be born. And *that* we know they haven't. We
> reduced it to a mathematical certainty long ago!"[2]

4

Part IV of this book illustrates why Malthus, regardless of his many
detractors, would now feel vindicated by history. As is shown in "Population Growth in the Twenty-First Century" (p. 165), world population is continuing to grow at the unmanageable rate of eighty
million plus per year, despite some successes in reducing birth rates
in China and elsewhere in the developing world. The earnest effort
of many governments to encourage birth control, together with a new
self-reliance among better-educated women in the developing countries (and thus their acceptance of family planning), has helped bring
total world growth rates down somewhat. But birth control information and assistance are not available everywhere, which is one
reason that global growth rates are still ominously elevated. Realistic
mid-range projections show world population rising from six billion
in 2000 to over nine billion by 2050—a 50 percent increase in only
fifty years. Such rapid growth, so long continued, is causing human
demands to overshoot not only the world's finite resource base but
also its environmental carrying capacity, with tragic results for our
own and future generations.

"Population and Food Supplies in the Twenty-First Century"
(p. 185) shows that this environmental overload is already causing
dramatic losses of much-needed cropland, due to salination, waterlogging, and erosion as well as to urban sprawl, road building, and
other effects of larger populations. Rangeland and fisheries are also

2. Charles Dickens, *The Chimes*, in *Works* (New York, 1911), Vol. 16, p. 97.

being exploited beyond their capacity for recovery. Meanwhile, a billion people are chronically malnourished; and in such densely populated countries as India, Bangladesh, Pakistan, Ethiopia, and Nigeria, where half of the children are already undernourished, hunger continues to increase along with the rapid growth in population.

"Population and Water Supplies in the Twenty-First Century" (p. 197) examines a part of the population/food equation that could hardly have seemed troubling to Malthus, living in a country of plentiful rainfall. But freshwater shortages may well be the most severe threat of all—not only to the human need for potable water but also to the needs of industry and agriculture. As populations grow, the demands for freshwater supplies of all sorts—surface water, groundwater, reclaimed water—are increasing. Meanwhile, many ancient aquifers (which are mainly fossil water, deposited over many centuries) are being overpumped for irrigation and are in danger of almost total depletion in the foreseeable future, threatening food production on irrigated lands. And irrigation itself, on which so much of world food production depends, can have deleterious after effects, which will eventually make the soil virtually worthless for agriculture.

"Population and Energy Supplies in the Twenty-First Century" (p. 205) surveys some of the ways that population growth causes energy-related problems—among them air pollution, global warming, depletion of fossil fuel supplies, and destruction of the ozone layer. These detrimental effects are due partly to voracious fuel consumption in the industrialized societies, but they are also due to the huge increase in energy demands required to double or triple food supplies in this century to feed the world's burgeoning population more equitably and more adequately. This disparity between increasing energy demands and diminishing traditional energy supplies impels a close look at newer or alternative (and less polluting) energy sources, including wind, solar, hydro, geothermal, and hydrogen power.

"Population and Environment in the Twenty-First Century" (p. 211) shows how severely overpopulation burdens the environment. It is increasingly clear even to casual observers that dense populations stress and degrade the long-term carrying capacity of the earth. The wealth of our earth is far less a matter of gold and silver than of freshwater, fertile soil, forests, fisheries, and clean air; these are the assets that sustain our lives and undergird our civilization. But that fundamental wealth is being squandered and plundered by a global population too numerous and too wasteful.

"Population and Social Dynamics in the Twenty-First Century" (p. 221) explores the kinds of social disruptions that are caused by population growth. Disputes over inadequate supplies of food, water, and other resources can destabilize governments, cause civil strife, and degenerate into social chaos. Meanwhile, existing religious or ethnic conflicts can be exacerbated by ongoing demographic pressures, causing riots, massacres, and "ethnic cleansing." They may also spur large-scale emigration to neighboring countries, which are often hostile to such massive immigration. Rapidly growing populations can also breed international conflicts over shared or common resources, such as water—conflicts that have implications for other nations, often far removed from the location of the struggle. In 2002 Thoraya Obaid, head of the United Nations' Population Fund, pointed out that rapidly increasing populations in the Middle East have resulted in very high proportions of young people there, many of them radicalized by "a growing sense of inequality and injustice," which, she warned, leads to extremism and terrorism. "There is no doubt," she said, "that demographics and population are linked to political instability," and she called for improved family-planning services, health services, and education.

"Some Contemporary Critics of Malthusianism" (p. 233) demonstrates that the initial nineteenth-century hostility to Malthusian thought continues to the present. Criticisms now come from those holding left-leaning social ideas or right-leaning capitalist doctrines and from those with religious objections to birth control. All of these critics operate on the assumption that despite the population explosion of the past half century, all is nevertheless well—or *could* be well, if the world would only heed their special prescriptions. They simply assert that there is no population problem, that overpopulation does not cause hunger, that all the talk about overpopulation is only a mask to conceal capitalist—or socialist—failures, that the world and its natural resources are to all intents and purposes infinite. Also, in some religions, any effort to limit population growth is considered sinful. However, the facts of the real world, as discussed in the other parts of this book, refute these ideas.

"Rethinking Endless Population Growth" (p. 247) addresses basic questions of what can be done about ever-increasing populations. The first requirement is that people recognize the nature of the problem. All too often we focus on the symptom rather than the basic malady, preferring to think only about increasing supplies of food and other human necessities, meanwhile ignoring the fundamental problem of ever-growing populations. But until we face up to the harsh reality of unmanageable population growth, we are ignoring an essential element of a two-sided predicament. Beyond mere recognition, population growth needs to be addressed as a treatable problem, which requires education and effective social action, including reliable and conveniently available means of birth control. This part of the book provides a variety of thoughtful responses to our demographic predicament, including population stabilization and a substantial reduction in global human numbers.

"Three Significant Postscripts" (p. 291) cites some of the many notable people and the scores of organizations that are now trying to alert the world to the dangers of overpopulation. Many scientists, statesmen, environmentalists, economists, physicians, business executives, feminists, ministers, writers, and academics have warned us repeatedly that failure to address adequately the problem of over-population has already had, and will continue to have, grave consequences for the whole world.

5

Are there not thousands in the world . . .
Who love their fellows even to the death,
And feel the giant agony of the world?

—John Keats

To the foregoing survey of current facts and opinions about over-population (all of which are discussed at length in this book), I would like to add a personal note. My wife and I once had the opportunity to spend two years traveling and teaching throughout the Far East, Asia, the Middle East, and Europe. From this and previous and sub-sequent experiences in North Africa and Central America, we came to understand, in a personal and emotive way, the deep gulf between our own well-being in America and the hardships of life in the devel-oping world.

From one deprived country to another, we continued to observe (but could never become accustomed to or reconciled to) the con-stant presence of poverty. In the developing world, human misery is ubiquitous and inescapable. In Calcutta, we followed the alleyways that straggle off in every direction, lined with tiny shacks built of metal scraps, pieces of old baskets, strips of wood, and gunny sacks. In the dim interiors of those shacks, small fires glowed through the smoke, and gaunt faces gazed out at children playing in the fetid, fly-infested streets. In Delhi, Bangkok, and Cairo, with their great numbers of people and crowds of roaming children; in Hong Kong in the thousands of squatters' shacks or in the miles of tenements where whole families live in a single small room or in the acres of sampans and junks lashed together to form the strange floating cities of Asia: dark, dense aquatic jungles of bamboo and fluttering rags—and human beings.

After that experience, seeing firsthand the human suffering in some of the poorest countries in the world, caused by too many people with too little sustenance, I was moved to write a book about it, called *The Silent Explosion*, that examines the causes and consequences of overpopulation. In his foreword, Sir Julian Huxley wrote, "The special value of Professor Appleman's book is that it reveals the moral nature of the population problem." As Huxley implied, the ability of some people to ignore the seriousness of this problem could be considered a moral as well as an intellectual failure.

Ironically, the world's poverty and misery are now most heavily concentrated in lands where previous generations had raised brilliant civilizations, at a time when the ancestors of the Europeans were still comparatively primitive. The Egyptians developed a complex and durable society thousands of years before the ancient Greeks. The splendid Gupta dynasty in India flourished five hundred years before Charlemagne. The Khmers developed a sophisticated civilization in Southeast Asia before William the Conqueror invaded England. The sumptuous Chinese cultures of the T'ang and Sung dynasties stretched over six centuries before the discovery of the New World. The Mayas, Toltecs, Aztecs, and Incas ruled rich empires in the Western Hemisphere long before Europeans arrived.

Time, the great destroyer, eventually leveled the grandeur of those ancient civilizations. Dominated and exploited by Western colonial powers, exhausted by wars, constrained by traditional forms and customs, skeptical of the European Enlightenment and wary of the Industrial Revolution, those societies did not "develop"; and their poverty-stricken lands gradually became, as Kipling once called them, "the dark places of the earth," seeming to have been "created by Providence in order to supply picturesque scenery."

Comparatively wealthy societies, including our own, unfortunately also have poor people; yet without minimizing their distress, it must be recognized that degrees of poverty vary greatly around the world. People accustomed to automobiles, refrigerators, televisions, computers, and air-conditioning find it hard to imagine the extent of the deprivation in Asian, African, and other third-world countries.

The reasons for the poverty of the developing countries are many and complicated. They stretch back into the obscurity of ancient history and out into the jigsaw relations of religion, law, education, politics, economics, and social custom. But one of the main reasons conditions are now *staying* so persistently bad is that the populations of those countries are growing rapidly, and therefore demands for all goods and services are increasing so fast that supplies cannot keep pace. In those places, the population explosion is no vague menace of the distant future. It is tangible and visible, here and now.

The population explosion is so grave and difficult a problem that many people have just closed their eyes and minds to it. Perhaps in no other social arena is denial so widespread. Such denial is sometimes motivated by vested interests; many people see personal, political, or ideological advantages to increasing the population. Capitalist entrepreneurs envision cheap labor, as well as more consumers and customers. Religious leaders foresee more followers and thus more influence. Politicians and militarists see more bodies and thus more power. All of these opportunists refuse to acknowledge the "giant agony of the world," nor do they respect the welfare or happiness of individual human beings.

Certain economists, for instance, stubbornly assert that natural resources are "limitless"—even though that word and that concept are meaningless in a finite world. I call these people cornucopian economists, because they propagate a myth of endless abundance. They also propose that the "demographic transition" from high to low population growth will automatically solve the population problem, even though such a transition faces formidable obstacles. And they claim that industrialization and development will by themselves solve the economic problems of the third-world countries, ignoring the economic, social, and political roadblocks to actual development—not to mention the environmental degradation that always accompanies it. What the cornucopian economists are advocating is a philosophy of "could," by which, they claim, they can fix everything—tomorrow. But if we are going to be practical about the life-and-death struggle with world poverty in our time, we must shake off the tranquilizing temptations of the philosophy of "could" and admit frankly that we "can" do only what we actually *do* succeed in doing.

Such an honest criterion makes it clear that the rosy illusions of the cornucopian economists are irresponsible. Their plans are grounded in the most precarious and improbable assumptions: that serious national and international tensions will not interrupt the progress they so confidently predict; that governments will efficiently use, not misuse, economic assistance; that provincial overlords will suddenly begin to act in the interest of the people they are now oppressing; that caste, class, and religious conflicts will somehow be reduced to insignificance; that peasants will abruptly forsake the "wisdom" of their ancestors in favor of foreigners' technical advice; that investors of capital will commit large sums of money to high-risk areas; that well-trained and dedicated corps of civil servants will suddenly spring out of nowhere, reject all corrupting influences, and apply themselves efficiently to the welfare of their communities. Such expectations are simply out of touch with reality.

Another formidable obstacle to sensible population limitation is the hierarchy of the Roman Catholic Church, which condemns birth control, calling it "an offense against the law of God and of nature." Most other religions disagree with this opinion, but the Catholic hierarchy, wielding the political power of large congregations, continues to oppose population limitation. Its influence is especially unfortunate in the United Nations, where for many years it has succeeded in weakening or preventing family-planning programs, despite the present suffering in the third world and the severe hardships that continuing overpopulation will inevitably bring to people everywhere.

Complicating this picture is the Catholic hierarchy's linking of birth control to abortion, so that United Nations' population programs can be further undermined by the accusation that they promote abortion—even when that is not true and even though birth control has been shown to *prevent* large numbers of abortions. On the abortion issue, the Catholic hierarchy is joined in an unlikely alliance with certain American fundamentalist Protestant groups, and together, by their strong influence on the Republican Party in particular, they have successfully pressured Republican administrations in Washington—from Eisenhower's to G. W. Bush's—to ignore the global population problem and to withhold family-planning contributions to the United Nations. In 2002 the United Nations' Population Fund stated that the Bush administration's withholding of the United States appropriation to United Nations' family planning aid "could mean two million unwanted pregnancies, 800,000 induced abortions, 4,700 maternal deaths, and 77,000 infant and child deaths." Thus an ostensibly spiritual message has been turned into a political tool—with harmful and even fatal results.

There is another obvious reason for Catholic opposition to family planning. Noting that, as Voltaire said, God is on the side of the big battalions, the Catholic hierarchy has promoted the expansion of its own membership with such unguarded political statements as this, from the journal of the Holy Name Society: "Unless there are some surprising changes in birth rates or marked shifts in immigration policy—neither likely—sooner or later Catholics will be the numerically dominating group of citizens in the United States." Or this statement from the Catholic Truth Society in London: "Our faithful Catholic mothers are doing a wonderful work for God. In time, if contraceptive practices continue to prevail amongst Protestants, their number will decrease and the Catholic race will prevail and thus England might again become what it once was, a Catholic country." *Dominating* and *prevail* are clearly political, not theological, terms—and, used in this way, they underline the critical importance of the American constitutional principle of the separation of church and state.[3]

In a world of diminishing distances and accelerating crises, the older, narrower concepts of self-interest have become obsolete. The traditional expedient of the wealthy societies—taking refuge behind national boundaries of affluence and, in case of emergency, sending out the gunboats—is no longer an adequate response to pressing world problems. A century ago, chaos, stagnation, or aggression in faraway places might not have been cause for concern; but in the increasingly interconnected polity and economy of the twenty-first century, they are often directly relevant to everyone's national and personal security. The only conceivably secure world now is a prospering one, for everybody.

The unit of survival is now the human species itself, and the unit of conscience should also be the human species: people *ought* to increase their sphere of moral awareness and concern to include the devastating effects of overpopulation around the world, and they ought to do what they can to solve such problems without further delay. That may sound excessive or bothersome to some people, living "normal" lives in wealthy and well-fed countries. But in global terms, their "normal" life is not at all normal. For many millions of the world's people, life remains, as it has always been, a vale of tears.

6

When Malthus died in 1834, the total population of the world barely exceeded one billion. If he were to return now, in the twenty-first century, he would find a world population that is well over six billion. He would be surprised at that, because he would find it hard to believe that food supplies had increased sufficiently to keep so many people alive. He would be far less surprised to hear that of those six billion people, one billion of them, as many as existed in his own time, are suffering from malnutrition and in danger of starvation. So despite two centuries of progress in agricultural productivity (which is now diminishing; see Part IV B), there is little in today's world situation to suggest that Malthus would now change his mind. In many third-world countries, there is simply not enough locally grown food to nourish the population adequately, and food from foreign sources is increasingly expensive and unaffordable, largely because

3. Ironically, by blocking implementation of birth-control programs in the developing countries, the Catholic hierarchy is partly responsible for high third-world growth rates and therefore partly responsible for the fact that Catholics are daily becoming a smaller and smaller fraction of the world's population.

of higher costs of oil and fertilizer. Meanwhile the world population keeps growing by over eighty million mouths per year.

Malthus would also be familiar with the other problems that are caused by large population increases: unemployment; shortages of housing, hospitals, schools, and teachers; inadequate sanitation and health care; social discontent; religious conflict; and civil and international wars. For all such reasons, most neo-Malthusian humanitarians consider population stabilization—and eventually significant population reduction—to be an urgent necessity for what Malthus hoped would be "the future improvement of society."

It has now become compellingly obvious that the world already has population growth rates that threaten hundreds of millions with starvation; therefore, urgent and effective efforts must be made to bring those growth rates down as much as humanly (and humanely) possible—eventually to zero or to negative levels. And since the world already has food shortages and at the same time the ability to raise more food, everything possible must be done to increase food supplies, and also the means to store and distribute such supplies more efficiently and more equitably. There is nothing mutually exclusive about these two social necessities; on the contrary, they can be mutually reinforcing.

Due largely to rapid population growth, human beings everywhere confront a future full of uncertainty and prodigious challenge; it is hard not to be discouraged in the face of such ominous conditions. But the same man who anticipated our present predicament also prescribed the only tenable response to it. As Malthus wrote: "Sufficient remains to be done for mankind, to animate us to the most unremitted exertion" (p. 111).

Part I
INFLUENCES ON MALTHUS

DAVID HUME

Of the Populousness of Antient Nations (1752)†

In general, we may observe, that the question with regard to the comparative populousness of ages or kingdoms implies very important consequences * * *. For as there is in all men, both male and female, a desire and power of generation more active than is ever universally exerted, the restraints, which it lyes under, must proceed from some difficulties in men's situation, which it belongs to a wise legislature carefully to observe and remove. Almost every man, who thinks he can maintain a family, will have one; and the human species, at this rate of propagation, wou'd more than double every generation, were every one coupled as soon as he comes to the age of puberty. How fast do mankind multiply in every colony or new settlement; where it is an easy matter to provide for a family; and where men are no way straitned or confin'd, as in long established governments? History tells us frequently of plagues, that have swept away the third or fourth part of a people: Yet in a generation or two, the destruction was not perceiv'd; and the society had again acquir'd their former number. The lands, that were cultivated, the houses built, the commodities rais'd, the riches acquir'd, enabled the people, who escap'd, immediately to marry, and to rear families, which supply'd the place of those who had perish'd. And for a like reason, every wise, just, and mild government, by rendering the condition of its subjects easy and secure, will always abound most in people, as well as in commodities and riches. A country, indeed, whose climate and soil are fitted for vines, will naturally be more populous than one, which produces only corn, and that more populous than one, which is only fitted for pasturage. But if every thing else be equal, it seems natural to expect, that wherever there are most happiness and virtue and the wisest institutions, there will also be most people.

*　*　*

† David Hume (1711–1776), Scottish philosopher and historian. The text is from Discourse X of his *Political Discourses*.

ROBERT WALLACE

A Dissertation on the Numbers of Mankind in Antient and Modern Times (1753)†

It will be proper to lay down some general maxims taken from nature and constant observation, which may be useful to guide us in a more particular comparison.

1. A rude and barbarous people, living by hunting, fishing, or pasturage, or on the spontaneous product of the earth, without agriculture, commerce and arts, can never be so numerous as a people inhabiting the same tracts of land, who are well skilled in agriculture and civilized by commerce: since uncultivated can never maintain so many inhabitants, as cultivated lands. In every country, there shall always be found a greater number of inhabitants, *cæteris paribus*, in proportion to the plenty of provisions it affords, as plenty will always encourage the generality of the people to marry.

* * *

2. As the earth could not be well peopled in rude and barbarous ages, neither are all countries, climates and soils, equally favourable to propagation.

* * *

3. Besides the nature of the climate or soil, the number of people in every country depends greatly on its political maxims and institutions concerning the division of lands.

* * *

Hence we may conclude, that when any antient nation divided its lands into small shares, and when even eminent citizens had but a few acres to maintain their families; tho' such a nation had but little commerce, and had learned only a few simple and more necessary arts, it must have abounded greatly in people. This was in a particular manner the case in *Rome* for several ages, as we shall see afterwards.

* * *

4. As the number of people in every nation depends most immediately on the number and fruitfulness of marriages, and the encouragement that is given to marry; where-ever the greatest care is taken in this respect, the number of people, *cæteris paribus*, shall be greatest; and a bad policy in this article must give a considerable check to propagation.

† Robert Wallace (1697–1771), Scottish clergyman and amateur economist.

Hence, in a debauched nation, addicted to sensuality and irregular amours, and where luxury and a high taste of delicate living prevails, the number of the people must be proportionally small, as their debauchery will hinder many from marrying, and their luxury and delicacy will render them less able to maintain families.

For the same reason, a nation shall be more populous in proportion as good morals and a simplicity of taste and manners prevail, or as the people are more frugal and virtuous.

5. As mankind can only be supported by the fruits of the earth and animal food, and it is only by agriculture, fishing and hunting, that food can be provided, to render the earth as populous as possible, these arts must be duly cherished, especially agriculture and fishing.

Hence, the more persons employ themselves in agriculture and fishing, and the arts which are necessary for managing them to greatest advantage, the world in general will be more populous; and as fewer hands are employed in this manner, there will be fewer people. * * *

Philosophers have been advising, and Divines calling upon mankind to cultivate frugality, temperance, simplicity, contentment with a little, and patience of labour, demonstrating, that these humble virtues are the only means by which they can expect to secure solid, lasting, and independent felicity. * * *

But the cultivation of these virtues not only makes individuals happy; but, from what has been maintained in the preceding *Dissertation*, appears further to be the surest way of rendering the earth populous, and making society flourish. 'Twas simplicity of taste, frugality, patience of labour, and contentment with a little, which made the world so populous in antient times. * * *

In this manner the most humble virtues are found to be not only consistent with, but greatly conducive to the populousness and grandeur of society.

BENJAMIN FRANKLIN

Observations Concerning the Increase of Mankind (1755)†

* * *

21. The importation of foreigners into a country that has as many inhabitants as the present employments and provisions for subsis-

---

† Benjamin Franklin (1706–1790), American statesman and Founding Father, who speculated on many of the social issues of his time. The text is from Selections 21 and 22 of his *Observations Concerning the Increase of Mankind, Peopling of Countries, etc.*

tence will bear, will be in the end no increase of people; unless the new comers have more industry and frugality than the natives, and then they will provide more Subsistence, and increase in the country; but they will gradually eat the natives out. Nor is it necessary to bring in foreigners to fill up any occasional vacancy in a country; for such vacancy (if the Laws are good) will soon be filled by natural generation. * * *

22. There is in short, no bound to the prolific nature of plants or animals, but what is made by their crowding and interfering with each others' means of subsistence. Was the face of the earth vacant of other plants, it might be gradually sowed and overspread with one kind only; as, for instance, with Fennel; and were it empty of other inhabitants, it might in a few Ages be replenish'd from one nation only; as for Instance, with *Englishmen*. Thus there are suppos'd to be now upwards of One Million *English* Souls in *North America*, (tho' 'tis thought scarce 80,000 have been brought over sea) and yet perhaps there is not one the fewer in *Britain*, but rather many more, on Account of the employment the Colonies afford to manufacturers at home. This million doubling, suppose but once in twenty-five years, will in another century be more than the people of *England*, and the greatest Number of *Englishmen* will be on this side the water. What an accession of Power to the *British* empire by the Sea as well as Land! What increase of trade and navigation! What numbers of ships and seamen! We have been here but little more than one hundred years, and yet the force of our Privateers in the late war, united, was greater, both in men and guns, than that of the whole *British* Navy in Queen *Elizabeth's* time. How important an affair then to *Britain*, is the present treaty for settling the bounds between her Colonies and the *French*, and how careful should she be to secure room enough, since on the room depends so much the increase of her people?

*   *   *

ADAM SMITH

An Inquiry into the Nature and Causes of the Wealth of Nations (1776)†

Though the wealth of a country should be very great, yet if it has been long stationary, we must not expect to find the wages of labour

† Adam Smith (1723–1790), Scottish economist and moral philosopher.

very high in it. The funds destined for the payment of wages, the revenue and stock of its inhabitants, may be of the greatest extent; but if they have continued for several centuries of the same, or very nearly of the same extent, the number of labourers employed every year could easily supply, and even more than supply, the number wanted the following year. There could seldom be any scarcity of hands, nor could the masters be obliged to bid against one another in order to get them. The hands, on the contrary, would, in this case, naturally multiply beyond their employment. * * *

Poverty, though it no doubt discourages, does not always prevent marriage. It seems even to be favourable to generation. A half-starved Highland woman frequently bears more than twenty children, while a pampered fine lady is often incapable of bearing any, and is generally exhausted by two or three. Barrenness, so frequent among women of fashion, is very rare among those of inferior station. Luxury in the fair sex, while it inflames perhaps the passion for enjoyment, seems always to weaken, and frequently to destroy altogether, the powers of generation.

But poverty, though it does not prevent the generation, is extremely unfavorable to the rearing of children. The tender plant is produced, but in so cold a soil and so severe a climate, soon withers and dies. It is not uncommon, I have been frequently told, in the Highlands of Scotland for a mother who has borne twenty children not to have two alive. * * * In some places one half the children born die before they are four years of age; in many places before they are seven; and in almost all places before they are nine or ten. This great mortality, however, will everywhere be found chiefly among the children of the common people, who cannot afford to tend them with the same care as those of better station. Though their marriages are generally more fruitful than those of people of fashion, a smaller proportion of their children arrive at maturity. In foundling hospitals, and among the children brought up by parish charities, the mortality is still greater than among those of the common people.

Every species of animals naturally multiplies in proportion to the means of their subsistence, and no species can ever multiply beyond it. But in civilised society it is only among the inferior ranks of people that the scantiness of subsistence can set limits to the further multiplication of the human species; and it can do so in no other way than by destroying a great part of the children which their fruitful marriages produce.

The liberal reward of labour, by enabling them to provide better for their children, and consequently to bring up a greater number, naturally tends to widen and extend those limits. It deserves to be remarked, too, that it necessarily does this as nearly as possible in the proportion which the demand for labour requires. If this demand is continually increasing, the reward of labour must necessarily encourage in such a manner the marriage and multiplication of labourers, as may enable them to supply that continually increasing demand by a continually increasing population. If the reward should at any time be less than what was requisite for this purpose, the deficiency of hands would soon raise it; and if it should at any time be more, their excessive multiplication would soon lower it to this necessary rate. The market would be so much under-stocked with labour in the one case, and so much over-stocked in the other, as would soon force back its price to that proper rate which the circumstances of the society required. It is in this manner that the demand for men, like that for any other commodity, necessarily regulates the production of men; quickens it when it goes on too slowly, and stops it when it advances too fast. * * *

CONDORCET

The Future Progress of the Human Mind (1795)†

If man can, with almost complete assurance, predict phenomena when he knows their laws, and if, even when he does not, he can still, with great expectation of success, forecast the future on the basis of his experience of the past, why, then, should it be regarded as a fantastic undertaking to sketch, with some pretence to truth, the future destiny of man on the basis of his history? The sole foundation for belief in the natural sciences is this idea, that the general laws directing the phenomena of the universe, known or unknown, are necessary and constant. Why should this principle be any less true for the development of the intellectual and moral faculties of man than for the other operations of nature? * * *

If we glance at the state of the world today we see first of all that in Europe the principles of the French constitution are already those of all enlightened men. We see them too widely propagated, too seriously professed, for priests and despots to prevent their gradual penetration even into the hovels of their slaves; there they will soon awaken in these slaves the remnants of their common sense and inspire them with that smouldering indignation which not even constant humiliation and fear can smother in the soul of the oppressed.

* * *

† Marie-Jean-Antoine-Nicolas de Caritat, Marquis de Condorcet (1743–1794), French mathematician and philosopher. The text is from the last chapter of his *Sketch for a Historical Picture of the Progress of the Human Mind*.

Let us turn to the enlightened nations of Europe, and observe the size of their present populations in relation to the size of their territories. Let us consider, in agriculture and industry the proportion that holds between labour and the means of subsistence, * * * new instruments, machines and looms can add to man's strength and can improve at once the quality and the accuracy of his productions, and can diminish the time and labour that has to be expended on them. The obstacles still in the way of this progress will disappear, accidents will be foreseen and prevented, the insanitary conditions that are due either to the work itself or to the climate will be eliminated.

A very small amount of ground will be able to produce a great quantity of supplies of greater utility or higher quality; more goods will be obtained for a smaller outlay; the manufacture of articles will be achieved with less wastage in raw materials and will make better use of them. Every type of soil will produce those things which satisfy the greatest number of needs; of several alternative ways of satisfying needs of the same order, that will be chosen which satisfies the greatest number of people and which requires least labour and least expenditure. So, without the need for sacrifice, methods of preservation and economy in expenditure will improve in the wake of progress in the arts of producing and preparing supplies and making articles from them.

So not only will the same amount of ground support more people, but everyone will have less work to do, will produce more, and satisfy his wants more fully.

With all this progress in industry and welfare which establishes a happier proportion between men's talents and their needs, each successive generation will have larger possessions, either as a result of this progress or through the preservation of the products of industry; and so, as a consequence of the physical constitution of the human race, the number of people will increase. Might there not then come a moment when these necessary laws begin to work in a contrary direction; when, the number of people in the world finally exceeding the means of subsistence, there will in consequence ensue a continual diminution of happiness and population, a true retrogression, or at best an oscillation between good and bad? In societies that have reached this stage will not this oscillation be a perennial source of more or less periodic disaster? Will it not show that a point has been attained beyond which all further improvement is impossible, that the perfectibility of the human race has after long years arrived at a term beyond which it may never go?

There is doubtless no-one who does not think that such a time is still very far from us; but will it ever arrive? It is impossible to pronounce about the likelihood of an event that will occur only when the human species will have necessarily acquired a degree of knowledge of which we can have no inkling. And who would take it upon himself to predict the condition to which the art of converting the elements to the use of man may in time be brought?

But even if we agree that the limit will one day arrive, nothing follows from it that is in the least alarming as far as either the happiness of the human race or its indefinite perfectibility is concerned; if we consider that, before all this comes to pass, the progress of reason will have kept pace with that of the sciences, and that the absurd prejudices of superstition will have ceased to corrupt and degrade the moral code by its harsh doctrines instead of purifying and elevating it, we can assume that by then men will know that, if they have a duty towards those who are not yet born, that duty is not to give them existence but to give them happiness; their aim should be to promote the general welfare of the human race or of the society in which they live or of the family to which they belong, rather than foolishly to encumber the world with useless and wretched beings. It is, then, possible that there should be a limit to the amount of food that can be produced, and, consequently, to the size of the population of the world, without this involving that untimely destruction of some of those creatures who have been given life, which is so contrary to nature and to social prosperity.

WILLIAM GODWIN

Of Avarice and Profusion (1797)†

Riches and poverty are in some degree necessarily incidental to the social existence of man. There is no alternative, but that men must either have their portion of labour assigned them by the society at large, and the produce collected into a common stock; or that each man must be left to exert the portion of industry, and cultivate the habits of economy, to which his mind shall prompt him.

*   *   *

Inequality * * * being to a certain extent unavoidable, it is the province of justice and virtue to counteract the practical evils which inequality has a tendency to produce. It is certain that men will differ from each other in their degrees of industry and economy. But it is not less certain, that the wants of one man are similar to the wants of another, and that the same things will conduce to the improvement and happiness of each, except so far as either is corrupted by

† William Godwin (1756–1836), British social philosopher. The text is from Essay II of his *The Enquirer: Reflections on Education, Manners and Literature*.

the oppressive and tyrannical condition of the society in which he is born. * * *

How far does the conduct of the rich man who lives up to his fortune on the one hand, and of the avaricious man on the other, contribute to the placing of human beings in the condition in which they ought to be placed?

* * * It is a gross and ridiculous error to suppose that the rich pay for any thing. There is no wealth in the world except this, the labour of man.[1] What is misnamed wealth, is merely a power vested in certain individuals by the institutions of society, to compel others to labour for their benefit. So much labour is requisite to produce the necessaries of life; so much more to produce those superfluities which at present exist in any country. Every new luxury is a new weight thrown into the scale. The poor are scarcely ever benefited by this. It adds a certain portion to the mass of their labour; but it adds nothing to their conveniences.[2] Their wages are not changed. They are paid no more now for the work of ten hours, than before for the work of eight. They support the burthen; but they come in for no share of the fruit. * * *

* * * Let us see what is the tendency of the conduct of the avaricious man in this respect.

He recognizes, in his proceedings at least, if not as an article of his creed, that great principle of austere and immutable justice, that the claims of the rich man are no more extensive than those of the poor, to the sumptuousness and pamperings of human existence. He watches over his expenditure with unintermitted scrupulosity; and, though enabled to indulge himself in luxuries, he has the courage to practice an entire self-denial.

It may be alleged indeed that, if he do not consume his wealth upon himself, neither does he impart it to another; he carefully locks it up, and pertinaciously withholds it from general use. But this point does not seem to have been rightly understood. The true development and definition of the nature of wealth have not been applied to illustrate it. Wealth consists in this only, the commodities raised and fostered by human labour. But he locks up neither corn, nor oxen, nor clothes, nor houses. These things are used and consumed by his contemporaries, as truly and to as great an extent, as if he were a begger. * * *

His conduct is much less pernicious to mankind, and much more nearly conformable to the unalterable principles of justice, than that of the man who disburses his income in what has been termed, a liberal and spirited style. * * *

Such appears to be the genuine result of the comparison between

1. *Political Justice*, Book VIII, Chap. II, octavo edition.
2. *Ibid.*

the votary of avarice and the man of profusion. It by no means follows from the preference we feel compelled to cede to the former, that he is not fairly chargeable with enormous mistakes. Money, though in itself destitute of any real value, is an engine enabling us to vest the actual commodities of life in such persons and objects, as our understandings may point out to us. This engine, which might be applied to most admirable purposes, the miser constantly refuses to employ. The use of wealth is no doubt a science attended with uncommon difficulties. But it is not less evident that, by a master in the science, it might be applied, to chear the miserable, to relieve the oppressed, to assist the manly adventurer, to advance science, and to encourage art. A rich man, guided by the genuine principles of virtue, would be munificent, though not with that spurious munificence that has so often usurped the name. It may however almost be doubted whether the conduct of the miser, who wholly abstains from the use of riches, be not more advantageous to mankind, than the conduct of the man who, with honorable intentions, is continually misapplying his wealth to what he calls public benefits and charitable uses.

* * *

This speculation upon the comparative merits of avarice and profusion, may perhaps be found to be of greater importance than at first sight might be imagined. It includes in it the first principles of morality, and of justice between man and man. It strikes at the root of a deception that has long been continued, and long proved a curse to all the civilised nations of the earth. It tends to familiarise the mind to those strict and severe principles of judging, without which our energy, as well as our usefulness, will lie in a very narrow compass. It contains the germs of a code of political science, and may perhaps be found intimately connected with the extensive diffusion of liberty and happiness.

Part II
SELECTIONS FROM MALTHUS' WORK

An Essay on the Principle of Population†

Preface

The following Essay owes its origin to a conversation with a friend, on the subject of Mr. Godwin's Essay on avarice and profusion, in his Enquirer. The discussion started the general question of the future improvement of society; and the Author at first sat down with an intention of merely stating his thoughts to his friend, upon paper, in a clearer manner than he thought he could do in conversation. But as the subject opened upon him, some ideas occurred which he did not recollect to have met with before; and as he conceived that every the least light, on a topic so generally interesting, might be received with candour, he determined to put his thoughts in a form for publication.

The Essay might undoubtedly have been rendered much more complete by a collection of a greater number of facts in elucidation of the general argument. But a long and almost total interruption from very particular business, joined to a desire (perhaps imprudent) of not delaying the publication much beyond the time that he originally proposed, prevented the Author from giving to the subject an undivided attention. He presumes, however, that the facts which he has adduced will be found to form no inconsiderable evidence for the truth of his opinion respecting the future improvement of mankind. As the Author contemplates this opinion at present, little more appears to him to be necessary than a plain statement, in addition to the most cursory view of society, to establish it.

It is an obvious truth, which has been taken notice of by many writers, that population must always be kept down to the level of the means of subsistence; but no writer that the Author recollects has inquired particularly into the means by which this level is effected: and it is a view of these means which forms, to his mind, the strongest obstacle in the way to any very great future improvement of society. He hopes it will appear that, in the discussion of this interesting subject, he is actuated solely by a love of truth, and not by any prejudices against any particular set of men, or of opinions. He professes to have read some of the speculations on the future improvement of society in a temper very different from a wish to find them visionary, but he has not acquired that command over his understanding which would enable him to believe what he wishes, without evidence, or to refuse his assent to what might be unpleasing, when accompanied with evidence.

The view which he has given of human life has a melancholy hue,

---

† This text of the *Essay on the Principle of Population* is Malthus' first essay of 1798; the typography and punctuation (and, in a few instances, spelling) have been modernized.

but he feels conscious that he has drawn these dark tints from a conviction that they are really in the picture, and not from a jaundiced eye or an inherent spleen of disposition. The theory of mind which he has sketched in the two last chapters accounts to his own understanding in a satisfactory manner for the existence of most of the evils of life, but whether it will have the same effect upon others must be left to the judgment of his readers.

If he should succeed in drawing the attention of more able men to what he conceives to be the principal difficulty in the way to the improvement of society and should, in consequence, see this difficulty removed, even in theory, he will gladly retract his present opinions and rejoice in a conviction of his error.

June 7, 1798

CHAPTER I

Question stated—Little prospect of a determination of it, from the enmity of the opposing parties—The principal argument against the perfectibility of man and of society has never been fairly answered—Nature of the difficulty arising from population—Outline of the principal argument of the essay.

The great and unlooked for discoveries that have taken place of late years in natural philosophy, the increasing diffusion of general knowledge from the extension of the art of printing, the ardent and unshackled spirit of inquiry that prevails throughout the lettered and even unlettered world, the new and extraordinary lights that have been thrown on political subjects which dazzle and astonish the understanding, and particularly that tremendous phenomenon in the political horizon, the French revolution, which, like a blazing comet, seems destined either to inspire with fresh life and vigour, or to scorch up and destroy the shrinking inhabitants of the earth, have all concurred to lead many able men into the opinion that we were touching on a period big with the most important changes, changes that would in some measure be decisive of the future fate of mankind.

It has been said that the great question is now at issue, whether man shall henceforth start forwards with accelerated velocity towards illimitable, and hitherto unconceived improvement, or be condemned to a perpetual oscillation between happiness and misery, and after every effort remain still at an immeasurable distance from the wished for goal.

Yet, anxiously as every friend of mankind must look forwards to the termination of this painful suspense, and eagerly as the inquiring mind would hail every ray of light that might assist its view into futurity, it is much to be lamented that the writers on each side of this momentous question still keep far aloof from each other. Their mutual arguments do not meet with a candid examination. The question is not brought to rest on fewer points, and even in theory scarcely seems to be approaching to a decision.

The advocate for the present order of things is apt to treat the sect of speculative philosophers either as a set of artful and designing knaves who preach up ardent benevolence and draw captivating pictures of a happier state of society only the better to enable them to destroy the present establishments and to forward their own deep-laid schemes of ambition, or as wild and madheaded enthusiasts whose silly speculations and absurd paradoxes are not worthy the attention of any reasonable man.

The advocate for the perfectibility of man and of society retorts on the defender of establishments a more than equal contempt. He brands him as the slave of the most miserable and narrow prejudices; or as the defender of the abuses of civil society only because he profits by them. He paints him either as a character who prostitutes his understanding to his interest, or as one whose powers of mind are not of a size to grasp any thing great and noble, who cannot see above five yards before him, and who must therefore be utterly unable to take in the views of the enlightened benefactor of mankind.

In this unamicable contest the cause of truth cannot but suffer. The really good arguments on each side of the question are not allowed to have their proper weight. Each pursues his own theory, little solicitous to correct or improve it by an attention to what is advanced by his opponents.

The friend of the present order of things condemns all political speculations in the gross. He will not even condescend to examine the grounds from which the perfectibility of society is inferred. Much less will he give himself the trouble in a fair and candid manner to attempt an exposition of their fallacy.

The speculative philosopher equally offends against the cause of truth. With eyes fixed on a happier state of society, the blessings of which he paints in the most captivating colours, he allows himself to indulge in the most bitter invectives against every present establishment, without applying his talents to consider the best and safest means of removing abuses and without seeming to be aware of the tremendous obstacles that threaten, even in theory, to oppose the progress of man towards perfection.

It is an acknowledged truth in philosophy that a just theory will always be confirmed by experiment. Yet so much friction and so many minute circumstances occur in practice, which it is next to impossible for the most enlarged and penetrating mind to foresee, that on few subjects can any theory be pronounced just, that has not stood the test of experience. But an untried theory cannot fairly be advanced as probable, much less as just, till all the arguments against it have been maturely weighed and clearly and consistently refuted.

I have read some of the speculations on the perfectibility of man and of society with great pleasure. I have been warmed and delighted with the enchanting picture which they hold forth. I ardently wish for such happy improvements. But I see great, and, to my understanding, unconquerable difficulties in the way to them. These difficulties it is my present purpose to state, declaring, at the same time, that so far from exulting in them, as a cause of triumph over the friends of innovation, nothing would give me greater pleasure than to see them completely removed.

The most important argument that I shall adduce is certainly not new. The principles on which it depends have been explained in part by Hume, and more at large by Dr. Adam Smith. It has been advanced and applied to the present subject, though not with its proper weight, or in the most forcible point of view, by Mr. Wallace, and it may probably have been stated by many writers that I have never met with. I should certainly therefore not think of advancing it again, though I mean to place it in a point of view in some degree different from any that I have hitherto seen, if it had ever been fairly and satisfactorily answered.

The cause of this neglect on the part of the advocates for the perfectibility of mankind is not easily accounted for. I cannot doubt the talents of such men as Godwin and Condorcet. I am unwilling to doubt their candour. To my understanding, and probably to that of most others, the difficulty appears insurmountable. Yet these men of acknowledged ability and penetration scarcely deign to notice it, and hold on their course in such speculations, with unabated ardour and undiminished confidence. I have certainly no right to say that they purposely shut their eyes to such arguments. I ought rather to doubt the validity of them, when neglected by such men, however forcibly their truth may strike my own mind. Yet in this respect it must be acknowledged that we are all of us too prone to err. If I saw a glass of wine repeatedly presented to a man, and he took no notice of it, I should be apt to think that he was blind or uncivil. A juster philosophy might teach me rather to think that my eyes deceived me and that the offer was not really what I conceived it to be.

In entering upon the argument I must premise that I put out of the question, at present, all mere conjectures, that is, all suppositions, the probable realization of which cannot be inferred upon any just philosophical grounds. A writer may tell me that he thinks man will ultimately become an ostrich. I cannot properly contradict him. But before he can expect to bring any reasonable person over to his opinion, he ought to shew that the necks of mankind have been gradually elongating, that the lips have grown harder and more prominent, that the legs and feet are daily altering their shape, and that the hair is beginning to change into stubs of feathers. And till the probability of so wonderful a conversion can be shewn, it is surely lost time and lost eloquence to expatiate on the happiness of man in such a state; to describe his powers, both of running and flying, to paint him in a condition where all narrow luxuries would be contemned, where he would be employed only in collecting the necessaries of life, and where, consequently, each man's share of labour would be light, and his portion of leisure ample.

I think I may fairly make two postulata.

First, That food is necessary to the existence of man.

Secondly, That the passion between the sexes is necessary and will remain nearly in its present state.

These two laws, ever since we have had any knowledge of mankind, appear to have been fixed laws of our nature, and, as we have not hitherto seen any alteration in them, we have no right to conclude that they will ever cease to be what they now are, without an immediate act of power in that Being who first arranged the system of the universe, and for the advantage of his creatures, still executes, according to fixed laws, all its various operations.

I do not know that any writer has supposed that on this earth man will ultimately be able to live without food. But Mr. Godwin has conjectured that the passion between the sexes may in time be extinguished. As, however, he calls this part of his work a deviation into the land of conjecture, I will not dwell longer upon it at present than to say that the best arguments for the perfectibility of man are drawn from a contemplation of the great progress that he has already made from the savage state and the difficulty of saying where he is to stop. But towards the extinction of the passion between the sexes, no progress whatever has hitherto been made. It appears to exist in as much force at present as it did two thousand or four thousand years ago. There are individual exceptions now as there always have been. But, as these exceptions do not appear to increase in number, it would surely be a very unphilosophical mode of arguing, to infer merely from the existence of an exception, that the exception would, in time, become the rule, and the rule the exception.

Assuming then, my postulata as granted, I say that the power of population is indefinitely greater than the power in the earth to produce subsistence for man.

Population, when unchecked, increases in a geometrical ratio. Subsistence increases only in an arithmetical ratio. A slight acquaintance with numbers will shew the immensity of the first power in comparison of the second.

By that law of our nature which makes food necessary to the life of man, the effects of these two unequal powers must be kept equal.

man cannot stop nature the laws of nature

This implies a strong and constantly operating check on population from the difficulty of subsistence. This difficulty must fall somewhere and must necessarily be severely felt by a large portion of mankind.

plenty of seeds, not enough room, or nutrition

Through the animal and vegetable kingdoms, nature has scattered the seeds of life abroad with the most profuse and liberal hand. She has been comparatively sparing in the room and the nourishment necessary to rear them. The germs of existence contained in this spot of earth, with ample food and ample room to expand in, would fill millions of worlds in the course of a few thousand years. Necessity, that imperious all pervading law of nature, restrains them within the prescribed bounds. The race of plants and the race of animals shrink under this great restrictive law. And the race of man cannot, by any efforts of reason, escape from it. Among plants and animals its effects are waste of seed, sickness, and premature death. Among mankind, misery and vice. The former, misery, is an absolutely necessary consequence of it. Vice is a highly probable consequence, and we therefore see it abundantly prevail, but it ought not, perhaps, to be called an absolutely necessary consequence. The ordeal of virtue is to resist all temptation to evil.

obstacles in perfectability of society

This natural inequality of the two powers of population and of production in the earth and that great law of our nature which must constantly keep their effects equal form the great difficulty that to me appears insurmountable in the way to the perfectibility of society. All other arguments are of slight and subordinate consideration in comparison of this. I see no way by which man can escape from the weight of this law which pervades all animated nature. No fancied equality, no agrarian regulations in their utmost extent, could remove the pressure of it even for a single century. And it appears, therefore, to be decisive against the possible existence of a society, all the members of which should live in ease, happiness, and comparative leisure, and feel no anxiety about providing the means of subsistence for themselves and families.

Consequently, if the premises are just, the argument is conclusive against the perfectibility of the mass of mankind.

I have thus sketched the general outline of the argument, but I will examine it more particularly, and I think it will be found that experience, the true source and foundation of all knowledge, invariably confirms its truth.

theory of perfectability of man is much influenced, but it is not possible, which is a view toward that comes from exper.

CHAPTER II

The different ratios in which population and food increase—The necessary effects of these different ratios of increase—Oscillation produced by them in the condition of the lower classes of society—

Reasons why this oscillation has not been so much observed as might be expected—Three propositions on which the general argument of the essay depends—The different states in which mankind have been known to exist proposed to be examined with reference to these three propositions.

I said that population, when unchecked, increased in a geometrical ratio, and subsistence for man in an arithmetical ratio.

Let us examine whether this position be just.

I think it will be allowed that no state has hitherto existed (at least that we have any account of) where the manners were so pure and simple, and the means of subsistence so abundant, that no check whatever has existed to early marriages, among the lower classes, from a fear of not providing well for their families, or among the higher classes, from a fear of lowering their condition in life. Consequently in no state that we have yet known has the power of population been left to exert itself with perfect freedom.

Whether the law of marriage be instituted or not, the dictate of nature and virtue seems to be an early attachment to one woman. Supposing a liberty of changing in the case of an unfortunate choice, this liberty would not affect population till it arose to a height greatly vicious; and we are now supposing the existence of a society where vice is scarcely known.

In a state therefore of great equality and virtue, where pure and simple manners prevailed, and where the means of subsistence were so abundant that no part of the society could have any fears about providing amply for a family, the power of population being left to exert itself unchecked, the increase of the human species would evidently be much greater than any increase that has been hitherto known.

In the United States of America, where the means of subsistence have been more ample, the manners of the people more pure, and consequently the checks to early marriages fewer than in any of the modern states of Europe, the population has been found to double itself in twenty-five years.

This ratio of increase, though short of the utmost power of population, yet as the result of actual experience, we will take as our rule, and say, that population, when unchecked, goes on doubling itself every twenty-five years or increases in a geometrical ratio.

Let us now take any spot of earth, this Island for instance, and see in what ratio the subsistence it affords can be supposed to increase. We will begin with it under its present state of cultivation.

If I allow that by the best possible policy, by breaking up more land and by great encouragements to agriculture, the produce of this

Island may be doubled in the first twenty-five years, I think it will be allowing as much as any person can well demand.

In the next twenty-five years, it is impossible to suppose that the produce could be quadrupled. It would be contrary to all our knowledge of the qualities of land. The very utmost that we can conceive is that the increase in the second twenty-five years might equal the present produce. Let us then take this for our rule, though certainly far beyond the truth, and allow that by great exertion, the whole produce of the Island might be increased every twenty-five years, by a quantity of subsistence equal to what it at present produces. The most enthusiastic speculator cannot suppose a greater increase than this. In a few centuries it would make every acre of land in the Island like a garden.

Yet this ratio of increase is evidently arithmetical.

It may be fairly said, therefore, that the means of subsistence increase in an arithmetical ratio. Let us now bring the effects of these two ratios together.

The population of the Island is computed to be about seven millions, and we will suppose the present produce equal to the support of such a number. In the first twenty-five years the population would be fourteen millions, and the food being also doubled, the means of subsistence would be equal to this increase. In the next twenty-five years the population would be twenty-eight millions, and the means of subsistence only equal to the support of twenty-one millions. In the next period the population would be fifty-six millions, and the means of subsistence just sufficient for half that number. And at the conclusion of the first century the population would be one hundred and twelve millions and the means of subsistence only equal to the support of thirty-five millions, which would leave a population of seventy-seven millions totally unprovided for.

A great emigration necessarily implies unhappiness of some kind or other in the country that is deserted. For few persons will leave their families, connections, friends, and native land, to seek a settlement in untried foreign climes, without some strong subsisting causes of uneasiness where they are, or the hope of some great advantages in the place to which they are going.

But to make the argument more general and less interrupted by the partial views of emigration, let us take the whole earth, instead of one spot, and suppose that the restraints to population were universally removed. If the subsistence for man that the earth affords was to be increased every twenty-five years by a quantity equal to what the whole world at present produces, this would allow the power of production in the earth to be absolutely unlimited and its ratio to increase much greater than we can conceive that any possible exertions of mankind could make it.

Taking the population of the world at any number, a thousand millions, for instance, the human species would increase in the ratio of—1, 2, 4, 8, 16, 32, 64, 128, 256, 512, &c. and subsistence as— 1, 2, 3, 4, 5, 6, 7, 8, 9, 10, &c. In two centuries and a quarter, the population would be to the means of subsistence as 512 to 10, in three centuries as 4096 to 13, and in two thousand years the difference would be almost incalculable, though the produce in that time would have increased to an immense extent.

No limits whatever are placed to the productions of the earth; they may increase for ever and be greater than any assignable quantity; yet still the power of population being a power of a superior order, the increase of the human species can only be kept commensurate to the increase of the means of subsistence by the constant operation of the strong law of necessity acting as a check upon the greater power. (nature)

The effects of this check remain now to be considered.

Among plants and animals the view of the subject is simple. They are all impelled by a powerful instinct to the increase of their species, and this instinct is interrupted by no reasoning or doubts about providing for their offspring. Wherever therefore there is liberty, the power of increase is exerted, and the super-abundant effects are repressed afterwards by want of room and nourishment, which is common to animals and plants, and among animals, by becoming the prey of others.

The effects of this check on man are more complicated. Impelled to the increase of his species by an equally powerful instinct, reason interrupts his career and asks him whether he may not bring beings into the world, for whom he cannot provide the means of subsistence. In a state of equality, this would be the simple question. In the present state of society, other considerations occur. Will he not lower his rank in life? Will he not subject himself to greater difficulties than he at present feels? Will he not be obliged to labour harder? and if he has a large family, will his utmost exertions enable him to support them? May he not see his offspring in rags and misery, and clamouring for bread that he cannot give them? And may he not be reduced to the grating necessity of forfeiting his independence and of being obliged to the sparing hand of charity for support?

These considerations are calculated to prevent, and certainly do prevent, a very great number in all civilized nations from pursuing the dictate of nature in an early attachment to one woman. And this restraint almost necessarily, though not absolutely so, produces vice. Yet in all societies, even those that are most vicious, the tendency to a virtuous attachment is so strong that there is a constant effort towards an increase of population. This constant effort as constantly

tends to subject the lower classes of the society to distress and to
prevent any great permanent amelioration of their condition.

The way in which these effects are produced seems to be this.

We will suppose the means of subsistence in any country just
equal to the easy support of its inhabitants. The constant effort
towards population, which is found to act even in the most vicious
societies, increases the number of people before the means of subsistence are increased. The food therefore which before supported
seven millions must now be divided among seven millions and a half
or eight millions. The poor consequently must live much worse, and
many of them be reduced to severe distress. The number of labourers
also being above the proportion of the work in the market, the price
of labour must tend toward a decrease, while the price of provisions
would at the same time tend to rise. The labourer therefore must
work harder to earn the same as he did before. During this season
of distress, the discouragements to marriage and the difficulty of
rearing a family are so great that population is at a stand. In the
mean time the cheapness of labour, the plenty of labourers, and the
necessity of an increased industry amongst them, encourage cultivators to employ more labour upon their land, to turn up fresh soil,
and to manure and improve more completely what is already in tillage, till ultimately the means of subsistence become in the same
proportion to the population as at the period from which we set out.
The situation of the labourer being then again tolerably comfortable,
the restraints to population are in some degree loosened, and the
same retrograde and progressive movements with respect to happiness are repeated.

This sort of oscillation will not be remarked by superficial observers, and it may be difficult even for the most penetrating mind to
calculate its periods. Yet that in all old states some such vibration
does exist, though from various transverse causes, in a much less
marked, and in a much more irregular manner than I have described
it, no reflecting man who considers the subject deeply can well
doubt.

Many reasons occur why this oscillation has been less obvious,
and less decidedly confirmed by experience, than might naturally be
expected.

One principal reason is that the histories of mankind that we pos-
ses are histories only of the higher classes. We have but few accounts
that can be depended upon of the manners and customs of that part
of mankind, where these retrograde and progressive movements
chiefly take place. A satisfactory history of this kind, of one people,
and of one period, would require the constant and minute attention
of an observing mind during a long life. Some of the objects of
enquiry would be, in what proportion to the number of adults was

the number of marriages, to what extent vicious customs prevailed in consequence of the restraints upon matrimony, what was the comparative mortality among the children of the most distressed part of the community and those who lived rather more at their ease, what were the variations in the real price of labour, and what were the observable differences in the state of the lower classes of society with respect to ease and happiness, at different times during a certain period.

Such a history would tend greatly to elucidate the manner in which the constant check upon population acts and would probably prove the existence of the retrograde and progressive movements that have been mentioned, though the times of their vibration must necessarily be rendered irregular, from the operation of many interrupting causes, such as the introduction or failure of certain manufactures, a greater or less prevalent spirit of agriculture enterprize, years of plenty, or years of scarcity, wars and pestilence, poor laws, the invention of processes for shortening labour without the proportional extension of the market for the commodity, and, particularly, the difference between the nominal and real price of labour, a circumstance which has perhaps more than any other contributed to conceal this oscillation from common view.

It very rarely happens that the nominal price of labour universally falls, but we well know that it frequently remains the same, while the nominal price of provisions has been gradually increasing. This is, in effect, a real fall in the price of labour, and during this period the condition of the lower orders of the community must gradually grow worse and worse. But the farmers and capitalists are growing rich from the real cheapness of labour. Their increased capitals enable them to employ a greater number of men. Work therefore may be plentiful, and the price of labour would consequently rise. But the want of freedom in the market of labour, which occurs more or less in all communities, either from parish laws, or the more general cause of the facility of combination among the rich, and its difficulty among the poor, operates to prevent the price of labour from rising at the natural period, and keeps it down some time longer; perhaps, till a year of scarcity, when the clamour is too loud, and the necessity too apparent to be resisted.

The true cause of the advance in the price of labour is thus concealed, and the rich affect to grant it as an act of compassion and favour to the poor, in consideration of a year of scarcity, and, when plenty returns, indulge themselves in the most unreasonable of all complaints, that the price does not again fall, when a little reflection would shew them that it must have risen long before but from an unjust conspiracy of their own.

But though the rich by unfair combinations contribute frequently to prolong a season of distress among the poor, yet no possible form of society could prevent the almost constant action of misery upon a great part of mankind, if in a state of inequality, and upon all, if all were equal.

The theory on which the truth of this position depends appears to me so extremely clear that I feel at a loss to conjecture what part of it can be denied.

That population cannot increase without the means of subsistence is a proposition so evident that it needs no illustration.

That population does invariably increase where there are the means of subsistence, the history of every people that have ever existed will abundantly prove.

And that the superior power of population cannot be checked without producing misery or vice, the ample portion of these too bitter ingredients in the cup of human life and the continuance of the physical causes that seem to have produced them bear too convincing a testimony.

But in order more fully to ascertain the validity of these three propositions, let us examine the different states in which mankind have been known to exist. Even a cursory review will, I think, be sufficient to convince us that these propositions are incontrovertible truths.

CHAPTER III

The savage or hunter state shortly reviewed—The shepherd state, or the tribes of barbarians that overran the Roman Empire—The superiority of the power of population to the means of subsistence— The cause of the great tide of Northern Emigration.

In the rudest state of mankind, in which hunting is the principal occupation and the only mode of acquiring food, the means of subsistence being scattered over a large extent of territory, the comparative population must necessarily be thin. It is said that the passion between the sexes is less ardent among the North American Indians than among any other race of men. Yet notwithstanding this apathy, the effort towards population, even in this people, seems to be always greater than the means to support it. This appears from the comparatively rapid population that takes place whenever any of the tribes happen to settle in some fertile spot and to draw nourishment from more fruitful sources than that of hunting, and it has been frequently remarked that when an Indian family has taken up its abode near any European settlement and adopted a more easy and civilized mode of life, that one woman has reared five or six, or more children, though in the savage state it rarely happens, that above one or two in a family grow up to maturity. The same observation has been made with regard to the Hottentots near the Cape. These facts prove the superior power of population to the means of subsistence in nations of hunters, and that this power always shews itself the moment it is left to act with freedom.

It remains to inquire whether this power can be checked, and its effects kept equal to the means of subsistence, without vice or misery.

The North American Indians, considered as a people, cannot justly be called free and equal. In all the accounts we have of them, and, indeed, of most other savage nations, the women are represented as much more completely in a state of slavery to the men than the poor are to the rich in civilized countries. One half the nation appears to act as Helots to the other half, and the misery that checks population falls chiefly, as it always must do, upon that part whose condition is lowest in the scale of society. The infancy of man in the simplest state requires considerable attention, but this necessary attention the women cannot give, condemned as they are to the inconveniences and hardships of frequent change of place and to the constant and unremitting drudgery of preparing every thing for the reception of their tyrannic lords. These exertions, sometimes during pregnancy or with children at their backs, must occasion frequent miscarriages, and prevent any but the most robust infants from growing to maturity. Add to these hardships of the women, the constant war that prevails among savages, and the necessity which they frequently labour under of exposing their aged and helpless parents, and of thus violating the first feelings of nature, and the picture will not appear very free from the blot of misery. In estimating the happiness of a savage nation, we must not fix our eyes only on the warrior in the prime of life: he is one of a hundred: he is the gentleman, the man of fortune, the chances have been in his favour; and many efforts have failed ere this fortunate being was produced, whose guardian genius should preserve him through the numberless dangers with which he would be surrounded from infancy to manhood. The true points of comparison between two nations, seem to be, the ranks in each which appear nearest to answer to each other. And in this view, I should compare the warriors in the prime of life with the gentlemen, and the women, children, and aged, with the lower classes of the community in civilized states.

May we not then fairly infer from this short review, or rather, from the accounts that may be referred to of nations of hunters, that their population is thin from the scarcity of food, that it would immediately increase if food was in greater plenty, and that, putting vice out of the question among savages, misery is the check that represses the superior power of population and keeps its effects equal to the means of subsistence. Actual observation and experience tell us that this check, with a few local and temporary exceptions, is constantly acting now upon all savage nations, and the theory indicates, that it probably acted with nearly equal strength a thousand years ago, and it may not be much greater a thousand years hence.

Of the manners and habits that prevail among nations of shepherds, the next state of mankind, we are even more ignorant than of the savage state. But that these nations could not escape the general lot of misery arising from the want of subsistence, Europe, and all the fairest countries in the world, bear ample testimony. Want was the goad that drove the Scythian shepherds from their native haunts, like so many famished wolves in search of prey. Set in motion by this all powerful cause, clouds of Barbarians seemed to collect from all points of the northern hemisphere. Gathering fresh darkness and terror as they rolled on, the congregated bodies at length obscured the sun of Italy and sunk the whole world in universal night. These tremendous effects, so long and so deeply felt throughout the fairest portions of the earth, may be traced to the simple cause of the superior power of population, to the means of subsistence.

It is well known that a country in pasture cannot support so many inhabitants as a country in tillage, but what renders nations of shepherds so formidable is the power which they possess of moving all together and the necessity they frequently feel of exerting this power in search of fresh pasture for their herds. A tribe that was rich in cattle had an immediate plenty of food. Even the parent stock might be devoured in a case of absolute necessity. The women lived in greater ease than among nations of hunters. The men bold in their united strength and confiding in their power of procuring pasture for their cattle by change of place, felt, probably, but few fears about providing for a family. These combined causes soon produced their natural and invariable effect on extended population. A more frequent and rapid change of place became then necessary. A wider and more extensive territory was successively occupied. A broader desolation extended all around them. Want pinched the less fortunate members of the society, and, at length, the impossibility of supporting such a number together became too evident to be resisted. Young scions were then pushed out from the parent-stock and instructed to explore fresh regions and to gain happier seats for themselves by their swords. "The world was all before them where to chuse." Restless from present distress, flushed with the hope of fairer prospects, and animated with the spirit of hardy enterprize, these daring adventurers were likely to become formidable adversaries to all who opposed them. The peaceful inhabitants of the countries on which they rushed could not long withstand the energy of men acting under such powerful motives of exertion. And when they fell in with any tribes like their own, the contest was a struggle for existence, and they fought with a desperate courage, inspired by the reflection that death was the punishment of defeat and life the prize of victory.

In these savage contests many tribes must have been utterly exterminated. Some probably perished by hardship and famine. Others, whose leading star had given them a happier direction, became great and powerful tribes, and, in their turns, sent off fresh adventurers in search of still more fertile seats. The prodigious waste of human life occasioned by this perpetual struggle for room and food was more than supplied by the mighty power of population, acting, in some degree, unshackled from the constant habit of emigration. The tribes that migrated towards the South, though they won these more fruitful regions by continual battles, rapidly increased in number and power, from the increased means of subsistence. Till at length the whole territory, from the confines of China to the shores of the Baltic, was peopled by a various race of Barbarians, brave, robust, and enterprising, inured to hardship, and delighting in war. Some tribes maintained their independence. Others ranged themselves under the standard of some barbaric chieftain who led them to victory after victory, and what was of more importance, to regions abounding in corn, wine, and oil, the long wished for consummation and great reward of their labours. An Alaric, an Attila, or a Zingis Khan, and the chiefs around them, might fight for glory, for the fame of extensive conquests; but the true cause that set in motion the great tide of northern emigration, and that continued to propel it till it rolled at different periods, against China, Persia, Italy, and even Egypt, was a scarcity of food, a population extended beyond the means of supporting it.

The absolute population at any one period, in proportion to the extent of territory, could never be great, on account of the unproductive nature of some of the regions occupied; but there appears to have been a most rapid succession of human beings, and as fast as some were mowed down by the scythe of war or of famine, others rose in increased numbers to supply their place. Among these bold and improvident Barbarians, population was probably but little checked, as in modern states, from a fear of future difficulties. A prevailing hope of bettering their condition by change of place, a constant expectation of plunder, a power even, if distressed, of selling their children as slaves, added to the natural carelessness of the barbaric character, all conspired to raise a population which remained to be repressed afterwards by famine or war.

Where there is any inequality of conditions, and among nations of shepherds this soon takes place, the distress arising from a scarcity of provisions, must fall hardest upon the least fortunate members of the society. This distress also must frequently have been felt by the women, exposed to casual plunder in the absence of their husbands, and subject to continual disappointments in their expected return.

But without knowing enough of the minute and intimate history of these people, to point out precisely on what part the distress for want of food chiefly fell, and to what extent it was generally felt, I think we may fairly say, from all the accounts that we have of nations of shepherds, that population invariably increased among them whenever, by emigration or any other cause, the means of subsistence were increased, and that a further population was checked, and the actual population kept equal to the means of subsistence, by misery and vice.

For independently of any vicious customs that might have prevailed amongst them with regard to women, which always operate as checks to population, it must be acknowledged I think, that the commission of war is vice, and the effect of it misery, and none can doubt the misery of want of food.

CHAPTER IV

State of civilized nations—Probability that Europe is much more populous now than in the time of Julius Caesar—Best criterion of population—Probable error of Hume in one of the criterion that he proposes as assisting in an estimate of population—Slow increase of population at present in most of the states of Europe—The two principal checks to population—The first, or preventive check examined with regard to England.

In examining the next state of mankind with relation to the question before us, the state of mixed pasture and tillage, in which with some variation in the proportions the most civilized nations must always remain, we shall be assisted in our review by what we daily see around us, by actual experience, by facts that come within the scope of every man's observation.

Notwithstanding the exaggerations of some old historians, there can remain no doubt in the mind of any thinking man that the population of the principal countries of Europe, France, England, Germany, Russia, Poland, Sweden, and Denmark is much greater than ever it was in former times. The obvious reason of these exaggerations is the formidable aspect that even a thinly peopled nation must have, when collected together and moving all at once in search of fresh seats. If to this tremendous appearance be added a succession at certain intervals of similar emigrations, we shall not be muct surprised that the fears of the timid nations of the South represented the North as a region absolutely swarming with human beings. A nearer and juster view of the subject at present enables us to see that the inference was as absurd as if a man in this country, who was continually meeting on the road droves of cattle from Wales and the North, was immediately to conclude that these countries were the most productive of all the parts of the kingdom.

The reason that the greater part of Europe is more populous now than it was in former times is that the industry of the inhabitants has made these countries produce a greater quantity of human subsistence. For I conceive that it may be laid down as a position not to be controverted, that taking a sufficient extent of territory to include within it exportation and importation, and allowing some variation for the prevalence of luxury or of frugal habits, that population constantly bears a regular proportion to the food that the earth is made to produce. In the controversy concerning the populousness of ancient and modern nations, could it be clearly ascertained that the average produce of the countries in question, taken altogether, is greater now than it was in the times of Julius Caesar, the dispute would be at once determined.

When we are assured that China is the most fertile country in the world, that almost all the land is in tillage, and that a great part of it bears two crops every year, and further, that the people live very frugally, we may infer with certainty that the population must be immense, without busying ourselves in inquiries into the manners and habits of the lower classes and the encouragements to early marriages. But these inquiries are of the utmost importance, and a minute history of the customs of the lower Chinese would be of the greatest use in ascertaining in what manner the checks to a further population operate; what are the vices, and what are the distresses that prevent an increase of numbers beyond the ability of the country to support.

Hume, in his essay on the populousness of ancient and modern nations, when he intermingles, as he says, an inquiry concerning causes with that concerning facts, does not seem to see with his usual penetration how very little some of the causes he alludes to could enable him to form any judgment of the actual population of ancient nations. If any inference can be drawn from them, perhaps it should be directly the reverse of what Hume draws, though I certainly ought to speak with great diffidence in dissenting from a man, who of all others on such subjects was the least likely to be deceived by first appearances. If I find that at a certain period in ancient history, the encouragements to have a family were great, that early marriages were consequently very prevalent, and that few persons remained single, I should infer with certainty that population was rapidly increasing, but by no means that it was then actually very great, rather, indeed, the contrary, that it was then thin and that there was room and food for a much greater number. On the other hand, if I find that at this period the difficulties attending a family were very great, that consequently few early marriages took place, and that a great number of both sexes remained single, I infer with certainty that population was at a stand, and probably because the actual population was very great in proportion to the fertility of the land and that there was scarcely room and food for more. The number of footmen, housemaids, and other persons remaining unmarried in modern states Hume allows to be rather an argument against their population. I should rather draw a contrary inference and consider it an argument of their fullness, though this inference is not certain, because there are many thinly inhabited states that are yet stationary in their population. To speak, therefore, correctly, perhaps it may be said that the number of unmarried persons in proportion to the whole number existing at different periods, in the same or different states will enable us to judge whether population at these periods was increasing, stationary, or decreasing, but will form no criterion by which we can determine the actual population.

There is, however, a circumstance taken notice of in most of the accounts we have of China that it seems difficult to reconcile with this reasoning. It is said that early marriages very generally prevail through all the ranks of the Chinese. Yet Dr. Adam Smith supposes that population in China is stationary. These two circumstances appear to be irreconcileable. It certainly seems very little probable that the population of China is fast increasing. Every acre of land has been so long in cultivation that we can hardly conceive there is any great yearly addition to the average produce. The fact, perhaps, of the universality of early marriages may not be sufficiently ascertained. If it be supposed true, the only way of accounting for the difficulty, with our present knowledge of the subject, appears to be that the redundant population, necessarily occasioned by the prevalence of early marriages, must be repressed by occasional famines, and by the custom of exposing children, which, in times of distress, is probably more frequent than is ever acknowledged to Europeans. Relative to this barbarous practice, it is difficult to avoid remarking that there cannot be a stronger proof of the distresses that have been felt by mankind for want of food, than the existence of a custom that thus violates the most natural principle of the human heart. It appears to have been very general among ancient nations, and certainly tended rather to increase population.

In examining the principal states of modern Europe, we shall find that though they have increased very considerably in population since they were nations of shepherds, yet that at present, their progress is but slow, and instead of doubling their numbers every twenty-five years they require three or four hundred years or more for that purpose. Some, indeed, may be absolutely stationary, and others even retrograde. The cause of this slow progress in population cannot be traced to a decay of the passion between the sexes. We have sufficient reason to think that this natural propensity exists still in undiminished vigour. Why then do not its effects appear in a rapid increase of the human species? An intimate view of the state of society in any one country in Europe, which may serve equally for all, will enable us to answer this question, and to say that a foresight of the difficulties attending the rearing of a family acts as a preventive check, and the actual distresses of some of the lower classes, by which they are disabled from giving the proper food and attention to their children, acts as a positive check to the natural increase of population.

England, as one of the most flourishing states of Europe, may be fairly taken for an example, and the observations made will apply with but little variation to any other country where the population increases slowly.

The preventive check appears to operate in some degree through all the ranks of society in England. There are some men, even in the highest rank, who are prevented from marrying by the idea of the expenses that they must retrench, and the fancied pleasures that they must deprive themselves of, on the supposition of having a family. These considerations are certainly trivial, but a preventive foresight of this kind has objects of much greater weight for its contemplation as we go lower.

A man of liberal education, but with an income only just sufficient to enable him to associate in the rank of gentlemen, must feel absolutely certain that if he marries and has a family he shall be obliged, if he mixes at all in society, to rank himself with moderate farmers and the lower class of tradesmen. The woman that a man of education would naturally make the object of his choice would be one brought up in the same tastes and sentiments with himself and used to the familiar intercourse of a society totally different from that to which she must be reduced by marriage. Can a man consent to place the object of his affection in a situation so discordant, probably, to her tastes and inclinations? Two or three steps of descent in society, particularly at this round of the ladder, where education ends and ignorance begins, will not be considered by the generality of people as a fancied and chimerical, but a real and essential evil. If society be held desireable, it surely must be free, equal, and reciprocal society, where benefits are conferred as well as received, and not such as the dependent finds with his patron or the poor with the rich.

These considerations undoubtedly prevent a great number in this rank of life from following the bent of their inclinations in an early attachment. Others, guided either by a stronger passion, or a weaker judgment, break through these restraints, and it would be hard indeed, if the gratification of so delightful a passion as virtuous love did not sometimes more than counterbalance all its attendant evils. But I fear it must be owned, that the more general consequences of such marriages, are rather calculated to justify than to repress the forebodings of the prudent.

The sons of tradesmen and farmers are exhorted not to marry, and generally find it necessary to pursue this advice till they are settled in some business or farm that may enable them to support a family. These events may not, perhaps, occur till they are far advanced in life. The scarcity of farms is a very general complaint in England. And the competition in every kind of business is so great that it is not possible that all should be successful.

The labourer who earns eighteen pence a day and lives with some degree of comfort as a single man, will hesitate a little before he divides that pittance among four or five, which seems to be but just sufficient for one. Harder fare and harder labour he would submit to for the sake of living with the woman that he loves, but he must feel conscious, if he thinks at all, that should he have a large family, and any ill luck whatever, no degree of frugality, no possible exertion of his manual strength could preserve him from the heart rending sensation of seeing his children starve, or of forfeiting his independence, and being obliged to the parish for their support. The love of independence is a sentiment that surely none would wish to be erased from the breast of man, though the parish law of England, it must be confessed, is a system of all others the most calculated gradually to weaken this sentiment, and in the end may eradicate it completely.

The servants who live in gentlemen's families have restraints that are yet stronger to break through in venturing upon marriage. They possess the necessaries, and even the comforts of life, almost in as great plenty as their masters. Their work is easy and their food luxurious compared with the class of labourers. And their sense of dependence is weakened by the conscious power of changing their masters, if they feel themselves offended. Thus comfortably situated at present, what are their prospects in marrying? Without knowledge or capital, either for business or farming, and unused, and therefore unable, to earn a subsistence by daily labour, their only refuge seems to be a miserable alehouse, which certainly offers no very enchanting prospect of a happy evening to their lives. By much the greater part, therefore, deterred by this uninviting view of their future situation, content themselves with remaining single where they are.

If this sketch of the state of society in England be near the truth, and I do not conceive that it is exaggerated, it will be allowed that the preventive check to population in this country operates, though with varied force, through all the classes of the community. The same observation will hold true with regard to all old states. The effects, indeed, of these restraints upon marriage are but too conspicuous in the consequent vices that are produced in almost every part of the world, vices that are continually involving both sexes in inextricable unhappiness.

CHAPTER V

The second, or positive check to population examined, in England—The true cause why the immense sum collected in England for the poor does not better their condition—The powerful tendency of the poor laws to defeat their own purpose—Palliative of the distresses of the poor proposed—The absolute impossibility from the fixed laws of our nature, that the pressure of want can ever be completely removed from the lower classes of society—All the checks to population may be resolved into misery or vice.

The positive check to population, by which I mean the check that represses an increase which is already begun, is confined chiefly, though not perhaps solely, to the lowest orders of society. This check is not so obvious to common view as the other I have mentioned, and to prove distinctly the force and extent of its operation would require, perhaps, more data than we are in possession of. But I believe it has been very generally remarked by those who have attended to bills of mortality that of the number of children who die annually, much too great a proportion belongs to those who may be supposed unable to give their offspring proper food and attention, exposed as they are occasionally to severe distress and confined, perhaps, to unwholesome habitations and hard labour. This mortality among the children of the poor has been constantly taken notice of in all towns. It certainly does not prevail in an equal degree in the country, but the subject has not hitherto received sufficient attention to enable any one to say that there are not more deaths in proportion among the children of the poor, even in the country, than among those of the middling and higher classes. Indeed, it seems difficult to suppose that a labourer's wife who has six children, and who is sometimes in absolute want of bread, should be able always to give them the food and attention necessary to support life. The sons and daughters of peasants will not be found such rosy cherubs in real life as they are described to be in romances. It cannot fail to be remarked by those who live much in the country that the sons of labourers are very apt to be stunted in their growth, and are a long while arriving at maturity. Boys that you would guess to be fourteen or fifteen, are upon inquiry, frequently found to be eighteen or nineteen. And the lads who drive plough, which must certainly be a healthy exercise, are very rarely seen with any appearance of calves to their legs; a circumstance which can only be attributed to a want either of proper or of sufficient nourishment.

To remedy the frequent distresses of the common people, the poor laws of England have been instituted; but it is to be feared that though they may have alleviated a little the intensity of individual misfortune, they have spread the general evil over a much larger surface. It is a subject often started in conversation and mentioned always as a matter of great surprise that notwithstanding the immense sum that is annually collected for the poor in England, there is still so much distress among them. Some think that the money must be embezzled, others that the church-wardens and over-seers consume the greater part of it in dinners. All agree that some how or other it must be very ill-managed. In short the fact that nearly three millions are collected annually for the poor and yet that their distresses are not removed is the subject of continual astonishment. But a man who sees a little below the surface of things would be very much more astonished if the fact were otherwise than it is observed to be, or even if a collection universally of eighteen shillings in the pound instead of four, were materially to alter it. I will state a case which I hope will elucidate my meaning.

Suppose, that by a subscription of the rich, the eighteen pence a day which men earn now was made up five shillings, it might be imagined, perhaps, that they would then be able to live comfortably and have a piece of meat every day for their dinners. But this would be a very false conclusion. The transfer of three shillings and six-pence a day to every labourer would not increase the quantity of meat in the country. There is not at present enough for all to have a decent share. What would then be the consequence? The com-petition among the buyers in the market of meat would rapidly raise the price from six pence or seven pence, to two or three shillings in the pound, and the commodity would not be divided among many more than it is at present. When an article is scarce, and cannot be distributed to all, he that can shew the most valid patent, that is, he that offers most money becomes the possessor. If we can suppose the competition among the buyers of meat to continue long enough for a greater number of cattle to be reared annually, this could only be done at the expense of the corn, which would be a very disadvan-tageous exchange, for it is well known that the country could not then support the same population, and when subsistence is scarce in proportion to the number of people, it is of little consequence whether the lowest members of the society possess eighteen pence or five shillings. They must at all events be reduced to live upon the hardest fare and in the smallest quantity.

It will be said, perhaps, that the increased number of purchasers in every article would give a spur to productive industry and that the whole produce of the island would be increased. This might in some degree be the case. But the spur that these fancied riches would give to population would more than counterbalance it, and the increased produce would be to be divided among a more than proportionately increased number of people. All this time I am supposing that the same quantity of work would be done as before. But this would not really take place. The receipt of five shillings a day, instead of eighteen pence, would make every man fancy himself comparatively rich and able to indulge himself in many hours or days of leisure. This would give a strong and immediate check to productive industry, and in a short time not only the nation would be poorer, but the lower classes themselves would be much more distressed than when they received only eighteen pence a day.

A collection from the rich of eighteen shillings in the pound, even if distributed in the most judicious manner, would have a little the same effect as that resulting from the supposition I have just made, and no possible contributions of sacrifices of the rich, particularly in money, could for any time prevent the recurrence of distress among the lower members of society whoever they were. Great changes might, indeed, be made. The rich might become poor, and some of the poor rich, but a part of the society must necessarily feel a difficulty of living, and this difficulty will naturally fall on the least fortunate members.

It may at first appear strange, but I believe it is true, that I cannot by means of money raise a poor man and enable him to live much better than he did before, without proportionably depressing others in the same class. If I retrench the quantity of food consumed in my house, and give him what I have cut off, I then benefit him, without depressing any but myself and family, who, perhaps, may be well able to bear it. If I turn up a piece of uncultivated land, and give him the produce, I then benefit both him and all the members of the society, because what he before consumed is thrown into the common stock, and probably some of the new produce with it. But if I only give him money, supposing the produce of the country to remain the same, I give him a title to a larger share of that produce than formerly, which share he cannot receive without diminishing the shares of others. It is evident that this effect, in individual instances, must be so small as to be totally imperceptible; but still it must exist, as many other effects do, which like some of the insects that people the air, elude our grosser perceptions.

Supposing the quantity of food in any country to remain the same for many years together, it is evident that this food must be divided according to the value of each man's patent,[1] or the sum of money that he can afford to spend in this commodity so universally in request. It is a demonstrative truth, therefore, that the patents of one set of men could not be increased in value without diminishing the value of the patents of some other set of men. If the rich were to subscribe and give five shillings a day to five hundred thousand men without retrenching their own tables, no doubt can exist that as these men would naturally live more at their ease and consume a greater quantity of provisions, there would be less food remaining to divide among the rest, and consequently each man's patent would be diminished in value or the same number of pieces of silver would purchase a smaller quantity of subsistence.

An increase of population without a proportional increase of food will evidently have the same effect in lowering the value of each man's patent. The food must necessarily be distributed in smaller quantities, and consequently a day's labour will purchase a smaller quantity of provisions. An increase in the price of provisions would arise either from an increase of population faster than the means of subsistence, or from a different distribution of the money of the society. The food of a country that has been long occupied, if it be increasing, increases slowly and regularly and cannot be made to answer any sudden demands, but variations in the distribution of the money of a society are not unfrequently occurring, and are undoubtedly among the causes that occasion the continual variations which we observe in the price of provisions.

The poor-laws of England tend to depress the general condition of the poor in these two ways. Their first obvious tendency is to increase population without increasing the food for its support. A poor man may marry with little or no prospect of being able to support a family in independence. They may be said therefore in some measure to create the poor which they maintain, and as the provisions of the country must, in consequence of the increased population, be distributed to every man in smaller proportions, it is evident that the labour of those who are not supported by parish assistance will purchase a smaller quantity of provisions than before and consequently more of them must be driven to ask for support.

Secondly, the quantity of provisions consumed in workhouses upon a part of the society that cannot in general be considered as the most valuable part diminishes the shares that would otherwise belong to more industrious and more worthy members, and thus in the same manner forces more to become dependent. If the poor in the workhouses were to live better than they now do, this new dis-

1. Mr. Godwin calls the wealth that a man receives from his ancestors a mouldy patent. It may, I think, very properly be termed a patent, but I hardly see the propriety of calling it a mouldy one, as it is an article in such constant use.

tribution of the money of the society would tend more conspicuously to depress the condition of those out of the workhouses by occasioning a rise in the price of provisions.

Fortunately for England, a spirit of independence still remains among the peasantry. The poor-laws are strongly calculated to eradicate this spirit. They have succeeded in part, but had they succeeded as completely as might have been expected, their pernicious tendency would not have been so long concealed.

Hard as it may appear in individual instances, dependent poverty ought to be held disgraceful. Such a stimulus seems to be absolutely necessary to promote the happiness of the great mass of mankind, and every general attempt to weaken this stimulus, however benevolent its apparent intention, will always defeat its own purpose. If men are induced to marry from a prospect of parish provision, with little or no chance of maintaining their families in independence, they are not only unjustly tempted to bring unhappiness and dependence upon themselves and children, but they are tempted, without knowing it, to injure all in the same class with themselves. A labourer who marries without being able to support a family may in some respects be considered as an enemy to all his fellow-labourers.

I feel no doubt whatever that the parish laws of England have contributed to raise the price of provisions and to lower the real price of labour. They have therefore contributed to impoverish that class of people whose only possession is their labour. It is also difficult to suppose that they have not powerfully contributed to generate that carelessness and want of frugality observable among the poor, so contrary to the disposition frequently to be remarked among petty tradesmen and small farmers. The labouring poor, to use a vulgar expression, seem always to live from hand to mouth. Their present wants employ their whole attention, and they seldom think of the future. Even when they have an opportunity of saving they seldom exercise it, but all that is beyond their present necessities goes, generally speaking, to the ale-house. The poor-laws of England may therefore be said to diminish both the power and the will to save among the common people, and thus to weaken one of the strongest incentives to sobriety and industry, and consequently to happiness.

It is a general complaint among master manufacturers that high wages ruin all their workmen, but it is difficult to conceive that these men would not save a part of their high wages for the future support of their families, instead of spending it in drunkenness and dissipation, if they did not rely on parish assistance for support in case of accidents. And that the poor employed in manufacturers consider this assistance as a reason why they may spend all the wages they earn and enjoy themselves while they can appears to be evident from the number of families that, upon the failure of any great manufactory, immediately fall upon the parish, when perhaps the wages earned in this manufactory while it flourished were sufficiently above the price of common country labour to have allowed them to save enough for their support till they could find some other channel for their industry.

A man who might not be deterred from going to the ale-house from the consideration that on his death, or sickness, he should leave his wife and family upon the parish might yet hesitate in thus dissipating his earnings if he were assured that, in either of these cases, his family must starve or be left to the support of casual bounty. In China, where the real as well as nominal price of labour is very low, sons are yet obliged by law to support their aged and helpless parents. Whether such a law would be adviseable in this country I will not pretend to determine. But it seems at any rate highly improper, by positive institutions, which render dependent poverty so general, to weaken that disgrace, which for the best and most humane reasons ought to attach to it.

The mass of happiness among the common people cannot but be diminished, when one of the strongest checks to idleness and dissipation is thus removed, and when men are thus allured to marry with little or no prospect of being able to maintain a family in independence. Every obstacle in the way of marriage must undoubtedly be considered as a species of unhappiness. But as from the laws of our nature some check to population must exist, it is better that it should be checked from a foresight of the difficulties attending a family and the fear of dependent poverty than that it should be encouraged, only to be repressed afterwards by want and sickness.

It should be remembered always that there is an essential difference between food and those wrought commodities, the raw materials of which are in great plenty. A demand for these last will not fail to create them in as great a quantity as they are wanted. The demand for food has by no means the same creative power. In a country where all the fertile spots have been seized, high offers are necessary to encourage the farmer to lay his dressing on land from which he cannot expect a profitable return for some years. And before the prospect of advantage is sufficiently great to encourage this sort of agricultural enterprize, and while the new produce is rising, great distresses may be suffered from the want of it. The demand for an increased quantity of subsistence is, with few exceptions, constant every where, yet we see how slowly it is answered in all those countries that have been long occupied.

The poor-laws of England were undoubtedly instituted for the most benevolent purpose, but there is great reason to think that they have not succeeded in their intention. They certainly mitigate some cases of very severe distress which might otherwise occur, yet the state of the poor who are supported by parishes, considered in all its circumstances, is very far from being free from misery. But one of the principal objections to them is that for this assistance which some of the poor receive, in itself almost a doubtful blessing, the whole class of the common people of England is subjected to a set of grating, inconvenient, and tyrannical laws, totally inconsistent with the genuine spirit of the constitution. The whole business of settlements, even in its present amended state, is utterly contradictory to all ideas of freedom. The parish persecution of men whose families are likely to become chargeable, and of poor women who are near lying-in, is a most disgraceful and disgusting tyranny. And the obstructions continually occasioned in the market of labour by these laws, have a constant tendency to add to the difficulties of those who are struggling to support themselves without assistance.

These evils attendant on the poor-laws are in some degree irremediable. If assistance be to be distributed to a certain class of people, a power must be given somewhere of discriminating the proper objects and of managing the concerns of the institutions that are necessary, but any great interference with the affairs of other people, is a species of tyranny, and in the common course of things the exercise of this power may be expected to become grating to those who are driven to ask for support. The tyranny of Justices, Churchwardens, and Overseers, is a common complaint among the poor, but the fault does not lie so much in these persons, who probably before they were in power were not worse than other people, but in the nature of all such institutions.

The evil is perhaps gone too far to be remedied, but I feel little doubt in my own mind that if the poor-laws had never existed, though there might have been a few more instances of very severe distress, yet that the aggregate mass of happiness among the common people would have been much greater than it is at present.

Mr. Pitt's Poor-bill has the appearance of being framed with benevolent intentions, and the clamour raised against it was in many respects ill directed and unreasonable. But it must be confessed that it possesses in a high degree the great and radical defect of all systems of the kind, that of tending to increase population without increasing the means for its support, and thus to depress the condition of those that are not supported by parishes, and, consequently, to create more poor.

To remove the wants of the lower classes of society is indeed an arduous task. The truth is that the pressure of distress on this part of a community is an evil so deeply seated that no human ingenuity can reach it. Were I to propose a palliative, and palliatives are all that the nature of the case will admit, it should be, in the first place, the total abolition of all the present parish-laws. This would at any rate give liberty and freedom of action to the peasantry of England, which they can hardly be said to possess at present. They would then be able to settle without interruption, wherever there was a prospect of a greater plenty of work and a higher price for labour. The market of labour would then be free, and those obstacles removed, which as things are now, often for a considerable time prevent the price from rising according to the demand.

Secondly, Premiums might be given for turning up fresh land, and all possible encouragements held out to agriculture above manufacturers, and to tillage above grazing. Every endeavour should be used to weaken and destroy all those institutions relating to corporations, apprenticeships, &c, which cause the labours of agriculture to be worse paid than the labours of trade and manufactures. For a country can never produce its proper quantity of food while these distinctions remain in favour of artizans. Such encouragements to agriculture would tend to furnish the market with an increasing quantity of healthy work, and at the same time, by augmenting the produce of the country, would raise the comparative price of labour and ameliorate the condition of the labourer. Being now in better circumstances, and seeing no prospect of parish assistance, he would be more able, as well as more inclined, to enter into associations for providing against the sickness of himself or family.

Lastly, for cases of extreme distress, county workhouses might be established, supported by rates upon the whole kingdom and free for persons of all counties, and indeed of all nations. The fare should be hard, and those that were able obliged to work. It would be desireable that they should not be considered as comfortable asylums in all difficulties, but merely as places where severe distress might find some alleviation. A part of these houses might be separated, or others built for a most beneficial purpose, which has not been unfrequently taken notice of, that of providing a place where any person, whether native or foreigner, might do a day's work at all times and receive the market price for it. Many cases would undoubtedly be left for the exertion of individual benevolence.

A plan of this kind, the preliminary of which should be an abolition of all the present parish laws, seems to be the best calculated to increase the mass of happiness among the common people in England. To prevent the recurrence of misery is, alas! beyond the power of man. In the vain endeavour to attain what in the nature of things is impossible, we now sacrifice not only possible but certain benefits. We tell the common people that if they will submit to a code of tyrannical regulations, they shall never be in want. They do submit to these regulations. They perform their part of the contract, but we do not, nay cannot, perform ours, and thus the poor sacrifice the valuable blessing of liberty and receive nothing that can be called an equivalent in return.

Notwithstanding then, the institution of the poor-laws in England, I think it will be allowed that considering the state of the lower classes altogether, both in the towns and in the country, the distresses which they suffer from the want of proper and sufficient food, from hard labour and unwholesome habitations, must operate as a constant check to incipient population.

To these two great checks to population, in all long occupied countries, which I have called the preventive and the positive checks, may be added vicious customs with respect to women, great cities, unwholesome manufactures, luxury, pestilence, and war.

All these checks may be fairly resolved into misery and vice. And that these are the true causes of the slow increase of population in all the states of modern Europe, will appear sufficiently evident from the comparatively rapid increase that has invariably taken place whenever these causes have been in any considerable degree removed.

CHAPTER VI

New colonies—Reasons of their rapid increase—North American Colonies—Extraordinary instance of increase in the back settlements—Rapidity with which even old states recover the ravages of war, pestilence, famine, or the convulsions of nature.

It has been universally remarked that all new colonies settled in healthy countries where there was plenty of room and food have constantly increased with astonishing rapidity in their population. Some of the colonies from ancient Greece, in no very long period, more than equalled their parent states in numbers and strength. And not to dwell on remote instances, the European settlements in the new world bear ample testimony to the truth of a remark which, indeed, has never, that I know of, been doubted. A plenty of rich land, to be had for little or nothing, is so powerful a cause of population as to overcome all other obstacles. No settlements could well have been worse managed than those of Spain in Mexico, Peru, and Quito. The tyranny, superstition, and vices of the mother-country were introduced in ample quantities among her children. Exorbitant taxes were exacted by the Crown. The most arbitrary restrictions were imposed on their trade. And the governors were not behind hand in rapacity and extortion for themselves as well as their master. Yet, under all these difficulties, the colonies made a quick progress in population. The city of Lima, founded since the conquest, is represented by Ulloa as containing fifty thousand inhabitants near fifty years ago. Quito, which had been but a hamlet of Indians, is represented by the same author as in his time equally populous. Mexico is said to contain a hundred thousand inhabitants, which, notwithstanding the exaggerations of the Spanish writers, is supposed to be five times greater than what it contained in the time of Montezuma.

In the Portuguese colony of Brazil, governed with almost equal tyranny, there were supposed to be, thirty years since, six hundred thousand inhabitants of European extraction.

The Dutch and French colonies, though under the government of exclusive companies of merchants, which, as Dr. Adam Smith says very justly, is the worst of all possible governments, still persisted in thriving under every disadvantage.

But the English North American colonies, now the powerful People of the United States of America, made by far the most rapid progress. To the plenty of good land which they possessed in common with the Spanish and Portuguese settlements, they added a greater degree of liberty and equality. Though not without some restrictions on their foreign commerce, they were allowed a perfect liberty of managing their own internal affairs. The political institutions that prevailed were favourable to the alienation and division of property. Lands that were not cultivated by the proprietor within a limited time were declared grantable to any other person. In Pennsylvania there was no right of primogeniture, and in the provinces of New England the eldest had only a double share. There were no tythes in any of the States, and scarcely any taxes. And on account of the extreme cheapness of good land a capital could not be more advantageously employed than in agriculture which at the same time that it supplies the greatest quantity of healthy work affords much the most valuable produce to the society.

The consequence of these favourable circumstances united was a rapidity of increase, probably without parallel in history. Throughout all the northern colonies, the population was found to double itself in 25 years. The original number of persons who had settled in the four provinces of new England in 1643, was 21,200.[2] Afterwards, it is supposed that more left them than went to them. In the year 1760, they were increased to half a million. They had therefore all along doubled their own number in 25 years. In New Jersey the period of doubling appeared to be 22 years; and in Rhode Island still less. In the back settlements, where the inhabitants applied themselves solely to agriculture, and luxury was not known, they were found to double their own number in 15 years, a most extraordinary instance

2. I take these facts from Dr. Price's two volumes of Observations [Richard Price, *Observations on Reversionary Payments* (1771), 2 vols. (*Editor*)], not having Dr. Styles's pamphlet, from which he quotes, by me.

of increase.[3] Along the sea coast, which would naturally be first inhabited, the period of doubling was about 35 years; and in some of the maritime towns, the population was absolutely at a stand.

These facts seem to shew that population increases exactly in the proportion that the two great checks to it, misery and vice, are removed and that there is not a truer criterion of the happiness and innocence of a people than the rapidity of their increase. The unwholesomeness of towns, to which some persons are necessarily driven from the nature of their trades, must be considered as a species of misery, and every the slightest check to marriage, from a prospect of the difficulty of maintaining a family, may be fairly classed under the same head. In short it is difficult to conceive any check to population which does not come under the description of some species of misery or vice.

The population of the thirteen American States before the war, was reckoned at about three millions. Nobody imagines that Great Britain is less populous at present for the emigration of the small parent stock that produced these numbers. On the contrary, a certain degree of emigration is known to be favourable to the population of the mother country. It has been particularly remarked that the two Spanish provinces from which the greatest number of people emigrated to America became in consequence more populous. Whatever was the original number of British Emigrants that increased so fast in the North American Colonies, let us ask, why does not an equal number produce an equal increase in the same time in Great Britain? The great and obvious cause to be assigned is the want of room and food, or, in other words, misery, and that this is a much more powerful cause even than vice appears sufficiently evident from the rapidity with which even old States recover the desolations of war, pestilence, or the accidents of nature. They are then for a short time placed a little in the situation of new states, and the effect is always answerable to what might be expected. If the industry of the inhabitants be not destroyed by fear or tyranny, subsistence will soon

3. In instances of this kind the powers of the earth appear to be fully equal to answer all the demands for food that can be made upon it by man. But we should be led into an error if we were thence to suppose that population and food ever really increase in the same ratio. The one is still a geometrical and the other an arithmetical ratio, that is, one increases by multiplication, and the other by addition. Where there are few people, and a great quantity of fertile land, the power of the earth to afford a yearly increase of food may be compared to a great reservoir of water, supplied by a moderate stream. The faster population increases, the more help will be got to draw off the water, and consequently an increasing quantity will be taken every year. But the sooner, undoubtedly, will the reservoir be exhausted, and the streams only remain. When acre has been added to acre, till all the fertile land is occupied, the yearly increase of food will depend upon the amelioration of the land already in possession; and even this moderate stream will be gradually diminishing. But population, could it be supplied with food, would go on with unexhausted vigour, and the increase of one period would furnish the power of a greater increase the next, and this without any limit.

increase beyond the wants of the reduced numbers, and the invariable consequence will be, that population which before, perhaps, was nearly stationary, will begin immediately to increase.

The fertile province of Flanders, which has been so often the seat of the most destructive wars, after a respite of a few years, has appeared always as fruitful and as populous as ever. Even the Palatinate lifted up its head again after the execrable ravages of Louis the Fourteenth. The effects of the dreadful plague in London in 1666 were not perceptible 15 or 20 years afterwards. The traces of the most destructive famines in China and Indostan are by all accounts very soon obliterated. It may even be doubted whether Turkey and Egypt are upon an average much less populous for the plagues that periodically lay them waste. If the number of people which they contain be less now than formerly, it is, probably, rather to be attributed to the tyranny and oppression of the government under which they groan, and the consequent discouragements to agriculture, than to the loss which they sustain by the plague. The most tremendous convulsions of nature, such as volcanic eruptions and earthquakes, if they do not happen so frequently as to drive away the inhabitants or to destroy their spirit of industry, have but a trifling effect on the average population of any state. Naples, and the country under Vesuvius, are still very populous, notwithstanding the repeated eruptions of that mountain. And Lisbon and Lima are now, probably, nearly in the same state with regard to population, as they were before the last earthquakes.

CHAPTER VII

A probable cause of epidemics—Extracts from Mr. Susmilch's tables—Periodical returns of sickly seasons to be expected in certain cases—Proportion of births to burials for short periods in any country an inadequate criterion of the real average increase of population—Best criterion of a permanent increase of population—Great frugality of living one of the causes of the famines of China and Indostan—Evil tendency of one of the clauses in Mr. Pitt's Poor Bill—Only one proper way of encouraging population—Causes of the happiness of nations—Famine, the last and most dreadful mode by which nature represses a redundant population—The three propositions considered as established.

By great attention to cleanliness, the plague seems at length to be completely expelled from London. But it is not improbable that among the secondary causes that produce even sickly seasons and epidemics ought to be ranked a crowded population and unwholesome and insufficient food. I have been led to this remark, by looking over some of the tables of Mr. Susmilch, which Dr. Price has extracted in one of his notes to the postscript on the controversy respecting the population of England and Wales. They are considered as very correct, and if such tables were general, they would throw great light on the different ways by which population is repressed and prevented from increasing beyond the means of subsistence in any country. I will extract a part in the tables, with Dr. Price's remarks.

IN THE KINGDOM OF PRUSSIA, AND DUKEDOM OF LITHUANIA

Annual Average	Births	Burials	Marriages	Proportion of Births to Marriages	Proportion of Births to Burials
10 Yrs. to 1702	21963	14718	5928	37 to 10	150 to 100
5 Yrs. to 1716	21602	11984	4968	37 to 10	180 to 100
5 Yrs. to 1756	28392	19154	5599	50 to 10	148 to 100

"N. B. In 1709 and 1710, pestilence carried off 247,733 of the inhabitants of this country, and in 1736 and 1737, epidemics prevailed, which again checked its increase."

It may be remarked, that the greatest proportion of births to burials, was in the five years after the great pestilence.

DUTCHY OF POMERANIA

Annual Average	Births	Burials	Marriages	Proportion of Births to Marriages	Proportion of Births to Burials
6 Yrs. to 1702	6540	4647	1810	36 to 10	140 to 100
6 Yrs. to 1708	7455	4208	1875	39 to 10	177 to 100
6 Yrs. to 1726	8432	5627	2131	39 to 10	150 to 100
4 Yrs. to 1756	12767	9281	2957	43 to 10	137 to 100

"In this instance the inhabitants appear to have been almost doubled in 56 years, no very bad epidemics having once interrupted the increase, but the three years immediately following the last period (to 1759) were years so sickly that the births were sunk to 10,229, and the burials raised to 15,068."

Is it not probable that in this case the number of inhabitants had increased faster than the food and the accommodations necessary to preserve them in health? The mass of the people would, upon this supposition, be obliged to live harder, and a greater number would be crowded together in one house, and it is not surely improbable that these were among the natural causes that produced the three sickly years. These causes may produced such an effect, though the country, absolutely considered, may not be extremely crowded and populous. In a country even thinly inhabited, if an increase of population takes place before more food is raised and more houses are built, the inhabitants must be distressed in some degree for room and subsistence. Were the marriages in England, for the next eight or ten years, to be more prolifick than usual, or even were a greater number of marriages than usual to take place, supposing the number of houses to remain the same, instead of five or six to a cottage, there must be seven or eight, and this, added to the necessity of harder living, would probably have a very unfavourable effect on the health of the common people.

NEUMARK OF BRANDENBURCH

Annual Average	Births	Burials	Marriages	Proportion of Births to Marriages	Proportion of Births to Burials
5 Yrs. to 1701	5433	3483	1436	37 to 10	155 to 100
5 Yrs. to 1726	7012	4254	1713	40 to 10	164 to 100
5 Yrs. to 1756	7978	5567	1891	42 to 10	143 to 100

"Epidemics prevailed for six years, from 1736, to 1741, which checked the increase."

DUKEDOM OF MAGDEBURGH

Annual Average	Births	Burials	Marriages	Proportion of Births to Marriages	Proportion of Births to Burials
5 Yrs. to 1702	6431	4103	1681	38 to 10	156 to 100
5 Yrs. to 1717	7590	5335	2076	36 to 10	142 to 100
5 Yrs. to 1756	8850	8069	2193	40 to 10	109 to 100

"The years 1738, 1740, 1750, and 1751, were particularly sickly."
For further information on this subject, I refer the reader to Mr. Susmilch's tables. The extracts that I have made are sufficient to shew the periodical though irregular returns of sickly seasons, and it seems highly probable that a scantiness of room and food was one of the principal causes that occasioned them.

It appears from the tables that these countries were increasing rather fast for old states, notwithstanding the occasional sickly seasons that prevailed. Cultivation must have been improving, and marriages, consequently, encouraged. For the checks to population appear to have been rather of the positive than of the preventive kind. When from a prospect of increasing plenty in any country, the weight that represses population is in some degree removed, it is highly probable that the motion will be continued beyond the operation of the cause that first impelled it. Or, to be more particular, when the increasing produce of a country, and the increasing demand for labour, so far ameliorate the condition of the labourer as greatly to encourage marriage, it is probable that the custom of early marriages will continue till the population of the country has gone beyond the increased produce, and sickly seasons appear to be the natural and necessary consequence. I should expect, therefore, that those countries where subsistence was increasing sufficiently at times to encourage population but not to answer all its demands, would be more subject to periodical epidemics than those where the population could more completely accommodate itself to the average produce.

An observation the converse of this will probably also be found true. In those countries that are subject to periodical sicknesses, the increase of population, or the excess of births above the burials, will be greater in the intervals of these periods than is usual, caeteris paribus, in the countries not so much subject to such disorders. If Turkey and Egypt have been nearly stationary in their average population for the last century, in the intervals of their periodical plagues, the births must have exceeded the burials in a greater proportion than in such countries as France and England.

The average proportion of births to burials in any country for a period of five or ten years will hence appear to be a very inadequate criterion by which to judge of its real progress in population. This proportion certainly shews the rate of increase during those five or ten years; but we can by no means thence infer what had been the increase for the twenty years before, or what would be the increase for the twenty years after. Dr. Price observes that Sweden, Norway, Russia, and the kingdom of Naples are increasing fast; but the extracts from registers that he has given are not for periods of sufficient extent to establish the fact. It is highly probable, however, that Sweden, Norway, and Russia are really increasing in their population, though not at the rate that the proportion of births to burials for the short periods that Dr. Price takes would seem to shew.[4] For five years, ending in 1777, the proportion of births to burials in the kingdom of Naples was 144 to 100, but there is reason to suppose that this proportion would indicate an increase much greater than would be really found to have taken place in that kingdom during a period of a hundred years.

Dr. Short compared the registers of many villages and market towns in England for two periods; the first from Queen Elizabeth to the middle of the last century, and the second from different years

4. See Dr. Price's Observation, 2 Vol. Postscript to the controversy on the population of England and Wales.

at the end of the last century to the middle of the present. And from a comparison of these extracts, it appears that in the former period the births exceeded the burials in the proportion of 124 to 100 but in the latter, only in the proportion of 111 to 100. Dr. Price thinks that the registers in the former period are not to be depended upon, but probably in this instance they do not give incorrect proportions. At least there are many reasons for expecting to find a greater excess of births above the burials in the former period than in the latter. In the natural progress of the population of any country, more good land will, caeteris paribus,[5] be taken into cultivation in the earlier stages of it than in the later. And a greater proportional yearly increase of produce will almost invariably be followed by a greater proportional increase of population. But besides this great cause, which would naturally give the excess of births above the burials greater at the end of Queen Elizabeth's reign than in the middle of the present century, I cannot help thinking that the occasional ravages of the plague in the former period must have had some tendency to increase this proportion. If an average of ten years had been taken in the intervals of the returns of this dreadful disorder, or if the years of plague had been rejected as accidental, the registers would certainly give the proportion of births to burials too high for the real average increase of the population. For some few years after the great plague in 1666, it is probable that there was a more than usual excess of births above burials, particularly if Dr. Price's opinion be founded, that England was more populous at the revolution (which happened only 22 years afterwards) than it is at present.

Mr. King, in 1693, stated the proportion of the births to the burials throughout the Kingdom, exclusive of London, as 115 to 100. Dr. Short makes it, in the middle of the present century, 111 to 100, including London. The proportion in France for five years, ending in 1774, was 117 to 100. If these statements are near the truth, and if there are no very great variations at particular periods in the proportions, it would appear that the population of France and England has accommodated itself very nearly to the average produce of each country. The discouragements to marriage, the consequent vicious habits, war, luxury, the silent though certain depopulation of large towns, and the close habitations and insufficient food of many of the poor, prevent population from increasing beyond the means of subsistence; and, if I may use an expression which certainly at first appears strange, supersede the necessity of great and ravaging epidemics to repress what is redundant. Were a wasting plague to sweep

---

5. I say caeteris paribus, because the increase of the produce of any country will always very greatly depend on the spirit of industry that prevails and the way in which it is directed. The knowledge and habits of the people, and other temporary causes, particularly the degree of civil liberty and equality existing at the time, must always have great influence in exciting and directing this spirit.

off two millions in England and six millions in France, there can be no doubt whatever that after the inhabitants had recovered from the dreadful shock, the proportion of births to burials would be much above what it is in either country at present.

In New Jersey, the proportion of births to deaths on an average of seven years, ending in 1743, was as 300 to 100. In France and England, taking the highest proportion, it is as 117 to 100. Great and astonishing as this difference is, we ought not to be so wonderstruck at it as to attribute it to the miraculous interposition of heaven. The causes of it are not remote, latent and mysterious; but near us, round about us, and open to the investigation of every inquiring mind. It accords with the most liberal spirit of philosophy to suppose that not a stone can fall, or a plant rise, without the immediate agency of divine power. But we know from experience that these operations of what we call nature have been conducted almost invariably according to fixed laws. And since the world began, the causes of population and depopulation have probably been as constant as any of the laws of nature with which we are acquainted.

The passion between the sexes has appeared in every age to be so nearly the same that it may always be considered, in algebraic language, as a given quantity. The great law of necessity which prevents population from increasing in any country beyond the food which it can either produce or acquire, is a law so open to our view, so obvious and evident to our understandings, and so completely confirmed by the experience of every age, that we cannot for a moment doubt it. The different modes which nature takes to prevent or repress a redundant population do not appear, indeed, to us so certain and regular, but though we cannot always predict the mode we may with certainty predict the fact. If the proportion of births to deaths for a few years, indicate an increase of numbers much beyond the proportional increased or acquired produce of the country, we may be perfectly certain that unless an emigration takes place, the deaths will shortly exceed the births, and that the increase that had taken place for a few years cannot be the real average increase of the population of the country. Were there no other depopulating causes, every country would, without doubt, be subject to periodical pestilences or famines.

The only true criterion of a real and permanent increase in the population of any country is the increase of the means of subsistence. But even this criterion is subject to some slight variations which are, however, completely open to our view and observations. In some countries population appears to have been forced, that is, the people have been habituated by degrees to live almost upon the smallest possible quantity of food. There must have been periods in such countries when population increased permanently, without an increase in the means of subsistence. China seems to answer to this description. If the accounts we have of it are to be trusted, the lower classes of people are in the habit of living almost upon the smallest possible quantity of food and are glad to get any putrid offals that European labourers would rather starve than eat. The law in China which permits parents to expose their children has tended principally thus to force the population. A nation in this state must necessarily be subject to famines. Where a country is so populous in proportion to the means of subsistence that the average produce of it is but barely sufficient to support the lives of the inhabitants, any deficiency from the badness of seasons must be fatal. It is probable that the very frugal manner in which the Gentoos are in the habit of living contributes in some degree to the famines of Indostan.

In America, where the reward of labour is at present so liberal, the lower classes might retrench very considerably in a year of scarcity without materially distressing themselves. A famine therefore seems to be almost impossible. It may be expected that in the progress of the population of America, the labourers will in time be much less liberally rewarded. The numbers will in this case permanently increase without a proportional increase in the means of subsistence.

In the different States of Europe there must be some variations in the proportion between the number of inhabitants and the quantity of food consumed, arising from the different habits of living that prevail in each State. The labourers of the South of England are so accustomed to eat fine wheaten bread that they will suffer themselves to be half starved before they will submit to live like the Scotch peasants. They might perhaps in time, by the constant operation of the hard law of necessity, be reduced to live even like the lower Chinese, and the country would then, with the same quantity of food, support a greater population. But to effect this must always be a most difficult, and every friend to humanity will hope, an abortive attempt. Nothing is so common as to hear of encouragements that ought to be given to population. If the tendency of mankind to increase be so great as I have represented it to be, it may appear strange that this increase does not come when it is thus repeatedly called for. The true reason is that the demand for a greater population is made without preparing the funds necessary to support it. Increase the demand for agricultural labour by promoting cultivation, and with it consequently increase the produce of the country, and ameliorate the condition of the labourer, and no apprehensions whatever need be entertained of the proportional increase of population. An attempt to effect this purpose in any other way is vicious, cruel, and tyrannical, and in any state of tolerable freedom cannot therefore succeed. It may appear to be the interest of the rulers, and the rich of a State, to force population and thereby lower the price of labour, and consequently the expense of fleets and armies and the cost of manufactures for foreign sale, but every attempt of the kind should be carefully watched and strenuously resisted by the friends of the poor, particularly when it comes under the deceitful garb of benevolence and is likely, on that account, to be cheerfully and cordially received by the common people.

I entirely acquit Mr. Pitt of any sinister intention in that clause of his poor bill which allows a shilling a week to every labourer for each child he has above three. I confess that before the bill was brought into Parliament, and for some time after, I thought that such a regulation would be highly beneficial; but further reflection on the subject has convinced me that if its object be to better the condition of the poor, it is calculated to defeat the very purpose which it has in view. It has no tendency that I can discover to increase the produce of the country, and if it tend to increase the population without increasing the produce, the necessary and inevitable consequence appears to be that the same produce must be divided among a greater number, and consequently that a day's labour will purchase a smaller quantity of provisions, and the poor therefore in general must be more distressed.

I have mentioned some cases where population may permanently increase without a proportional increase in the means of subsistence. But it is evident that the variation in different States, between the food and the numbers supported by it, is restricted to a limit beyond which it cannot pass. In every country, the population of which is not absolutely decreasing, the food must be necessarily sufficient to support, and to continue, the race of labourers.

Other circumstances being the same, it may be affirmed that countries are populous according to the quantity of human food which they produce, and happy according to the liberality with which that food is divided, or the quantity which a day's labour will purchase. Corn countries are more populous than pasture countries, and rice countries more populous that corn countries. The lands in England are not suited to rice, but they would all bear potatoes; and Dr. Adam Smith observes that if potatoes were to become the favourite vegetable food of the common people, and if the same quantity of land was employed in their culture as is now employed in the culture of corn, the country would be able to support a much greater population, and would consequently in a very short time have it.

The happiness of a country does not depend absolutely upon its poverty or its riches, upon its youth or its age, upon its being thinly or fully inhabited, but upon the rapidity with which it is increasing, upon the degree in which the yearly increase of food approaches to the yearly increase of an unrestricted population. This approximation is always the nearest in new colonies, where the knowledge and industry of an old State operate on the fertile unappropriated land of a new one. In other cases, the youth or the age of a State is not in this respect of very great importance. It is probable that the food of Great Britain is divided in as great plenty to the inhabitants at the present period as it was two thousand, three thousand, or four thousand years ago. And there is reason to believe that the poor and thinly inhabited tracts of the Scotch Highlands are as much distressed by an overcharged population as the rich and populous province of Flanders.

Were a country never to be over-run by a people more advanced in arts, but left to its own natural progress in civilization; from the time that its produce might be considered as an unit, to the time that it might be considered as a million, during the lapse of many hundred years there would not be a single period when the mass of the people could be said to be free from distress, either directly or indirectly, for want of food. In every State in Europe, since we have first had accounts of it, millions and millions of human existences have been repressed from this simple cause; though perhaps in some of these States, an absolute famine has never been known.

Famine seems to be the last, the most dreadful resource of nature. The power of population is so superior to the power in the earth to produce subsistence for man, that premature death must in some shape or other visit the human race. The vices of mankind are active and able ministers of depopulation. They are the precursors in the great army of destruction, and often finish the dreadful work themselves. But should they fail in this war of extermination, sickly seasons, epidemics, pestilence, and plague, advance in terrific array and sweep off their thousands and ten thousands. Should success be still incomplete, gigantic inevitable famine stalks in the rear, and with one mighty blow, levels the population with the food of the world.

Must it not then be acknowledged by an attentive examiner of the histories of mankind, that in every age and in every State in which man has existed, or does now exist,

That the increase of population is necessarily limited by the means of subsistence.

That population does invariably increase when the means of subsistence increase. And that the superior power of population is repressed, and the actual population kept equal to the means of subsistence, by misery and vice.

CHAPTER VIII

Mr. Wallace—Error of supposing that the difficulty arising from population is at a great distance—Mr. Condorcet's sketch of the

progress of the human mind—Period when the oscillation, mentioned by Mr. Condorcet, ought to be applied to the human race.

To a person who draws the preceding obvious inferences from a view of the past and present state of mankind, it cannot but be a matter of astonishment that all the writers on the perfectibility of man and of society who have noticed the argument of an overcharged population treat it always very slightly and invariably represent the difficulties arising from it as at a great and almost immeasurable distance. Even Mr. Wallace, who thought the argument itself of so much weight as to destroy his whole system of equality, did not seem to be aware that any difficulty would occur from this cause till the whole earth had been cultivated like a garden and was incapable of any further increase of produce. Were this really the case, and were a beautiful system of equality in other respects practicable, I cannot think that our ardour in the pursuit of such a scheme ought to be damped by the contemplation of so remote a difficulty. An event at such a distance might fairly be left to providence; but the truth is that if the view of the argument given in this essay be just, the difficulty, so far from being remote, would be imminent and immediate. At every period during the progress of cultivation, from the present moment to the time when the whole earth was become like a garden, the distress for want of food would be constantly pressing on all mankind, if they were equal. Though the produce of the earth might be increasing every year, population would be increasing much faster, and the redundancy must necessarily be repressed by the periodical or constant action of misery or vice.

Mr. Condorcet's *Esquisse d'un tableau historique des progrès de l'esprit humain* was written, it is said, under the pressure of that cruel proscription which terminated in his death. If he had no hopes of its being seen during his life and of its interesting France in his favour, it is a singular instance of the attachment of a man to principles which every day's experience was so fatally for himself contradicting. To see the human mind in one of the most enlightened nations of the world, and after a lapse of some thousand years, debased by such a fermentation of disgusting passions, of fear, cruelty, malice, revenge, ambition, madness, and folly as would have disgraced the most savage nation in the most barbarous age must have been such a tremendous shock to his ideas of the necessary and inevitable progress of the human mind that nothing but the firmest conviction of the truth of his principles, in spite of all appearances, could have withstood.

This posthumous publication is only a sketch of a much larger work which he proposed should be executed. It necessarily, therefore, wants that detail and application which can alone prove

the truth of any theory. A few observations will be sufficient to shew
how completely the theory is contradicted when it is applied to the
real, and not to an imaginary, state of things.

In the last division of the work, which treats of the future progress
of man towards perfection, he says, that comparing, in the different
civilized nations of Europe, the actual population with the extent of
territory, and observing their cultivation, their industry, their divi-
sions of labour, and their means of subsistence, we shall see that it
would be impossible to preserve the same means of subsistence, and,
consequently, the same population, without a number of individuals
who have no other means of supplying their wants than their industry. Having allowed the necessity of such a class of men, and advert-
ing afterwards to the precarious revenue of those families that would
depend so entirely on the life and health of their chief,[6] he says, very
justly, "There exists then, a necessary cause of inequality, of dependence, and even of misery, which menaces, without ceasing, the
most numerous and active class of our societies." The difficulty is
just and well stated, and I am afraid that the mode by which he
proposes it should be removed, will be found inefficacious. By the
application of calculations to the probabilities of life and the interest
of money, he proposes that a fund should be established which
should assure to the old an assistance, produced, in part, by their
own former savings, and, in part, by the savings of individuals who
in making the same sacrifice die before they reap the benefit of it.
The same or a similar fund should give assistance to women and
children who lose their husbands or fathers and afford a capital to
those who were of an age to found a new family, sufficient for the
proper development of their industry. These establishments he
observes, might be made in the name and under the protection of
the society. Going still further, he says that by the just application
of calculations, means might be found of more completely preserving
a state of equality, by preventing credit from being the exclusive
privilege of great fortunes, and yet giving it a basis equally solid, and
by rendering the progress of industry, and the activity of commerce,
less dependent on great capitalists.

Such establishments and calculations may appear very promising
upon paper, but when applied to real life they will be found to be
absolutely nugatory. Mr. Condorcet allows that a class of people
which maintains itself entirely by industry is necessary to every state.
Why does he allow this? No other reason can well be assigned than
that he conceives that the labour necessary to procure subsistence
for an extended population will not be performed without the goad

---

6. To save time and long quotations, I shall here give the substance of some of Mr. Condorcet's sentiments, and hope I shall not misrepresent them, but I refer the reader to the
   work itself, which will amuse, if it does not convince him.

of necessity. If by establishments of this kind this spur to industry be removed, if the idle and the negligent are placed upon the same footing with regard to their credit, and the future support of their wives and families, as the active and industrious, can we expect to see men exert that animated activity in bettering their condition which now forms the master spring of public prosperity? If an inquisition were to be established to examine the claims of each individual and to determine whether he had or had not exerted himself to the utmost, and to grant or refuse assistance accordingly, this would be little else than a repetition upon a larger scale of the English poor laws and would be completely destructive of the true principles of liberty and equality.

But independent of this great objection to these establishments, and supposing for a moment that they would give no check to productive industry, by far the greatest difficulty remains yet behind.

Were every man sure of a comfortable provision for a family, almost every man would have one, and were the rising generation free from the "killing frost" of misery, population must rapidly increase. Of this Mr. Condorcet seems to be fully aware himself, and after having described further improvements, he says,

"But in this progress of industry and happiness, each generation will be called to more extended enjoyments, and in consequence, by the physical constitution of the human frame, to an increase in the number of individuals. Must not there arrive a period then, when these laws, equally necessary, shall counteract each other? When the increase of the number of men surpassing their means of subsistence, the necessary result must be either a continual diminution of happiness and population, a movement truly retrograde, or at least a kind of oscillation between good and evil? In societies arrived at this term, will not this oscillation be a constantly subsisting cause of periodical misery? Will it not mark the limit when all further amelioration will become impossible, and point out that term to the perfectibility of the human race which it may reach in the course of ages, but can never pass?"

He then adds,

"There is no person who does not see how very distant such a period is from us, but shall we ever arrive at it? It is equally impossible to pronounce for or against the future realization of an event which cannot take place but at an era when the human race will have attained improvements, of which we can at present scarcely form a conception."

Mr. Condorcet's picture of what may be expected to happen when the number of men shall surpass the means of their subsistence, is justly drawn. The oscillation which he describes will certainly take place and will without doubt be a constantly subsisting cause of periodical misery. The only point in which I differ from Mr. Condorcet with regard to this picture is the period when it may be applied to the human race. Mr. Condorcet thinks that it cannot possibly be applicable but at an era extremely distant. If the proportion between the natural increase of population and food which I have geven be in any degree near the truth, it will appear, on the contrary, that the period when the number of men surpass their means of subsistence has long since arrived, and that this necessary oscillation, this constantly subsisting cause of periodical misery, has existed ever since we have had any histories of mankind, does exist at present, and will for ever continue to exist, unless some decided change take place in the physical constitution of our nature.

Mr. Condorcet, however, goes on to say that should the period which he conceives to be so distant ever arrive, the human race, and the advocates for the perfectibility of man, need not be alarmed at it. He then proceeds to remove the difficulty in a manner which I profess not to understand. Having observed that the ridiculous prejudices of superstition would by that time have ceased to throw over morals a corrupt and degrading austerity, he alludes either to a promiscuous concubinage, which would prevent breeding, or to something else as unnatural. To remove the difficulty in this way will surely, in the opinion of most men, be to destroy that virtue and purity of manners which the advocates of equality and of the perfectibility of man profess to be the end and object of their views.

CHAPTER IX

Mr. Condorcet's conjecture concerning the organic perfectibility of man, and the indefinite prolongation of human life—Fallacy of the argument, which infers an unlimited progress from a partial improvement, the limit of which cannot be ascertained, illustrated in the breeding of animals, and the cultivation of plants.

The last question which Mr. Condorcet proposes for examination is the organic perfectibility of man. He observes that if the proofs which have been already given and which, in their development, will receive greater force in the work itself, are sufficient to establish the indefinite perfectibility of man upon the supposition of the same natural faculties and the same organization which he has at present, what will be the certainty, what the extent of our hope, if this organization, these natural faculties themselves, are susceptible of amelioration?

From the improvement of medicine, from the use of more wholesome food and habitations, from a manner of living which will improve the strength of the body by exercise without impairing it by excess, from the destruction of the two great causes of the degradation of man, misery and too great riches, from the gradual removal of transmissible and contagious disorders by the improvement of physical knowledge, rendered more efficacious by the progress of reason and of social order, he infers that though man will not absolutely become immortal, yet that the duration between his birth and natural death will increase without ceasing, will have no assignable term, and may properly be expressed by the word indefinite. He then defines this word to mean either a constant approach to an unlimited extent, without ever reaching it, or an increase in the immensity of ages to an extent greater than any assignable quantity.

But surely the application of this term in either of these senses to the duration of human life is in the highest degree unphilosophical and totally unwarranted by any appearances in the laws of nature. Variations from different causes are essentially distinct from a regular and unretrograde increase. The average duration of human life will to a certain degree vary from healthy or unhealthy climates, from wholesome or unwholesome food, from virtuous or vicious manners, and other causes, but it may be fairly doubted whether there is really the smallest perceptible advance in the natural duration of human life since first we have had any authentic history of man. The prejudices of all ages have indeed been directly contrary to this supposition, and though I would not lay much stress upon these prejudices, they will in some measure tend to prove that there has been no marked advance in an opposite direction.

It may perhaps be said that the world is yet so young, so completely in its infancy, that it ought not to be expected that any difference should appear so soon.

If this be the case, there is at once an end of all human science. The whole train of reasonings from effects to causes will be destroyed. We may shut our eyes to the book of nature, as it will no longer be of any use to read it. The wildest and most improbable conjectures may be advanced with as much certainty as the most just and sublime theories, founded on careful and reiterated experiments. We may return again to the old mode of philosophizing and make facts bend to systems, instead of establishing systems upon facts. The grand and consistent theory of Newton will be placed upon the same footing as the wild and eccentric hypotheses of Descartes. In short, if the laws of nature are thus fickle and inconstant, if it can be affirmed and be believed that they will change, when for ages and ages they have appeared immutable, the human mind will no longer have any incitements to inquiry, but must remain fixed in inactive torpor, or amuse itself only in bewildering dreams and extravagant fancies.

The constancy of the laws of nature and of effects and causes is the foundation of all human knowledge, though far be it from me to

say that the same power which framed and executes the laws of
nature, may not change them all "in a moment, in the twinkling of
an eye." Such a change may undoubtedly happen. All that I mean to
say is that it is impossible to infer it from reasoning. If without any
previous observable symptoms or indications of a change, we can
infer that a change will take place, we may as well make any assertion
whatever and think it as unreasonable to be contradicted in affirming
that the moon will come in contact with the earth to-morrow, as in
saying that the sun will rise at its usual time.

With regard to the duration of human life, there does not appear
to have existed from the earliest ages of the world to the present
moment the smallest permanent symptom or indication of increasing
prolongation.[7] The observable effects of climate, habit, diet, and
other causes, on length of life have furnished the pretext for asserting
its indefinite extension; and the sandy foundation on which the argument rests is that because the limit of human life is undefined;
because you cannot mark its precise term, and say so far exactly shall
it go and no further; that therefore its extent may increase for ever,
and be properly termed indefinite or unlimited. But the fallacy and
absurdity of this argument will sufficiently appear from a slight examination of what Mr. Condorcet calls the organic perfectibility, or
degeneration, of the race of plants and animals, which he says may
be regarded as one of the general laws of nature.

I am told that it is a maxim among the improvers of cattle that you
may breed to any degree of nicety you please, and they found this
maxim upon another, which is that some of the offspring will possess

7. Many, I doubt not, will think that the attempting gravely to controvert so absurd a paradox
as the immortality of man on earth, or indeed even the perfectibility of man and society,
is a waste of time and words, and that such unfounded conjectures are best answered by
neglect. I profess, however, to be of a different opinion. When paradoxes of this kind are
advanced by ingenious and able men, neglect has no tendency to convince them of their
mistakes. Priding themselves on what they conceive to be a mark of the reach and size of
their own understandings, of the extent and comprehensiveness of their views; they will
look upon this neglect merely as an indication of poverty and narrowness in the mental
exertions of their contemporaries; and only think that the world is not yet prepared to
receive their sublime truths.

On the contrary, a candid investigation of these subjects, accompanied with a perfect
readiness to adopt any theory warranted by sound philosophy, may have a tendency to
convince them that in forming improbable and unfounded hypotheses, so far from enlarging the bounds of human science, they are contracting it, so far from promoting the
improvement of the human mind, they are obstructing it; they are throwing us back again
almost into the infancy of knowledge and weakening the foundations of that mode of
philosophising, under the auspices of which, science has of late made such rapid advances.
The present rage for wide and unrestrained speculation seems to be a kind of mental
intoxication, arising, perhaps, from the great and unexpected discoveries which have been
made of late years, in various branches of science. To men elate and giddy with such
successes, every thing appeared to be within the grasp of human powers; and under this
illusion, they confounded subjects where no real progress could be proved, with those
where the progress had been marked, certain, and acknowledged. Could they be persuaded
to sober themselves with a little severe and chastized thinking, they would see, that the
cause of truth and of sound philosophy cannot but suffer by substituting wild flights and
unsupported assertions for patient investigation and well-authenticated proofs.

the desirable qualities of the parents in a greater degree. In the famous Leicestershire breed of sheep, the object is to procure them with small heads and small legs. Proceeding upon these breeding maxims, it is evident that we might go on till the heads and legs were evanescent quantities, but this is so palpable an absurdity that we may be quite sure that the premises are not just and that there really is a limit, though we cannot see it or say exactly where it is. In this case, the point of the greatest degree of improvement, or the smallest size of the head and legs, may be said to be undefined, but this is very different from unlimited, or from indefinite, in Mr. Condorcet's acceptation of the term. Though I may not be able in the present instance to mark the limit at which further improvement will stop, I can very easily mention a point at which it will not arrive. I should not scruple to assert that were the breeding to continue for ever, the head and legs of these sheep would never be so small as the head and legs of a rat.

It cannot be true, therefore, that among animals some of the off-spring will possess the desirable qualities of the parents in a greater degree, or that animals are indefinitely perfectible.

The progress of a wild plant to a beautiful garden flower is perhaps more marked and striking than any thing that takes place among animals, yet even here it would be the height of absurdity to assert that the progress was unlimited or indefinite. One of the most obvious features of the improvement is the increase of size. The flower has grown gradually larger by cultivation. If the progress were really unlimited it might be increased ad infinitum, but this is so gross an absurdity that we may be quite sure that among plants as well as among animals there is a limit to improvement, though we do not exactly know where it is. It is probable that the gardeners who contend for flower prizes have often applied stronger dressing without success. At the same time, it would be highly presumptuous in any man to say that he had seen the finest carnation or anemone that could ever be made to grow. He might however assert without the smallest chance of being contradicted by a future fact, that no carnation or anemone could ever by cultivation be increased to the size of a large cabbage; and yet there are assignable quantities much greater than a cabbage. No man can say that he has seen the largest ear of wheat or the largest oak that could ever grow; but he might easily, and with perfect certainty, name a point of magnitude, at which they would not arrive. In all these cases therefore, a careful distinction should be made, between an unlimited progress and a progress where the limit is merely undefined.

It will be said, perhaps, that the reason why plants and animals cannot increase indefinitely in size is that they would fall by their own weight. I answer, how do we know this but from experience?

from experience of the degree of strength with which these bodies are formed. I know that a carnation, long before it reached the size of a cabbage, would not be supported by its stalk, but I only know this from my experience of the weakness and want of tenacity in the materials of a carnation stalk. There are many substances in nature of the same size that would support as large a head as a cabbage.

The reasons of the mortality of plants are at present perfectly unknown to us. No man can say why such a plant is annual, another biennial, and another endures for ages. The whole affair in all these cases, in plants, animals, and in the human race, is an affair of experience, and I only conclude that man is mortal because the invariable experience of all ages has proved the mortality of those materials of which his visible body is made.

What can we reason but from what we know.

Sound philosophy will not authorize me to alter this opinion of the mortality of man on earth, till it can be clearly proved that the human race has made, and is making, a decided progress towards an illimitable extent of life. And the chief reason why I adduced the two particular instances from animals and plants was to expose and illustrate, if I could, the fallacy of that argument which infers an unlimited progress, merely because some partial improvement has taken place, and that the limit of this improvement cannot be precisely ascertained.

The capacity of improvement in plants and animals, to a certain degree, no person can possibly doubt. A clear and decided progress has already been made; and yet I think it appears that it would be highly absurd to say that this progress has no limits. In human life, though there are great variations from different causes, it may be doubted whether, since the world began, any organic improvement whatever in the human frame can be clearly ascertained. The foundations therefore, on which the arguments for the organic perfectibility of man rest, are unusually weak and can only be considered as mere conjectures. It does not, however, by any means seem impossible that by an attention to breed, a certain degree of improvement similar to that among animals might take place among men. Whether intellect could be communicated may be a matter of doubt; but size, strength, beauty, complexion, and perhaps even longevity are in a degree transmissible. The error does not seem to lie in supposing a small degree of improvement possible, but in not discriminating between a small improvement, the limit of which is undefined, and an improvement really unlimited. As the human race however could not be improved in this way without condemning all the bad specimens to celibacy, it is not probable that an attention to breed should ever become general; indeed, I know of no well-directed attempts of this kind, except in the ancient family of the Bickerstaffs, who are said to have been very successful in whitening the skins and increasing the height of their race by prudent marriages, particularly by that very judicious cross with Maud, the milk-maid, by which some capital defects in the constitutions of the family were corrected.

It will not be necessary, I think, in order more completely to shew the improbability of any approach in man towards immortality on earth, to urge the very great additional weight that an increase in the duration of life would give to the argument of population.

Mr. Condorcet's book may be considered not only as a sketch of the opinions of a celebrated individual, but of many of the literary men in France at the beginning of the revolution. As such, though merely a sketch, it seems worthy of attention.

CHAPTER X

Mr. Godwin's system of equality—Error of attributing all the vices of mankind to human institutions—Mr. Godwin's first answer to the difficulty arising from population totally insufficient—Mr. Godwin's beautiful system of equality supposed to be realized—Its utter destruction simply from the principle of population in so short a time as thirty years.

In reading Mr. Godwin's ingenious and able work on political justice, it is impossible not to be struck with the spirit and energy of his style, the force and precision of some of his reasonings, the ardent tone of his thoughts, and particularly with that impressive earnestness of manner which gives an air of truth to the whole. At the same time, it must be confessed that he has not proceeded in his enquiries with the caution that sound philosophy seems to require. His conclusions are often unwarranted by his premises. He fails sometimes in removing the objections which he himself brings forward. He relies too much on general and abstract propositions which will not admit of application. And his conjectures certainly far outstrip the modesty of nature.

The system of equality which Mr. Godwin proposes is without doubt by far the most beautiful and engaging of any that has yet appeared. An amelioration of society to be produced merely by reason and conviction wears much more the promise of permanence than any change effected and maintained by force. The unlimited exercise of private judgment is a doctrine inexpressibly grand and captivating and has a vast superiority over those systems where every individual is in a manner the slave of the public. The substitution of benevolence as the master-spring and moving principle of society, instead of self-love, is a consummation devoutly to be wished. In short, it is impossible to contemplate the whole of this fair structure without emotions of delight and admiration, accompanied with ardent longing for the period of its accomplishment. But alas! that moment can never arrive. The whole is little better than a dream, a beautiful phantom of the imagination. These "gorgeous palaces" of happiness and immortality, these "solemn temples" of truth and virtue will dissolve, "like the baseless fabric of a vision," when we awaken to real life and contemplate the true and genuine situation of man on earth.

Mr. Godwin, at the conclusion of the third chapter of his eighth book, speaking of population, says, "There is a principle in human society, by which population is perpetually kept down to the level of the means of subsistence. Thus among the wandering tribes of America and Asia, we never find through the lapse of ages that population has so increased as to render necessary the cultivation of the earth." This principle, which Mr. Godwin thus mentions as some mysterious and occult cause and which he does not attempt to investigate, will be found to be the grinding law of necessity, misery, and the fear of misery.

The great error under which Mr. Godwin labours throughout his whole work is the attributing almost all the vices and misery that are seen in civil society to human institutions. Political regulations and the established administration of property are with him the fruitful sources of all evil, the hotbeds of all the crimes that degrade mankind. Were this really a true state of the case, it would not seem a hopeless task to remove evil completely from the world, and reason seems to be the proper and adequate instrument for effecting so great a purpose. But the truth is, that though human institutions appear to be the obvious and obtrusive causes of much mischief to mankind, yet in reality they are light and superficial, they are mere feathers that float on the surface, in comparison with those deeper seated causes of impurity that corrupt the springs and render turbid the whole stream of human life.

Mr. Godwin, in his chapter on the benefits attendant on a system of equality, says, "The spirit of oppression, the spirit of servility, and the spirit of fraud, these are the immediate growth of the established administration of property. They are alike hostile to intellectual improvement. The other vices of envy, malice, and revenge are their inseparable companions. In a state of society where men lived in the midst of plenty and where all shared alike the bounties of nature, these sentiments would inevitably expire. The narrow principle of selfishness would vanish. No man being obliged to guard his little store or provide with anxiety and pain for his restless wants, each would lose his individual existence in the thought of the general good. No man would be an enemy to his neighbour, for they would have no subject of contention, and, of consequence, philanthropy would resume the empire which reason assigns her. Mind would be delivered from her perpetual anxiety about corporal support, and free to expatiate in the field of thought, which is congenial to her. Each would assist the enquiries of all."

This would indeed be a happy state. But that it is merely an imaginary picture, with scarcely a feature near the truth, the reader, I am afraid, is already too well convinced.

Man cannot live in the midst of plenty. All cannot share alike the bounties of nature. Were there no established administration of property, every man would be obliged to guard with force his little store. Selfishness would be triumphant. The subjects of contention would be perpetual. Every individual mind would be under a constant anxiety about corporal support, and not a single intellect would be left free to expatiate in the field of thought.

How little Mr. Godwin has turned the attention of his penetrating mind to the real state of man on earth will sufficiently appear from the manner in which he endeavours to remove the difficulty of an overcharged population. He says, "The obvious answer to this objection, is, that to reason thus is to foresee difficulties at a great distance. Three fourths of the habitable globe is now uncultivated. The parts already cultivated are capable of immeasureable improvement. Myriads of centuries of still increasing population may pass away, and the earth be still found sufficient for the subsistence of its inhabitants."

I have already pointed out the error of supposing that no distress and difficulty would arise from an overcharged population before the earth absolutely refused to produce any more. But let us imagine for a moment Mr. Godwin's beautiful system of equality realized in its utmost purity, and see how soon this difficulty might be expected to press under so perfect a form of society. A theory that will not admit of application cannot possibly be just.

Let us suppose all the causes of misery and vice in this island removed. War and contention cease. Unwholesome trades and manufactories do not exist. Crowds no longer collect together in great and pestilent cities for purposes of court intrigue, of commerce, and vicious gratifications. Simple, healthy, and rational amusements take place of drinking, gaming, and debauchery. There are no towns sufficiently large to have any prejudicial effects on the human constitution. The greater part of the happy inhabitants of this terrestrial paradise live in hamlets and farm-houses scattered over the face of the country. Every house is clean, airy, sufficiently roomy, and in a healthy situation. All men are equal. The labours of luxury are at end. And the necessary labours of agriculture are shared amicably among all. The number of persons, and the produce of the island, we suppose to be the same as at present. The spirit of benevolence,

guided by impartial justice, will divide this produce among all the
members of the society according to their wants. Though it would
be impossible that they should all have animal food every day, yet
vegetable food, with meat occasionally, would satisfy the desires of
a frugal people and would be sufficient to preserve them in health,
strength, and spirits.

Mr. Godwin considers marriage as a fraud and a monopoly. Let
us suppose the commerce of the sexes established upon principles
of the most perfect freedom. Mr. Godwin does not think himself that
this freedom would lead to a promiscuous intercourse, and in this I
perfectly agree with him. The love of variety is a vicious, corrupt,
and unnatural taste and could not prevail in any great degree in a
simple and virtuous state of society. Each man would probably select
himself a partner to whom he would adhere as long as that adherence
continued to be the choice of both parties. It would be of little consequence, according to Mr. Godwin, how many children a woman
had or to whom they belonged. Provisions and assistance would
spontaneously flow from the quarter in which they abounded, to the
quarter that was deficient.[8] And every man would be ready to furnish
instruction to the rising generation according to his capacity.

I cannot conceive a form of society so favourable upon the whole
to population. The irremediableness of marriage, as it is at present
constituted, undoubtedly deters many from entering into that state.
An unshackled intercourse on the contrary would be a most powerful
incitement to early attachments, and as we are supposing no anxiety
about the future support of children to exist, I do not conceive that
there would be one woman in a hundred, of twenty three, without a
family.

With these extraordinary encouragements to population, and every
cause of depopulation, as we have supposed, removed, the numbers
would necessarily increase faster than in any society that has ever
yet been known. I have mentioned, on the authority of a pamphlet
published by a Dr. Styles and referred to by Dr. Price, that the inhabitants of the back settlements of America doubled their numbers in
fifteen years. England is certainly a more healthy country than the
back settlements of America, and as we have supposed every house
in the island to be airy and wholesome, and the encouragements to
have a family greater even than with the back settlers, no probable
reason can be assigned why the population should not double itself
in less, if possible, than fifteen years. But to be quite sure that we
do not go beyond the truth, we will only suppose the period of doubling to be twenty-five years, a ratio of increase which is well known

8. *Enquiry concerning Political Justice*, Book 8, p. 504. [Malthus' note. The editor has
   expanded this and some others of Malthus' notes to include full bibliographical information.]

to have taken place throughout all the Northern States of America.

There can be little doubt that the equalization of property which we have supposed, added to the circumstance of the labour of the whole community being directed chiefly to agriculture, would tend greatly to augment the produce of the country. But to answer the demands of a population increasing so rapidly, Mr. Godwin's calculation of half an hour a day for each man would certainly not be sufficient. It is probable that the half of every man's time must be employed for this purpose. Yet with such, or much greater exertions, a person who is acquainted with the nature of the soil in this country, and who reflects on the fertility of the lands already in cultivation, and the barrenness of those that are not cultivated, will be very much disposed to doubt whether the whole average produce could possibly be doubled in twenty-five years from the present period. The only chance of success would be the ploughing up all the grazing countries and putting an end almost entirely to the use of animal food. Yet a part of this scheme might defeat itself. The soil of England will not produce much without dressing, and cattle seem to be necessary to make that species of manure which best suits the land. In China it is said that the soil in some of the provinces is so fertile as to produce two crops of rice in the year without dressing. None of the lands in England will answer to this description.

Difficult, however, as it might be to double the average produce of the island in twenty-five years, let us suppose it effected. At the expiration of the first period therefore, the food, though almost entirely vegetable, would be sufficient to support in health the doubled population of fourteen millions.

During the next period of doubling, where will the food be found to satisfy the importunate demands of the increasing numbers? Where is the fresh land to turn up? where is the dressing necessary to improve that which is already in cultivation? There is no person with the smallest knowledge of land, but would say that it was impossible that the average produce of the country could be increased during the second twenty-five years by a quantity equal to what it at present yields. Yet we will suppose this increase, however improbable, to take place. The exuberant strength of the argument allows of almost any concession. Even with this concession, however, there would be seven millions at the expiration of the second term, unprovided for. A quantity of food equal to the frugal support of twenty-one millions, would be to be divided among twenty-eight millions.

Alas! what becomes of the picture where men lived in the midst of plenty, where no man was obliged to provide with anxiety and pain for his restless wants, where the narrow principle of selfishness did not exist, where Mind was delivered from her perpetual anxiety about corporal support and free to expatiate in the field of thought which is congenial to her? This beautiful fabric of imagination vanishes at the severe touch of truth. The spirit of benevolence, cherished and invigorated by plenty, is repressed by the chilling breath of want. The hateful passions that had vanished, reappear. The mighty law of self-preservation expels all the softer and more exalted emotions of the soul. The temptations to evil are too strong for human nature to resist. The corn is plucked before it is ripe, or secreted in unfair proportions, and the whole black train of vices that belong to false-hood are immediately generated. Provisions no longer flow in for the support of the mother with a large family. The children are sickly from insufficient food. The rosy flush of health gives place to the pallid cheek and hollow eye of misery. Benevolence yet lingering in a few bosoms makes some faint expiring struggles, till at length self-love resumes his wonted empire and lords it triumphant over the world.

No human institutions here existed, to the perverseness of which Mr. Godwin ascribes the original sin of the worst men.[9] No opposition had been produced by them between public and private good. No monopoly had been created of those advantages which reason directs to be left in common. No man had been goaded to the breach of order by unjust laws. Benevolence had established her reign in all hearts; and yet in so short a period as within fifty years, violence, oppression, falsehood, misery, every hateful vice, and every form of distress, which degrade and sadden the present state of society, seem to have been generated by the most imperious circumstances, by laws inherent in the nature of man, and absolutely independent of all human regulations.

If we are not yet too well convinced of the reality of this melan-choly picture, let us but look for a moment into the next period of twenty-five years, and we shall see twenty-eight millions of human beings without the means of support; and before the conclusion of the first century, the population would be one hundred and twelve millions, and the food only sufficient for thirty-five millions, leaving seventy-seven millions unprovided for. In these ages want would be indeed triumphant, and rapine and murder must reign at large; and yet all this time we are supposing the produce of the earth absolutely unlimited, and the yearly increase greater than the boldest specu-lator can imagine.

This is undoubtedly a very different view of the difficulty arising from population from that which Mr. Godwin gives when he says, "Myriads of centuries of still increasing population may pass away, and the earth be still found sufficient for the subsistence of its inhab-itants."

9. *Ibid.*, p. 340.

I am sufficiently aware that the redundant twenty-eight millions, or seventy-seven millions, that I have mentioned, could never have existed. It is a perfectly just observation of Mr. Godwin that "There is a principle in human society, by which population is perpetually kept down to the level of the means of subsistence." The sole question is, what is this principle? Is it some obscure and occult cause? Is it some mysterious interference of heaven, which at a certain period, strikes the men with impotence, and the women with barrenness? Or is it a cause open to our researches, within our view, a cause which has constantly been observed to operate, though with varied force, in every state in which man has been placed? Is it not a degree of misery, the necessary and inevitable result of the laws of nature, which human institutions, so far from aggravating, have tended considerably to mitigate, though they never can remove?

It may be curious to observe, in the case that we have been supposing, how some of the laws which at present govern civilized society would be successively dictated by the most imperious necessity. As man, according to Mr. Godwin, is the creature of the impressions to which he is subject, the goadings of want could not continue long, before some violations of public or private stock would necessarily take place. As these violations increased in number and extent, the more active and comprehensive intellects of the society would soon perceive that while population was fast increasing, the yearly produce of the country would shortly begin to diminish. The urgency of the case would suggest the necessity of some immediate measures to be taken for the general safety. Some kind of convention would then be called and the dangerous situation of the country stated in the strongest terms. It would be observed that while they lived in the midst of plenty, it was of little consequence who laboured the least, or who possessed the least, as every man was perfectly willing and ready to supply the wants of his neighbour. But that the question was no longer whether one man should give to another that which he did not use himself; but whether he should give to his neighbour the food which was absolutely necessary to his own existence. It would be represented that the number of those that were in want very greatly exceeded the number and means of those who should supply them; that these pressing wants, which from the state of the produce of the country could not all be gratified, had occasioned some flagrant violations of justice; that these violations had already checked the increase of food, and would, if they were not by some means or other prevented, throw the whole community in confusion; that imperious necessity seemed to dictate that a yearly increase of produce should, if possible, be obtained at all events; that in order to effect this first, great, and indispensible purpose, it would be adviseable to make a more complete division of land, and to secure every man's stock against violation by the most powerful sanctions, even by death itself.

It might be urged perhaps by some objectors, that, as the fertility of the land increased and various accidents occurred, the share of some men might be much more than sufficient for their support, and that when the reign of self-love was once established, they would not distribute their surplus produce without some compensation in return. It would be observed in answer, that this was an inconvenience greatly to be lamented, but that it was an evil which bore no comparison to the black train of distresses, that would inevitably be occasioned by the insecurity of property: that the quantity of food which one man could consume was necessarily limited by the narrow capacity of the human stomach; that it was not certainly probable that he should throw away the rest; but that even if he exchanged his surplus food for the labour of others, and made them in some degree dependent on him, this would still be better than that these others should absolutely starve.

It seems highly probable, therefore, that an administration of property, not very different from that which prevails in civilized States at present, would be established as the best, though inadequate, remedy for the evils which were pressing on the society.

The next subject that would come under discussion, intimately connected with the preceding, is the commerce between the sexes. It would be urged by those who had turned their attention to the true cause of the difficulties under which the community laboured, that while every man felt secure that all his children would be well provided for by general benevolence, the powers of the earth would be absolutely inadequate to produce food for the population which would inevitably ensue; that even, if the whole attention and labour of the society were directed to this sole point, and if, by the most perfect security of property and every other encouragement that could be thought of, the greatest possible increase of produce were yearly obtained, yet still, that the increase of food would by no means keep pace with the much more rapid increase of population; that some check to population therefore was imperiously called for; that the most natural and obvious check seemed to be, to make every man provide for his own children; that this would operate in some respect as a measure and guide, in the increase of population; as it might be expected that no man would bring beings into the world for whom he could not find the means of support; that where this notwithstanding was the case, it seemed necessary, for the example of others, that the disgrace and inconvenience attending such a conduct, should fall upon the individual who had thus inconsiderately plunged himself and innocent children in misery and want.

The institution of marriage, or at least of some express or implied obligation on every man to support his own children, seemed to be the natural result of these reasonings in a community under the difficulties that we have supposed.

The view of these difficulties presents us with a very natural origin of the superior disgrace which attends a breach of chastity in the woman, than in the man. It could not be expected that women should have resources sufficient to support their own children. When therefore a woman was connected with a man who had entered into no compact to maintain her children, and aware of the inconveniences that he might bring upon himself, had deserted her, these children must necessarily fall for support upon the society, or starve. And to prevent the frequent recurrence of such an inconvenience, as it would be highly unjust to punish so natural a fault by personal restraint or infliction, the men might agree to punish it with disgrace. The offence is besides more obvious and conspicuous in the woman, and less liable to any mistake. The father of a child may not always be known, but the same uncertainty cannot easily exist with regard to the mother. Where the evidence of the offence was most complete, and the inconvenience to the society at the same time the greatest, there, it was agreed, that the largest share of blame should fall. The obligation on every man to maintain his children, the society would enforce if there were occasion; and the greater degree of inconvenience or labour to which a family would necessarily subject him, added to some portion of disgrace which every human being must incur, who leads another into unhappiness, might be considered as a sufficient punishment for the man.

That a woman should at present be almost driven from society for an offence which men commit nearly with impunity, seems to be undoubtedly a breach of natural justice. But the origin of the custom, as the most obvious and effectual method of preventing the frequent recurrence of a serious inconvenience to a community, appears to be natural, though not perhaps perfectly justifiable. This origin, however, is now lost in the new train of ideas which the custom has since generated. What at first might be dictated by state necessity is now supported by female delicacy; and operates with the greatest force on that part of society where, if the original intention of the custom were preserved, there is the least real occasion for it.

When these two fundamental laws of society, the security of property and the institution of marriage, were once established, inequality of conditions must necessarily follow. Those who were born after the division of property, would come into a world already possessed. If their parents, from having too large a family, could not give them sufficient for their support, what are they to do in a world where every thing is appropriated? We have seen the fatal effects that would result to a society if every man had a valid claim to an equal share of the produce of the earth. The members of a family which was grown too large for the original division of land appropriated to it could not then demand a part of the surplus produce of others, as a debt of justice. It has appeared that from the inevitable laws of our nature, some human beings must suffer from want. These are the unhappy persons who, in the great lottery of life, have drawn a blank. The number of these claimants would soon exceed the ability of the surplus produce to supply. Moral merit is a very difficult distinguishing criterion, except in extreme cases. The owners of surplus produce would in general seek some more obvious mark of distinction. And it seems both natural and just, that except upon particular occasions, their choice should fall upon those who were able, and professed themselves willing, to exert their strength in procuring a further surplus produce; and thus at once benefitting the community and enabling these proprietors to afford assistance to greater numbers. All who were in want of food would be urged by imperious necessity to offer their labour in exchange for this article so absolutely essential to existence. The fund appropriated to the maintenance of labour would be the aggregate quantity of food possessed by the owners of land beyond their own consumption. When the demands upon this fund were great and numerous, it would naturally be divided in very small shares. Labour would be ill paid. Men would offer to work for a bare subsistence, and the rearing of families would be checked by sickness and misery. On the contrary, when this fund was increasing fast, when it was great in proportion to the number of claimants, it would be divided in much larger shares. No man would exchange his labour without receiving an ample quantity of food in return. Labourers would live in ease and comfort and would consequently be able to rear a numerous and vigorous offspring.

On the state of this fund, the happiness or the degree of misery prevailing among the lower classes of people in every known State at present chiefly depends. And on this happiness or degree of misery depends the increase, stationariness, or decrease of population.

And thus it appears that a society constituted according to the most beautiful form that imagination can conceive, with benevolence for its moving principle instead of self-love, and with every evil disposition in all its members corrected by reason and not force, would, from the inevitable laws of nature, and not from any original depravity of man, in a very short period degenerate into a society constructed upon a plan not essentially different from that which prevails in every known State at present; I mean, a society divided into a class of proprietors, and a class of labourers, and with self-love the main-spring of the great machine.

In the supposition I have made, I have undoubtedly taken the increase of population smaller, and the increase of produce greater, than they really would be. No reason can be assigned, why, under the circumstances I have supposed, population should not increase faster than in any known instance. If then we were to take the period of doubling at fifteen years, instead of twenty-five years, and reflect upon the labour necessary to double the produce in so short a time, even if we allow it possible, we may venture to pronounce with certainty that if Mr. Godwin's system of society was established in its utmost perfection, instead of myriads of centuries, not thirty years could elapse before its utter destruction from the simple principle of population.

I have taken no notice of emigration for obvious reasons. If such societies were instituted in other parts of Europe, these countries would be under the same difficulties with regard to population, and could admit no fresh members into their bosoms. If this beautiful society were confined to this island, it must have degenerated strangely from its original purity, and administer but a very small portion of the happiness it proposed; in short, its essential principle must be completely destroyed before any of its members would voluntarily consent to leave it and live under such governments as at present exist in Europe, or submit to the extreme hardships of first settlers in new regions. We well know from repeated experience how much misery and hardship men will undergo in their own country before they can determine to desert it, and how often the most tempting proposals of embarking for new settlements have been rejected by people who appeared to be almost starving.

CHAPTER XI

Mr. Godwin's conjecture concerning the future extinction of the passion between the sexes—Little apparent grounds for such a conjecture—Passion of love not inconsistent either with reason or virtue.

We have supposed Mr. Godwin's system of society once completely established. But it is supposing an impossibility. The same causes in nature which would destroy it so rapidly, were it once established, would prevent the possibility of its establishment. And upon what grounds we can presume a change in these natural causes, I am utterly at a loss to conjecture. No move towards the extinction of the passion between the sexes has taken place in the five or six thousand years that the world has existed. Men in the decline of life have in all ages declaimed a passion which they have ceased to feel, but with as little reason as success. Those who from coldness of constitutional temperament have never felt what love is, will surely be allowed to be very incompetent judges with regard to the power of this passion to contribute to the sum of pleasurable sensations in life. Those who have spent their youth in criminal excesses and have prepared for themselves, as the comforts of their age corporal debility and mental remorse may well inveigh against such pleasures as vain and futile, and unproductive of lasting satisfaction. But the pleasures of pure love will bear the contemplation of the most improved reason, and the most exalted virtue. Perhaps there is scarcely a man who has once experienced the genuine delight of virtuous love, however great his intellectual pleasures may have been, that does not look back to the period as the sunny spot in his whole life, where his imagination loves to bask, which he recollects and contemplates with the fondest regrets, and which he would most wish to live over again. The superiority of intellectual to sensual pleasures consists rather in their filling up more time, in their having a larger range, and in their being less liable to satiety, than in their being more real and essential.

Intemperance in every enjoyment defeats its own purpose. A walk in the finest day through the most beautiful country, if pursued too far, ends in pain and fatigue. The most wholesome and invigorating food, eaten with an unrestrained appetite, produces weakness instead of strength. Even intellectual pleasures, though certainly less liable than others to satiety, pursued with too little intermission, debilitate the body and impair the vigour of the mind. To argue against the reality of these pleasures from their abuse seems to be hardly just. Morality, according to Mr. Godwin, is a calculation of consequences, or, as Archdeacon Paley very justly expresses it, the will of God, as collected from general expediency. According to either of these definitions, a sensual pleasure not attended with the probability of unhappy consequences does not offend against the laws of morality, and if it be pursued with such a degree of temperance as to leave the most ample room for intellectual attainments, it must undoubtedly add to the sum of pleasurable sensations in life. Virtuous love, exalted by friendship, seems to be that sort of mixture of sensual and intellectual enjoyment particularly suited to the nature of man, and most powerfully calculated to awaken the sympathies of the soul and produce the most exquisite gratifications.

Mr. Godwin says, in order to shew the evident inferiority of the pleasures of sense, "Strip the commerce of the sexes of all its attendant circumstances,[1] and it would be generally despised." He might as well say to a man who admired trees: strip them of their spreading branches and lovely foliage, and what beauty can you see in a bare pole? But it was the tree with the branches and foliage, and not without them, that excited admiration. One feature of an object may be as distinct, and excite as different emotions, from the aggregate,

1. *Ibid.*, Book I, Chapter 5, p. 73.

as any two things the most remote, as a beautiful woman and a map of Madagascar. It is "the symmetry of person, the vivacity, the voluptuous softness of temper, the affectionate kindness of feelings, the imagination and the wit" of a woman that excite the passion of love, and not the mere distinction of her being a female. Urged by the passion of love, men have been driven into acts highly prejudicial to the general interests of society, but probably they would have found no difficulty in resisting the temptation, had it appeared in the form of a woman with no other attractions whatever but her sex. To strip sensual pleasures of all their adjuncts, in order to prove their inferiority, is to deprive a magnet of some of its most essential causes of attraction, and then to say that it is weak and inefficient.

In the pursuit of every enjoyment, whether sensual or intellectual, Reason, that faculty which enables us to calculate consequences, is the proper corrective and guide. It is probable therefore that improved reason will always tend to prevent the abuse of sensual pleasures, though it by no means follows that it will extinguish them.

I have endeavored to expose the fallacy of that argument which infers an unlimited progress from a partial improvement, the limits of which cannot be exactly ascertained. It has appeared, I think, that there are many instances in which a decided progress has been observed, where yet it would be a gross absurdity to suppose that progress indefinite. But towards the extinction of the passion between the sexes, no observable progress whatever has hitherto been made. To suppose such an extinction, therefore, is merely to offer an unfounded conjecture, unsupported by any philosophical probabilities.

It is a truth, which history I am afraid makes too clear, that some men of the highest mental powers have been addicted not only to a moderate, but even to an immoderate indulgence in the pleasures of sensual love. But allowing, as I should be inclined to do, notwithstanding numerous instances to the contrary, that great intellectual exertions tend to diminish the empire of this passion over man, it is evident that the mass of mankind must be improved more highly than the brightest ornaments of the species at present before any difference can take place sufficient sensibly to affect population. I would by no means suppose that the mass of mankind has reached its term of improvement, but the principal argument of this essay tends to place in a strong point of view the improbability that the lower classes of people in any country should ever be sufficiently free from want and labour to obtain any high degree of intellectual improvement.

CHAPTER XII

Mr. Godwin's conjecture concerning the indefinite prolongation of human life—Improper inference drawn from the effects of mental stimulants on the human frame, illustrated in various instances—Conjectures not founded on any indications in the past, not to be considered as philosophical conjectures—Mr. Godwin's and Mr. Condorcet's conjecture respecting the approach of man towards immortality on earth, a curious instance of the inconsistency of scepticism.

Mr. Godwin's conjecture respecting the future approach of man towards immortality on earth seems to be rather oddly placed in a chapter which professes to remove the objection to his system of equality from the principle of population. Unless he supposes the passion between the sexes to decrease faster than the duration of life increases, the earth would be more encumbered than ever. But leaving this difficulty to Mr. Godwin, let us examine a few of the appearances from which the probable immortality of man is inferred.

To prove the power of the mind over the body, Mr. Godwin observes, "How often do we find a piece of good news dissipating a distemper? How common is the remark that those accidents which are to the indolent a source of disease are forgotten and extirpated in the busy and active? I walk twenty miles in an indolent and half determined temper and am extremely fatigued. I walk twenty miles full of ardour, and with a motive that engrosses my soul, and I come in as fresh and as alert as when I began my journey. Emotions excited by some unexpected word, by a letter that is delivered to us, occasions the most extraordinary revolutions in our frame, accelerates the circulation, causes the heart to palpitate, the tongue to refuse its office, and has been known to occasion death by extreme anguish or extreme joy. There is nothing indeed of which the physician is more aware than of the power of the mind in assisting or retarding convalescence."

The instances here mentioned, are chiefly instances of the effects of mental stimulants on the bodily frame. No person has ever for a moment doubted the near, though mysterious connection of mind and body. But it is arguing totally without knowledge of the nature of stimulants to suppose, either that they can be applied continually with equal strength, or if they could be so applied for a time, that they would not exhaust and wear out the subject. In some of the cases here noticed, the strength of the stimulus depends upon its novelty and unexpectedness. Such a stimulus cannot, from its nature, be repeated often with the same effect, as it would by repetition lose that property which gives it its strength.

In the other case, the argument is from a small and partial effect to a great and general effect, which will in numberless instances be found to be a very fallacious mode of reasoning. The busy and active man may in some degree counteract, or what is perhaps nearer the truth, may disregard those slight disorders of frame, which fix the attention of a man who has nothing else to think of; but this does not tend to prove that activity of mind will enable a man to disregard a high fever, the smallpox, or the plague.

The man who walks twenty miles with a motive that engrosses his soul does not attend to his slight fatigue of body when he comes in; but double his motive, and set him to walk another twenty miles, quadruple it, and let him start a third time, and so on; and the length of his walk will ultimately depend upon muscle and not mind. Powel, for a motive of ten guineas, would have walked further probably than Mr. Godwin, for a motive of half a million. A motive of uncommon power acting upon a frame of moderate strength, would, perhaps, make the man kill himself by his exertions, but it would not make him walk an hundred miles in twenty-four hours. This statement of the case shews the fallacy of supposing that the person was really not at all tired in his first walk of twenty miles, because he did not appear to be so, or, perhaps, scarcely felt any fatigue himself. The mind cannot fix its attention strongly on more than one object at once. The twenty thousand pounds so engrossed his thoughts, that he did not attend to any slight soreness of foot or stiffness of limb. But had he been really as fresh and as alert as when he first set off, he would be able to go the second twenty miles with as much ease as the first, and so on, the third, &c., which leads to a palpable absurdity. When a horse of spirit is nearly half tired, by the stimulus of the spur, added to the proper management of the bit, he may be put so much upon his mettle, that he would appear to a stander-by as fresh and as high spirited as if he had not gone a mile. Nay, probably the horse himself, while in the heat and passion occasioned by this stimulus, would not feel any fatigue; but it would be strangely contrary to all reason and experience to argue from such an appearance that if the stimulus were continued, the horse would never be tired. The cry of a pack of hounds will make some horses, after a journey of forty miles on the road, appear as fresh, and as lively, as when they first set out. Were they then to be hunted, no perceptible abatement would at first be felt by their riders in their strength and spirits, but towards the end of a hard day, the previous fatigue would have its full weight and effect, and make them tire sooner. When I have taken a long walk with my gun and met with no success, I have frequently returned home feeling a considerable degree of uncomfortableness from fatigue. Another day, perhaps, going over nearly the same extent of ground with a good deal of sport, I have come home fresh and alert. The difference in the sensation of fatigue upon coming in, on the different days, may have been very striking, but on the following mornings I have found no such difference. I have not perceived that I was less stiff in my limbs, or less footsore, on the morning after the day of the sport, than on the other morning.

In all these cases, stimulants upon the mind seem to act rather by taking off the attention from the bodily fatigue, than by really and truly counteracting it. If the energy of my mind had really counteracted the fatigue of my body, why should I feel tired the next morning? If the stimulus of the hounds had as completely overcome the fatigue of the journey in reality, as it did in appearance, why should the horse be tired sooner than if he had not gone the forty miles? I happen to have a very bad fit of the toothache at the time I am writing this. In the eagerness of composition, I every now and then, for a moment or two, forget it. Yet I cannot help thinking that the process which causes the pain is still going forwards, and that the nerves which carry the information of it to the brain are even during these moments demanding attention and room for their appropriate vibrations. The multiplicity of vibrations of another kind may perhaps prevent their admission, or overcome them for a time when admitted, till a shoot of extraordinary energy puts all other vibrations to the rout, destroys the vividness of my argumentative conceptions, and rides triumphant in the brain. In this case, as in the others, the mind seems to have little or no power in counteracting, or curing the disorder, but merely possesses a power, if strongly excited, of fixing its attention on other subjects.

I do not, however, mean to say that a sound and vigorous mind has no tendency whatever to keep the body in a similar state. So close and intimate is the union of mind and body that it would be highly extraordinary if they did not mutually assist each other's functions. But, perhaps, upon a comparison, the body has more effect upon the mind, than the mind upon the body. The first object of the mind is to act as purveyor to the wants of the body. When these wants are completely satisfied, an active mind is indeed apt to wander further, to range over the fields of science, or sport in the regions of imagination, to fancy that it has "shuffled off this mortal coil," and is seeking its kindred element. But all these efforts are like the vain exertions of the hare in the fable. The slowly moving tortoise, the body, never fails to overtake the mind, however widely and extensively it may have ranged, and the brightest and most energetic intellects, unwillingly as they may attend to the first or second summons, must ultimately yield the empire of the brain to the calls of hunger, or sink with the exhausted body in sleep.

It seems as if one might say with certainty that if a medicine could be found to immortalize the body, there would be no fear of its being accompanied by the immortality of the mind. But the immortality of the mind by no means seems to infer the immortality of the body. On the contrary, the greatest conceivable energy of mind would probably exhaust and destroy the strength of the body. A temperate vigour of mind appears to be favourable to health, but very great intellectual exertions tend rather, as has been often observed, to wear out the scabbard. Most of the instances which Mr. Godwin has brought to prove the power of the mind over the body, and the consequent probability of the immortality of man, are of this latter description, and could such stimulants be continually applied, instead of tending to immortalize, they would tend very rapidly to destroy the human frame.

The probable increase of the voluntary power of man over his animal frame comes next under Mr. Godwin's consideration, and he concludes by saying that the voluntary power of some men, in this respect, is found to extend to various articles in which other men are impotent. But this is reasoning against an almost universal rule from a few exceptions; and these exceptions seem to be rather tricks, than powers that may be exerted to any good purpose. I have never heard of any man who could regulate his pulse in a fever, and doubt much, if any of the persons here alluded to have made the smallest perceptible progress in the regular correction of the disorders of their frames and the consequent prolongation of their lives.

Mr. Godwin says, "Nothing can be more unphilosophical than to conclude, that, because a certain species of power is beyond the train of our present observation, that it is beyond the limits of the human mind." I own my ideas of philosophy are in this respect widely different from Mr. Godwin's. The only distinction that I see between a philosophical conjecture and the assertions of the Prophet Mr. Brothers is, that one is founded upon indications arising from the train of our present observations, and the other, has no foundation at all. I expect that great discoveries are yet to take place in all the branches of human science, particularly in physics; but the moment we leave past experience as the foundation of our conjectures concerning the future; and still more, if our conjectures absolutely contradict past experience, we are thrown upon a wide field of uncertainty, and any one supposition is then just as good as another. If a person were to tell me that men would ultimately have eyes and hands behind them as well as before them, I should admit the usefulness of the addition, but should give as a reason for my disbelief of it, that I saw no indications whatever in the past from which I could infer the smallest probability of such a change. If this be not allowed a valid objection, all conjectures are alike, and all equally philosophical. I own it appears to me that in the train of our present observations, there are no more genuine indications that man will become immortal upon earth, than that he will have four eyes and four hands, or that trees will grow horizontally instead of perpendicularly.

It will be said, perhaps, that many discoveries have already taken place in the world that were totally unforeseen and unexpected. This I grant to be true; but if a person had predicted these discoveries without being guided by any analogies or indications from past facts, he would deserve the name of seer or prophet, but not of philosopher. The wonder that some of our modern discoveries would excite in the savage inhabitants of Europe in the times of Theseus and Achilles proves but little. Persons almost entirely unacquainted with the powers of a machine cannot be expected to guess at its effects. I am far from saying that we are at present by any means fully acquainted with the powers of the human mind; but we certainly know more of this instrument than was known four thousand years ago; and therefore, though not to be called competent judges, we are certainly much better able than savages to say what is, or is not, within its grasp. A watch would strike a Savage with as much surprize as a perpetual motion; yet one is to us a most familiar piece of mechanism and the other has constantly eluded the efforts of the most acute intellects. In many instances we are now able to perceive the causes which prevent an unlimited improvement in those inventions which seemed to promise fairly for it at first. The original improvers of telescopes would probably think that as long as the size of the specular and the length of the tubes could be increased, the powers and advantages of the instrument would increase; but experience has since taught us, that the smallness of the field, the deficiency of light, and the circumstance of the atmosphere being magnified prevent the beneficial results that were to be expected from telescopes of extraordinary size and power. In many parts of knowledge, man has been almost constantly making some progress; in other parts, his efforts have been invariably baffled. The Savage would not probably be able to guess at the causes of this mighty difference. Our further experience has given us some little insight into these causes, and has therefore enabled us better to judge, if not of what we are to expect in future, at least of what we are not to expect, which, though negative, is a very useful piece of information.

As the necessity of sleep seems rather to depend upon the body than the mind, it does not appear how the improvement of the mind can tend, very greatly to supersede this "conspicuous infirmity." A man who by great excitements on his mind is able to pass two or three nights without sleep, proportionably exhausts the vigour of his body, and this diminution of health and strength will soon disturb the operations of his understanding, so that by these great efforts he appears to have made no real progress whatever in superseding the necessity of this species of rest.

There is certainly a sufficiently marked difference in the various characters of which we have some knowledge, relative to the energies of their minds, their benevolent pursuits, &c. to enable us to judge whether the operations of intellect have any decided effect in prolonging the duration of human life. It is certain that no decided effect of this kind has yet been observed. Though no attention of any kind has ever produced such an effect as could be construed into the smallest semblance of an approach towards immortality, yet of the two, a certain attention to the body seems to have more effect in this respect than an attention to the mind. The man who takes his temperate meals and his bodily exercise with scrupulous regularity, will generally be found more healthy than the man who, very deeply engaged in intellectual pursuits, often forgets for a time these bodily cravings. The citizen who has retired, and whose ideas, perhaps, scarcely soar above or extend beyond his little garden, puddling all the morning about his borders of box, will, perhaps, live as long as the philosopher whose range of intellect is the most extensive, and whose views are the clearest of any of his contemporaries. It has been positively observed by those who have attended to the bills of mortality that women live longer upon an average than men, and, though I would not by any means say that their intellectual faculties are inferior, yet, I think, it must be allowed that from their different education, there are not so many women as men who are excited to vigorous mental exertion.

As in these and similar instances, or to take a larger range, as in the great diversity of characters that have existed during some thousand years, no decided difference has been observed in the duration of human life from the operation of intellect, the mortality of man on earth seems to be as completely established, and exactly upon the same grounds, as any one, the most constant, of the laws of nature. An immediate act of power in the Creator of the Universe might, indeed, change one or all of these laws, either suddenly or gradually, but without some indications of such a change, and such indications do not exist, it is just as unphilosophical to suppose that the life of man may be prolonged beyond any assignable limits, as to suppose that the attraction of the earth will gradually be changed into repulsion and that stones will ultimately rise instead of fall or that the earth will fly off at a certain period to some more genial and warmer sun.

The conclusion of this chapter presents us, undoubtedly, with a very beautiful and desireable picture, but from fancy and not imagined with truth, it fails of that interest in the heart which nature and probability can alone give.

I cannot quit this subject without taking notice of these conjectures of Mr. Godwin and Mr. Condorcet concerning the indefinite prolongation of human life, as a very curious instance of the longing of the soul after immortality. Both these gentlemen have rejected the light of revelation which absolutely promises eternal life in another state. They have also rejected the light of natural religion, which to the ablest intellects in all ages, has indicated the future existence of the soul. Yet so congenial is the idea of immortality to the mind of man that they cannot consent entirely to throw it out of their systems. After all their fastidious skepticisms concerning the only probable mode of immortality, they introduce a species of immortality of their own, not only completely contradictory to every law of philosophical probability, but in itself in the highest degree, narrow, partial, and unjust. They suppose that all the great, virtuous, and exalted minds that have ever existed or that may exist for some thousands, perhaps millions of years, will be sunk in annihilation, and that only a few beings, not greater in number than can exist at once upon the earth, will be ultimately crowned with immortality. Had such a tenet been advanced as a tenet of revelation I am very sure that all the enemies of religion, and probably Mr. Godwin and Mr. Condorcet among the rest, would have exhausted the whole force of their ridicule upon it, as the most puerile, the most absurd, the poorest, the most pitiful, the most iniquitously unjust, and, consequently, the most unworthy of the Deity that the superstitious folly of man could invent.

What a strange and curious proof do these conjectures exhibit of the inconsistency of skepticism! For it should be observed that there is a very striking and essential difference between believing an assertion which absolutely contradicts the most uniform experience, and an assertion which contradicts nothing, but is merely beyond the power of our present observation and knowledge.[2] So diversified are the natural objects around us, so many instances of mighty power daily offer themselves to our view, that we may fairly presume that there are many forms and operations of nature which we have not yet observed, or which, perhaps, we are not capable of observing with our present confined inlets of knowledge. The resurrection of a spiritual body from a natural body does not appear in itself a more wonderful instance of power than the germination of a blade of wheat

---

2. When we extend our view beyond this life, it is evident that we can have no other guides than authority, or conjecture, and perhaps, indeed, an obscure and undefined feeling. What I say here, therefore, does not appear to me in any respect to contradict what I said before, when I observed that it was unphilosophical to expect any specifick event that was not indicated by some kind of analogy in the past. In ranging beyond the bourne from which no traveller returns, we must necessarily quit this rule; but with regard to events that may be expected to happen on earth, we can seldom quit it consistently with true philosophy. Analogy has, however, as I conceive, great latitude. For instance, man has discovered many of the laws of nature: analogy seems to indicate that he will discover many more; but no analogy seems to indicate that he will discover a sixth sense, or a new species of power in the human mind, entirely beyond the train of our present observations.

from the grain, or of an oak from an acorn. Could we conceive an intelligent being so placed as to be conversant only with inanimate or full grown objects, and never to have witnessed the process of vegetation or growth; and were another being to shew him two little pieces of matter, a grain of wheat, and an acorn, to desire him to examine them, to analize them if he pleased, and endeavour to find out their properties and essences; and then to tell him, that however trifling these little bits of matter might appear to him, that they possessed such curious powers of selection, combination, arrangement, and almost of creation, that upon being put into the ground, they would cause, amongst all the dirt and moisture that surrounded them, those parts which best suited their purpose, that they would collect and arrange these parts with wonderful taste, judgment, and execution, and would rise up into beautiful forms, scarcely in any respect analogous to the little bits of matter which were first placed in the earth, I feel very little doubt that the imaginary being which I have supposed would hesitate more, would require better authority, and stronger proofs, before he believed these strange assertions, than if he had been told that a being of mighty power, who had been the cause of all that he saw around him, and of that existence of which he himself was conscious, would, by a great act of power upon the death and corruption of human creatures, raise up the essence of thought in an incorporeal, or at least invisible form, to give it a happier existence in another state.

The only difference, with regard to our own apprehensions, that is not in favour of the latter assertion is that the first miracle[3] we have repeatedly seen, and the last miracle we have not seen. I admit the full weight of this prodigious difference, but surely no man can hesitate a moment in saying that, putting Revelation out of the question, the resurrection of a spiritual body from a natural body, which may be merely one among the many operations of nature which we cannot see, is an event indefinitely more probable than the immortality of man on earth, which is not only an event of which no symptoms or indications have yet appeared, but is a positive contradiction

---

3. The powers of selection, combination, and transmutation, which every seed shews, are truely miraculous. Who can imagine that these wonderful faculties are contained in these little bits of matter? To me it appears much more philosophical to suppose that the mighty God of nature is present in full energy in all these operations. To this all powerful Being, it would be equally easy to raise an oak without an acorn as with one. The preparatory process of putting seeds into the ground is merely ordained for the use of man, as one among the various other excitements necessary to awaken matter into mind. It is an idea that will be found consistently equally with the natural phenomena around us, with the various events of human life, and with the successive Revelations of God to man, to suppose that the world is a mighty process for the creation and formation of mind. Many vessels will necessarily come out of this great furnace in wrong shapes. These will be broken and thrown aside as useless; while those vessels whose forms are full of truth, grace, and loveliness will be wafted into happier situations nearer the presence of the mighty maker.

to one of the most constant of the laws of nature that has ever come within the observation of man.

I ought perhaps again to make an apology to my readers for dwelling so long upon a conjecture which many, I know, will think too absurd and improbable to require the least discussion. But if it be as improbable and as contrary to the genuine spirit of philosophy as I own I think it is, why should it not be shewn to be so in a candid examination? A conjecture, however improbable on the first view of it, advanced by able and ingenious men, seems at least to deserve investigation. For my own part I feel no disinclination whatever to give that degree of credit to the opinion of the probable immortality of man on earth, which the appearances that can be brought in support of it deserve. Before we decide upon the utter improbability of such an event, it is but fair impartially to examine these appearances; and from such an examination I think we may conclude that we have rather less reason for supposing that the life of man may be indefinitely prolonged, than that trees may be made to grow indefinitely high, or potatoes indefinitely large.[4]

CHAPTER XIII

Error of Mr. Godwin in considering man too much in the light of a being merely rational—In the compound being, man, the passions will always act as disturbing forces in the decisions of the understanding—Reasonings of Mr. Godwin on the subject of coercion—Some truths of a nature not to be communicated from one man to another.

In the chapter which I have been examining, Mr. Godwin professes to consider the objection to his system of equality from the principle of population. It has appeared, I think clearly, that he is greatly erroneous in his statement of the distance of this difficulty, and that instead of myriads of centuries, it is really not thirty years, or even thirty days, distant from us. The supposition of the approach of man to immortality on earth is certainly not of a kind to soften the difficulty. The only argument, therefore, in the chapter which has any tendency to remove the objection is the conjecture concerning the extinction of the passion between the sexes, but as this is a mere conjecture, unsupported by the smallest shadow of proof, the force of the objection may be fairly said to remain unimpaired, and it is undoubtedly of sufficient weight of itself completely to overturn Mr. Godwin's whole system of equality. I will, however, make one or

---

4. Though Mr. Godwin advances the idea of the indefinite prolongation of human life merely as a conjecture, yet as he has produced some appearances, which in his conception favour the supposition, he must certainly intend that these appearances should be examined and this is all that I have meant to do.

two observations on a few of the prominent parts of Mr. Godwin's reasonings which will contribute to place in a still clearer point of view the little hope that we can reasonably entertain of those vast improvements in the nature of man and of society which he holds up to our admiring gaze in his political justice.

Mr. Godwin considers man too much in the light of a being merely intellectual. This error, at least such I conceive it to be, pervades his whole work and mixes itself with all his reasonings. The voluntary actions of men may originate in their opinions, but these opinions will be very differently modified in creatures compounded of a rational faculty and corporal propensities from what they would be in beings wholly intellectual. Mr. Godwin in proving that sound reasoning and truth are capable of being adequately communicated, examines the proposition first practically, and then adds, "Such is the appearance which this proposition assumes, when examined in a loose and practical view. In strict consideration it will not admit of debate. Man is a rational being, &c."[5] So far from calling this a strict consideration of the subject, I own I should call it the loosest and most erroneous way possible, of considering it. It is the calculating the velocity of a falling body in vacuo, and persisting in it, that it would be the same through whatever resisting mediums it might fall. This was not Newton's mode of philosophizing. Very few general propositions are just in application to a particular subject. The moon is not kept in her orbit round the earth, nor the earth in her orbit round the sun, by a force that varies merely in the inverse ratio of the squares of the distances. To make the general theory just in application to the revolutions of these bodies, it was necessary to calculate accurately, the disturbing force of the sun upon the moon, and of the moon upon the earth; and till these disturbing forces were properly estimated, actual observations on the motions of these bodies would have proved that the theory was not accurately true.

I am willing to allow that every voluntary act is preceded by a decision of the mind, but it is strangely opposite to what I should conceive to be the just theory upon the subject, and a palpable contradiction to all experience, to say that the corporal propensities of man do not act very powerfully, as disturbing forces, in these decisions. The question, therefore, does not merely depend upon whether a man may be made to understand a distinct proposition or be convinced by an unanswerable argument. A truth may be brought home to his conviction as a rational being, though he may determine to act contrary to it, as a compound being. The cravings of hunger, the love of liquor, the desire of possessing a beautiful woman will urge men to actions, of the fatal consequences of which, to the gen-

5. *Ibid.*, p. 89.

eral interests of society, they are perfectly well convinced, even at
the very time they commit them. Remove their bodily cravings, and
they would not hesitate a moment in determining against such
actions. Ask them their opinion of the same conduct in another person, and they would immediately reprobate it. But in their own case,
and under all the circumstances of their situation with these bodily
cravings, the decision of the compound being is different from the
conviction of the rational being.

If this be the just view of the subject, and both theory and experience unite to prove that it is, almost all Mr. Godwin's reasonings
on the subject of coercion in his 7th chapter will appear to be
founded on error. He spends some time in placing in a ridiculous
point of view the attempt to convince a man's understanding and to
clear up a doubtful proposition in his mind, by blows. Undoubtedly
it is both ridiculous and barbarous, and so is cockfighting; but one
has little more to do with the real object of human punishments than
the other. One frequent (indeed much too frequent) mode of punishment is death. Mr. Godwin will hardly think this intended for
conviction, at least it does not appear how the individual or the society could reap much future benefit from an understanding enlightened in this manner.

The principal objects which human punishments have in view are
undoubtedly restraint and example, restraint, or removal of an individual member whose vicious habits are likely to be prejudicial to
the society. And example, which by expressing the sense of the community with regard to a particular crime, and by associating more
nearly and visibly, crime and punishment, holds out a moral motive
to dissuade others from the commission of it.

Restraint, Mr. Godwin thinks, may be permitted as a temporary
expedient, though he reprobates solitary imprisonment, which has
certainly been the most successful, and, indeed, almost the only
attempt towards the moral amelioration of offenders. He talks of the
selfish passions that are fostered by solitude and of the virtues generated in society. But surely these virtues are not generated in the
society of a prison. Were the offender confined to the society of able
and virtuous men he would probably be more improved than in solitude. But is this practicable? Mr. Godwin's ingenuity is more frequently employed in finding out evils than in suggesting practical
remedies.

Punishment, for example, is totally reprobated. By endeavouring
to make examples too impressive and terrible, nations have indeed
been led into the most barbarous cruelties, but the abuse of any
practice is not a good argument against its use. The indefatigable
pains taken in this country to find out a murder, and the certainty
of its punishment, has powerfully contributed to generate that sen-

timent which is frequent in the mouths of the common people, that a murder will sooner or later come to light; and the habitual horror in which murder is in consequence held, will make a man, in the agony of passion, throw down his knife for fear he should be tempted to use it in the gratification of his revenge. In Italy, where murderers by flying to a sanctuary are allowed more frequently to escape, the crime has never been held in the same detestation and has consequently been more frequent. No man, who is at all aware of the operation of moral motives, can doubt for a moment, that if every murder in Italy had been invariably punished, the use of the stilletto in transports of passion would have been comparatively but little known.

That human laws either do, or can, proportion the punishment accurately to the offence, no person will have the folly to assert. From the inscrutability of motives the thing is absolutely impossible, but this imperfection, though it may be called a species of injustice, is no valid argument against human laws. It is the lot of man, that he will frequently have to chuse between two evils; and it is a sufficient reason for the adoption of any institution, that it is the best mode that suggests itself of preventing greater evils. A continual endeavour should undoubtedly prevail to make these institutions as perfect as the nature of them will admit. But nothing is so easy, as to find fault with human institutions; nothing so difficult, as to suggest adequate practical improvements. It is to be lamented that more men of talents employ their time in the former occupation than in the latter.

The frequency of crime among men, who, as the common saying is, know better, sufficiently proves, that some truths may be brought home to the conviction of the mind without always producing the proper effect upon the conduct. There are other truths of a nature that perhaps never can be adequately communicated from one man to another. The superiority of the pleasures of intellect to those of sense Mr. Godwin considers as a fundamental truth. Taking all circumstances into consideration, I should be disposed to agree with him; but how am I to communicate this truth to a person who has scarcely ever felt intellectual pleasure. I may as well attempt to explain the nature and beauty of colours to a blind man. If I am ever so laborious, patient, and clear, and have the most repeated opportunities of expostulation, any real progress toward the accomplishment of my purpose seems absolutely hopeless. There is no common measure between us. I cannot proceed step by step: it is a truth of a nature absolutely incapable of demonstration. All that I can say is that the wisest and best men in all ages had agreed in giving the preference very greatly to the pleasures of intellect; and that my own experience completely confirmed the truth of their decisions; that I had found sensual pleasures vain, transient, and continually attended with tedium and disgust; but that intellectual pleasures appeared to me ever fresh and young, filled up all my hours satisfactorily, gave a new zest to life, and diffused a lasting serenity over my mind. If he believe me, it can only be from respect and veneration for my authority: it is credulity, and not conviction. I have not said any thing, nor can any thing be said of a nature to produce real conviction. The affair is not an affair of reasoning, but of experience. He would probably observe in reply, what you say may be very true with regard to yourself and many other good men, but for my own part I feel very differently upon the subject. I have very frequently taken up a book, and almost as frequently gone to sleep over it; but when I pass an evening with a gay party, or a pretty woman, I feel alive, and in spirits, and truly enjoy my existence.

Under such circumstances, reasoning and arguments are not instruments from which success can be expected. At some future time perhaps, real satiety of sensual pleasures, or some accidental impressions that awakened the energies of his mind, might effect that, in a month, which the most patient and able expostulations, might be incapable of effecting in forty years.

CHAPTER XIV

Mr. Godwin's five propositions respecting political truth, on which his whole work hinges, not established—Reasons we have for supposing from the distress occasioned by the principle of population, that the vices, and moral weakness of man can never be wholly eradicated—Perfectibility, in the sense in which Mr. Godwin uses the term, not applicable to man—Nature of the real perfectibility of man illustrated.

If the reasonings of the preceding chapter are just, the corollaries respecting political truth, which Mr. Godwin draws from the proposition, that the voluntary actions of men originate in their opinions, will not appear to be clearly established. These corollaries are, "Sound reasoning and truth, when adequately communicated, must always be victorious over error: Sound reasoning and truth are capable of being so communicated:Truth is omnipotent: The vices and moral weakness of man are not invincible: Man is perfectible, or in other words, susceptible of perpetual improvement."

The first three propositions may be considered a complete syllogism. If by adequately communicated, be meant such a conviction as to produce an adequate effect upon the conduct, the major may be allowed and the minor denied. The consequent, or the omnipotence of truth, of course falls to the ground. If by adequately communicated be meant merely the conviction of the rational faculty, the major must be denied, the minor will be only true in cases capable of demonstration, and the consequent equally falls. The fourth proposition, Mr. Godwin calls the preceding proposition, with a slight variation in the statement. If so, it must accompany the preceding proposition in its fall. But it may be worth while to inquire, with reference to the principal argument of this essay, into the particular reasons which we have for supposing that the vices and moral weakness of man can never be wholly overcome in this world.

Man, according to Mr. Godwin, is a creature formed what he is by the successive impressions which he has received, from the first moment that the germ from which he sprung was animated. Could he be placed in a situation where he was subject to no evil impressions whatever, though it might be doubted whether in such a situation virtue could exist, vice would certainly be banished. The great bent of Mr. Godwin's work on political justice, if I understand it rightly, is to shew that the greater part of the vices and weaknesses of men proceed from the injustice of their political and social institutions, and that if these were removed and the understandings of men more enlightened, there would be little or no temptation in the world to evil. As it has been clearly proved, however (at least as I think), that this is entirely a false conception, and that independent of any political or social institutions whatever, the greater part of mankind, from the fixed and unalterable laws of nature, must ever be subject to the evil temptations arising from want, besides other passions; it follows from Mr. Godwin's definition of man that such impressions, and combinations of impressions, cannot be afloat in the world without generating a variety of bad men. According to Mr. Godwin's own conception of the formation of character, it is surely as improbable that under such circumstances all men will be virtuous as that sixes will come up a hundred times following upon the dice. The great variety of combinations upon the dice in a repeated succession of throws appears to me not inaptly to represent the great variety of character that must necessarily exist in the world, supposing every individual to be formed what he is by that combination of impressions which he has received since his first existence. And this comparison will, in some measure, shew the absurdity of supposing, that exceptions will ever become general rules; that extraordinary and unusual combinations will be frequent; or that the individual instances of great virtue which have appeared in all ages of the world will ever prevail universally.

I am aware that Mr. Godwin might say that the comparison is in one respect inaccurate, that in the case of the dice, the preceding causes, or rather the chances respecting the preceding causes, were always the same, and that therefore I could have no good reason for supposing that a greater number of sixes would come up in the next hundred times of throwing than in the preceding same number of throws. But, that man had in some sort a power of influencing those causes that formed character, and that every good and virtuous man that was produced, by the influence which he must necessarily have, rather increased the probability that another such virtuous character would be generated, whereas the coming up of sixes upon the dice once, would certainly not increase the probability of their coming up a second time. I admit this objection to the accuracy of the comparison, but it is only partially valid. Repeated experience has assured us that the influence of the most virtuous character will rarely prevail against very strong temptations to evil. It will undoubtedly affect some, but it will fail with a much greater number. Had Mr. Godwin succeeded in his attempt to prove that these temptations to evil could by the exertions of man be removed, I would give up the comparison; or at least allow that a man might be so far enlightened with regard to the mode of shaking his elbow, that he would be able to throw sixes every time. But as long as a great number of those impressions which form character, like the nice motions of the arm, remain absolutely independent of the will of man; though it would be the height of folly and presumption to attempt to calculate the relative proportions of virtue and vice at the future periods of the world; it may be safely asserted that the vices and moral weakness of mankind, taken in the mass, are invincible.

The fifth proposition is the general deduction from the four former and will consequently fall, as the foundations which support it have given way. In the sense in which Mr. Godwin understands the term perfectible, the perfectibility of man cannot be asserted, unless the preceding propositions could have been clearly established. There is, however, one sense which the term will bear, in which it is, perhaps, just. It may be said with truth that man is always susceptible of improvement, or that there never has been, or will be, a period of his history in which he can be said to have reached his possible acme of perfection. Yet it does not by any means follow from this, that our efforts to improve man will always succeed, or even that he will ever make, in the greatest number of ages, any extraordinary strides towards perfection. The only inference that can be drawn is that the precise limit of his improvement cannot possibly be known. And I cannot help again reminding the reader of a distinction which, it appears to me, ought particularly to be attended to in the present question: I mean, the essential difference there is between an unlimited improvement and an improvement the limit of which cannot be ascertained. The former is an improvement not applicable to man under the present laws of his nature. The latter, undoubtedly, is applicable.

The real perfectibility of man may be illustrated, as I have men-

tioned before, by the perfectibility of a plant. The object of the enterprising florist is, as I conceive, to unite size, symmetry, and beauty
of colour. It would surely be presumptuous in the most successful
improver to affirm that he possessed a carnation in which these qualities existed in the greatest possible state of perfection. However
beautiful his flower may be, other care, other soil, or other suns
might produce one still more beautiful. Yet, although he may be
aware of the absurdity of supposing that he has reached perfection;
and though he may know by what means he attained that degree of
beauty in the flower which he at present possesses, yet he cannot be
sure that by pursuing similar means, rather increased in strength, he
will obtain a more beautiful blossom. By endeavouring to improve
one quality, he may impair the beauty of another. The richer mould
which he would employ to increase the size of his plant would probably burst the calyx and destroy at once its symmetry. In a similar
manner, the forcing manure used to bring about the French revolution, and to give a greater freedom and energy to the human mind,
has burst the calyx of humanity, the restraining bond of all society;
and however large the separate petals have grown, however strongly
or even beautifully a few of them have been marked, the whole is at
present a loose, deformed, disjointed mass, without union, symmetry, or harmony of colouring.

Were it of consequence to improve pinks and carnations, though
we could have no hope of raising them as large as cabbages, we might
undoubtedly expect, by successive efforts, to obtain more beautiful
specimens than we at present possess. No person can deny the
importance of improving the happiness of the human species. Even
the least advance in this respect is highly valuable. But an experiment
with the human race is not like an experiment upon inanimate
objects. The bursting of a flower may be a trifle. Another will soon
succeed it. But the bursting of the bonds of society is such a separation of parts as cannot take place without giving the most acute
pain to thousands, and a long time may elapse, and much misery
may be endured, before the wound grows up again.

As the five propositions which I have been examining may be considered as the corner stones of Mr. Godwin's fanciful structure, and,
indeed, as expressing the aim and bent of his whole work, however
excellent much of his detached reasoning may be, he must be considered as having failed in the great object of his undertaking.
Besides the difficulties arising from the compound nature of man,
which he has by no means sufficiently smoothed, the principal argument against the perfectibility of man and society remains whole and
unimpaired from any thing that he has advanced. And as far as I can
trust my own judgment, this argument appears to be conclusive not
only against the perfectibility of man, in the enlarged sense in which

Mr. Godwin understands the term, but against any very marked and striking change for the better, in the form and structure of general society, by which I mean any great and decided amelioration of the condition of the lower classes of mankind, the most numerous and, consequently, in a general view of the subject, the most important part of the human race. Were I to live a thousand years, and the laws of nature to remain the same, I should little fear, or rather little hope, a contradiction from experience in asserting that no possible sacrifices or exertions of the rich, in a country which had been long inhabited, could for any time place the lower classes of the community in a situation equal, with regard to circumstances, to the situation of the common people about thirty years ago in the northern States of America.

The lower classes of people in Europe may at some future period be much better instructed than they are at present; they may be taught to employ the little spare time they have in many better ways than at the ale-house; they may live under better and more equal laws than they have ever hitherto done, perhaps, in any country; and I even conceive it possible, though not probable, that they may have more leisure; but it is not in the nature of things, that they can be awarded such a quantity of money or subsistence, as will allow them all to marry early, in the full confidence that they shall be able to provide with ease for a numerous family.

CHAPTER XV

Models too perfect, may sometimes rather impede than promote improvement—Mr. Godwin's essay on avarice and profusion— Impossibility of dividing the necessary labour of a society amicably among all—Invectives against labour may produce present evil, with little or no chance of producing future good—An accession to the mass of agricultural labour must always be an advantage to the labourer.

Mr. Godwin in the preface to his Enquirer drops a few expressions which seem to hint at some change in his opinions since he wrote the Political Justice; and as this is a work now of some years' standing, I should certainly think that I had been arguing against opinions which the author had himself seen reason to alter, but that in some of the essays of the Enquirer, Mr. Godwin's peculiar mode of thinking appears in as striking a light as ever.

It has been frequently observed that though we cannot hope to reach perfection in any thing, yet that it must always be advantageous to us to place before our eyes the most perfect models. This observation has a plausible appearance, but is very far from being generally true. I even doubt its truth in one of the most obvious exemplifications that would occur. I doubt whether a very young painter would receive so much benefit from an attempt to copy a highly finished and perfect picture as from copying one where the outlines were more strongly marked and the manner of laying on the colours was more easily discoverable. But in cases where the perfection of the model is a perfection of a different and superior nature from that towards which we should naturally advance, we shall not always fail in making any progress towards it, but we shall in all probability impede the progress which we might have expected to make had we not fixed our eyes upon so perfect a model. A highly intellectual being, exempt from the infirm calls of hunger or sleep, is undoubtedly a much more perfect existence than man, but were man to attempt to copy such a model, he would not only fail in making any advances towards it; but by unwisely straining to imitate what was inimitable, he would probably destroy the little intellect which he was endeavouring to improve.

The form and structure of society which Mr. Godwin describes is as essentially distinct from any forms of society which have hitherto prevailed in the world, as a being that can live without food or sleep is from a man. By improving society in its present form, we are making no more advances towards such a state of things as he pictures, than we should make approaches towards a line, with regard to which we were walking parallel. The question therefore is whether, by looking to such a form of society as our polar star, we are likely to advance or retard the improvement of the human species? Mr. Godwin appears to me to have decided this question against himself in his essay on avarice and profusion in the Enquirer.

Dr. Adam Smith has very justly observed that nations as well as individuals grow rich by parsimony and poor by profusion, and that therefore every frugal man was a friend and every spend-thrift an enemy to his country. The reason he gives is that what is saved from revenue is always added to stock, and is therefore taken from the maintenance of labour that is generally unproductive and employed in the maintenance of labour that realizes itself in valuable commodities. No observation can be more evidently just. The subject of Mr. Godwin's essay is a little similar in its first appearance, but in essence is as distinct as possible. He considers the mischief of profusion as an acknowledged truth, and therefore makes his comparison between the avaricious man, and the man who spends his income. But the avaricious man of Mr. Godwin is totally a distinct character, at least with regard to his effect upon the prosperity of the state, from the frugal man of Dr. Adam Smith. The frugal man in order to make more money saves from his income and adds to his

capital, and this capital he either employs himself in the maintenance of productive labour, or he lends it to some other person who
will probably employ it in the way. He benefits the state because he
adds to its general capital, and because wealth employed as capital
not only sets in motion more labour, than when spent as income,
but the labour is besides of a more valuable kind. But the avaricious
man of Mr. Godwin locks up his wealth in a chest and sets in motion
no labour of any kind, either productive or unproductive. This is so
essential a difference that Mr. Godwin's decision in his essay appears
at once as evidently false as Dr. Adam Smith's position is evidently
true. It could not, indeed, but occur to Mr. Godwin, that some present inconvenience might arise to the poor, from thus locking up the
funds destined for the maintenance of labour. The only way,
therefore, he had of weakening this objection was to compare the
two characters chiefly with regard to their tendency to accelerate the
approach of that happy state of cultivated equality, on which he says
we ought always to fix our eyes as our polar star.

I think it has been proved in the former parts of this essay that
such a state of society is absolutely impracticable. What consequences then are we to expect from looking to such a point as our
guide and polar star in the great sea of political discovery? Reason
would teach us to expect no other than winds perpetually adverse,
constant but fruitless toil, frequent shipwreck, and certain misery.
We shall not only fail in making the smallest real approach towards
such a perfect form of society; but by wasting our strength of mind
and body in a direction in which it is impossible to proceed, and by
the frequent distress which we must necessarily occasion by our
repeated failures, we shall evidently impede that degree of improvement in society which is really attainable.

It has appeared that a society constituted according to Mr. Godwin's system must, from the inevitable laws of our nature, degenerate
into a class of proprietors and a class of labourers, and that the substitution of benevolence for self-love as the moving principle of society, instead of producing the happy effects that might be expected
from so fair a name, would cause the same pressure of want to be
felt by the whole of society which is now felt only by a part. It is to
the established administration of property and to the apparently narrow principle of self-love that we are indebted for all the noblest
exertions of human genius, all the finer and more delicate emotions
of the soul, for everything, indeed, that distinguishes the civilized
from the savage state; and no sufficient change has as yet taken place
in the nature of civilized man, to enable us to say that he either is,
or ever will be, in a state when he may safely throw down the ladder
by which he has risen to this eminence.

If in every society that has advanced beyond the savage state, a class of proprietors and a class of labourers[6] must necessarily exist, it is evident that, as labour is the only property of the class of labourers, every thing that tends to diminish the value of this property must tend to diminish the possessions of this part of society. The only way that a poor man has of supporting himself in independence is by the exertion of his bodily strength. This is the only commodity he has to give in exchange for the necessaries of life. It would hardly appear then that you benefit him by narrowing the market for this commodity, by decreasing the demand for labour, and lessening the value of the only property that he possesses.

Mr. Godwin would perhaps say that the whole system of barter and exchange is a vile and iniquitous traffic. If you would essentially relieve the poor man, you should take a part of his labour upon yourself, or give him your money without exacting so severe a return for it. In answer to the first method proposed, it may be observed that even if the rich could be persuaded to assist the poor in this way, the value of the assistance would be comparatively trifling. The rich, though they think themselves of great importance, bear but a small proportion in point of numbers to the poor, and would therefore relieve them but of a small part of their burdens by taking a share. Were all those that are employed in the labours of luxuries, added to the number of those employed in producing necessaries; and could these necessary labours be amicably divided among all, each man's share might indeed be comparatively light; but desirable as such an amicable division would undoubtedly be, I cannot conceive any practical principle[7] according to which it could take place. It has been shewn that the spirit of benevolence, guided by the strict impartial justice that Mr. Godwin describes, would, if vigorously acted upon, depress in want and misery the whole human race. Let us examine what would be the consequence if the proprietor were to retain a decent share for himself, but to give the rest away to the poor without exacting a task from them in return. Not to mention the idleness and the vice that such a proceeding, if general, would

6. It should be observed that the principal argument of this essay only goes to prove the necessity of a class of proprietors and a class of labourers, but by no means infers that the present great inequality of property is either necessary or useful to society. On the contrary, it must certainly be considered as an evil, and every institution that promotes it is essentially bad and impolitic. But whether a government could with advantage to society actively interfere to repress inequality of fortunes, may be a matter of doubt. Perhaps the generous system of perfect liberty adopted by Dr. Adam Smith and the French economists would be ill exchanged for any system of restraint.

7. Mr. Godwin seems to have but little respect for practical principles; but I own it appears to me, that he is a much greater benefactor to mankind, who points out how an inferior good may be attained, than he who merely expatiates on the deformity of the present state of society and the beauty of a different state, without pointing out a practical method, that might be immediately applied, of accelerating our advances from the one to the other.

probably create in the present state of society, and the great risk there would be of diminishing the produce of land, as well as the labours of luxury, another objection yet remains.

It has appeared that from the principle of population more will always be in want than can be adequately supplied. The surplus of the rich man might be sufficient for three, but four will be desirous to obtain it. He cannot make this selection of three out of the four without conferring a great favour on those that are the objects of his choice. These persons must consider themselves as under a great obligation to him and as dependent upon him for their support. The rich man would feel his power and the poor man his dependence, and the evil effects of these two impressions on the human heart are well known. Though I perfectly agree with Mr. Godwin therefore in the evil of hard labour, yet I still think it a less evil, and less calculated to debase the human mind, than dependence, and every history of man that we have ever read, places in a strong point of view the danger to which that mind is exposed, which is intrusted with constant power.

In the present state of things, and particularly when labour is in request, the man who does a day's work for me confers full as great an obligation upon me as I do upon him. I possess what he wants, he possesses what I want. We make an amicable exchange. The poor man walks erect in conscious independence; and the mind of his employer is not vitiated by a sense of power.

Three or four hundred years ago, there was undoubtedly much less labour in England, in proportion to the population, than at present, but there was much more dependence, and we probably should not now enjoy our present degree of civil liberty if the poor, by the introduction of manufactures, had not been enabled to give something in exchange for the provisions of the great Lords, instead of being dependent upon their bounty. Even the greatest enemies of trade and manufactures, and I do not reckon myself a very determined friend to them, must allow that when they were introduced into England, liberty came in their train.

Nothing that has been said tends in the most remote degree to undervalue the principle of benevolence. It is one of the noblest and most godlike qualities of the human heart, generated perhaps, slowly and gradually from self-love, and afterwards intended to act as a general law, whose kind office it should be to soften the partial deformities, to correct the asperities, and to smooth the wrinkles of its parent; and this seems to be the analogy of all nature. Perhaps there is no one general law of nature that will not appear, to us at least, to produce partial evil; and we frequently observe at the same time, some bountiful provision, which acting as another general law, corrects the inequalities of the first.

The proper office of benevolence is to soften the partial evils arising from self-love, but it can never be substituted in its place. If no man were to allow himself to act till he had completely determined that the action he was about to perform was more conducive than any other to the general good, the most enlightened minds would hesitate in perplexity and amazement; and the unenlightened would be continually committing the grossest mistakes.

As Mr. Godwin, therefore, has not laid down any practical principle according to which the necessary labours of agriculture might be amicably shared among the whole class of labourers, by general invectives against employing the poor he appears to pursue an unattainable good through much present evil. For if every man who employs the poor ought to be considered as their enemy, and as adding to the weight of their oppressions, and if the miser is for this reason to be preferred to the man who spends his income, it follows that any number of men who now spend their incomes might, to the advantage of society, be converted into misers. Suppose then that a hundred thousand persons who now employ ten men each were to lock up their wealth from general use, it is evident, that a million of working men of different kinds would be completely thrown out of all employment. The extensive misery that such an event would produce in the present state of society, Mr. Godwin himself could hardly refuse to acknowledge, and I question whether he might not find some difficulty in proving that a conduct of this kind tended more than the conduct of those who spend their incomes to "place human beings in the condition in which they ought to be placed."

But Mr. Godwin says that the miser really locks up nothing, that the point has not been rightly understood, and that the true development and definition of the nature of wealth have not been applied to illustrate it. Having defined therefore wealth, very justly, to be the commodities raised and fostered by human labour, he observes that the miser locks up neither corn, nor oxen, nor clothes, nor houses. Undoubtedly he does not really lock up these articles, but he locks up the power of producing them, which is virtually the same. These things are certainly used and consumed by his contemporaries, as truly and to as great an extent, as if he were a beggar; but not to as great an extent, as if he had employed his wealth in turning up more land, in breeding more oxen, in employing more taylors, and in building more houses. But supposing, for a moment, that the conduct of the miser did not tend to check any really useful produce, how are all those who are thrown out of employment to obtain patents which they may shew in order to be awarded a proper share of the food and raiment produced by the society? This is the unconquerable difficulty.

I am perfectly willing to concede to Mr. Godwin that there is much

more labour in the world than is really necessary, and that, if the
lower classes of society could agree among themselves never to work
more than six or seven hours in the day, the commodities essential
to human happiness might still be produced in as great abundance
as at present. But it is almost impossible to conceive that such an
agreement could be adhered to. From the principle of population,
some would necessarily be more in want than others. Those that had
large families would naturally be desirous of exchanging two hours
more of their labour for an ampler quantity of subsistence. How are
they to be prevented from making this exchange? It would be a violation of the first and most sacred property that a man possesses, to
attempt, by positive institutions, to interfere with his command over
his own labour.

Till Mr. Godwin, therefore, can point out some practical plan
according to which the necessary labour in a society might be equitably divided, his invectives against labour, if they were attended to,
would certainly produce much present evil without approximating
us to that state of cultivated equality to which he looks forward as
his polar star, and which, he seems to think, should at present be
our guide in determining the nature and tendency of human actions.
A mariner guided by such a polar star is in danger of shipwreck.

Perhaps there is no possible way in which wealth could in general
be employed so beneficially to a state, and particularly to the lower
orders of it, as by improving and rendering productive that land
which to a farmer would not answer the expence of cultivation. Had
Mr. Godwin exerted his energetic eloquence in painting the superior
worth and usefulness of the character who employed the poor in this
way, to him who employed them in narrow luxuries, every enlightened man must have applauded his efforts. The increasing demand
for agricultural labour must always tend to better the condition of
the poor; and if the accession of work be of this kind, so far is it from
being true that the poor would be obliged to work ten hours for the
same price that they before worked eight, that the very reverse would
be the fact; and a labourer might then support his wife and family
as well by the labour of six hours, as he could before by the labour
of eight.

The labour created by luxuries, though useful in distributing the
produce of the country without vitiating the proprietor by power or
debasing the labourer by dependence, has not, indeed, the same
beneficial effects on the state of the poor. A great accession of work
from manufacturers, though it may raise the price of labour even
more than an increasing demand for agricultural labour; yet, as in
this case, the quantity of food in the country may not be proportionably increasing, the advantage to the poor will be but temporary, as
the price of provisions must necessarily rise in proportion to the price

of labour. Relative to this subject, I cannot avoid venturing a few remarks on a part of Dr. Adam Smith's *Wealth of Nations*, speaking at the same time with that diffidence which I ought certainly to feel in differing from a person so justly celebrated in the political world.

CHAPTER XVI

Probable error of Dr. Adam Smith in representing every increase of the revenue or stock of a society as an increase in the funds for the maintenance of labour—Instances where an increase of wealth can have no tendency to better the condition of the labouring poor—England has increased in riches without a proportional increase in the funds for the maintenance of labour—The state of the poor in China would not be improved by an increase of wealth from manufactures.

The professed object of Dr. Adam Smith's inquiry is the nature and causes of the wealth of nations. There is another inquiry, however, perhaps still more interesting, which he occasionally mixes with it, I mean an inquiry into the causes which affect the happiness of nations or the happiness and comfort of the lower orders of society, which is the most numerous class in every nation. I am sufficiently aware of the near connection of these two subjects, and that the causes which tend to increase the wealth of a State tend also, generally speaking, to increase the happiness of the lower classes of the people. But perhaps Dr. Adam Smith has considered these two inquiries as still more nearly connected than they really are; at least he has not stopped to take notice of those instances where the wealth of a society may increase (according to his definition of wealth) without having any tendency to increase the comforts of the labouring part of it. I do not mean to enter into a philosophical discussion of what constitutes the proper happiness of man, but shall merely consider two universally acknowledged ingredients, health, and the command of the necessaries and conveniences of life.

Little or no doubt can exist that the comforts of the labouring poor depend upon the increase of the funds destined for the maintenance of labour, and will be very exactly in proportion to the rapidity of this increase. The demand for labour which such increase would occasion, by creating a competition in the market, must necessarily raise the value of labour, and, till the additional number of hands required were reared, the increased funds would be distributed to the same number of persons as before the increase, and therefore every labourer would live comparatively at his ease. But perhaps Dr. Adam Smith errs in representing every increase of the revenue or stock of a society as an increase of these funds. Such surplus stock or revenue will, indeed, always be considered by the individual possessing it as an additional fund from which he may maintain more labour; but it will not be a real and effectual fund for the maintenance of an additional number of labourers, unless the whole, or at least a great part of this increase of the stock or revenue of the society, be convertible into a proportional quantity of provisions; and it will not be so convertible where the increase has arisen merely from the produce of labour, and not from the produce of land. A distinction will in this case occur, between the number of hands which the stock of the society could employ, and the number which its territory can maintain.

To explain myself by an instance. Dr. Adam Smith defines the wealth of a nation to consist in the annual produce of its land and labour. This definition evidently includes manufactured produce, as well as the produce of the land. Now supposing a nation for a course of years was to add what it saved from its yearly revenue to its manufacturing capital solely, and not to its capital employed upon land, it is evident that it might grow richer according to the above definition, without a power of supporting a greater number of labourers, and therefore, without an increase in the real funds for the maintenance of labour. There would, notwithstanding, be a demand for labour from the power which each manufacturer would possess, or at least think he possessed, of extending his old stock in trade or of setting up fresh works. This demand would of course raise the price of labour, but if the yearly stock of provisions in the country was not increasing, this rise would soon turn out to be merely nominal, as the price of provisions must necessarily rise with it. The demand for manufacturing labourers might, indeed, entice many from agriculture and thus tend to diminish the annual produce of the land, but we will suppose any effect of this kind to be compensated by improvements in the instruments of agriculture, and the quantity of provisions therefore to remain the same. Improvements in manufacturing machinery would of course take place, and this circumstance, added to the greater number of hands employed in manufactures, would cause the annual produce of the labour of the country to be upon the whole greatly increased. The wealth therefore of the country would be increasing annually, according to the definition, and might not, perhaps, be increasing very slowly.

The question is whether wealth, increasing in this way, has any tendency to better the condition of the labouring poor. It is a self-evident proposition that any general rise in the price of labour, the stock of provisions remaining the same, can only be a nominal rise, as it must very shortly be followed by a proportional rise in provisions. The increase in the price of labour therefore, which we have supposed, would have little or no effect in giving the labouring poor a greater command over the necessaries and conveniences of life. In this respect they would be nearly in the same state as before. In one other respect they would be in a worse state. A greater proportion of them would be employed in manufactures, and fewer, consequently, in agriculture. And this exchange of professions will be allowed, I think, by all, to be very unfavourable in respect of health, one essential ingredient of happiness, besides the greater uncertainty of manufacturing labour, arising from the capricious taste of man, the accidents of war, and other causes.

It may be said, perhaps, that such an instance as I have supposed could not occur, because the rise in the price of provisions would immediately turn some additional capital into the channel of agriculture. But this is an event which may take place very slowly, as it should be remarked that a rise in the price of labour had preceded the rise of provisions, and would therefore impede the good effects upon agriculture, which the increased value of the produce of the land might otherwise have occasioned.

It might also be said, that the additional capital of the nation would enable it to import provisions sufficient for the maintenance of those whom its stock could employ. A small country with a large navy, and great inland accommodations for carriage, such as Holland, may indeed import and distribute an effectual quantity of provisions; but the price of provisions must be very high to make such an importation and distribution answer in large countries less advantageously circumstanced in this respect.

An instance, accurately such as I have supposed, may not, perhaps, ever have occurred, but I have little doubt that instances nearly approximating to it may be found without any very laborious search. Indeed I am strongly inclined to think that England herself, since the revolution, affords a very striking elucidation of the argument in question.

The commerce of this country, internal as well as external, has certainly been rapidly advancing during the last century. The exchangeable value in the market of Europe of the annual produce of its land and labour has, without doubt, increased very considerably. But upon examination it will be found that the increase has been chiefly in the produce of labour and not in the produce of land, and therefore, though the wealth of the nation has been advancing with a quick pace, the effectual funds for the maintenance of labour have been increasing very slowly, and the result is such as might be expected. The increasing wealth of the nation has had little or no tendency to better the condition of the labouring poor. They have not, I believe, a greater command of the necessaries and conveniences of life, and a much greater proportion of them than at the period of the revolution is employed in manufactures and crowded together in close and unwholesome rooms.

Could we believe the statement of Dr. Price that the population of England has decreased since the revolution, it would even appear that the effectual funds for the maintenance of labour had been declining during the progress of wealth in other respects. For I conceive that it may be laid down as a general rule that if the effectual funds for the maintenance of labour are increasing, that is, if the territory can maintain as well as the stock employ a greater number of labourers, this additional number will quickly spring up, even in spite of such wars as Dr. Price enumerates. And consequently, if the population of any country has been stationary or declining, we may safely infer that however it may have advanced in manufacturing wealth, its effectual funds for the maintenance of labour cannot have increased.

It is difficult, however, to conceive that the population of England has been declining since the revolution, though every testimony concurs to prove that its increase, if it has increased, has been very slow. In the controversy which the question has occasioned, Dr. Price undoubtedly appears to be much more completely master of his subject, and to possess more accurate information than his opponents. Judging simply from this controversy, I think one should say that Dr. Price's point is nearer being proved than Mr. Howlett's. Truth probably lies between the two statements, but this supposition makes the increase of population since the revolution to have been very slow in comparison with the increase of wealth.

That the produce of the land has been decreasing, or even that it has been absolutely stationary during the last century, few will be disposed to believe. The inclosure of commons and waste lands certainly tends to increase the food of the country, but it has been asserted with confidence that the inclosure of common fields has frequently had a contrary effect, and that large tracts of land which formerly produced great quantities of corn, by being converted into pasture, both employ fewer hands and feed fewer mouths than before their inclosure. It is, indeed, an acknowledged truth, that pasture land produces a smaller quantity of human subsistence than corn land of the same natural fertility, and could it be clearly ascertained that from the increased demand for butcher's meat of the best quality, and its increased price in consequence, a greater quantity of good land has annually been employed in grazing, the diminution of human subsistence, which this circumstance would occasion, might have counterbalanced the advantages derived from the inclosure of waste lands and the general improvements in husbandry.

It scarcely need be remarked that the high price of butcher's meat at present, and its low price formerly, were not caused by the scarcity in the one case or the plenty in the other, but by the different expence sustained at the different periods, in preparing cattle for the market. It is, however, possible that there might have been more cattle a hundred years ago in the country than at present; but no doubt can be entertained that there is much more meat of a superior quality brought to market at present than ever there was. When the price of butcher's meat was very low, cattle were reared chiefly upon waste lands; and except for some of the principal markets, were probably killed with but little other fatting. The veal that is sold so cheap in some distant counties at present, bears little other resemblance than the name to that which is bought in London. Formerly, the price of butcher's meat would not pay for rearing, and scarcely for feeding cattle on land that would answer in tillage; but the present price will not only pay for fatting cattle on the very best land, but will even allow of the rearing many on land that would bear good crops of corn. The same number of cattle, or even the same weight of cattle at the different periods when killed, will have consumed (if I may be allowed the expression) very different quantities of human subsistence. A fatted beast may in some respects be considered, in the language of the French economists, as an unproductive labourer; he has added nothing to the value of the raw produce that he has consumed. The present system of grazing undoubtedly tends more than the former system to diminish the quantity of human subsistence in the country, in proportion to the general fertility of the land.

I would not by any means be understood to say that the former system either could or ought to have continued. The increasing price of butcher's meat is a natural and inevitable consequence of the general progress of cultivation; but I cannot help thinking, that the present great demand for butcher's meat of the best quality, and the quantity of good land that is in consequence annually employed to produce it, together with the great number of horses at present kept for pleasure, are the chief causes that have prevented the quantity of human food in the country from keeping pace with the generally increased fertility of the soil; and a change of custom in these respects would, I have little doubt, have a very sensible effect on the quantity of subsistence in the country, and consequently on its population.

The employment of much of the most fertile land in grazing, the improvements in agricultural instruments, the increase of large farms, and particularly the diminution of the number of cottages throughout the kingdom, all concur to prove that there are not probably so many persons employed in agricultural labour now as at the period of the revolution. Whatever increase of population, therefore, has taken place, must be employed almost wholly in manufactures, merely from the caprice of fashion, such as the adoption of muslins instead of silks, or of shoe-strings and covered buttons, instead of buckles and metal buttons, combined with the restraints in the mar-

ket of labour arising from corporation and parish laws, have frequently driven thousands on charity for support. The great increase
of the poor rates is, indeed, of itself a strong evidence that the poor
have not a greater command of the necessaries and conveniences of
life, and if to the consideration that their condition in this respect is
rather worse than better, be added the circumstance that a much
greater proportion of them is employed in large manufactories, unfavourable both to health and virtue, it must be acknowledged that the
increase of wealth of late years, has had no tendency to increase the
happiness of the labouring poor.

That every increase of the stock of revenue of a nation cannot be
considered as an increase of the real funds for the maintenance of
labour and, therefore, cannot have the same good effect upon the
condition of the poor will appear in a strong light if the argument be
applied to China.

Dr. Adam Smith observes that China has probably long been as
rich as the nature of her laws and institutions will admit, but that
with other laws and institutions, and if foreign commerce were had
in honour, she might still be much richer. The question is, would
such an increase of wealth be an increase of the real funds for the
maintenance of labour, and consequently, tend to place the lower
classes of people in China in a state of greater plenty?

It is evident, that if trade and foreign commerce were held in great
honour in China, from the plenty of labourers, and the cheapness
of labour she might work up manufactures for foreign sale to an
immense amount. It is equally evident that from the great bulk of
provisions and the amazing extent of her inland territory she could
not in return import such a quantity as would be any sensible addition to the annual stock of subsistence in the country. Her immense
amount of manufactures, therefore, she would exchange chiefly for
luxuries collected from all parts of the world. At present it appears
that no labour whatever is spared in the production of food. The
country is rather over peopled in proportion to what its stock can
employ, and labour is, therefore, so abundant, that no pains are
taken to abridge it. The consequence of this is, probably, the greatest
production of food that the soil can possibly afford, for it will be
generally observed that processes for abridging labour, though they
may enable a farmer to bring a certain quantity of grain cheaper to
market, tend rather to diminish than increase the whole produce;
and in agriculture, therefore, may in some respects be considered
rather as private, than public advantages.

An immense capital could not be employed in China in preparing
manufactures for foreign trade without taking off so many labourers
from agriculture as to alter this state of things, and in some degree
to diminish the produce of the country. The demand for manufac-

turing labourers would naturally raise the price of labour, but as the quantity of subsistence would not be increased, the price of provisions would keep pace with it, or even more than keep pace with it if the quantity of provisions were really decreasing. The country would be evidently advancing in wealth, the exchangeable value of the annual produce of its land and labour would be annually augmented, yet the real funds for the maintenance of labour would be stationary, or even declining, and, consequently, the increasing wealth of the nation would rather tend to depress than to raise the condition of the poor. With regard to the command over the necessaries and comforts of life, they would be in the same or rather worse state than before; and a great part of them would have exchanged the healthy labours of agriculture, for the unhealthy occupations of manufacturing industry.

The argument, perhaps, appears clearer when applied to China, because it is generally allowed that the wealth of China has been long stationary. With regard to any other country it might be always a matter of dispute at which of the two periods compared, wealth was increasing the fastest, as it is upon the rapidity of the increase of wealth at any particular period that Dr. Adam Smith says the condition of the poor depends. It is evident, however, that two nations might increase exactly with the same rapidity in the exchangeable value of the annual produce of their land and labour, yet if one had applied itself chiefly to agriculture, and the other chiefly to commerce, the funds for the maintenance of labour, and consequently the effect of the increase of wealth in each nation, would be extremely different. In that which had applied itself chiefly to agriculture, the poor would live in great plenty, and population would rapidly increase. In that which had applied itself chiefly to commerce, the poor would be comparatively but little benefited and consequently population would increase slowly.

CHAPTER XVII

Question of the proper definition of the wealth of a state—Reason given by the French Economists for considering all manufacturers as unproductive labourers, not the true reason—The labour of artificers and manufacturers sufficiently productive to individuals, though not to the state—A remarkable passage in Dr. Price's two volumes of observations—Error of Dr. Price in attributing the happiness and rapid population of America, chiefly, to its peculiar state of civilization—No advantage can be expected from shutting our eyes to the difficulties in the way to the improvement of society.

A question seems naturally to arise here whether the exchangeable value of the annual produce of the land and labour be the proper

definition of the wealth of a country, or whether the gross produce
of the land, according to the French economists, may not be a more
accurate definition. Certain it is that every increase of wealth,
according to the definition of the economists, will be an increase of
the funds for the maintenance of labour, and consequently will
always tend to ameliorate the condition of the labouring poor,
though an increase of wealth, according to Dr. Adam Smith's definition, will by no means invariably have the same tendency. And yet
it may not follow from this consideration that Dr. Adam Smith's
definition is not just. It seems in many respects improper to exclude
the clothing and lodging of a whole people from any part of their
revenue. Much of it may, indeed, be of very trivial and unimportant
value in comparison with the food of the country, yet still it may be
fairly considered as a part of its revenue, and, therefore, the only
point in which I should differ from Dr. Adam Smith, is where he
seems to consider every increase of the revenue or stock of a society
as an increase of the funds for the maintenance of labour, and consequently as tending always to ameliorate the condition of the poor.

   The fine silks and cottons, the laces, and other ornamental luxuries of a rich country may contribute very considerably to augment
the exchangeable value of its annual produce; yet they contribute
but in a very small degree to augment the mass of happiness in the
society, and it appears to me that it is with some view to the real
utility of the produce that we ought to estimate the productiveness
or unproductiveness of different sorts of labour. The French economists consider all labour employed in manufactures as unproductive. Comparing it with the labour employed upon land, I should be
perfectly disposed to agree with them, but not exactly for the reasons
which they give. They say that labour employed upon land is productive because the produce, over and above completely paying the
labourer and the farmer, affords a clear rent to the landlord, and that
the labour employed upon a piece of lace is unproductive because it
merely replaces the provisions that the workman had consumed, and
the stock of his employer, without affording any clear rent whatever.
But supposing the value of the wrought lace to be such, as that
besides paying in the most complete manner the workman and his
employer, it could afford a clear rent to a third person; it appears to
me that in comparison with the labour employed upon land, it would
be still as unproductive as ever. Though according to the reasoning
used by the French economists, the man employed in the manufacture of lace would, in this case, seem to be a productive labourer;
yet according to their definition of the wealth of a state, he ought
not to be considered in that light. He will have added nothing to the
gross produce of the land: he has consumed a portion of this gross
produce, and has left a bit of lace in return; and though he may sell

this bit of lace for three times the quantity of provisions that he consumed whilst he was making it, and thus be a very productive labourer with regard to himself; yet he cannot be considered as having added by his labour to any essential part of the riches of the state. The clear rent, therefore, that a certain produce can afford, after paying the expences of procuring it, does not appear to be the sole criterion by which to judge of the productiveness or unproductiveness to a state of any particular species of labour.

Suppose that two hundred thousand men, who are now employed in producing manufactures that only tend to gratify the vanity of a few rich people, were to be employed upon some barren and uncultivated lands, and to produce only half the quantity of food that they themselves consumed; they would be still more productive labourers with regard to the state than they were before, though their labour, so far from affording a rent to a third person, would but half replace the provisions used in obtaining the produce. In their former employment they consumed a certain portion of the food of the country and left in return some silks and laces. In their latter employment they consumed the same quantity of food and left in return provision for a hundred thousand men. There can be little doubt which of the two legacies would be the most really beneficial to the country, and it will, I think, be allowed that the wealth which supported the two hundred thousand men while they were producing silks and laces would have been more usefully employed in supporting them while they were producing the additional quantity of food.

A capital employed upon land may be unproductive to the individual that employs it and yet be highly productive to the society. A capital employed in trade, on the contrary, may be highly productive to the individual and yet be almost totally unproductive to the society; and this is the reason why I should call manufacturing labour unproductive in comparison of that which is employed in agriculture, and not for the reason given by the French economists. It is indeed almost impossible to see the great fortunes that are made in trade, and the liberality with which so many merchants live, and yet agree in the statement of the economists, that manufacturers can only grow rich by depriving themselves of the funds destined for their support. In many branches of trade the profits are so great as would allow of a clear rent to a third person; but as there is no third person in the case, and as all the profits centre in the master manufacturer or merchant, he seems to have a fair chance of growing rich without much privation; and we consequently see large fortunes acquired in trade by persons who have not been remarked for their parsimony.

Daily experience proves that the labour employed in trade and manufactures is sufficiently productive to individuals, but it certainly is not productive in the same degree to the state. Every accession to

the food of a country tends to the immediate benefit of the whole
society; but the fortunes made in trade tend but in a remote and
uncertain manner to the same end, and in some respects have even
a contrary tendency. The home trade of consumption is by far the
most important trade of every nation. China is the richest country
in the world, without any other. Putting then, for a moment, foreign
trade out of the question, the man who by an engenious manufacture
obtains a double portion out of the old stock of provisions will certainly not be so useful to the state as the man who, by his labour,
adds a single share to the former stock. The consumable commodities of silks, laces, trinkets, and expensive furniture are undoubtedly
a part of the revenue of the society; but they are the revenue only of
the rich, and not of the society in general. An increase in this part
of the revenue of a state, cannot therefore be considered of the same
importance as an increase of food, which forms the principal revenue
of the great mass of the people.

Foreign commerce adds to the wealth of a state, according to Dr.
Adam Smith's definition, though not according to the definition of
the economists. Its principal use, and the reason probably that it has
in general been held in such high estimation, is that it adds greatly
to the external power of a nation or to its power of commanding the
labour of other countries; but it will be found, upon a near examination, to contribute but little to the increase of the internal funds
for the maintenance of labour, and consequently but little to the
happiness of the greatest part of society. In the natural progress of
a state towards riches, manufactures and foreign commerce would
follow, in their order, the high cultivation of the soil. In Europe, this
natural order of things has been inverted, and the soil has been cultivated from the redundancy of manufacturing capital, instead of
manufactures rising from the redundancy of capital employed upon
land. The superior encouragement that has been given to the industry of the towns, and the consequent higher price that is paid for the
labour of artificers, than for the labour of those employed in husbandry, are probably the reasons why so much soil in Europe remains
uncultivated. Had a different policy been pursued throughout
Europe, it might undoubtedly have been much more populous than
at present, and yet not be more incumbered by its population.

I cannot quit this curious subject of the difficulty arising from
population, a subject that appears to me to deserve a minute investigation and able discussion much beyond my power to give it, without taking notice of an extraordinary passage in Dr. Price's two
volumes of Observations. Having given some tables on the probabilities of life in towns and in the country, he says,[8] "From this com-

8. Richard Price, *Observations on Reversionary Payments* (1771), Volume 2, p. 243.

parison, it appears with how much truth great cities hae been called the graves of mankind. It must also convince all who consider it, that according to the observation at the end of the fourth essay in the former volume, it is by no means strictly proper to consider our diseases as the original intention of nature. They are, without doubt, in general our own creation. *Were there a country where the inhabitants led lives entirely natural and virtuous, few of them would die without measuring out the whole period of present existence allotted to them; pain and distemper would be unknown among them, and death would come upon them like a sleep, in consequence of no other cause than gradual and unavoidable decay."*

I own that I felt myself obliged to draw a very opposite conclusion from the facts advanced in Dr. Price's two volumes. I had for some time been aware that population and food increased in different ratios, and a vague opinion had been floating in my mind that they could only be kept equal by some species of misery or vice, but the perusal of Dr. Price's two volumes of Observations, after that opinion had been conceived, raised it at once to conviction. With so many facts in his view to prove the extraordinary rapidity with which population increases when unchecked, and with such a body of evidence before him to elucidate even the manner by which the general laws of nature repress a redundant population, it is perfectly inconceivable to me how he could write the passage that I have quoted. He was a strenuous advocate for early marriages as the best preservative against vicious manners. He had no fanciful conceptions about the extinction of the passion between the sexes, like Mr. Godwin, nor did he ever think of eluding the difficulty in the ways hinted at by Mr. Condorcet. He frequently talks of giving the prolifick powers of nature room to exert themselves. Yet with these ideas, that his understanding could escape from the obvious and necessary inference that an unchecked population would increase beyond comparison faster than the earth, by the best directed exertions of man, could produce food for its support, appears to me as astonishing as if he had resisted the conclusion of one of the plainest propositions of Euclid.

Dr. Price, speaking of the different stages of the civilized state, says, "The first, or simple stages of civilization, are those which favour most the increase and the happiness of mankind." He then instances the American colonies, as being at that time in the first and happiest of the states that he had described, and as affording a very striking proof of the effects of the different stages of civilization on population. But he does not seem to be aware that the happiness of the Americans depended much less upon their peculiar degree of civilization than upon the peculiarity of their situation as new colonies, upon their having a great plenty of fertile uncultivated land. In parts of Norway, Denmark, or Sweden, or in this country two or three hundred years ago, he might have found perhaps nearly the same degree of civilization, but by no means the same happiness or the same increase of population. He quotes himself a statute of Henry the Eighth, complaining of the decay of tillage, and the enhanced price of provisions, "whereby a marvellous number of people were rendered incapable of maintaining themselves and families." The superior degree of civil liberty which prevailed in America contributed, without doubt, its share to promote the industry, happiness, and population of these states, but even civil liberty, all powerful as it is, will not create fresh land. The Americans may be said, perhaps, to enjoy a greater degree of civil liberty, now they are an independent people, than while they were in subjection to England, but we may be perfectly sure that population will not long continue to increase with the same rapidity as it did then.

A person who contemplated the happy state of the lower classes of people in America twenty years ago, would naturally wish to retain them for ever in that state, and might think, perhaps, that by preventing the introduction of manufactures and luxury he might effect his purpose; but he might as reasonably expect to prevent a wife or mistress from growing old by never exposing her to the sun or air. The situation of new colonies, well governed, is a bloom of youth that no efforts can arrest. There are, indeed, many modes of treatment in the political, as well as animal body, that contribute to accelerate or retard the approaches of age, but there can be no chance of success, in any mode that could be divised, for keeping either of them in perpetual youth. By encouraging the industry of the towns more than the industry of the country, Europe may be said, perhaps, to have brought on a premature old age. A different policy in this respect would infuse fresh life and vigour into every state. While from the law of primogeniture, and other European customs, land bears a monopoly price, a capital can never be employed in it with much advantage to the individual; and therefore it is not probable that the soil should be properly cultivated. And though in every civilized state, a class of proprietors and a class of labourers must exist; yet one permanent advantage would always result from a nearer equalization of property. The greater the number of proprietors, the smaller must be the number of labourers; a greater part of society would be in the happy state of possessing property, and a smaller part in the unhappy state of possessing no other property than their labour. But the best directed exertions, though they may alleviate, can never remove the pressure of want, and it will be difficult for any person who contemplates the genuine situation of man on earth, and the general laws of nature, to suppose it possible that any, the most enlightened efforts, could place mankind in a state where "few would die without measuring out the whole period of present existence allotted to them; where pain and distemper would be unknown among them; and death would come upon them like a sleep, in consequence of no other cause than gradual and unavoidable decay."

It is undoubtedly a most disheartening reflection that the great obstacle in the way to any extraordinary improvement in society is of a nature that we can never hope to overcome. The perpetual tendency in the race of man to increase beyond the means of subsistence is one of the general laws of animated nature which we can have no reason to expect will change. Yet discouraging as the contemplation of this difficulty must be to those whose exertions are laudably directed to the improvement of the human species, it is evident that no possible good can arise from any endeavours to slur it over or keep it in the back ground. On the contrary, the most baleful mischiefs may be expected from the unmanly conduct of not daring to face truth because it is unpleasing. Independently of what relates to this great obstacle, sufficient yet remains to be done for mankind to animate us to the most unremitted exertion. But if we proceed without a thorough knowledge and accurate comprehension of the nature, extent, and magnitude of the difficulties we have to encounter, or if we unwisely direct our efforts towards an object in which we cannot hope for success, we shall not only exhaust our strength in fruitless exertions and remain at as great a distance as ever from the summit of our wishes, but we shall be perpetually crushed by the recoil of this rock of Sisyphus.

CHAPTER XVIII

The constant pressure of distress on man, from the principle of population, seems to direct our hopes to the future—State of trial inconsistent with our ideas of the foreknowledge of God—The world, probably, a mighty process for awakening matter into mind—Theory of the formation of mind—Excitements from the wants of the body—Excitements from the operation of general laws—Excitements from the difficulties of life arising from the principle of population.

The view of human life which results from the contemplation of the constant pressure of distress on man from the difficulty of subsistence, by shewing the little expectation that he can reasonably entertain of perfectibility on earth, seems strongly to point his hopes to the future. And the temptations to which he must necessarily be exposed from the operation of those laws of nature which we have been examining, would seem to represent the world in the light in which it has been frequently considered, as a state of trial and school of virtue preparatory to a superior state of happiness. But I hope I shall be pardoned if I attempt to give a view in some degree different of the situation of man on earth, which appears to me to be more consistent with the various phenomena of nature which we observe around us and more consonant to our ideas of the power, goodness, and foreknowledge of the Deity.

It cannot be considered as an unimproving exercise of the human mind to endeavour to "Vindicate the ways of God to man" if we proceed with a proper distrust of our own understandings and a just sense of our insufficiency to comprehend the reason of all that we see, if we hail every ray of light with gratitude, and when no light appears, think that the darkness is from within and not from without, and bow with humble deference to the supreme wisdom of him whose "thoughts are above our thoughts" "as the heavens are high above the earth."

In all our feeble attempts, however, to "find out the Almighty to perfection," it seems absolutely necessary that we should reason from nature up to nature's God and not presume to reason from God to nature. The moment we allow ourselves to ask why some things are not otherwise, instead of endeavouring to account for them as they are, we shall never know where to stop; we shall be led into the grossest and most childish absurdities; all progress in the knowledge of the ways of Providence must necessarily be at an end; and the study will even cease to be an improving exercise of the human mind. Infinite power is so vast and incomprehensible an idea that the mind of man must necessarily be bewildered in the contemplation of it. With the crude and puerile conceptions which we sometimes form of this attribute of the Deity, we might imagine that God could call into being myriads and myriads of existences, all free from pain and imperfection, all eminent in goodness and wisdom, all capable of the highest enjoyments, and unnumbered as the points throughout infinite space. But when from these vain and extravagant dreams of fancy, we turn our eyes to the book of nature, where alone we can read God as he is, we see a constant succession of sentient beings, rising apparently from so many specks of matter, going through a long and sometimes painful process in this world, but many of them attaining, ere the termination of it, such high qualities and powers as seem to indicate their fitness for some superior state. Ought we not then to correct our crude and puerile ideas of Infinite Power from the contemplation of what we actually see existing? Can we judge of the Creator but from his creation? And unless we wish to exalt the power of God at the expence of his goodness, ought we not to conclude that even to the Great Creator, Almighty as he is, a certain process may be necessary, a certain time (or at least what appears to us as time) may be requisite, in order to form beings with those exalted qualities of mind which will fit them for his high purposes?

A state of trial seems to imply a previously formed existence that does not agree with the appearance of man in infancy and indicates something like suspicion and want of foreknowledge, inconsistent with those ideas which we wish to cherish of the Supreme Being. I should be inclined, therefore, as I have hinted before in a note, to consider the world and this life as the mighty process of God, not for the trial, but for the creation and formation of mind, a process necessary to awaken inert, chaotic matter into spirit, to sublimate the dust of the earth into soul, to elicit an ethereal spark from the clod of clay. And in this view of the subject, the various impressions and excitements which man receives through life may be considered as the forming hand of his Creator, acting by general laws, and awakening his sluggish existence, by the animating touches of the Divinity, into a capacity of superior enjoyment. The original sin of man is the torpor and corruption of the chaotic matter in which he may be said to be born.

It could answer no good purpose to enter into the question whether mind be a distinct substance from matter, or only a finer form of it. The question is, perhaps, after all, a question merely of words. Mind is as essentially mind, whether formed from matter or any other substance. We know from experience that soul and body are most intimately united, and every appearance seems to indicate that they grow from infancy together. It would be a supposition attended with very little probability to believe that a complete and full formed spirit existed in every infant, but that it was clogged and impeded in its operations during the first twenty years of life by the weakness, or hebetude, of the organs in which it was enclosed. As we shall all be disposed to agree that God is the creator of mind as well as of body, and as they both seem to be forming and unfolding themselves at the same time, it cannot appear inconsistent either with reason or revelation, if it appear to be consistent with phenomena of nature, to suppose that God is constantly occupied in forming mind out of matter and that the various impressions that man receives through life is the process for that purpose. The employment is surely worthy of the highest attributes of the Deity.

This view of the state of man on earth will not seem to be unattended with probability, if, judging from the little experience we have of the nature of mind, it shall appear upon investigation that the phenomena around us, and the various events of human life, seem peculiarly calculated to promote this great end, and especially if, upon this supposition, we can account, even to our own narrow understandings, for many of those roughnesses and inequalities in life which querulous man too frequently makes the subject of his complaint against the God of nature.

The first great awakeners of the mind seem to be the wants of the body.[9] They are the first stimulants that rouse the brain of infant man into sentient activity, and such seems to be the sluggishness of original matter that unless by a peculiar course of excitements other wants, equally powerful, are generated, these stimulants seem, even afterwards, to be necessary to continue that activity which they first awakened. The savage would slumber for ever under his tree unless he were roused from his torpor by the cravings of hunger or the pinchings of cold, and the exertions that he makes to avoid these evils, by procuring food and building himself a covering, are the exercises which form and keep in motion his faculties, which otherwise would sink into listless inactivity. From all that experience has taught us concerning the structure of the human mind, if those stimulants to exertion, which arise from the wants of the body, were removed from the mass of mankind, we have much more reason to think that they would be sunk to the level of brutes, from a deficiency of excitements, than that they would be raised to the rank of philosophers by the possession of leisure. In those countries where nature is the most redundant in spontaneous produce the inhabitants will not be found the most remarkable for acuteness of intellect. Necessity has been with great truth called the mother of invention. Some of the noblest exertions of the human mind have been set in motion by the necessity of satisfying the wants of the body. Want has not unfrequently given wings to the imagination of the poet, pointed the flowing periods of the historian, and added acuteness to the researches of the philosopher, and though there are undoubtedly many minds at present so far improved by the various excitements of knowledge or of social sympathy that they would not relapse into listlessness if their bodily stimulants were removed, yet it can scarcely be doubted that these stimulants could not be withdrawn from the mass of mankind without producing a general and fatal torpor, destructive of all the germs of future improvement.

Locke, if I recollect, says that the endeavour to avoid pain rather than the pursuit of pleasure is the great stimulus to action in life, and that in looking to any particular pleasure, we shall not be roused into action in order to obtain it, till the contemplation of it has continued so long as to amount to a sensation of pain or uneasiness under the absence of it. To avoid evil and to pursue good seem to be the great duty and business of man, and this world appears to be peculiarly calculated to afford opportunity of the most unremitted exertion of this kind, and it is by this exertion, by these stimulants, that mind is formed. If Locke's idea be just, and there is great reason

---

9. It was my intention to have entered at some length into this subject as a kind of second part to the essay. A long interruption, from particular business, has obliged me to lay aside this intention, at least for the present. I shall now, therefore, only give a sketch of a few of the leading circumstances that appear to me to favour the general supposition that I have advanced.

to think that it is, evil seems to be necessary to create exertion, and exertion seems evidently necessary to create mind.

The necessity of food for the support of life gives rise, probably, to a greater quantity of exertion than any other want, bodily or mental. The supreme Being has ordained that the earth shall not produce food in great quantities till much preparatory labour and ingenuity has been exercised upon its surface. There is no conceivable connection to our comprehensions, between the seed and the plant or tree that rises from it. The Supreme Creator might, undoubtedly, raise up plants of all kinds for the use of his creatures without the assistance of those little bits of matter, which we call seed, or even without the assisting labour and attention of man. The processes of ploughing and clearing the ground, of collecting and sowing seeds, are not surely for the assistance of God in his creation, but are made previously necessary to the enjoyment of the blessings of life, in order to rouse man into action and form his mind to reason.

To furnish the most unremitted excitements of this kind, and to urge man to further the gracious designs of Providence by the full cultivation of the earth, it has been ordained that population should increase much faster than food. This general law (as it has appeared in the former parts of this essay) undoubtedly produces much partial evil, but a little reflection may perhaps satisfy us that it produces a great overbalance of good. Strong excitements seem necessary to create exertion, and to direct this exertion, and form the reasoning faculty, it seems absolutely necessary that the Supreme Being should act always according to general laws. The constancy of the laws of nature, or the certainty with which we may expect the same effect from the same causes, is the foundation of the faculty of reason. If in the ordinary course of things, the finger of God were frequently visible, or to speak more correctly, if God were frequently to change his purpose (for the finger of God is, indeed, visible in every blade of grass that we see), a general and fatal torpor of the human faculties would probably ensue, even the bodily wants of mankind would cease to stimulate them to exertion, could they not reasonably expect that if their efforts were well directed they would be crowned with success. The constancy of the laws of nature is the foundation of the industry and foresight of the husbandman, the indefatigable ingenuity of the artificer, the skilful researches of the physician and anatomist, and the watchful observation and patient investigation of the natural philosopher. To this constancy we owe all the greatest and noblest efforts of intellect. To this constancy we owe the immortal mind of a Newton.

As the reasons, therefore, for the constancy of the laws of nature seem, even to our understandings, obvious and striking, if we return to the principle of population and consider man as he really is, inert, sluggish, and averse from labour unless compelled by necessity (and it is surely the height of folly to talk of man, according to our crude fancies, of what he might be), we may pronounce with certainty that the world would not have been peopled but for the superiority of the power of population to the means of subsistence. Strong and constantly operative as this stimulus is on man to urge him to the cultivation of the earth, if we still see that cultivation proceeds very slowly, we may fairly conclude that a less stimulus would have been insufficient. Even under the operation of this constant excitement, savages will inhabit countries of the greatest natural fertility for a long period before they betake themselves to pasturage or agriculture. Had population and food increased in the same ratio, it is probable that man might never have emerged from the savage state. But supposing the earth once well peopled, an Alexander, a Julius Caesar, a Tamerlane, or a bloody revolution might irrecoverably thin the human race and defeat the great designs of the Creator. The ravages of a contagious disorder would be felt for ages, and an earthquake might unpeople a region for ever. The principle according to which population increases prevents the vices of mankind or the accidents of nature, the partial evils arising from general laws, from obstructing the high purpose of the creation. It keeps the inhabitants of the earth always fully up to the level of the means of subsistence, and is constantly acting upon man as a powerful stimulus, urging him to the further cultivation of the earth, and to enable it consequently to support a more extended population. But it is impossible that this law can operate and produce the effects apparently intended by the Supreme Being without occasioning partial evil. Unless the principle of population were to be altered, according to the circumstances of each separate country (which would not only be contrary to our universal experience, with regard to the laws of nature, but would contradict even our own reason, which sees the absolute necessity of general laws, for the formation of intellect), it is evident that the same principle which, seconded by industry, will people a fertile region in a few years must produce distress in countries that have been long inhabited.

It seems, however, every way probable that even the acknowledged difficulties occasioned by the law of population tend rather to promote than impede the general purpose of Providence. They excite universal exertion and contribute to that infinite variety of situations, and consequently of impressions, which seems upon the whole favourable to the growth of mind. It is probable that too great or too little excitement, extreme poverty, or too great riches may be alike unfavourable in this respect. The middle regions of society seem to be best suited to intellectual improvement, but it is contrary to the analogy of all nature to expect that the whole of society can be a middle region. The temperate zones of the earth seem to be the most favourable to the mental and corporeal energies of man, but all cannot be temperate zones. A world warmed and enlightened but by one sun must from the laws of matter have some parts chilled by perpetual frosts and others scorched by perpetual heats. Every piece of matter lying on a surface must have an upper and an under side; all the particles cannot be in the middle. The most valuable parts of an oak to a timber merchant are not either the roots or the branches, but these are absolutely necessary to the existence of the middle part, or stem, which is the object in request. The timber merchant could not possibly expect to make an oak grow without roots or branches, but if he could find out a mode of cultivation which would cause more of the substance to go to stem, and less to root and branch, he would be right to exert himself in bringing such a system into general use.

In the same manner, though we cannot possibly expect to exclude riches and poverty from society, yet if we could find out a mode of government by which the numbers in the extreme regions would be lessened and the numbers in the middle regions increased, it would be undoubtedly our duty to adopt it. It is not, however, improbable that as in the oak, the roots and branches could not be diminished very greatly without weakening the vigorous circulation of the sap in the stem, so in society the extreme parts could not be diminished beyond a certain degree without lessening that animated exertion throughout the middle parts which is the very cause that they are the most favourable to the growth of intellect. If no man could hope to rise or fear to fall in society, if industry did not bring with it its reward and idleness its punishment, the middle parts would not certainly be what they now are. In reasoning upon this subject, it is evident that we ought to consider chiefly the mass of mankind and not individual instances. There are undoubtedly many minds, and there ought to be many, according to the chances, out of so great a mass that, having been vivified early by a peculiar course of excitements, would not need the constant action of narrow motives to continue them in activity. But if we were to review the various useful discoveries, the valuable writings, and other laudable exertions of mankind, I believe we should find that more were to be attributed to the narrow motives that operate upon the many than to the apparently more enlarged motives that operate upon upon the few.

Leisure is without doubt highly valuable to man, but taking man as he is, the probability seems to be that in the greater number of instances it will produce evil rather than good. It has been not unfrequently remarked that talents are more common among younger brothers than among elder brothers, but it can scarcely be imagined that younger brothers are, upon an average, born with a greater original susceptibility of parts. The difference, if there really is any observable difference, can only arise from their different situations. Exertion and activity are in general absolutely necessary in the one case and are only optional in the other.

That the difficulties of life contribute to generate talents, every day's experience must convince us. The exertions that men find it necessary to make in order to support themselves or families, frequently awaken faculties that might otherwise have lain for ever dormant, and it has been commonly remarked that new and extraordinary situations generally create minds adequate to grapple with the difficulties in which they are involved.

CHAPTER XIX

The sorrows of life necessary to soften and humanize the heart— The excitements of social sympathy often produce characters of a higher order than the mere possesssors of talents—Moral evil probably necessary to the production of moral excellence—Excitements from intellectual wants continually kept up by the infinite variety of nature, and the obscurity that involves metaphysical subjects— The difficulties in Revelation to be accounted for upon this principle—The degree of evidence which the scriptures contain, probably, best suited to the improvement of the human faculties, and the moral amelioration of mankind—The idea that mind is created by excitements, seems to account for the existence of natural and moral evil.

The sorrows and distresses of life form another class of excitements which seem to be necessary, by a peculiar train of impressions, to soften and humanize the heart, to awaken social sympathy, to generate all the Christian virtues, and to afford scope for the ample exertion of benevolence. The general tendency of an uniform course of prosperity is rather to degrade than exalt the character. The heart that has never known sorrow itself will seldom be feelingly alive to the pains and pleasures, the wants and wishes, of its fellow beings. It will seldom be overflowing with that warmth of brotherly love, those kind and amiable affections, which dignify the human character even more than the possession of the highest talents. Talents, indeed, though undoubtedly a very prominent and fine feature of mind, can by no means be considered as constituting the whole of it. There are many minds which have not been exposed to those excitements that usually form talents, that have yet been vivified to a high degree by the excitements of social sympathy. In every rank of life, in the lowest as frequently as in the highest, characters are to be found overflowing with the milk of human kindness, breathing love towards God and man, and though without those peculiar powers of mind called talents, evidently holding a higher rank in the scale of beings than many who possess them. Evangelical charity, meekness, piety, and all that class of virtues distinguished particularly by the name of Christian virtues do not seem necessarily to include abilities, yet a soul possessed of these amiable qualities, a soul awakened and vivified by these delightful sympathies, seems to hold a nearer commerce with the skies than mere acuteness of intellect.

The greatest talents have been frequently misapplied and have produced evil proportionate to the extent of their powers. Both reason and revelation seem to assure us that such minds will be condemned to eternal death, but while on earth, these vicious instruments performed their part in the great mass of impressions, by the disgust and abhorrence which they excited. It seems highly probable that moral evil is absolutely necessary to the production of moral excellence. A being with only good placed in view may be justly said to be impelled by a blind necessity. The pursuit of good in this case can be no indication of virtuous propensities. It might be said, perhaps, that Infinite Wisdom cannot want such an indication as outward action, but would foreknow with certainty whether the being would chuse good or evil. This might be a plausible argument against a state of trial, but will not hold against the supposition that mind in this world is in a state of formation. Upon this idea, the being that has seen moral evil and has felt disapprobation and disgust at it is essentially different from the being that has seen only good. They are pieces of clay that have received distinct impressions: they must, therefore, necessarily be in different shapes; or, even if we allow them both to have the same lovely form of virtue, it must be acknowledged that one has undergone the further process, necessary to give firmness and durability to its substance, while the other is still exposed to injury, and liable to be broken by every accidental impulse. An ardent love and admiration of virtue seems to imply the existence of something opposite to it, and it seems highly probable that the same beauty of form and substance, the same perfection of character, could not be generated without the impressions of disapprobation which arise from the spectacle of moral evil.

When the mind has been awakened into activity by the passions and the wants of the body, intellectual wants arise; and the desire of knowledge and the impatience under ignorance form a new and important class of excitements. Every part of nature seems peculiarly calculated to furnish stimulants to mental exertion of this kind, and to offer inexhaustible food for the most unremitted inquiry. Our immortal Bard says of Cleopatra—

> Custom cannot stale
> Her infinite variety.

the expression, when applied to any one object, may be considered
as a poetical amplification, but it is accurately true when applied to
nature. Infinite variety seems, indeed, eminently her characteristic
feature. The shades that are here and there blended in the picture
give spirit, life, and prominence to her exuberant beauties, and those
roughnesses and inequalities, those inferior parts that support the
superior, though they sometimes offend the fastidious microscopic
eye of short sighted man, contribute to the symmetry, grace, and fair
proportion of the whole.

The infinite variety of the forms and operations of nature, besides
tending immediately to awaken and improve the mind by the variety
of impressions that it creates, opens other fertile sources of improvement by offering so wide and extensive a field for investigation and
research. Uniform, undiversified perfection could not possess the
same awakening powers. When we endeavour then to contemplate
the system of the universe, when we think of the stars as the suns
of other systems scattered throughout infinite space, when we reflect
that we do not probably see a millionth part of those bright orbs that
are beaming light and life to unnumbered worlds, when our minds
unable to grasp the immeasurable conception sink, lost and confounded, in admiration at the mighty incomprehensible power of the
Creator, let us not querulously complain that all climates are not
equally genial, that perpetual spring does not reign throughout the
year, that all God's creatures do not possess the same advantages,
that clouds and tempests sometimes darken the natural world and
vice and misery the moral world, and that all the works of the creation are not formed with equal perfection. Both reason and experience seem to indicate to us that the infinite variety of nature (and
variety cannot exist without inferior parts, or apparent blemishes) is
admirably adapted to further the high purpose of the creation and
to produce the greatest possible quantity of good.

The obscurity that involves all metaphysical subjects appears to
me in the same manner peculiarly calculated to add to that class of
excitements which arise from the thirst of knowledge. It is probable
that man, while on earth, will never be able to attain complete satisfaction on these subjects; but this is by no means a reason that he
should not engage in them. The darkness that surrounds these interesting topics of human curiosity may be intended to furnish endless
motives to intellectual activity and exertion. The constant effort to
dispel this darkness, even if it fail of success, invigorates and
improves the thinking faculty. If the subjects of human inquiry were
once exhausted, mind would probably stagnate; but the infinitely
diversified forms and operations of nature, together with the endless
food for speculation which metaphysical subjects offer, prevent the
possibility that such a period should ever arrive.

It is by no means one of the wisest sayings of Solomon that "there is no new thing under the sun." On the contrary, it is probable that were the present system to continue for millions of years, continual additions would be making to the mass of human knowledge, and yet perhaps it may be a matter of doubt whether what may be called the capacity of mind be in any marked and decided manner increasing. A Socrates, a Plato, or an Aristotle, however confessedly inferior in knowledge to the philosophers of the present day, do not appear to have been much below them in intellectual capacity. Intellect rises from a speck, continues in vigour only for a certain period, and will not perhaps admit while on earth of above a certain number of impressions. These impressions may, indeed, be infinitely modified, and from these various modifications, added probably to a difference in the susceptibility of the original germs,[1] arise the endless diversity of character that we see in the world; but reason and experience seem both to assure us, that the capacity of individual minds does not increase in proportion to the mass of existing knowledge. The finest minds seem to be formed rather by efforts at original thinking, by endeavours to form new combinations, and to discover new truths, than by passively receiving the impressions of other men's ideas. Could we suppose the period arrived, when there was no further hope of future discoveries, and the only employment of mind was to acquire pre-existing knowledge, without any efforts to form new and original combinations; though the mass of human knowledge were a thousand times greater than it is at present, yet it is evident that one of the noblest stimulants to mental exertion would have ceased; the finest feature of intellect would be lost; every thing allied to genius would be at an end; and it appears to be impossible, that, under such circumstances, any individuals could possess the same intellectual energies as were possessed by a Locke, a Newton, or a Shakespear, or even by a Socrates, a Plato, an Aristotle, or a Homer.

If a revelation from heaven of which no person could feel the smallest doubt were to dispel the mists that now hang over metaphysical subjects, were to explain the nature and structure of mind, the affections and essences of all substances, the mode in which the Supreme Being operates in the works of the creation, and the whole plan and scheme of the Universe, such an accession of knowledge so obtained, instead of giving additional vigour and activity to the human mind, would in all probability tend to repress future exertion and to damp the soaring wings of intellect.

1. It is probable that no two grains of wheat are exactly alike, Soil undoubtedly makes the principal difference in the blades that spring up, but probably not all. It seems natural to suppose some sort of difference in the original germs that are afterwards awakened into thought, and the extraordinary difference of susceptibility in very young children seems to confirm the supposition.

For this reason I have never considered the doubts and difficulties that involve some parts of the sacred writings as any argument against their divine original. The Supreme Being might undoubtedly have accompanied his revelations to man by such a succession of miracles, and of such a nature, as would have produced universal overpowering conviction and have put an end at once to all hesitation and discussion. But weak as our reason is to comprehend the plans of the Great Creator, it is yet sufficiently strong to see the most striking objections to such a revelation. From the little we know of the structure of the human understanding, we must be convinced that an overpowering conviction of this kind, instead of tending to the improvement and moral amelioration of man, would act like the touch of a torpedo on all intellectual exertion and would almost put an end to the existence of virtue. If the scriptural denunciations of eternal punishment were brought home with the same certainty to every man's mind as that the night will follow the day, this one vast and gloomy idea would take such full possession of the human faculties as to leave no room for any other conceptions, the external actions of men would be all nearly alike, virtuous conduct would be no indication of virtuous disposition, vice and virtue would be blended together in one common mass, and though the all-seeing eye of God might distinguish them they must necessarily make the same impressions on man, who can judge only from external appearances. Under such a dispensation, it is difficult to conceive how human beings could be formed to a detestation of moral evil, and a love and admiration of God, and of moral excellence.

Our ideas of virtue and vice are not, perhaps, very accurate and well-defined; but few, I think, would call an action really virtuous which was performed simply and solely from the dread of a very great punishment or the expectation of a very great reward. The fear of the Lord is very justly said to be the beginning of wisdom, but the end of wisdom is the love of the Lord and the admiration of moral good. The denunciations of future punishment contained in the scriptures seem to be well calculated to arrest the progress of the vicious and awaken the attention of the careless, but we see from repeated experience that they are not accompanied with evidence of such a nature as to overpower the human will and to make men lead virtuous lives with vicious dispositions, merely from a dread of hereafter. A genuine faith, by which I mean a faith that shews itself in all the virtues of a truly Christian life, may generally be considered as an indication of an amiable and virtuous disposition, operated upon more by love than by pure unmixed fear.

When we reflect on the temptations to which man must necessarily be exposed in this world, from the structure of his frame, and the operation of the laws of nature, and the consequent moral certainty that many vessels will come out of this mighty creative furnace in wrong shapes, it is perfectly impossible to conceive that any of these creatures of God's hand can be condemned to eternal suffering. Could we once admit such an idea, all our natural conceptions of goodness and justice would be completely overthrown, and we could no longer look up to God as a merciful and righteous Being. But the doctrine of life and immortality which was brought to light by the gospel, the doctrine that the end of righteousness is everlasting life, but that the wages of sin are death, is in every respect just and merciful, and worthy of the Great Creator. Nothing can appear more consonant to our reason than that those beings which come out of the creative process of the world in lovely and beautiful forms, should be crowned with immortality, while those which come out misshapen, those whose minds are not suited to a purer and happier state of existence, should perish and be condemned to mix again with their original clay. Eternal condemnation of this kind may be considered as a species of eternal punishment, and it is not wonderful that it should be represented sometimes under images of suffering. But life and death, salvation and destruction, are more frequently opposed to each other in the New Testament than happiness and misery. The Supreme Being would appear to us in a very different view if we were to consider him as pursuing the creatures that had offended him with eternal hate and torture, instead of merely condemning to their original insensibility those beings that, by the operation of general laws, had not been formed with qualities suited to a purer state of happiness.

Life is, generally speaking, a blessing independent of a future state. It is a gift which the vicious would not always be ready to throw away, even if they had no fear of death. The partial pain, therefore, that is inflicted by the Supreme Creator, while he is forming numberless beings to a capacity of the highest enjoyments, is but as the dust of the balance in comparison of the happiness that is communicated, and we have every reason to think that there is no more evil in the world than what is absolutely necessary as one of the ingredients in the mighty process.

The striking necessity of general laws for the formation of intellect will not in any respect be contradicted by one or two exceptions, and these evidently not intended for partial purposes, but calculated to operate upon a great part of mankind, and through many ages. Upon the idea that I have given of the formation of mind, the infringement of the general laws of nature, by a divine revelation, will appear in the light of the immediate hand of God mixing new ingredients in the mighty mass, suited to the particular state of the process, and calculated to give rise to a new and powerful train of impressions, tending to purify, exalt, and improve the human mind. The miracles that accompanied these revelations when they had once excited the attention of mankind, and rendered it a matter of most interesting discussion, whether the doctrine was from God or man, had performed their part, had answered the purpose of the Creator; and these communications of the divine will were afterwards left to make their way by their own intrinsic excellence and by operating as moral motives, gradually to influence and improve, and not to overpower and stagnate the faculties of man.

It would be undoubtedly presumptuous to say that the Supreme Being could not possibly have effected his purpose in any other way than that which he has chosen; but as the revelation of the divine will which we possess is attended with some doubts and difficulties, and as our reason points out to us the strongest objections to a revelation which would force immediate, implicit, universal belief, we have surely just cause to think that these doubts and difficulties are no argument against the divine origin of the scriptures, and that the species of evidence which they possess is best suited to the improvement of the human faculties and the moral amelioration of mankind.

The idea that the impressions and excitements of this world are the instruments with which the Supreme Being forms matter into mind, and that the necessity of constant exertion to avoid evil and to pursue good is the principal spring of these impressions and excitements, seems to smooth many of the difficulties that occur in a contemplation of human life, and appears to me to give a satisfactory reason for the existence of natural and moral evil, and, consequently, for that part of both, and it certainly is not a very small part, which arises from the principle of population. But, though upon this supposition, it seems highly improbable that evil should ever be removed from the world, yet it is evident that this impression would not answer the apparent purpose of the Creator, it would not act so powerfully as an excitement to exertion, if the quantity of it did not diminish or increase with the activity or the indolence of man. The continual variations in the weight and in the distribution of this pressure keep alive a constant expectation of throwing it off.

> Hope springs eternal in the human breast,
> Man never is, but always to be blest.

Evil exists in the world not to create despair but activity. We are not patiently to submit to it, but to exert ourselves to avoid it. It is not only the interest but the duty of every individual to use his utmost efforts to remove evil from himself and from as large a circle as he can influence, and the more he exercises himself in this duty, the more wisely he directs his efforts, and the more successful these efforts are, the more he will probably improve and exalt his own mind and the more completely does he appear to fulfil the will of his Creator.

An Essay on the Principle of Population: From the Revised Edition (1803–)†

Preface

* * *

Throughout the whole of the present work I have so far differed in principle from the former, as to suppose the action of another check to population which does not come under the head either of vice or misery; and, in the latter part I have endeavoured to soften some of the harshest conclusions of the first Essay. In doing this, I hope that I have not violated the principles of just reasoning; nor expressed any opinion respecting the probable improvement of society, in which I am not borne out by the experience of the past. To those who still think that any check to population whatever would be worse than the evils which it would relieve, the conclusions of the former Essay will remain in full force: and if we adopt this opinion we shall be compelled to acknowledge, that the poverty and misery which prevailed among the lower classes of society are absolutely irremediable.

* * *

Book IV. Of Our Future Prospects Respecting the Removal or Mitigation of the Evils Arising from the Principle of Population

CHAPTER I. OF MORAL RESTRAINT, AND OUR OBLIGATION TO PRACTISE THIS VIRTUE

As it appears that, in the actual state of every society which has come within our review, the natural progress of population has been constantly and powerfully checked; and as it seems evident that no improved form of government, no plans of emigration, no benevolent institutions, and no degree or direction of national industry, can prevent the continued action of a great check to population in some form or other; it follows that we must submit to it as an inevitable law of nature; and the only inquiry that remains is, how it may take place with the least possible prejudice to the virtue and happiness of human society.

All the immediate checks to population, which have been observed to prevail in the same and different countries, seem to be resolvable into moral restraint, vice and misery; and if our choice be confined

---

† The *Essay* was greatly enlarged in its second edition (see Introduction) and went through six editions in Malthus' lifetime. The text is from the seventh edition, which appeared posthumously but was Malthus' work.

to these three, we cannot long hesitate in our decision respecting which it would be most eligible to encourage.

In the first edition of this essay I observed, that as from the laws of nature it appeared, that some check to population must exist, it was better that this check should arise from a foresight of the difficulties attending a family and the fear of dependent poverty, than from the actual presence of want and sickness. This idea will admit of being pursued farther; and I am inclined to think that, from the prevailing opinions respecting population, which undoubtedly originated in barbarous ages, and have been continued and circulated by that part of every community which may be supposed to be interested in their support, we have been prevented from attending to the clear dictates of reason and nature on this subject.

Natural and moral evil seem to be the instruments employed by the Deity in admonishing us to avoid any mode of conduct which is not suited to our being, and will consequently injure our happiness. If we are intemperate in eating and drinking, our health is disordered; if we indulge the transports of anger, we seldom fail to commit acts of which we afterwards repent; if we multiply too fast, we die miserably of poverty and contagious diseases. The laws of nature in all these cases are similar and uniform. They indicate to us that we have followed these impulses too far, so as to trench upon some other law, which equally demands attention. * * *

From the inattention of mankind hitherto to the consequences of increasing too fast, it must be presumed, that these consequences are not so immediately and powerfully connected with the conduct which leads to them, as in the other instances; but the delayed knowledge of particular effects does not alter their nature, or our obligation to regulate our conduct accordingly, as soon as we are satisfied of what this conduct ought to be. * * *

* * * It is of the very utmost importance to the happiness of mankind, that population should not increase too fast; but it does not appear, that the object to be accomplished would admit of any considerable diminution in the desire of marriage. It is clearly the duty of each individual not to marry till he has a prospect of supporting his children; but it is at the same time to be wished that he should retain undiminished his desire of marriage, in order that he may exert himself to realise this prospect, and be stimulated to make provision for the support of greater numbers.

It is evidently therefore regulation and direction which are required with regard to the principle of population, not diminution or alteration. And if moral restraint be the only virtuous mode of avoiding the incidental evils arising from this principle, our obligation to practise it will evidently rest exactly upon the same foundation as our obligation to practise any of the other virtues.

Whatever indulgence we may be disposed to allow to occasional failures in the discharge of a duty of acknowledged difficulty, yet of the strict line of duty we cannot doubt. Our obligation not to marry till we have a fair prospect of being able to support our children will appear to deserve the attention of the moralist, if it can be proved that an attention to this obligation is of most powerful effect in the prevention of misery; and that, if it were the general custom to follow the first impulse of nature, and marry at the age of puberty, the universal prevalence of every known virtue in the greatest conceivable degree, would fail of rescuing society from the most wretched and desperate state of want, and all the diseases and famines which usually accompany it.

*   *   *

CHAPTER III. OF THE ONLY EFFECTUAL MODE OF IMPROVING THE CONDITION OF THE POOR

*   *   *

The object of those who really wish to better the condition of the lower classes of society must be to raise the relative proportion between the price of labour and the price of provisions, so as to enable the labourer to command a larger share of the necessaries and comforts of life. We have hitherto principally attempted to attain this end by encouraging the married poor and consequently increasing the number of labourers, and overstocking the market with a commodity which we still say that we wish to be dear. It would seem to have required no great spirit of divination to foretell the certain failure of such a plan of proceeding. There is nothing however like experience. It has been tried in many different countries, and for many hundred years, and the success has always been answerable to the nature of the scheme. It is really time now to try something else.

When it was found that oxygen, or pure vital air, would not cure consumptions as was expected, but rather aggravated their symptoms, trial was made of an air of the most opposite kind. I wish we had acted with the same philosophical spirit in our attempts to cure the disease of poverty; and having found that the pouring in of fresh supplies of labour only tended to aggravate the symptoms, had tried what would be the effect of withholding a little these supplies.

In all old and fully-peopled states it is from this method, and this alone, that we can rationally expect any essential and permanent melioration in the condition of the labouring classes of the people.

In an endeavour to raise the proportion of the quantity of provisions to the number of consumers in any country, our attention would naturally be first directed to the increasing of the absolute quantity of provisions; but finding that, as fast as we did this, the number of consumers more than kept pace with it, and that with all our exertions we were still as far as ever behind, we should be convinced that our efforts directed only in this way would never succeed. It would appear to be setting the tortoise to catch the hare. Finding, therefore, that from the laws of nature we could not proportion the food to the population, our next attempt should naturally be to proportion the population to the food. If we can persuade the hare to go to sleep the tortoise may have some chance of overtaking her.

We are not, however, to relax our efforts in increasing the quantity of provisions, but to combine another effort with it; that of keeping the population, when once it has been overtaken, at such a distance behind as to effect the relative proportion which we desire; and thus unite the two grand *desiderata*, a great actual population and a state of society in which abject poverty and dependence are comparatively but little known; two objects which are far from being incompatible.

If we be really serious in what appears to be the object of such general research, the mode of essentially and permanently bettering the condition of the poor, we must explain to them the true nature of their situation, and show them that the withholding of the supplies of labour is the only possible way of really raising its price, and that they themselves, being the possessors of this commodity, have alone the power to do this.

*   *   *

CHAPTER VIII. PLAN OF THE GRADUAL ABOLITION OF THE POOR LAWS PROPOSED

If the principles in the preceding chapters should stand the test of examination, and we should ever feel the obligation of endeavouring to act upon them, the next inquiry would be in what way we ought practically to proceed. The first grand obstacle which presents itself in this country is the system of the poor-laws, which has been justly stated to be an evil in comparison of which the national debt, with all its magnitude of terror, is of little moment.[1] The rapidity with which the poor's rates have increased of late years presents us indeed with the prospect of such an extraordinary proportion of paupers in the society as would seem to be incredible in a nation flourishing in arts, agriculture, and commerce, and with a government

---

1. *Reports of the society for bettering the Condition of the Poor.*

which has generally been allowed to be the best that has hitherto stood the test of experience.[2]

* * *

I have reflected much on the subject of the poor-laws, and hope therefore that I shall be excused in venturing to suggest a mode of their gradual abolition to which I confess that at present I can see no material objection. Of this indeed I feel nearly convinced that, should we ever become so fully sensible of the widespreading tyranny, dependence, indolence, and unhappiness which they create as seriously to make an effort to abolish them, we shall be compelled by a sense of justice to adopt the principle, if not the plan, which I shall mention. It seems impossible to get rid of so extensive a system of support, consistently with humanity, without applying ourselves directly to its vital principle, and endeavouring to counteract that deeply-seated cause which occasions the rapid growth of all such establishments and invariably renders them inadequate to their object.

As a previous step even to any considerable alteration in the present system, which would contract or stop the increase of the relief to be given, it appears to me that we are bound in justice and honour formally to disclaim the *right* of the poor to support.

To this end, I should propose a regulation to be made, declaring that no child born from any marriage, taking place after the expiration of a year from the date of the law, and no illegitimate child born two years from the same date, should ever be entitled to parish assistance. And to give a more general knowledge of this law, and to enforce it more strongly on the minds of the lower classes of people, the clergyman of each parish should, after the publication of banns, read a short address stating the strong obligation on every man to support his own children; the impropriety, and even immorality, of marrying without a prospect of being able to do this; the evils which had resulted to the poor themselves from the attempt which had been made to assist by public institutions in a duty which ought to be exclusively appropriated to parents; and the absolute necessity which had at length appeared of abandoning all such institutions, on account of their producing effects totally opposite to those which were intended.

This would operate as a fair, distinct, and precise notice, which no man could well mistake; and, without pressing hard on any par-

---

2. If the poor's rates continue increasing as rapidly as they have done on the average of the last ten years, how melancholy are our future prospects! The system of the poor-laws has been justly stated by the French to be *la plate politique de l'Angleterre la plus devorante*. (Comté de Mendicité.)

ticular individuals, would at once throw off the rising generation from that miserable and helpless dependence upon the government and the rich, the moral as well as physical consequences of which are almost incalculable.

After the public notice which I have proposed had been given, and the system of poor-laws had ceased with regard to the rising generation, if any man chose to marry, without a prospect of being able to support a family, he should have the most perfect liberty so to do. Though to marry, in this case, is, in my opinion, clearly an immoral act, yet it is not one which society can justly take upon itself to prevent or punish; because the punishment provided for it by the laws of nature falls directly and most severely upon the individual who commits the act, and through him, only more remotely and feebly, on the society. When nature will govern and punish for us, it is a very miserable ambition to wish to snatch the rod from her hand and draw upon ourselves the odium of executioner. To the punishment therefore of nature he should be left, the punishment of want. He has erred in the face of a most clear and precise warning, and can have no just reason to complain of any person but himself when he feels the consequences of his error. All parish assistance should be denied him; and he should be left to the uncertain support of private charity. He should be taught to know that the laws of nature, which are the laws of God, had doomed him and his family to suffer for disobeying their repeated admonitions; that he had no claim of *right* on society for the smallest portion of food, beyond that which his labour would fairly purchase; and that if he and his family were saved from feeling the natural consequences of his imprudence he would owe it to the pity of some kind benefactor, to whom, therefore, he ought to be bound by the strongest ties of gratitude.

If this system were pursued, we need be under no apprehensions that the number of persons in extreme want would be beyond the power and the will of the benevolent to supply. The sphere for the exercise of private charity would, probably, not be greater than it is at present; and the principal difficulty would be to restrain the hand of benevolence from assisting those in distress in so indiscriminate a manner as to encourage indolence and want of foresight in others.

With regard to illegitimate children, after the proper notice had been given, they should not be allowed to have any claim to parish assistance, but be left entirely to the support of private charity. If the parents desert their child, they ought to be made answerable for the crime. The infant is, comparatively speaking, of little value to the society, as others will immediately supply its place. * * *

CHAPTER IX. OF THE MODES OF CORRECTING THE PREVAILING
OPINIONS ON POPULATION

It is not enough to abolish all the positive institutions which encourage population; but we must endeavour, at the same time, to correct the prevailing opinions which have the same, or perhaps even a more powerful effect. This must necessarily be a work of time; and can only be done by circulating juster notions on these subjects in writing and conversation; and by endeavouring to impress as strongly as possible on the public mind that it is not the duty of man simply to propagate his species, but to propagate virtue and happiness; and that, if he has not a tolerably fair prospect of doing this, he is by no means called upon to leave descendants.

*   *   *

The fairest chance of accomplishing this end would probably be by the establishment of a system of parochial education upon a plan similar to that proposed by Adam Smith.[3] In addition to the usual subjects of instruction, and those which he has mentioned, I should be disposed to lay considerable stress on the frequent explanation of the real state of the lower classes of society as affected by the principle of population, and their consequent dependence on themselves for the chief part of their happiness of misery. * * *

The principal argument which I have heard advanced against a system of national education in England is, that the common people would be put in a capacity to read such works as those of Paine, and that the consequences would probably be fatal to government. But on this subject I agree most cordially with Adam Smith in thinking that an instructed and well-informed people would be much less likely to be led away by inflammatory writings, and much better able to detect the false declamation of interested and ambitious demagogues, than an ignorant people. * * *

In most countries, among the lower classes of people, there appears to be something like a standard of wretchedness, a point below which they will not continue to marry and propagate their species. This standard is different in different countries, and is formed by various concurring circumstances of soil, climate, government, degree of knowledge, and civilisation, etc. The principal circumstances which contribute to raise it are liberty, security of property, the diffusion of knowledge, and a taste for the conveniences and the comforts of life. Those which contribute principally to lower it are despotism and ignorance.

In an attempt to better the condition of the labouring classes of society our object should be to raise this standard as high as possible,

3. *Wealth of Nations.*

by cultivating a spirit of independence, a decent pride, and a taste
for cleanliness and comfort. The effect of a good government in
increasing the prudential habits and personal respectability of the
lower classes of society has already been insisted on; but certainly
this effect will always be incomplete without a good system of education; and, indeed, it may be said that no government can approach
to perfection that does not provide for the instruction of the people.
The benefits derived from education are among those which may be
enjoyed without restriction of numbers; and, as it is in the power of
governments to confer these benefits, it is undoubtedly their duty to
do it.

CHAPTER XIV. OF OUR RATIONAL EXPECTATIONS RESPECTING THE FUTURE IMPROVEMENT OF SOCIETY

*   *   *

It is less the object of the present work to propose new plans of
improving society than to inculcate the necessity of resting contented with that mode of improvement which already has in part
been acted upon as dictated by the course of nature, and of not
obstructing the advances which would otherwise be made in this
way.

It would be undoubtedly highly advantageous that all our positive
institutions, and the whole tenour of our conduct to the poor, should
be such as actively to co-operate with that lesson of prudence incul-
cated by the common course of human events; and if we take upon
ourselves sometimes to mitigate the natural punishments of imprudence, that we could balance it by increasing the rewards of an opposite conduct. But much would be done if merely the institutions
which directly tend to encourage marriage were gradually changed,
and we ceased to circulate opinions and inculcate doctrines which
positively counteract the lessons of nature.

The limited good which it is sometimes in our power to effect, is
often lost by attempting too much, and by making the adoption of
some particular plan essentially necessary even to a partial degree of
success. In the practical application of the reasonings of this work,
I hope that I have avoided this error. I wish to press on the recollec-
tion of the reader that, though I may have given some new views of
old facts, and may have indulged in the contemplation of a considerable degree of *possible* improvement, that I might not shut out that
prime cheerer hope; yet in my expectations of probable improvement
and in suggesting the means of accomplishing it, I have been very
cautious. * * *

From a review of the state of society in former periods compared with the present, I should certainly say that the evils resulting from the principle of population have rather diminished than increased, even under the disadvantage of an almost total ignorance of the real cause. And if we can indulge the hope that this ignorance will be gradually dissipated, it does not seem unreasonable to expect that they will be still further diminished. The increase of absolute population, which will of course take place, will evidently tend but little to weaken this expectation, as everything depends upon the relative proportion between population and food, and not on the absolute number of people. In the former part of this work it appeared that the countries which possessed the fewest people often suffered the most from the effects of the principle of population; and it can scarcely be doubted that, taking Europe throughout, fewer famines and fewer diseases arising from want have prevailed in the last century than in those which preceded it.

On the whole, therefore, though our future prospects respecting the mitigation of the evils arising from the principle of population may not be so bright as we could wish, yet they are far from being entirely disheartening, and by no means preclude that gradual and progressive improvement in human society which, before the late wild speculations on this subject, was the object of rational expectation. To the laws of property and marriage, and to the apparent narrow principle of self-interest which prompts each individual to exert himself in bettering his condition, we are indebted for all the noblest exertions of human genius, for everything that distinguishes the civilised from the savage state. A strict inquiry into the principle of population obliges us to conclude that we shall never be able to throw down the ladder by which we have risen to this eminence; but it by no means proves that we may not rise higher by the same means. The structure of society, in its great features, will probably always remain unchanged. We have every reason to believe that it will always consist of a class of proprietors and a class of labourers; but the condition of each, and the proportion which they bear to each other, may be so altered as greatly to improve the harmony and beauty of the whole. It would indeed be a melancholy reflection that, while the views of physical science are daily enlarging, so as scarcely to be bounded by the most distant horizon, the science of moral and political philosophy should be confined within such narrow limits, or at best be so feeble in its influence, as to be unable to counteract the obstacles to human happiness arising from a single cause. But however formidable these obstacles may have appeared in some parts of this work, it is hoped that the general result of the inquiry is such as not to make us give up the improvement of human society in despair. The partial good which seems to be attainable is worthy of all our exertions; is sufficient to direct our efforts, and animate our prospects. And although we cannot expect that the virtue and happiness of mankind will keep pace with the brilliant career of physical discovery; yet, if we are not wanting to ourselves, we may confidently indulge the hope that, to no unimportant extent, they will be influenced by its progress and will partake in its success.

Part III
NINETEENTH-CENTURY
COMMENT

WILLIAM GODWIN

Of Population (1820)†

Preface

When I wrote my Enquiry concerning Political Justice, I flattered
myself that there was no mean probability that I should render an
important service to mankind. * * *

The book I produced seemed for some time fully to answer in its
effects the most sanguine expectations I had conceived from it. I
could not complain that it "fell dead-born from the press," or that it
did not awaken a considerable curiosity among my countrymen. * * *
Among other phenomena of the kind, I hailed the attack of Mr.
Malthus. I believed, that the Essay on Population, like other erroneous and exaggerated representations of things, would soon find its
own level.

In this I have been hitherto disappointed. * * * Finding therefore,
that whatever arguments have been produced against it by others, it
still holds on its prosperous career, and has not long since appeared
in the impressive array of a Fifth Edition, I cannot be contented to
go out of the world, without attempting to put into a permanent form
what has occurred to me on the subject. * * *

Between the advantages and disadvantages attendant on the state
of man on earth there is one thing that seems decisively to turn the
balance in favour of the former. Man is to a considerable degree the
artificer of his own fortune. We can apply our reflections and our
ingenuity to the remedy of whatever we regret. Speaking in a general
way, and within certain liberal and expansive limitations, it should
appear that there is no evil under which the human species can
labour, that man is not competent to cure. * * * Man, in the most
dejected condition in which a human being can be placed, has still
something within him which whispers him, "I belong to a world that
is worth living in."

Such was, and was admitted to be the state of the human species,
previously to the appearance of the Essay on Population. Now let us
see how, under the ascendancy of Mr. Malthus's theory, all this is
completely reversed.

The great error of those who sought to encourage and console
their fellow-beings in this vale of tears, was, we are told, in supposing
that any thing that we could do, could be of substantial benefit in
remedying the defects of our social existence. "Human institutions

---

† William Godwin (1756–1836), British social philosopher. The present text is from his *Of
Population: An Enquiry concerning the Power of Increase in the Numbers of Mankind.*

are light and superficial, mere feathers that float upon the surface."
The enemy that hems us in, and reduces our condition to despair,
is no other than "the laws of Nature, which are the laws of God."

Nor is this by any means the worst of the case. The express object
of Mr. Malthus's writing was to prove how pernicious was their error,
who aimed at any considerable and essential improvement in human
society. The only effectual checks upon that excess of population,
which, if unchecked, would be sufficient in no long time to people
all the stars, are vice and misery. The main and direct moral and
lesson of the Essay on Population, is passiveness. * * *

Till Mr. Malthus wrote, political writers and sages had courage.
They said, "The evils we suffer are from ourselves; let us apply ourselves with assiduity and fortitude to the cure of them." This courage
was rapidly descending, by the progress of illumination and intellect,
to a very numerous portion of mankind; and the sober and consid-
erate began deliberately to say, "Let us endeavour to remedy the evils
of political society, and mankind may then be free and contented
and happy." Mr. Malthus has placed himself in the gap. He has
proclaimed, with a voice that has carried astonishment and terror
into the hearts of thousands, the accents of despair. He has said,
The evils of which you complain, do not lie within your reach to
remove: they come from the laws of nature, and the unalterable
impulse of human kind.

But Mr. Malthus does not stop here. He presents us with a code
of morality conformable to his creed.

This code consists principally of negatives.

We must not preach up private charity. For charity, "if exerted at
all, will necessarily lead" to pernicious consequences.

We must not preach up frugality. For the "waste among the rich,
and the horses kept by them merely for their pleasure, operate like
granaries, and tend rather to benefit than to injure the lower classes
of society."

We must deny that the poor, whatever may be the causes of degree
or their distress, "have a right to support."

We must maintain that every man "has a right to do what he will
with his own."

We must preach down marriage. We must affirm that no man has
a right to marry, without a fair "prospect of being able to support a
family." "They should not have families, if they cannot support
them." And this rule is strictly to govern our treatment of the married
man in distress. "To the punishment of Nature he should be left, the
punishment of want. He should be taught to know that the laws of
Nature, which are the laws of God, have doomed him and his family
to suffer for disobeying their repeated admonitions."

What havock do these few maxims make with the old received notions of morality!

It has not been enough attended to, how complete a revolution the Essay on Population proposes to effect in human affairs. Mr. Malthus is the most daring and gigantic of all innovators.

To omit all other particulars, if we embrace his creed, we must have a new religion, and a new God.

FRANCIS PLACE

Illustrations and Proofs of the Principle of Population (1822)†

* * * If * * * it were once clearly understood, that it was not disreputable for married persons to avail themselves of such precautionary means as would, without being injurious to health, or destructive of female delicacy, prevent conception, a sufficient check might at once be given to the increase of population beyond the means of subsistence; vice and misery, to a prodigious extent, might be removed from society, and the object of Mr. Malthus, Mr. Godwin, and of every philanthropic person, be promoted, by the increase of comfort, of intelligence, and of moral conduct, in the mass of the population.

The course recommended will, I am fully persuaded, at some period by pursued by the people, even if left to themselves. The intellectual progress they have for several years past been making, the desire for information of all kinds, which is abroad in the world, and particularly in this country, cannot fail to lead them to the discovery of the true causes of their poverty and degradation, not the least of which they will find to be in overstocking the market with labour, by too rapidly producing children, and for which they will not fail to find and to apply remedies.

*   *   *

Mr. Malthus seems to shrink from discussing the propriety of preventing conception, not so much it may be supposed from the abhorrence which he or any reasonable man can have to the practice, as from the possible fear of encountering the prejudices of others * * *. It is time, however, that those who really understand the cause of a redundant, unhappy, miserable, and considerably vicious popula-

† Francis Place (1771–1854), British reformer. The text is from pages 165–75 of his *Illustrations and Proofs of the Principle of Population* (London, 1822).

tion, and the means of preventing the redundancy, should clearly, freely, openly, and fearlessly point out the means. It is "childish" to shrink from proposing or developing any means, however repugnant they may at first appear to be; our only care should be, that we do not in removing one evil introduce another of greater magnitude. * * * Mr. Malthus has, however, set the question of continence in a very clear point of view; he says, "it may be objected, that, by endeavouring to urge the duty of moral restraint" "we may increase the quantity of vice relating to the sex. I should be extremely sorry to say any thing which could either directly or remotely be construed unfavorably to the cause of virtue; but *I certainly cannot think that the vices which relate to the sex are the only vices which are to be considered in a moral question, or that they are even the greatest and most degrading to the human character.* They can rarely or never be committed without producing unhappiness somewhere or other, and, therefore, ought always to be strongly reprobated. But there are other vices, the effects of which are still more pernicious; and there are other situations which lead more certainly to moral offences than refraining from marriage. *Powerful as may be the temptations to a breach of chastity, I am inclined to think that they are impotent in comparison with the temptations arising from continued distress.* A large class of women and many men, I have no doubt, pass a considerable part of their lives consistently with the laws of chastity; but I believe *there will be found very few who pass through the ordeal of squalid and* HOPELESS *poverty, or even of long-continued embarrassed circumstances, without a great moral degradation of character.*"[1]

NASSAU W. SENIOR

Two Lectures on Population (1829)†

* * * In my introductory Lecture I sketched what appeared to me an outline of those laws in the following proposition:—"That the population of a given district is limited only by moral or physical evil, or by deficiency in the means of obtaining those articles of wealth; or, in other words, those necessaries, decencies, and luxuries, which the habits of the individuals of each class of the inhabitants of that district lead them to require."

The only modification which subsequent reflection induces me to apply to this proposition is, to substitute for the word "deficiency,"

---

1. Malthus, *An Essay on Population*, Everyman's Library ed., Vol. II, p. 175 [*Editor*].
† Nassau William Senior (1790–1864), British political economist. The text is from his *Selected Writings on Economics*.

the words, "the apprehension of a deficiency." My reasons for this substitution are: first, that the actual deficiency of necessaries is a branch of physical evil; and, secondly, that it is not the existence of a deficiency, but the *fear* of its existence which is the principal check to population, so far as necessaries are concerned, and the sole check as respects decencies and luxuries.

But before I take this proposition in detail, I feel that I ought to explain, as precisely as I can, what I mean by the words, necessaries, decencies, and luxuries; terms which have been used ever since the moral sciences first attracted attention in this country, but have never, within my knowledge, been defined.

It is scarcely necessary to remind you, that they are relative terms, and that some person must always be assigned, with reference to whom a given commodity or service is a luxury, a decency, or a necessary.

By *necessaries* then, I express those things, the use of which is requisite to keep a given individual in the health and strength essential to his going through his habitual occupations.

By *decencies*, those things which a given individual must use in order to preserve his existing rank in society.

Everything else of which a given individual makes use; or, in other words, all that portion of his consumption which is not essential to his health and strength, or to the preservation of his existing rank in society, I term *luxury*.

* * *

The check from an apprehended deficiency of luxuries is but slight. The motives, perhaps I might say the instincts, that prompt the human race to marriage, are too powerful to be much restrained by the fear of losing conveniences, unconnected with health or station in society.

The fear of losing decencies, or perhaps more frequently the hope to acquire, by a longer accumulation during celibacy the means of purchasing the decencies of a higher social rank, is a check of far more importance. Want of actual necessaries is seldom apprehended by any except the poorest classes in any country. And in England, though it sometimes is felt, it probably is anticipated by none. When an Englishman stands hesitating between love and prudence, a family really starving is not among his terrors. Against actual want he knows that he has the fence of the poor laws. But, however humble his desires, he cannot contemplate, without anxiety, a probability that the income which supported his social rank while single, may be insufficient to maintain it when he is married; that he may be unable to give to his children the advantages of education which he enjoyed himself; in short, that he may lose his caste. * * *

Supposing our population to have increased, as would be the case by the beginning of the next century, to one hundred millions, about an acre and a half would be allotted to each family; and, as I before observed, I think that allotment might be sufficient. But it can scarcely be supposed, that three roods would be enough, which would be their allotment in twenty-five years more, or granting that to be enough, it cannot be supposed that at the end of a further term of doubling a family of four persons could live on the produce of a rood and a half.

* * * Where the evil is the loss of luxuries, or even of decencies, it is trifling in the first instance, and bearable in the second. But in the case which I am supposing, the only prudential check would be an apprehended deficiency of necessaries; and that deficiency, in the many instances in which it would be incurred, would be the positive check in its most frightful form. It would be incurred not only in consequence of that miscalculation of chances to which all men are subject, and certainly those not the least so, who are anxious to marry, but through accidents against which no human prudence can guard. A *single* bad harvest may be provided against, but a succession of unfavourable seasons, and such successions do occur, must reduce such a people to absolute famine. When such seasons affect a nation indulging in considerable superfluous expenditure, they are relieved by a temporary sacrifice of that superfluity. The grain consumed in ordinary years by our breweries and distilleries is a store always at hand to supply a scarcity, and the same may be said of the large quantity of food used for the support of domestic animals, but applicable to human subsistence. To these resources may be added the importation from abroad of necessaries instead of luxuries, and the materials of luxury; of corn, for instance, instead of wine.

It appears, therefore, that habits of considerable superfluous expenditure afford the only permanent protection against a population pressing so closely on the means of subsistence, as to be continually incurring the misery of the positive checks. And as these habits can exist only in an opulent society, it appears to me equally clear, that as a nation advances in opulence, the positive checks are likely to be superseded by the preventive. If this be true, the evil of a redundant population, or to speak more intelligibly, of a population too numerous to be adequately and regularly supplied with necessaries, is likely to diminish in the progress of improvement. As wealth increases, what were the luxuries of one generation become the decencies of their successors. Not only a taste for additional comfort and convenience, but a feeling of degradation in their absence becomes more and more widely diffused. The increase, in many respects, of the productive powers of labour, must enable increased comforts to be enjoyed by increased numbers, and as it is the more beneficial, so it appears to me to be the more natural course of events, that increased comfort should not only accompany, but rather precede, increase of numbers.

*   *   *

If it be conceded, that there exists in the human race a natural tendency to rise from barbarism to civilization, and that the means of subsistence are proportionally more abundant in a civilized than in a savage state, and neither of these propositions can be denied, it must follow that there is a natural tendency in subsistence to increase in a greater ratio than population.

But, although Mr. Malthus has perhaps fallen into the exaggeration which is natural to a discoverer, his error, if it be one, does not affect the practical conclusions which place him, as a benefactor to mankind, on a level with Adam Smith. Whether, in the absence of disturbing causes, it be the tendency of subsistence or of population to advance with greater rapidity, is a question of slight importance, if it be acknowledged that human happiness or misery depend principally on their relative advance, and that there are causes, and causes within human control, by which that advance can be regulated.

These are propositions which Mr. Malthus has established by facts and reasonings, which, opposed as they were to long-rooted prejudice, and assailed by every species of sophistry and clamour, are now so generally admitted, that they have become rather matter of allusion than of formal statement.* * *

HARRIET MARTINEAU

Illustrations of Political Economy (1832)†

*   *   *

"Our resources are so improved that I would fain hope the best; and yet our numbers increase in full proportion, so that we had not need waste any of our capital."

"I think not indeed. I have been visiting every station on the coast and in the islands, and I find the same state of things everywhere,—a prosperity so unusual in these districts, that the people think their fortune secure for ever, while they are hastening, by every possible means, the approach of distress."

† Harriet Martineau (1802–1876), British novelist and popular writer on economic subjects whose fictional representation of Malthusian thought gave it a wide audience. The text is from Number 4, Chapter 4 of her *Illustrations of Political Economy* (London, 1832).

"I hope you find the farms and pastures improving with the fishery?" observed Angus.—"Everything depends upon the food keeping pace with the employment."

"The farms are improving to the utmost that skill and labour can make them improve. There is the powerful stimulus of an increasing demand, while there are increasing facilities of production. There is more manure, there are better implements, and more cattle: so that some farms produce actually double what they did when the fishery began."

Angus shook his head, observing that this was not enough.

"They have done their best already in the way of increase," said he. "They may be improved for some time to come, and to a great degree; but each improvement yields a less return: so that they will be further and further perpetually from again producing double in ten years; and all this time the consumers are increasing at a much quicker rate."

"Not double in ten years surely?" said Ella.

"Certainly not; but say twenty, thirty, fifty, a hundred, any number of years you choose;—still, as the number of people doubles itself for ever, while the produce of the land does not, the people must increase faster than the produce. If corn produced corn without being wedded to the soil, the rate of increase might be the same with that of the human race. Then two sacks of barley might grow out of one, and two more again out of each of those two—proceeding from one to two, four, eight, sixteen, thirty-two, sixty-four, and so on."

"If capital could be made to increase in this way, I see, Angus, that there could never be too many people in the world, or in our little world, Garveloch."

"Or if, on the other hand, human production could be kept down to the same rate with the production of our fields, we need have no fear of a deficiency of food. If the number of producers increased only in proportion to the increase of food, there would be no distress of the kind our islands were formerly afflicted with, and may be afflicted with again. But nobody thinks of establishing such a proportion; and in the meanwhile, food is yielded, though in larger quantities, in less and less proportions, while the eaters go on doubling and doubling their numbers perpetually."

*   *   *

"There is no need to do here as the Romans did," said Mr. Mackenzie, "and as many other nations have done—no need to offer bounties for the increase of population."

"I think not indeed," said Ella. "It seems a thing to be checked, rather than encouraged."

"All depends on time and circumstances, Ella. When Noah and

his little tribe stepped out of the ark into a desolated world, the great object was to increase the number of beings, who might gather and enjoy the fruits which the earth yielded, in an abundance over-powering to the few who were there to consume."

*   *   *

"In some of the best settlements I saw in America, the increase of capital and of people went on at a rate that would scarcely be believed in an old country."

"And that of the people the fastest, I suppose?"

"Of course: but still capital was far a-head, though the population is gaining upon it every year. When the people first went, they found nothing but capital—all means of production and no consumers but themselves. They raised corn in the same quantity from certain fields every year. There was too much corn at first in one field for a hundred months; but this hundred became two, four, eight, sixteen hundred, and so on, till more and more land was tilled, the people still spreading over it, and multiplying perpetually."

"And when all is tilled, and they still multiply," said Ella, "they must improve their land more and more."

"And still," said Angus, "the produce will fall behind more and more, as every improvement, every outlay of capital yields a less return. Then they will be in the condition of an old country, like England, where many are but half fed, where many prudent determine not to marry, and where the imprudent must see their children pine in hunger, or waste under disease till they are ready to be carried off by the first attack of illness."

*   *   *

FRIEDRICH ENGELS

Outlines of a Critique of Political Economy (1844)†

Malthus * * * asserts that population constantly exerts pressure on the means of subsistence; that as production is increased, population increases in the same proportion; and that the inherent tendency of population to multiply beyond the available means of subsistence is the cause of all poverty and all vice. For if there are too many people, then in one way or another they must be eliminated; they must die, either by violence or through starvation. When this has happened, however, a gap appears once more, and this is immediately filled by other propagators of population, so that the old

† Friedrich Engels (1820–1895), German socialist. The translation is from Ronald L. Meek, ed., *Marx and Engels on the Population Bomb* (Berkeley, Calif., 1971).

poverty begins anew. Moreover, this is the case under all conditions—not only in the civilized but also in the natural state of man. The savages of New Holland, who live *one* to the square mile, suffer just as much from overpopulation as England. In short, if we want to be logical, we have to recognize *that the earth was already over-populated when only one man existed.* Now the consequence of this theory is that since it is precisely the poor who constitute this surplus population, nothing ought to be done for them, except to make it as easy as possible for them to starve to death; to convince them that this state of affairs cannot be altered and that there is no salvation for their entire class other than that they should propagate as little as possible * * *

Is it necessary for me to give any more details of this vile and infamous doctrine, this repulsive blasphemy against man and nature, or to follow up its consequences any further? Here, brought before us at last, is the immorality of the economists in its highest form. What were all the wars and horrors of the monopoly system when compared with this theory? And it is precisely this theory which is the cornerstone of the liberal system of free trade, whose fall will bring the whole edifice down with it. For once competition has here been proved to be the cause of misery, poverty and crime, who will still dare to say a word in its defense?

* * * If, however, it is a fact that every adult produces more than he can himself consume, that children are like trees, returning abundantly the expenditure laid out on them—and surely these are facts?—one would imagine that every worker ought to be able to produce far more than he needs, and that the community ought therefore to be glad to furnish him with everything that he requires; one would imagine that a large family would be a most desirable gift to the community. But the economists, with their crude outlook, know no other equivalent apart from that which is paid over to them in tangible hard cash. They are so firmly entangled in their contradictions that they are just as little concerned with the most striking facts as they are with the most scientific principles.

We shall destroy the contradiction simply by resolving it. With the fusion of those interests which now conflict with one another, there will disappear the antithesis between surplus population in one place and surplus wealth in another, and also the wonderful phenomenon—more wonderful than all the wonders of all the religions put together—that a nation must starve to death from sheer wealth and abundance; and there will disappear too the crazy assertion that the earth does not possess the power to feed mankind. * * *

The Malthusian theory, however, was an absolutely necessary transitional stage, which has taken us infinitely further forward. Thanks to this theory, as also thanks to economics in general, our attention has been drawn to the productive power of the soil and of humanity, so that now, having triumphed over this economic despair, we are forever secure from the fear of overpopulation. From this theory we derive the most powerful economic arguments in favor of a social reorganization; for even if Malthus were altogether right, it would still be necessary to carry out this reorganization immediately, since only this reorganization, only the enlightenment of the masses which it can bring with it, can make possible that moral restraint upon the instinct for reproduction which Malthus himself puts forward as the easiest and most effective countermeasure against overpopulation. Thanks to this theory we have come to recognize in the dependence of man upon competitive conditions his most complete degradation. It has shown us that in the last analysis private property has turned man into a commodity, whose production and consumption also depend only on demand; that the system of competition has thereby slaughtered, and is still slaughtering today, millions of people—all this we have seen, and all this impels us to do away with this degradation of humanity by doing away with private property, competition and conflicting interests.

However, in order to deprive the general fear of overpopulation of all foundation, let us return once again to the question of the relation of productive power to population. Malthus puts forward a calculation upon which his whole system is based. Population increases in geometrical progression—$1+2+4+8+16+32$, etc. The productive power of the land increases in arithmetical progression—$1+2+3+4+5+6$. The difference is obvious and horrifying—but is it correct? Where has it been proved that the productivity of the land increases in arithmetical progression? The area of land is limited—that is perfectly true. But the labor power to be employed on this area increases together with the population; and even if we assume that the increase of output associated with this increase of labor is not always proportionate to the latter, there still remains a third element—which the economists, however, never consider as important—namely, science, the progress of which is just as limitless and at least as rapid as that of population. For what great advances is the agriculture of this century obliged to chemistry alone—and indeed to two men alone, Sir Humphry Davy and Justus Liebig? But science increases at least as fast as population; the latter increases in proportion to the size of the previous generation, and science advances in proportion to the body of knowledge passed down to it by the previous generation, that is, in the most normal conditions it also grows in geometrical progression—and what is impossible for science? But it is ridiculous to speak of overpopulation while "the valley of the Mississippi alone contains enough waste land to accommodate the whole population of Europe," while altogether only one-third of

the earth can be described as cultivated, and while the productivity
of this third could be increased sixfold and more merely by applying
improvements which are already known.

JOHN STUART MILL

Principles of Political Economy (1848)†

In all countries which have passed a very early stage in the progress
of agriculture, every increase in the demand for food, occasioned by
increased population, will always, unless there is a simultaneous
improvement in production, diminish the share which on a fair division would fall to each individual. An increased production, in
default of unoccupied tracts of fertile land, or of fresh improvements tending to cheapen commodities, can never be obtained but
by increasing the labor in more than the same proportion. The population must either work harder, or eat less, or obtain their usual
food by sacrificing a part of their other customary comforts. Whenever this necessity is postponed, it is because the improvements
which facilitate production continue progressive; because the con-
trivances of mankind for making their labor more effective, keep up
an equal struggle with nature, and extort fresh resources from her
reluctant powers as fast as human necessities occupy and engross
the old.

From this, results the important corollary, that the necessity of
restraining population is not, as many persons believe, peculiar to a
condition of great inequality of property. A greater number of people
cannot, in any given state of civilization, be collectively so well provided for as a smaller. The niggardliness of nature, not the injustice
of society, is the cause of the penalty attached to overpopulation. An
unjust distribution of wealth does not even aggravate the evil, but,
at most, causes it to be somewhat earlier felt. It is in vain to say, that
all mouths which the increase of mankind calls into existence, bring
with them hands. The new mouths require as much food as the old
ones, and the hands do not produce as much. If all instruments of
production were held in joint property by the whole people, and the
produce divided with perfect equality among them, and if in a society
thus constituted, industry were as energetic and the produce as
ample as at present, there would be enough to make all the existing
population extremely comfortable; but when that population had

† John Stuart Mill (1806–1873), British philosopher and political economist. In the text,
  the first excerpt is from Book I, Chapter 13. Section 2; the subsequent excerpts are from
  Book II, Chapters 11–13.

doubled itself, as, with the existing habits of the people, under such an encouragement, it undoubtedly would, in little more than twenty years, what would then be their condition? Unless the arts of production were in the same time improved in so unexampled a degree as to double the productive power of labor—the inferior soils which must be resorted to, and the more laborious and scantily remunerative cultivation which must be employed on the superior soils, to procure food for so much larger a population, would, by an insuperable necessity, render every individual in the community poorer than before. If the population continued to increase at the same rate, a time would soon arrive when no one would have more than mere necessaries, and, soon after, a time when no one would have a sufficiency of those, and the further increase of population would be arrested by death.

*   *   *

Chapter XI. Of Wages

Wages, like other things, may be regulated either by competition or by custom. In this country there are few kinds of labor of which the remuneration would not be lower than it is, if the employer took the full advantage of competition. Competition, however, must be regarded, in the present state of society, as the principal regulator of wages, and custom or individual character only as a modifying circumstance, and that in a comparatively slight degree.

Wages, then, depend mainly upon the demand and supply of labor; or as it is often expressed, on the proportion between population and capital. * * *

* * * But dearness or cheapness of food, when of a permanent character, and capable of being calculated on beforehand, may affect wages. In the first place, if the laborers have, as if often the case, no more than enough to keep them in working condition, and enable them barely to support the ordinary number of children, it follows that if food grows permanently dearer without a rise of wages, a greater number of the children will prematurely die; and thus wages will ultimately be higher, but only because the number of people will be smaller, than if food had remained cheap. But, secondly, even though wages were high enough to admit of food's becoming more costly without depriving the laborers and their families of necessaries; though they could bear, physically speaking, to be worse off, perhaps they would not consent to be so. They might have habits of comfort which were to them as necessaries, and sooner than forego which, they would put an additional restraint on their power of multiplication; so that wages would rise, not by increase of deaths but

by diminution of births. In these cases, then, wages do adapt themselves to the price of food, though after an interval of almost a generation. * * *

The converse case occurs when, by improvements in agriculture, the repeal of corn laws, or other such causes, the necessaries of the laborers are cheapened, and they are enabled with the same wages, to command greater comforts than before. Wages will not fall immediately; it is even possible that they may rise; but they will fall at last, so as to leave the laborers no better off than before, unless, during this interval of prosperity, the standard of comfort regarded as indispensable by the class, is permanently raised. * * *

§ 3. Wages depend, then, on the proportion between the number of the laboring population, and the capital or other funds devoted to the purchase of labor; we will say, for shortness, the capital. If wages are higher at one time or place than at another, if the subsistence and comfort of the class of hired laborers are more ample, it is for no other reason than because capital bears a greater proportion to population. It is not the absolute amount of accumulation or of production, that is of importance to the laboring class; it is not the amount even of the funds destined for distribution among the laborers: it is the proportion between those funds and the numbers among whom they are shared. The condition of the class can be bettered in no other way than by altering that proportion to their advantage: and every scheme for their benefit, which does not proceed on this as its foundation, is, for all permanent purposes, a delusion.

*   *   *

Except, therefore, in the very peculiar cases which I have just noticed, of which the only one of any practical importance is that of a new colony, or a country in circumstances equivalent to it; it is impossible that population should increase at its utmost rate without lowering wages. Nor will the fall be stopped at any point, short of that which either by its physical or its moral operation, checks the increase of population. In no old country, therefore, does population increase at anything like its utmost rate; in most, at a very moderate rate: in some countries not at all. These facts are only to be accounted for in two ways. Either the whole number of births which nature admits of, and which happen in some circumstances, do not take place; or if they do, a large proportion of those who are born, die. The retardation of increase results either from mortality or prudence; from Mr. Malthus's positive, or from his preventive check: and one or the other of these must and does exist, and very powerfully too, in all old societies. Wherever population is not kept down by the prudence either of individuals or of the state, it is kept down by starvation or disease.

* * * [W]hile there is a growing sensitiveness to the hardships of the poor, and a ready disposition to admit claims in them upon the good offices of other people, there is an all but universal unwillingness to face the real difficulty of their position, or advert at all to the conditions which nature has made indispensable to the improvement of their physical lot. Discussions on the condition of the laborers, lamentations over its wretchedness, denunciations of all who are supposed to be indifferent to it, projects of one kind or another for improving it, were in no country and in no time of the world so rife as in the present generation; but there is a tacit agreement to ignore totally the law of wages, or to dismiss it in a parenthesis, with such terms as "hard-hearted Malthusianism;" as if it were not a thousand times more hard-hearted to tell human beings that they may, than that they may not, call into existence swarms of creatures who are sure to be miserable, and most likely to be depraved; and forgetting that the conduct, which it is reckoned so cruel to disapprove, is a degrading slavery to a brute instinct in one of the persons concerned, and most commonly, in the other, helpless submission to a revolting abuse of power.

* * * I ask, then, is it true, or not, that if their numbers were fewer they would obtain higher wages? This is the question, and no other: and it is idle to divert attention from it, by attacking any incidental position of Malthus or some other writer, and pretending that to refute that, is to disprove the principle of population. Some, for instance, have achieved an easy victory over a passing remark of Mr. Malthus, hazarded chiefly by way of illustration, that the increase of food may perhaps be assumed to take place in an arithmetical ratio, while population increases in a geometrical: when every candid reader knows that Mr. Malthus laid no stress on this unlucky attempt to give numerical precision to things which do not admit of it, and every person capable of reasoning must see that it is wholly superfluous to his argument. * * *

Chapter XIII. The Remedies for Low Wages Further Considered

§ 1. By what means, then, is poverty to be contended against? How is the evil of low wages to be remedied? * * * Poverty, like most social evils, exists because men follow their brute instincts without due consideration. But society is possible, precisely because man is not necessarily a brute. Civilization in every one of its aspects is a struggle against the animal instincts. Over some even of the strongest of them, it has shown itself capable of acquiring abundant control. It has artificialized large portions of mankind to such an extent, that of many of their most natural inclinations they have scarcely a vestige or a remembrance left. If it has not brought the instinct of population under as much restraint as is needful, we must remember that it has never seriously tried. What efforts it has made, have mostly been in the contrary direction. Religion, morality, and statesmanship have vied with one another in incitements to marriage, and to the multiplication of the species, so it be but in wedlock. Religion has not even yet discontinued its encouragements. The Roman Catholic clergy (of any other clergy it is unnecessary to speak, since no other have any considerable influence over the poorer classes) everywhere think it their duty to promote marriage, in order to prevent fornication. * * * While a man who is intemperate in drink, is discountenanced and despised by all who profess to be moral people, it is one of the chief grounds made use of in appeals to the benevolent, that the applicant has a large family and is unable to maintain them.[1]

One cannot wonder that silence on this great department of human duty should produce unconsciousness of moral obligations, when it produces oblivion of physical facts. That it is possible to delay marriage, and to live in abstinence while unmarried, most people are willing to allow: but when persons are once married, the idea, in this country, never seems to enter anyone's mind that having or not having a family, or the number of which it shall consist, is amenable to their own control. One would imagine that children were rained down upon married people, direct from heaven, without their being art or part in the matter; that it was really, as the common phrases have it, God's will, and not their own, which decided the numbers of their offspring. * * *

§ 2. Those who think it hopeless that the laboring classes should be induced to practise a sufficient degree of prudence in regard to the increase of their families, because they have hitherto stopped short of that point, show an inability to estimate the ordinary principles of human action. Nothing more would probably be necessary to secure that result, than an opinion generally diffused that it was desirable. As a moral principle, such an opinion has never yet existed in any country: it is curious that it does not so exist in countries in which, from the spontaneous operation of individual forethought, population is, comparatively speaking, efficiently repressed. What is practised as prudence, is still not recognized as duty; the talkers and writers are mostly on the other side, even in France, where a sentimental horror of Malthus is almost as rife as in this country. * * *

But let us try to imagine what would happen if the idea became general among the laboring class, that the competition of too great numbers was the principal cause of their poverty; so that every

---

1. Little improvement can be expected in morality until the producing of large families is regarded with the same feelings as drunkenness or any other physical excess. But while the aristocracy and clergy are foremost to set the example of this kind of incontinence what can be expected from the poor?

laborer looked (with Sismondi) upon every other who had more than the number of children which the circumstances of society allowed to each, as doing him a wrong—as filling up the place which he was entitled to share. Anyone who supposes that this state of opinion would not have a great effect on conduct, must be profoundly ignorant of human nature; can never have considered how large a portion of the motives which induce the generality of men to take care even of their own interests, is derived from regard for opinion—from the expectation of being disliked or despised for not doing it. * * *

If the opinion were once generally established among the laboring class that their welfare required a due regulation of the numbers of families, the respectable and well-conducted of the body would conform to the prescription, and only those would exempt themselves from it, who were in the habit of making light of social obligations generally; and there would be then an evident justification for converting the moral obligation against bringing children into the world who are a burden to the community, into a legal one; just as in many other cases of the progress of opinion, the law ends by enforcing against recalcitrant minorities, obligations which to be useful must be general, and which, from a sense of their utility, a large majority have voluntarily consented to take upon themselves. There would be no need, however, of legal sanctions, if women were admitted, as on all other grounds they have the clearest title to be, to the same rights of citizenship with men. Let them cease to be confined by custom to one physical function as their means of living and their source of influence, and they would have for the first time an equal voice with men in what concerns that function: and of all the improvements in reserve for mankind which it is now possible to foresee, none might be expected to be so fertile as this in almost every kind of moral and social benefit.

*   *   *

§ 3. For the purpose therefore of altering the habits of the laboring people, there is need of a twofold action, directed simultaneously upon their intelligence and their poverty. An effective national education of the children of the laboring class, is the first thing needful: and, coincidently with this, a system of measures which shall (as the Revolution did in France) extinguish extreme poverty for one whole generation.

CHARLES DARWIN

The Origin of Species (1859)†

Geometrical Ratio of Increase

A struggle for existence inevitably follows from the high rate at which all organic beings tend to increase. Every being, which during its natural lifetime produces several eggs or seeds, must suffer destruction during some period of its life, and during some season or occasional year, otherwise, on the principle of geometrical increase, its numbers would quickly become so inordinately great that no country could support the product. Hence, as more individuals are produced than can possibly survive, there must in every case be a struggle for existence, either one individual with another of the same species, or with the individuals of distinct species, or with the physical conditions of life. It is the doctrine of Malthus applied with manifold force to the whole animal and vegetable kingdoms; for in this case there can be no artificial increase of food, and no prudential restraint from marriage. Although some species may be now increasing, more or less rapidly, in numbers, all cannot do so, for the world would not hold them.[1]

There is no exception to the rule that every organic being naturally increases at so high a rate, that, if not destroyed, the earth would be soon be covered by the progeny of a single pair. Even slow-breeding man has doubled in twenty-five years, and at this rate, in less than a thousand years, there would literally not be standing room for his progeny. Linnæus has calculated that if an annual plant produced only two seeds—and there is no plant so unproductive as this—and their seedlings next year produced two, and so on, then in twenty years there should be a million plants: The elephant is reckoned the slowest breeder of all known animals, and I have taken some pains to estimate its probable minimum rate of natural increase; it will be safest to assume that it begins breeding when thirty years old, and goes on breeding till ninety years old, bringing forth six young in the interval, and surviving till one hundred years old, if this be so, after a period of from 740 to 750 years there would be nearly nineteen

---

† Charles Robert Darwin (1809–1882), British scientist. The text is from Chapter 3 of the seventh edition of *The Origin of Species*.

1. Cf. Darwin's remark in his autobiography: "In October 1838, that is, fifteen months after I had begun my systematic enquiry, I happened to read for amusement Malthus on *Population*, and being well prepared to appreciate the struggle for existence which everywhere goes on from long-continued observation of the habits of animals and plants, it at once struck me that under these circumstances favourable variations would tend to be preserved, and unfavourable ones to be destroyed. The result of this would be the formation of new species. Here, then, I had at last got a theory by which to work." (*The Autobiography of Charles Darwin, 1809–1882*, Nora Barlow, ed., [New York, 1969,] p. 120) [*Editor*].

million elephants alive, descended from the first pair.

But we have better evidence on this subject than mere theoretical calculations, namely, the numerous recorded cases of the astonishingly rapid increase of various animals in a state of nature, when circumstances have been favourable to them during two or three following seasons. Still more striking is the evidence from our domestic animals of many kinds which have run wild in several parts of the world; if the statements of the rate of increase of slow-breeding cattle and horses in South America, and latterly in Australia, had not been well authenticated, they would have been incredible. So it is with plants; cases could be given of introduced plants which have become common throughout whole islands in a period of less than ten years. Several of the plants, such as the cardoon and a tall thistle, which are now the commonest over the whole plains of La Plata, clothing square leagues of surface almost to the exclusion of every other plant, have been introduced from Europe; and there are plants which now range in India, as I hear from Dr. Falconer, from Cape Comorin to the Himalaya, which have been imported from America since its discovery. In such cases, and endless others could be given, no one supposes, that the fertility of the animals or plants has been suddenly and temporarily increased in any sensible degree. The obvious explanation is that the conditions of life have been highly favourable, and that there has consequently been less destruction of the old and young, and that nearly all the young have been enabled to breed. Their geometrical ratio of increase, the result of which never fails to be surprising, simply explains their extraordinarily rapid increase and wide diffusion in their new homes.

In a state of nature almost every full-grown plant annually produces seed, and amongst animals there are very few which do not annually pair. Hence we may confidently assert, that all plants and animals are tending to increase at a geometrical ratio,—that all would rapidly stock every station in which they could anyhow exist,— and that this geometrical tendency to increase must be checked by destruction at some period of life. Our familiarity with the larger domestic animals tends, I think, to mislead us: we see no great destruction falling on them, but we do not keep in mind that thousands are annually slaughtered for food, and that in a state of nature an equal number would have somehow to be disposed of.

The only difference between organisms which annually produce eggs or seeds by the thousand, and those which produce extremely few, is, that the slow-breeders would require a few more years to people, under favourable conditions, a whole district, let it be ever so large. The condor lays a couple of eggs and the ostrich a score, and yet in the same country the condor may be the more numerous of the two; the Fulmar petrel lays but one egg, yet it is believed to be the most numerous bird in the world. One fly deposits hundreds of eggs, and another, like the hippobosca, a single one; but this difference does not determine how many individuals of the two species can be supported in a district. A large number of eggs is of some importance to those species which depend on a fluctuating amount of food, for it allows them rapidly to increase in number. But the real importance of a large number of eggs or seeds is to make up for much destruction at some period of life; and this period in the great majority of cases is an early one. If an animal can in any way protect its own eggs or young, a small number may be produced, and yet the average stock be fully kept up; but if many eggs or young are destroyed, many must be produced, or the species will become extinct. It would suffice to keep up the full number of a tree, which lived on an average for a thousand years, if a single seed were produced once in a thousand years, supposing that this seed were never destroyed, and could be ensured to germinate in a fitting place. So that, in all cases, the average number of any animal or plant depends only indirectly on the number of its eggs or seeds.

In looking at Nature, it is most necessary to keep the foregoing considerations always in mind—never to forget that every single organic being may be said to be striving to the utmost to increase in numbers; that each lives by a struggle at some period of its life; that heavy destruction inevitably falls either on the young or old, during each generation or at recurrent intervals. Lighten any check, mitigate the destruction ever so little, and the number of the species will almost instantaneously increase to any amount.* * *

KARL MARX

Capital (1867)†

If the reader reminds me of Malthus, whose "Essay on Population" appeared in 1798, I remind him that this work in its first form is nothing more than a schoolboyish, superficial plagiary of De Foe, Sir James Steuart, Townsend, Franklin, Wallace, &c., and does not contain a single sentence thought out by himself. The great sensation this pamphlet caused, was due solely to party interest. The French Revolution had found passionate defenders in the United Kingdom; the "principle of population," slowly worked-out in the eighteenth century, and then, in the midst of a great social crisis, proclaimed with drums and trumpets as the infallible antidote to the

† Karl Marx (1818–1883), German economist. The text is from a footnote to Part VII, Chapter 25, Section I (trans. Samuel Moore and Edward Aveling).

teachings of Condorcet, &c., was greeted with jubilance by the English oligarchy as the great destroyer of all hankerings after human development. Malthus, hugely astonished at his success, gave himself to stuffing into his book materials superficially compiled, and adding to it new matter, not discovered but annexed by him. Note further: Although Malthus was a parson of the English State Church, he had taken the monastic vow of celibacy—one of the conditions of holding a Fellowship in Protestant Cambridge University: "Socios collegiorum maritos esse non permittimus, sed statim postquam quis uxorem duxerit, socius collegii desinat esse." (Reports of Cambridge University Commission, p. 172.) This circumstance favourably distinguishes Malthus from the other Protestant parsons, who have shuffled off the command enjoining celibacy of the priesthood and have taken, "Be fruitful and multiply," as their special Biblical mission in such a degree that they generally contribute to the increase of population to a really unbecoming extent, whilst they preach at the same time to the labourers the "principle of population." It is characteristic that the economic fall of man, the Adam's apple, the urgent appetite, "the checks which tend to blunt the shafts of Cupid," as Parson Townsend waggishly puts it, that this delicate question was and is monopolised by the Reverends of Protestant Theology, or rather of the Protestant Church. With the exception of the Venetian monk, Ortes, an original and clever writer, most of the population-theory teachers are Protestant parsons. For instance, Bruckner, "Théorie du Système animal," Leyden, 1767, in which the whole subject of the modern population theory is exhausted, and to which the passing quarrel between Quesnay and his pupil, the elder Mirabeau, furnished ideas on the same topic; then Parson Wallace, Parson Townsend, Parson Malthus and his pupil, the arch-Parson Thomas Chalmers, to say nothing of lesser reverend scribblers in this line. Originally, political economy was studied by philosophers like Hobbes, Locke, Hume; by business men and statesmen, like Thomas More, Temple, Sully, De Witt, North, Law, Vanderlint, Cantillon, Franklin; and especially, and with the greatest success, by medical men like Petty, Barbon, Mandeville, Quesnay. Even in the middle of the eighteenth century, the Rev. Mr. Tucker, a notable economist of his time, excused himself for meddling with the things of Mammon. Later on, and in truth with this very "principle of population," struck the hour of the Protestant parsons. Petty, who regarded the population as the basis of wealth, and was, like Adam Smith, an outspoken foe to parsons, says, as if he had a presentiment of their bungling interference, "that Religion best flourishes when the Priests are most mortified, as was before said of the Law, which best flourisheth when lawyers have least to do." He advises the Protestant priests, therefore if they once for all, will not follow the Apostle Paul and "mortify" themselves by celibacy, "not to breed more Churchmen than the Benefices, as they now stand shared out, will receive, that is to say, if there be places for about twelve thousand in England and Wales, it will not be safe to breed up 24,000 ministers, for then the twelve thousand which are unprovided for, will seek ways how to get themselves a livelihood, which they cannot do more easily than by persuading the people that the twelve thousand incumbents do poison or starve their souls, and misguide them in their way to Heaven." (Petty; "A Treatise on Taxes and Contributions, London, 1667," p. 57.) * * *

GEORGE BERNARD SHAW

Fabian Essays (1889)†

All economic analyses begin with the cultivation of the earth. To the mind's eye of the astronomer the earth is a ball spinning in space without ulterior motives. To the bodily eye of the primitive cultivator it is a vast green plain, from which, by sticking a spade into it, wheat and other edible matters can be made to spring. * * *

* * * According to our hypothesis, the inland sea of cultivation has now spread into the wilderness so far that at its margin the return to a man's labour for a year is only £500. But as there is always a flood tide in that sea, caused by the incessant increase of population, the margin will not stop there: it will at last encroach upon every acre of cultivable land, rising to the snow line on the mountains and falling to the coast of the actual salt water sea, but always reaching the barrenest places last of all, because the cultivators are still, as ever, on the make, and will not break bad land when better is to be had. * * *

* * * In current economic terms the price is regulated by supply and demand. As the demand for land intensifies by the advent of fresh proletarians, the price goes up; and the bargains are made more stringent. Tenants' rights, instead of being granted in perpetuity, and so securing for ever to the tenant the increase due to unforeseen improvements in production, are granted on leases for finite terms, at the expiration of which the landlord can revise the terms or eject the tenant. The payments rise until the original head rents and quit rents appear insignificant in comparison with the incomes reaped by the intermediate tenant right holders or middlemen. Sooner or later the price of tenant right will rise so high that the actual cultivator

† George Bernard Shaw (1856–1950), British playwright and Fabian Socialist. The text is from his contribution, titled "Economic," to the *Fabian Essays*, Shaw, ed., (London, 1889).

will get no more of the produce than suffices him for subsistence. At that point there is an end of sub-letting tenant rights. The land's absorption of the proletarians as tenants paying more than the economic rent stops.

And now, what is the next proletarian to do? For all his forerunners we have found a way of escape: for him there seems none. The board is at the door, inscribed 'Only standing room left'; and it might well bear the more poetic legend, *Lasciate ogni speranza, voi ch' entrate*. This man, born a proletarian, must die a proletarian, and leave his destitution as an only inheritance to his son. It is not yet clear that there is ten days life in him; for whence is his subsistence to come if he cannot get at the land? Food he must have, and clothing; and both promptly. There is food in the market, and clothing also; but not for nothing: hard money must be paid for it, and paid on the nail too; for he who has no property gets no credit. Money then is a necessity of life; and money can only be procured by selling commodities. This presents no difficulty to the cultivators of the land, who can raise commodities by their labour; but the proletarian, being landless, has neither commodities nor means of producing them. Sell something he must. Yet he has nothing to sell—except himself. The idea seems a desperate one; but it proves quite easy to carry out. The tenant cultivators of the land have not strength enough or time enough to exhaust the productive capacity of their holdings. If they could buy men in the market for less than these men's labour would add to the produce, then the purchase of such men would be a sheer gain. It would indeed be only a purchase in form: the men would literally cost nothing, since they would produce their own price, with a surplus for the buyer. Never in the history of buying and selling was there so splendid a bargain for buyers as this. Aladdin's uncle's offer of new lamps for old ones was in comparison a catchpenny. Accordingly, the proletarian no sooner offers himself for sale than he finds a rush of bidders for him, each striving to get the better of the others by offering to give him more and more of the produce of his labour, and to content themselves with less and less surplus. But even the highest bidder must have some surplus, or he will not buy. The proletarian, in accepting the highest bid, sells himself openly into bondage. He is not the first man who has done so; for it is evident that his forerunners, the purchasers of tenant right, had been enslaved by the proprietors who lived on the rents paid by them. But now all the disguise falls off; the proletarian renounces not only the fruit of his labour, but also his right to think for himself and to direct his industry as he pleases. The economic change is merely formal: the moral change is enormous. Soon the new direct traffic in men overspreads the whole market, and takes the place formerly held by the traffic in tenant rights. * * *

* * * It was the increase of population that spread cultivation and civilization from the centre to the snow line, and at last forced men to sell themselves to the lords of the soil: it is the same force that continues to multiply men so that their exchange value falls slowly and surely until it disappears altogether—until even black chattel slaves are released as not worth keeping in a land where men of all colours are to be had for nothing. This is the condition of our English labourers today: they are no longer even dirt cheap: they are value-less, and can be had for nothing. * * * That is just the case of every member of the proletariat who could be replaced by one of the unemployed today. Their wage is not the price of themselves: for they are worth nothing: it is only their keep. For bare subsistence wages you can get as much common labour as you want, and do what you please with it within the limits of a criminal code which is sure to be interpreted by a proprietary-class judge-in your favour. * * *

Over Population

The introduction of the capitalistic system is a sign that the exploitation of the labourer toiling for a bare subsistence wage has become one of the chief arts of life among the holders of tenant rights. It also produces a delusive promise of endless employment which blinds the proletariat to those disastrous consequences of rapid multiplication which are obvious to the small cultivator and peasant proprietor. But indeed the more you degrade the workers, robbing them of all artistic enjoyment, and all chance of respect and admiration from their fellows, the more you throw them back, reckless, on the one pleasure and the one human tie left to them—the gratification of their instinct for producing fresh supplies of men. You will applaud this instinct as divine until at last the excessive supply becomes a nuisance: there comes a plague of men; and you suddenly discover that the instinct is diabolic, and set up a cry of 'over population'. But your slaves are beyond caring for your cries: they breed like rabbits; and their poverty breeds filth, ugliness, dishonesty, disease, obscenity, drunkenness, and murder. In the midst of the riches which their labour piles up for you, their misery rises up too and stifles you. You withdraw in disgust to the other end of the town from them; you appoint special carriages on your railways and special seats in your churches and theatres for them; you set your life apart from theirs by every class barrier you can devise; and yet they swarm about you still: your face gets stamped with your habitual loathing and suspicion of them: your ears get so filled with the language of the vilest of them that you break into it when you lose your self-control: they poison your life as remorselessly as you have sacrified theirs heartlessly. You begin to believe intensely in the devil. Then comes the terror of their revolting; the drilling and arming of bodies of them to keep down the rest; the prison, the hospital, paroxysms of frantic coercion, followed by paroxysms of frantic charity. And in the meantime, the population continues to increase!

Part IV
MALTHUS IN THE
TWENTY-FIRST CENTURY

A. Population Growth in the Twenty-First Century: A New Look At Malthus

THE UNITED NATIONS POPULATION FUND

Footprints and Milestones: Population and Environmental Change (2001)†

Over three and a half million years ago, two of modern humanity's ancestors left their footprints in the sand near what is now Laetoli in the United Republic of Tanzania. This couple was walking barefoot along a plain. Their people probably numbered in the hundreds or thousands and possessed very rudimentary implements. Only a remarkable chain of coincidences preserved their trail for our current inspection and wonder.

Today the footprints of humanity are impossible to miss. Human activity has affected every part of the planet, no matter how remote, and every ecosystem, from the simplest to the most complex. Our choices and interventions have transformed the natural world, posing both great possibilities and extreme dangers for the quality and sustainability of our civilizations, and for the intricate balances of nature.

Our numbers have doubled since 1960 to 6.1 billion, with growth mostly in poorer countries. Consumption expenditures have more than doubled since 1970, with increases mostly in richer countries. During this time, we have created wealth on an unimaginable scale, yet half the world still exists on less than $2 a day. We have learned how to extract resources for our use, but not how to deal with the resulting waste: emissions of carbon dioxide, for example, grew 12 times between 1900 and 2000. In the process we are changing the world's climate. The great questions for the 21st century are whether

† The text is from *The State of the World Population 2001* (New York, 2001). Reprinted by permission of The United Nations Population Fund.

the activities of the 20th century have set us on a collision course with the environment, and if so, what can we do about it? * * *

Water

Water may be the resource that defines the limits of sustainable development. The supply of fresh water is essentially fixed, and the balance between humanity's demands and available quantity is already precarious.

* * *

While global population has tripled over the past 70 years, water use has grown six-fold. Worldwide, 54 per cent of the annual available fresh water is being used, two thirds of it for agriculture. By 2025 it could be 70 per cent because of population growth alone, or—if per capita consumption everywhere reached the level of more developed countries—90 per cent.

In the year 2000, 508 million people lived in 31 water-stressed or water-scarce countries. By 2025, 3 billion people will be living in 48 such countries. By 2050, 4.2 billion people (over 45 per cent of the global total) will be living in countries that cannot meet the requirement of 50 liters of water per person each day to meet basic human needs.

Many countries use unsustainable means to meet their water needs, depleting local aquifers. The water tables under some cities in China, Latin America and South Asia are declining over one metre per year. Water from seas and rivers is also being diverted to meet the growing needs of agriculture and industry, with sometimes-disastrous effects. In 1997, the Yellow River in China ran dry for a record 226 days.

* * *

In developing countries, 90–95 per cent of sewage and 70 per cent of industrial wastes are dumped untreated into surface waters where they pollute the water supply. In many industrial countries, chemical run-off from fertilizers and pesticides, and acid rain from air pollution require expensive and energy-intensive filtration and treatment to restore acceptable water quality.

Purely technological solutions to water scarcity are likely to have limited effect. Desalinized seawater is expensive and now accounts for less than 1 per cent of the water people consume.

Protecting water supplies from pollutants, restoring natural flow patterns to river systems, managing irrigation and chemical use, and curbing industrial air pollution are vital steps to improving water quality and availability.

Food

In many countries, population growth has raced ahead of food production in recent years. Between 1985 and 1995, food production lagged behind population growth in 64 of 105 developing countries studied, with Africa faring the worst.

Australia, Europe and North America have large surpluses of food for export and are probably capable of expanding food production. However, there are questions over the long-term sustainability of intensive agricultural practices.

Most of the developing world is classified as "low-income, food deficit countries" by the Food and Agriculture Organization of the United Nations (FAO). These countries do not produce enough food to feed their people and cannot afford to import sufficient amounts to close the gap. In these countries, some 800 million people are chronically malnourished and 2 billion people lack food security.

Food production capacities in many poor countries are deteriorating due to soil degradation, chronic water shortages, inappropriate agricultural practices and rapid population growth.* * *

To accommodate the nearly 8 billion people expected on earth by 2025 and improve their diets, the world will have to double food production, and improve distribution to ensure that people do not go hungry. Since available cropland is shrinking, most production will have to come from higher yields rather than new cultivation. However, new high-yielding crop varieties require specialized fertilizers and pesticides, which may disturb the ecological balance and create new disease and pest problems.

*　*　*

Climate Change

In the 20th century, human population quadrupled—from 1.6 billion to 6.1 billion, and carbon dioxide emissions, which trap heat in the atmosphere, grew 12-fold—from 534 million metric tons in 1900 to 6.59 billion metric tons in 1997.

The Intergovernmental Panel on Climate Change (IPCC) estimates that the earth's atmosphere will warm by as much as 5.8 degrees Celsius over the coming century, a rate unmatched over the past 10,000 years. The panel's "best estimate" scenario projects a sea-level rise of about half a metre by 2100.

In 1995, the 20 per cent of the world's population living in countries with the highest per capita fossil-fuel carbon dioxide emissions contributed 63 per cent of the total global emissions. The 20 per cent in the lowest-emission countries contributed just 2 per cent of the total. The United States, with only 4.6 per cent of the world's population, produces one fourth of global greenhouse gas emissions.

*   *   *

Forests, Habitat and Biodiversity

In the last few decades as population growth has peaked, deforestation rates have reached the highest levels in history.

Since tropical forests contain an estimated 50 per cent of the world's remaining biodiversity, their destruction is particularly devastating. At current rates of deforestation, the last significant primary tropical forest could be harvested within 50 years, causing irreversible loss of species. Tropical deforestation also contributes to the build-up of carbon dioxide in the atmosphere.

While sustainable forestry holds some promise, projected increases in population growth over the next few decades will present challenges and difficult choices. Many of the countries that contain the largest blocks of remaining tropical forest are also those with the highest population growth rates.

One key to preserving remaining forests and biodiversity may be the integration of reproductive health and family planning programmes with park and forest management efforts.

*   *   *

LESTER R. BROWN

The Population Challenge (1999)†

During the last half-century, world population has more than doubled, climbing from 2.5 billion in 1950 to 5.9 billion in 1998. Those of us born before 1950 are members of the first generation to witness a doubling of world population. Stated otherwise, there has been more growth in population since 1950 than during the 4 million preceding years since our early ancestors first stood upright.[1]

---

† Lester R. Brown (b. 1934) is president of the Earth Policy Institute. The text is from Chapter 1 of Brown, Gary Gardner, and Brian Halweil's *Beyond Malthus: Nineteen Dimensions of the Population Challenge* (New York, 1999). Reprinted by permission of W. W. Norton & Company.

1. All population data in this paper, including per capita calculations, are from U.S. Bureau of the Census, *International Data Base*, electronic database, Suitland, MD, updated 30 November 1998, and from United Nations, *World Population Prospects: The 1998 Revision* (New York: December 1998) unless otherwise stated. We use Census data for the years 1950 to 1999 and U.N. data for the years 2000 to 2050. Although the two data sets do not differ substantially, Census provides annual data from 1950 to 1999 while United

This unprecedented surge in population, combined with rising individual consumption, is pushing our claims on the planet beyond its natural limits. Water tables are falling on every continent as demand exceeds the sustainable yield of aquifers. Our growing appetite for seafood has taken oceanic fisheries to their limits and beyond. Collapsing fisheries tell us we can go no further. The Earth's temperature is rising, promising changes in climate that we cannot even anticipate. And we have inadvertently launched the greatest extinction of plant and animal species since the dinosaurs disappeared.

Great as the population growth of the last half-century has been, it is far from over. U.N. demographers project an increase over the next half-century of another 2.8 billion people, somewhat fewer than the 3.6 billion added during the half-century now ending. In contrast to the last 50 years, however, all of the 2.8 billion will be added in the developing world, much of which is already densely populated.

Even as we anticipate huge further increases in population, encouraging demographic news seems to surface regularly. Fertility rates, the average number of children born to a woman, have fallen steadily in most countries in recent decades. Twice in the last 10 years the United Nations has moderated its projections of global population growth, first in 1996 and then again in 1998. Unfortunately, part of the latter decline in population projections is due to rising mortality rather then declining fertility.[2]

In contrast to the projected doublings and triplings for some developing countries, populations are stable or even declining in some 32 industrial nations. Compared with the situation at mid-century, when nearly all signs pointed to galloping population increases for the foreseeable future, today's demographic picture is decidedly more complex.

* * * Despite the many encouraging demographic trends, the need to stabilize global population is as urgent as ever. Although the rate of population growth is slowing, the world is still adding some 80 million people per year. And the number of young people coming of reproductive age—those between 15 and 24 years old—will be far larger during the early part of the next century than ever before. Through their reproductive choices, this group will heavily influence whether population is stabilized sooner rather than later, and with less rather than more suffering.[3]

In addition, population growth has already surpassed sustainable

Nations only provides data for every five years. However, the United Nations provides the latest projections to 2050, incorporating the most recent demographic surveys.

2. Fertility rates from United Nations, op. cit. note 1; moderation of past U.N. projections from Thomas Büettner, Population Division, Department of Economic and Social Affairs, United Nations, New York, discussion with Brian Halweil, 5 December 1998.

3. Annual addition from Bureau of Census, op, cit. note 1; number of people coming of reproductive age from United Nations, op. cit. note 1.

limits on a number of environmental fronts. From cropland and water availability to climate change and unemployment, population growth exacerbates existing problems, making them more difficult to manage. The intersection of the arrival of a series of environmental limits and a potentially huge expansion in the number of people subject to those limits makes the turn of the century a unique time in world demographic history.

* * *

In this respect, we are part of a long tradition dating back to 1798 when Thomas Malthus, a British clergyman and intellectual, warned in his "Essay on the Principle of Population" of the check on population growth provided by what he believed were coming constraints on food supplies. Noting that population grows exponentially while food supply grows only arithmetically, Malthus foresaw massive food shortages and famine as an inevitable consequence of population growth.[4]

Critics of Malthus point out that his pessimistic scenario never unfolded. His supporters believe he was simply ahead of his time. On the bicentennial of Malthus' legendary essay, and in an era of environmental decline, we find his focus on the connection between resource supply and population growth to be particularly useful. We move beyond Malthus's focus on food, however, to look at several resources—such as water and forests—whose supply may be insufficient to support projected increases in population. We also examine social phenomena including disease and education, and analyze the effect of population growth on these.

The results of our analysis offer further evidence that we are approaching—and increasingly broaching—any number of natural limits. We know that close to a tenth of world food production relies on the overpumping of groundwater, and that continuing this practice will mean a substantial decline in food production at some point in the future. We know that both atmospheric carbon dioxide concentrations and the Earth's surface temperature are rising. We know that we are the first species in the planet's history to trigger a mass extinction, and we admit that we do not understand the consequences of such a heavy loss of plant and animal species. In short, we know enough to understand that the growth in our numbers and the scale of our activities is already redirecting the natural course of our planet, and that this new direction will in turn affect us.

The relationship between these natural limits and population growth becomes clear if we contrast key trends projected for the next half-century with those of the last one. For example, since 1950 we

---

4. Thomas Robert Malthus, *An Essay on the Principle of Population (1798)*, from the Norton Critical Edition, ed. by Philip Appleman (New York: W. W. Norton & Company, 1976).

have seen a near fivefold growth in the oceanic fish catch and a doubling in the supply of fish per person, but people born today may well see the catch per person cut in half as population grows during their lifetimes. Marine biologists now believe we may have "hit the wall" in oceanic fisheries and that the oceans cannot sustain a catch any larger than todays.[5]

Similarly, the finite area that can be cultivated for grain is a worrisome natural limit as population increases. Grainland per person has been shrinking since mid-century, but the drop projected for the next 50 years means the world will have less grainland per person than India has today. Future population growth is likely to reduce this key number in many societies to the point where they will no longer be able to feed themselves. Countries such as Ethiopia, India, Iran, Nigeria, and Pakistan will see grainland per person shrink by 2050 to less than one tenth of a hectare (one fourth of an acre)—far smaller than a typical suburban building lot in the United States.[6]

Meanwhile, with the amount of fresh water produced each year essentially fixed by nature, population growth shrinks the water available per person and results in severe shortages in some areas. Countries now experiencing this include China and India, as well as scores of smaller ones. As irrigation water is diverted to industrial and residential uses, the resultant water shortages could drop food production per person in many countries below the survival level.

The fast-deteriorating water situation in India was described in July 1998 in one of India's leading newspapers, the *Hindustan Times:* "If our population continues to grow as it is now . . . it is certain that a major part of the country would be in the grip of a severe water famine in 10 to 15 years." The article goes on to reflect an emerging sense of desperation. "Only a bitter dose of compulsory family planning can save the coming generation from the fast-approaching Malthusian catastrophe." Among other things, this comment appears to implicitly recognize the emerging conflict between the reproductive rights of the current generation and the survival rights of the next generation.[7]

As difficult as it is to imagine the addition of another 2.8 billion people to the world's population, it is even harder to grasp the effects of the rising affluence of a growing population. As we look back over the last half-century, we see that world fuelwood use doubled, paper

5. U.N. Food and Agriculture Organization (FAO), *Yearbook of Fishery Statistics: Catches and Landings* (Rome: various years); 1990–97 data from FAO, Rome, letters to Worldwatch, 11 November 1998; FAO, *The State of World Fisheries and Aquaculture* (Rome: 1997).
6. U.S. Department of Agriculture (USDA), *Production, Supply, and Distribution,* electronic database, Washington, DC, updated December 1998.
7. Ajay Khudania, "India Struggles with Fading Water Supply," *Hindustan Times,* 20 July 1998.

use increased nearly sixfold, grain consumption nearly tripled, water use tripled, and fossil fuel burning increased some fourfold.[8]

The relative contribution of population growth and rising affluence to the growth in demand for various resources varies widely. With fuelwood use, most of the doubled use is accounted for by population growth. With paper, in contrast, rising affluence is primarily responsible for the growth in use. For grain, population accounts for most of the growth, since consumption per person has risen only 30 percent since 1950. Similarly with water. For fossil fuels, the growth in use is rather evenly divided between population growth and rising consumption.

Any meaningful assessment of the future pressures on resources must take into account both population growth and rises in affluence. Consumption per person of various resources among societies can vary from 5 to 1 for grain, as between the United States and India, for example, to easily 20 to 1 for energy. While population growth in some 32 countries has stabilized, and many more countries have stabilization as a goal, no country at any level of affluence has announced or even seriously contemplated limits on consumption per person.[9]

*   *   *

The challenge to nations presented by continuing rapid population growth is not limited to natural resources. It also includes social and economic needs, including education, housing, and jobs. During the last half-century, the world has fallen further and further behind in creating jobs, leading to record levels of unemployment and underemployment. Unfortunately, over the next 50 years the number of entrants into the job market will be even greater, pushing the ranks of unemployment to levels that could be politically destabilizing. And as homelessness is already a serious problem in most large Third World cities, the housing situation for additional urban dwellers is increasingly dismal.

The Earth is more crowded today than ever before. And although our numbers continue to grow, the size of the planet on which we live remains the same. Future population growth has the potential

8. Fuelwood from FAO, *FAOSTAT Statistics Database*, <http://apps.fao.org>, viewed 5 July 1998; paper from International Institute for Environment and Development, *Towards a Sustainable Paper Cycle* (London: 1996), and from FAO, op. cit. this note; water from Sandra Postel, *Pillar of Sand* (New York: W. W. Norton & Company, in press); fossil fuels 1950–70 from United Nations, *World Energy Supplies* 1950–74 (New York: 1976), and from United Nations, *Energy Statistics Yearbook* (New York: various years); fossil fuels 1970–95 from U.S. Department of Energy (DOE), Energy Information Administration (EIA), Office of Energy Markets and End Use, *International Statistics Database*, provided by Linda Doman at DOE, EIA, letter to Worldwatch, 5 August 1998; grain from USDA, op. cit. note 6.
9. Grain from USDA, op. cit. note 6; energy for DOE, op. cit. note 8.

to further degrade and deplete resources, such as topsoil, ground-water, and forest cover, as well as to reduce the resources available to each person. Moreover, population growth strains the capacity of governments to provide basic social services, such as education and health care, for each citizen. This combination of environmental deg-radation and social shortfalls can ultimately result in any number of unpleasant scenarios that can undermine future progress.

*   *   *

WILLIAM R. CATTON JR.

Overshoot (1982)†

*   *   *

Today mankind is locked into stealing ravenously from the future. That is what this book is about. It is not just a book about famine or hunger. Famine in the modern world must be read as one of several symptoms reflecting a deeper malady in the human condition—namely, diachronic competition, a relationship whereby contempo-rary well-being is achieved at the expense of our descendants. By our sheer numbers, by the state of our technological development, and by being oblivious to differences between a method that achieved lasting increments of human carrying capacity and one that achieves only temporary supplements, we have made satisfaction of today's human aspirations dependent upon massive deprivation for posterity.

*   *   *

We live in a world where it is becoming increasingly evident that, for quite non-political reasons, governments and politicians cannot achieve the paradise they have habitually promised. Political habits persist, though, and people have seen their leaders continuing to dangle before them the kinds of carrots ordinary men and women know are becoming unattainable. The result has been erosion of faith in political processes. As that faith disintegrates, societies all over the world are floundering, or becoming dictatorial.

*   *   *

† William R. Catton Jr. (b. 1926) is professor emeritus of sociology at Washington State University. The text is from his *Overshoot: The Ecological Basis of Revolutionary Change* (Urbana and Chicago, 1982). Reprinted by permission of the University of Illinois Press.

The alternative to chaos is to abandon the illusion that all things are possible. Mankind has learned to manipulate many of nature's forces, but neither as individuals nor as organized societies can human beings attain outright omnipotence. Many of us remain, to this day, beneficiaries of the once-New World's myth of limitlessness. But circumstances have ceased to be as they were when that myth made sense. Unless we discard our belief in limitlessness, all of us are in danger of becoming its victims.

In today's world it is imperative that all of us learn the following core principle:

> Human society is inextricably part of a global biotic community, and in that community human dominance has had and is having self-destructive consequences.

That principle is the basis of the non-political obstacles that now frustrate human societal aspirations everywhere on earth. The obstacles are non-political because they are not uniquely human. * * * Other dominant species before us have also been unavoidably self-destructive. We and our leaders need to understand such examples and to avail ourselves of the light they cast on our own history and our own situation. They exemplify a stark fact about life which we desperately need to grasp—and we need to see that grasping it will actually help us to adjust sanely to an unwelcome but inescapable future.

Because we haven't known these things, we, the human species, are inexorably tightening the two jaws of a vise around our fragile civilization. * * * There are already more human beings alive than the world's *renewable* resources can perpetually support. We have built complex societies that therefore *depend* on rapid use of exhaustible resources. Depletion of resources we don't know how to do without is *reducing* this finite planet's carrying capacity for our species. That is one jaw of the closing vise. The other is the accumulation of harmful substances that are unavoidably created by our life processes. There are so many of us, using so much technology, that these substances accumulate too fast for the global ecosystem to reprocess them; in fact, by overloading the natural reprocessing systems we are even breaking down their already limited capacity to set things right for us.

* * *

Origins of Man's Future

We are already living on an overloaded world. Our future will be a product of that fact; that fact is a product of our past. Our first order of business, then, is to make clear to ourselves how we got where we are and why our present situation entails a certain kind of future.

To this purpose, consider the information about the human saga. * * * It is the story of a world that has again and again approached the condition of being saturated with human inhabitants, only to have the limit raised by human ingenuity.

The first several rounds of limit-raising were accomplished by a series of technological breakthroughs that took almost two million years. These breakthroughs enabled human populations repeatedly to take over for human use portions of the earth's total life-supporting capacity that had previously supported other species. The most recent episode of limit-raising has had much more spectacular results, although it enlarged human carrying capacity by a fundamentally different method: the drawing down of finite reservoirs of materials that do not replace themselves within any human time frame. Thus its results *cannot be permanent*. This fact puts mankind out on a limb which the activities of modern life are busily sawing off.

*   *   *

The Drawdown Method

About 1800 A.D., a new phase in the ecological history of humanity began. Carrying capacity was tremendously (but temporarily) augmented by a quite different method; takeover gave way to drawdown. A conspicuous and unprecedentedly large acceleration of human population increase got under way as *Homo sapiens* began to supersede agrarian living with industrial living.

Industrialization made use of fossil energy. Machinery powered by the combustion of coal, and later oil, enabled man to do things on a scale never before possible. New, large, elaborate tools could now be made, some of which enhanced the effectiveness of the farming that of course had to continue. Products of farm and factory could be transported in larger quantity for greater distances. Eventually the tapping of this "new" energy source resulted in the massive application of chemical fertilizers to agricultural lands. Yields per acre increased, and in time acreages applied to the growing of food for humans were substantially increased—first by eliminating draft animals and their requirements for pasture land, but also by reclaiming land through irrigation, etc.

This time mankind was not merely taking away from competitors an additional portion of the earth's life-supporting capacity. (He was still doing this, and still not recognizing that this was what he had always done. But—worse—he was now also not recognizing the true nature of something else he was doing on a vast scale. So man was painting himself into a corner.) This time, the human carrying capacity of the planet was being supplemented by digging up energy that had been stored underground millions of years ago, captured from sunlight which fell upon the earth's green plants long before this world had supported any mammals, let alone humans, or even pre-human primates. The solar energy had been captured by photosynthesis in plants that grew and died and were buried during the Carboniferous period, without the efforts of any farmers. (As we shall see in the next chapter, the fact that no farm labor had to be paid to raise the Carboniferous vegetation, and that no investments in farm machinery used to grow those prehistoric "crops" had to be amortized, etc., helped get us into our present predicament.)

Carrying capacity was this time being augmented by drawing down a finite reservoir of the remains of prehistoric organisms. This was therefore going to result in a *temporary* extension of carrying capacity; in contrast, previous enlargements had been essentially permanent, as well as cumulative.

Being impermanent, this rise in apparent carrying capacity begged one enormously important question: What happens if population, as usual, increases until it nearly fills this temporarily expanded set of opportunities, and then, because the expansion was only temporary, the world finds itself (like the Indians on their shrunken territories) with a population excess? What are the implications of a carrying capacity deficit for mankind's future? What happens, for example, when supplies of oil become scarce, when tractor fuel becomes unavailable or prohibitively expensive, and when farmers again have to take ¼ to ⅓ of the land on which they now raise food for humans and convert it instead to raising feed for draft animals?

Such questions were not asked as long as we viewed our world with a pre-ecological paradigm. The myth of limitlessness dominated people's minds. Had anyone conceived such implausible-seeming questions in the Age of Exuberance, the answer might have seemed equally incredible: post-exuberant nations and individuals would have a compulsive need to deny the facts so as to deny their own redundancy.

*   *   *

The growth and progress upon which we looked back with such pride had *committed* mankind to living on a scale that exceeds the sustainable carrying capacity of this finite planet, and the leaders of nations continued to devote far more effort toward attempting to prolong overshoot than toward undoing it. Reluctance to face facts was driving us to make bad matters worse. The faster the present generation draws down the fossil energy legacy upon which persistently exuberant lifestyles now depend, the less opportunity posterity will have to live in anything like the same way or the same numbers. Yet most contemporary political proposals for solving problems of economic stagnation or inequity amount to plans for speeding up the rate of drawdown of non-renewable resources.[1]

Invisible Acreage

The truth of these statements is implicit in the concept of "ghost acreage." Georg Borgstrom, a food scientist at Michigan State University, devoted a whole chapter of his 1965 book, *The Hungry Planet*, to this subject. A number of nations have seemed to get away with exceeding the human carrying capacity of their own land, but Borgstrom pointed out that they had only been able to do so by drawing upon carrying capacity that was "invisible"—i.e., located elsewhere on the planet. The food required by such a nation's population comes only partly from the harvest of "visible acreage"—farm and pasture land within the nation's borders. A very substantial fraction comes from net imports of food. Not all the imports come from other countries; some are obtained from the sea. Borgstrom therefore subdivided "ghost acreage" into two components, "trade acreage" and "fish acreage." By each phrase he simply expressed, in terms of land area, the additional farming that would have been needed to provide from internal sources the net portion of a nation's sustenance actually derived from sources outside its boundaries and in excess of its own carrying capacity. As we shall see, a third component must be recognized if we are to understand fully the part played by ghost acreage in the life of modern man.

* * *

As an island in space, the world could not rely on imports from else*where*; nevertheless, it was already heavily dependent upon imports from else*when*. That we were importing from the past becomes clear when we logically extend Borgstrom's ghost acreage concept to include a third component. Technological progress had made mankind heavily dependent upon imports of energy from prehistoric sources. Man's use of fossil fuels has been another instance of reliance on phantom carrying capacity.

The energy we obtain from coal, petroleum, and natural gas can

1. For example, American officials urge Saudi Arabia to keep oil output high to help stabilize the world economy in the face of shortages from other sources; the administration pushes through Congress a proposal for an Energy Mobilization Board with powers to "cut red tape" (i.e., bypass environmental protection legislation) when energy-related projects such as pipelines, oil refineries, synthetic fuel factories, etc., are at stake; the government "deregulates" natural gas and petroleum prices partly to "give incentives" to "producers."

be expressed as "fossil acreage"—the number of additional acres of farmland that would have been needed to grow organic fuels with equivalent energy content. Mankind originally did rely on organic fuels, chiefly wood. Wood was a renewable resource, though even in the world's once vast forests it grew in limited quantity. Access to vast but non-renewable deposits of coal and petroleum came to be mistaken by peoples and nations as an opportunity for permanently transcending limits set by the finite supplies of organic fuel.

* * *

The "abundance" of this fossil energy was due to man's readiness to withdraw and spend it thousands of times faster than nature had deposited it in the earth's savings. And the energy from fossil fuels was cheap only because no workers had been paid (or slaves maintained) to grow the vegetation from which coal and oil had been formed. * * * If gasoline and other fossil fuels had been thirteen times as costly, we would never have fallen into the trap of reorganizing our social systems around their abundant use. Our overcommitment to dependence on fossil acreage was the result of the temporarily low cost of energy from antiquity. Because the low cost *was* temporary, it was an unrealistic basis for a way of life.

* * *

Recognition of the social significance of physical energy remained almost nil among politicians and social scientists until depleted resources began failing to meet persistently exuberant demand. But in a book called *Energy and Society*, whose enormous importance was insufficiently realized when it was published just a decade after the end of World War II, Fred Cottrell of Miami University in Ohio made clear the fact that "man can exist only where he is able to replace the energy he uses up in the process of living. He must regularly be in control of energy equal to or in excess of this minimum. A permanent deficit makes life impossible."[2] Full comprehension of the information and a thorough understanding of the reasoning in Cottrell's vital but neglected book would have shown the salience of Borgstrom's "ghost acreage" concept for the post-exuberant world. It was important to consider not just the food that keeps human bodies alive, but the energy of *all* kinds used by the mechanical extensions of man's bodily apparatus. * * * Throughout the world, vast quantities of machinery driven by vast quantities of fossil energy had become indispensable for doing the things that had become part of human living during four centuries of exuberance.

2. Fred Cottrell, *Energy and Society* (New York, 1955), p. 4.

Precarious Way of Life

Any nation that realized its self-sufficiency had fallen to less than 10 percent would almost certainly sense the precariousness of its existence. Borgstrom did not cite any nation whose visible acreage met as little as 10 percent of its needs. In energy terms, however, the condition of the post-exuberant *world* had become precarious in just that way. The human species, through technological progress, had made itself more than 90 percent dependent on phantom carrying capacity—a term we must now define. Phantom carrying capacity means either the illusory or the extremely precarious capacity of an environment to support a given life form or a given way of living. It can be quantitatively expressed as that portion of a population that cannot be permanently supported when temporarily available resources become unavailable.

Although the living generation did not realize that it was 90 percent redundant, the effects of dependence on phantom carrying capacity were beginning to be noticeable and disturbing. The reason for these effects remained unacknowledged, due to the continued grip of obsolete concepts on our thinking.

* * *

The Real Error

Malthus did indeed err, but not in the way that has been commonly supposed. He rightly discerned "the power of population" to increase exponentially "if unchecked." He rightly noted that population growth ordinarily is *not* unchecked. He saw that it was worth inquiring into the means by which the exponential growth tendency is normally checked. He was perceptive in attaching the label "misery" to some of the ramifications of these means. Where he was wrong was in supposing that the means worked fully and immediately. (That *this* was his error has not been seen by those who reject his views.)

Being himself under the impression that it was not possible for the human load to exceed the earth's carrying capacity, Malthus enabled those who came after him to go on misconstruing continued impressive growth as evidence against, rather than as evidence for, his basic ideas. Carrying capacity was a concept almost clear to Malthus. He even sensed that the carrying capacities of earth's regions had been repeatedly enlarged by human cultural progress.[3] If he was

3. This is evident in the following passages from the 1798 Essay (Philip Appleman, ed., *An Essay on the Principle of Population: A Norton Critical Edition*; 1976, pp. 27, 29, 31): "In the rudest state of mankind, in which hunting is the principal occupation and the only mode of acquiring food, the means of subsistence being scattered over a large extent of territory, the comparative population must necessarily be thin." "It is well known that a

not yet able to make clear to himself and his readers the distinction between means of enlarging carrying capacity and means of over-shooting it, we do ourselves a serious disservice by perpetuating his shortcoming. And we do just such a disservice by continuing to mis-take overshoot for progress, supposing drawdown to be no different from takeover. By erring thus we prolong and deepen our predica-ment.

Despite Malthus's belief to the contrary, it *is* possible to exceed an environment's carrying capacity—temporarily. Many species have done it. A species with as long an interval between generations as is characteristic of ours, and with cultural as well as biological appe-tites, can be expected to do it. Our largest per capita demands upon the world's resources only begin to be asserted years after we are born. Resource depletion sufficient to thwart our children's grown-up aspirations was not far enough advanced when our parents were begetting, gestating, and bearing us to deter them from thus adding to the human load.

By not quite seeing that carrying capacity *can* be temporarily over-shot, Malthus understated life's perils. He thus enabled both the admirers and the detractors of his admonitory writings to neglect the effects of overshoot—environmental degradation and carrying capacity reduction. While this fell short of sustaining exponential growth of would-be consumers, it was, even so, a far brighter pros-pect than carrying capacity *reduction*.

*　*　*

Chronic dissatisfaction and yearning breed millenarian cults. Peo-ple need not have suffered actual material deprivation; heightened desires can produce equivalent dissatisfaction. The neo-exuberant "revolution of rising expectations," together with the deterioration of the worldwide ecological basis for fulfilling such expanding hopes, have tended to foster millenarian beliefs and activities.

* * * Our understanding of such developments in the modern con-text can be enlarged by taking a comparative look at the cargo cults in the Pacific island societies studied extensively by anthropologists. To the pre-literate Melanesian peoples in the Pacific islands, Euro-pean society was unseen and baffling. The Europeans who came to the islands brought strange ways and imported many material things. The processes by which these goods had been produced, the type of social organization and equipment which enabled them to be pro-duced in such quantity and variety remained unseen and unknown.

---

country in pasture cannot support so many inhabitants as a country in tillage. . . ." "The reason that the greater part of Europe is more populous now than it was in former times is that the industry of the inhabitants has made these countries produce a greater quantity of human subsistence."

It was apparent to the islanders that European people had some secret magic; they obtained abundant cargoes of material objects without laboring to create them.

*   *   *

Space Age Cargo Cults

The cults that won Cargoist adherents among the citizens of advanced nations were not always obviously religious. The Type II belief held that great technological breakthroughs would inevitably occur in the near future, and would enable man to continue indefinitely expanding the world's human carrying capacity. This was a mere faith in a faith, like stock-market speculation; it had no firmer basis than naive statistical extrapolation—the uncritical supposition that past technological advances could be taken as representative samples of an inherently unending series of comparable achievements. Such a faith overlooked the fact that man's ostensible "enlargement" of the world's productivity in the past had mainly consisted of successive *diversions* of the world's life-supporting processes from use by other species to use by man. *   *   *

Technological optimism manifested itself in several pious hopes, enumerated below.

I. "UNLIMITED" FOOD

Enthusiasm for the Green Revolution was merely a special case of this cult of great technological breakthroughs. It believed that the crucial breakthrough had already been achieved (by development of high-yield strains of wheat and rice), and that now vigorous missionary effort throughout the hungry nations would convince their peoples to raise these superior crop varieties. Such an attitude was just another expression of inability to understand, or reluctance to perceive, the finiteness of the biosphere. Believers in this "breakthrough" were unable to see that further extension of the human irruption was going to be a problem aggravated, not a problem solved. They could not even see that the high-yield grains either would hasten the exhaustion of the soils on which they were grown or would intensify agriculture's precarious dependence upon a chemical fertilizer industry. Cultivation of renewable resources such as food was becoming heavily dependent upon continuing depletion of exhaustible resources like petroleum and minerals. Man's efforts to enlarge carrying capacity by agricultural progress were thus making the old takeover method dependent upon the treacherous drawdown method.

2. "UNLIMITED" ALTERNATIVES

In response to the worldwide shortfall of energy supplies under bur-geoning demand, economists extolled "resource substitution" as the answer. The man in the street tended to believe that somehow "new sources" of energy would be tapped, to make us "self-sufficient" by some vague target date—1980 at first, then 1990, then. . . . These were some of the millenarian pipe-dreams that arose to assuage post-exuberant anxieties. * * *

3. "UNLIMITED" ENERGY

In earlier times occasional dedicated eccentrics who pipe-dreamed of violating the laws of physics tried to invent "perpetual motion" machines—to provide energy, supposedly, without consuming any fuel. These impossible devices had always seemed like an ideal means to perpetuate limitlessness. Now, in what we had thought were more sophisticated times, Cargoists permitted themselves to believe in the same sort of absurdity by talking glibly of the "breeder reactor" as a device that not only would generate vast quantities of energy but also would, in the process, "produce more fuel than it consumes." It would *not* do that, of course. The illusion that it would, and therefore that mankind could expect to continue treating the world as limitless, arose from careless phrasing that fostered mis-understanding of rather simple physical facts.

*   *   *

5. OTHER TECHNOLOGICAL ESCAPES

The belief that emigration by space ship to unpopulated worlds would exempt us from the consequences of overshooting this world's carrying capacity flourished briefly when the Space Age was begin-ning, but it was no more realistic than postwar construction of "air-strips" by Melanesians. * * * Believers in extraterrestrial emigration as a solution to irrupting population never seemed to do the simple arithmetic to estimate the prodigious tonnage of space vehicles and impossible quantities of fuel it would take to boost up to escape velocity the earth's yearly increment of population (some 70 million human beings), plus the supplies they would need on their long jour-ney to some *hypothetically inhabitable* other planet. We are, of course, talking of exporting 70 million people per year for the rest of their lives, never to return. In the entire Apollo program of manned lunar landings, five pairs of astronauts spent a total of just over 23 man-days on the moon. If we could hope to hold the line on earthly population by exporting our growth to a planet no more inaccessible than the moon (as Europe once exported surplus people to the New World), it would take more than 60,000 Apollo-type launchings *every day* to do it! Even if that were not absurdly infeasible, scientific space research had quickly undercut any illusions of escape by this means, for the two most plausible planetary destinations, Venus and Mars, were shown by space probe photography and telemetry to be impossible environments for massive colonization by human refugees from the post-exuberant earth.

*   *   *

Paradigm versus Paradigm

The world, man's place in it, and a host of policy issues all look different when viewed in ecological terms than when viewed in traditional, pre-ecological perspectives. Let us therefore now try to encompass the new ecological paradigm in a few sentences, and then explicitly contrast it with the dangerously obsolete worldview it must replace. The ecological paradigm clearly recognizes the following basic ideas:

E1. Human beings are just one species among many species that are interdependently involved in biotic communities.

E2. Human social life is shaped by intricate linkages of cause and effect (and feedback) in the web of nature, and because of these, purposive human actions have many unintended consequences.

E3. The world we live in is finite, so there are potent physical and biological limits constraining economic growth, social progress, and other aspects of human living.

E4. However much the inventiveness of *Homo sapiens* or the power of *Homo colossus* may seem for a while to transcend carrying capacity limits, nature has the last word.

These precepts stand in sharp contradiction to some assumptions deeply imbedded in Western thoughtways by 400 years of exuberance. That is why the ecological paradigm has so little political acceptance, and why it has had so little influence upon public policy.

*   *   *

B. Population and Food Supplies in the Twenty-First Century

GARY GARDNER

Shrinking Fields (1996)†

Some 4,400 years ago, the city-states of ancient Sumer in modern-day Iraq faced an unsettling dilemma. Farmland was gradually accumulating salt, the byproduct of evaporating irrigation water. Almost imperceptibly, the salt began to poison the rich soil, and over time harvests tapered off.

Until 2400 BC, Sumerians had managed the problem of dwindling yields by cultivating new land, thereby ensuring the consistent food surpluses needed to support their armies and bureaucracies. But now they had reached the limits of agricultural expansion. And over the next three centuries, accumulating salts drove crop yields down more than 40 percent. The crippled production, combined with an evergrowing population, led to shrinking food reserves, which in turn reduced the ranks of soldiers and civil servants. By 1800 BC, Sumerian agriculture had effectively collapsed, and this once glorious civilization faded into obscurity.[1]

The decline of ancient Sumer holds valuable lessons for today's policymakers, who essentially follow the age-old practice of cultivating cropland until it is exhausted or taken for a new purpose. Around the world today, farmland continues to be devoured or damaged, with little appreciation of its finitude. Urban expansion, loss of irrigation water, and ongoing wear and tear to soils all claim

† Gary Gardner (b. 1958) is director of research at the Worldwatch Institute. The text is from his *Shrinking Fields: Cropland Loss in a World of Eight Billion* (Worldwatch Paper 131, July 1996). Reprinted by permission of the Worldwatch Institute.
1. Clive Ponting, "Historical Perspectives on Sustainable Development," *Environment*, November 1990.

valuable cropland each year. And since 1981 grainland, the base of
world food production, has steadily disappeared. As opportunities
to cultivate new lands dwindle, cropland losses loom increasingly
large.

The casual official attitude toward cropland loss and degradation
is largely a consequence of farmers' mesmerizing success with intensive cultivation. Starting in the 1960s, yields, especially of grain, rose
so rapidly that they outweighed the simultaneous losses of arable
land. Since 1984, however, growth in grain yields has slowed—dramatically so in the 1990s—and yield increases no longer fully compensate for the steady elimination of grainland. As in ancient Sumer,
sluggish productivity and loss of land are draining food reserves:
global grain stocks have fallen steadily since 1993, hitting a record
low in 1996.

The double blow to food production—a shrinking supply of quality
cropland, and lethargic growth in yields—comes on the eve of the
largest increase in food demand in human history. In 25 years, farmers will be asked to feed 7.9 billion people, 39 percent more than
they do today. Nine of every ten new births will occur in developing
countries, where grain self-sufficiency fell from 96 percent in 1969–
71 to 88 percent in 1993–95. In addition, economic expansion in
poor countries will allow millions to move from a monotonous diet
heavy in starches to varied meals that include livestock products,
fruits and vegetables, and foods prepared with vegetable oil. While
these foods offer benefits to consumers and farmers, they also
require more land to produce. As people become wealthier, they have
a disproportionate effect on cropland because they draw on food
stocks more heavily than the poor do.[2]

The imminent jump in demand for food would seem to dictate
protection of agricultural resources—especially cropland—but it has
not yet had that effect. Losses of cropland continue to be serious,
and they show no signs of abating. Land-tight China, for example,
lost nearly 4 million hectares of cropland on a net basis—roughly 3
percent of the total cropped area—between 1987 and 1992. Some
of the land was claimed by expanding cities, a source of attrition that
is projected to remain active: China hopes to build 600 *new* cities
by 2010, thus doubling the number it has now. Net losses in the
United States between 1982 and 1992 totaled an area larger than
the state of New Jersey, just under 2 million hectares. Meanwhile,
growth in irrigated cropland—the source of more than half of
increased global production between the mid-1960s and the mid-

2. Lester R. Brown et al., *Vital Signs 1996: The Trends that are Shaping Our Future* (New
York: W. W. Norton, 1996).

1980s—has plateaued, and millions of hectares irrigated with non-renewable groundwater will almost certainly be lost from production. Finally, degradation of farmland continues largely unabated, threatening a repetition of the toll exacted since World War II. Between 1945 and 1990, erosion, salination, waterlogging, and other degradation eliminated from production an area equal to the cropland of two Canadas. In an increasingly land-tight world, and with demand for food rising dramatically, losses of this magnitude cannot be repeated without grave consequences.

*   *   *

For millennia, cities have expanded into neighboring fields and orchards as their populations required more space for living, working, and playing. When land was plentiful, such expansion was easily accommodated, as farmers simply moved on to new plots. Today, cities are expanding rapidly, and because little new land is available for cultivation in the world's most crowded regions, cropland losses from urban expansion are typically net losses. Indeed, in many countries, the price for new industry, roads, houses, and recreational facilities can increasingly be measured in hectares of lost cropland.

Many competing claims to land are linked to the global rise of urbanization. Population growth and a preference for city life combined with economic—often environmentally rooted—problems in rural areas have caused a massive demographic shift to the world's urban areas. While fewer than 30 percent of the world's people lived in cities in 1950, more than 45 percent do today, and by 2025, the urban share of global population is expected to surpass 60 percent. The move to cities is not limited to the 100 or so megacities that receive the greatest attention; the fastest urban expansion is found in the 30,000 or so medium-sized cities in developing countries, where little or no planning guides the growth process.[3]

Because many cities were founded in agricultural areas, urban expansion often paves over farmland. The threat to cropland can be substantial: more than half of all U.S. agricultural production, for example, comes from counties on the edge of cities. Moreover, cropland near cities is often highly fertile. In the United States just over 18 percent of all rural land is classified as prime farmland; but within 50 miles of the largest urban areas, 27 percent is prime. And because development of agricultural land is rarely reversed,

3. Department of Economic and Social Information and Policy Analysis, United Nations, *World Urbanization Prospects: the 1992 Revision* (New York, 1993); fastest urban expansion from Eugene Linden, "The Exploding Cities of the Developing World," *Foreign Affairs*, January/February 1996.

encroachment represents a permanent loss of a principal agricultural resource.[4]

*   *   *

Mass adoption of an automobile-centered transport system entails land costs that are often not appreciated. In the seven Asian nations for which road data are available, road area would need to expand by more than 4 million hectares to handle the increase in cars newly registered between 1989 and 1994 without increasing congestion. If these additional roads were built, and if three-quarters of the area were taken from cropland, area sufficient to satisfy the grain needs of some 30 million people would be lost. The likelihood that a large share of the new road space would come from cropland is high, given the lack of spare land in Asia, and because roads and agriculture are most economical and function best on the same kind of terrain, typically, flat valley bottoms.[5]

*   *   *

Without a large increase in cropped area or a dramatic surge in yields, ongoing population pressures and continuing losses of cropland will literally squeeze the agricultural land base dry. Yet the potential for expansion is small, especially compared with the coming need for increased production.

Given projected increases in population in coming decades, the amount of cropland per person will certainly continue to fall. Today's grain area per person of 0.12 hectares will drop to 0.10 hectares by 2010, and to 0.09 hectares by 2020, assuming that grain area stabilizes at 700 million hectares. Every person added to the human family, and every hectare of land lost, places additional pressure on scientists and farmers to grow more on less land. Whether scientists and farmers can once again compensate for the shrinking area per person as they did before 1985 remains to be seen. Meanwhile, as grain area per person ratchets downward, the need to protect the crop-land base becomes more pressing.[6]

*   *   *

4. Dipasis Bhadra and Antonio Salazar P. Brandao, "Urbanization, Agricultural Development, and Land Allocation," World Bank Discussion Paper 201 (Washington, D.C.: World Bank, 1993).
5. Road estimates based on data in International Road Federation, *World Road Statistics 1989–1993* (Washington, D.C., 1994) and American Automobile Manufacturers Association, *World Motor Vehicle Data* (Washington, D.C., 1995).
6. Projection made using population data from Francis Urban and Ray Nightingale, "World Population by Country and Region, 1950–90 and Projections to 2050" (Washington, D.C.: Economic Research Service, USDA, April 1993).

LESTER R. BROWN

Eradicating Hunger: A Growing Challenge (2001)†

In 1974, U.S. Secretary of State Henry Kissinger made a pledge at the World Food Conference in Rome: "By 1984, no man, woman, or child would go to bed hungry." Those attending the conference, including many political leaders and ministers of agriculture, came away inspired by this commitment to end hunger.[1]

More than 26 years later, hunger is still very much part of the social landscape. Today, 1.1 billion of the world's 6 billion people are undernourished and underweight. Hunger and the fear of starvation quite literally shape their lives.

* * *

The alarming extent of hunger in the world today comes after a half-century during which world food output nearly tripled. The good news is that the share of population that is hungry is diminishing in all regions except Africa. Since 1980, both East Asia and Latin America have substantially reduced the number and the share of their populations that are hungry. In the Indian subcontinent, results have been mixed, with the number of hungry continuing to increase but the share declining slightly. In Africa, however, both the number and the share of hungry people have increased since 1980.[2]

* * *

These gains in eradicating hunger in East Asia and Latin America leave most of the world's hungry concentrated in two regions: the Indian subcontinent and sub-Saharan Africa. In India, with more than a billion people, 53 percent of all children are undernourished. In Bangladesh, the share is 56 percent. And in Pakistan, it is 38 percent. In Africa, the share of children who are undernourished has increased from 26 percent in 1980 to 28 percent today. In Ethiopia, 48 percent of all children are underweight. In Nigeria, the most populous country in Africa, the figure is 39 percent.[3]

† Lester R. Brown (b. 1934) is president of the Earth Policy Institute. The text is from Brown, Christopher Flavin, and Hilary French, *State of the World 2001* (New York, 2001). Reprinted by permission of W. W. Norton & Company.
1. Henry Kissinger, speech delivered at the First World Food Summit Conference, Rome, 5–16 November 1974.
2. Figure of 1.1 billion hungry is a Worldwatch estimate from U.N. Administrative Committee on Coordination, Sub-Committee on Nutrition (UN ACC/SCN), in collaboration with International Food Policy Research Institute (IFPRI), *Fourth Report on the World Nutrition Situation* (Geneva: 1999).
3. UN ACC/SCN, op. cit. note 2, 94–96.

*   *   *

Demographically, most of the world's poor live in countries where populations continue to grow rapidly, countries where poverty and population growth are reinforcing each other. The Indian subcontinent, for example, is adding 21 million people a year, the equivalent of another Australia. India's population has nearly tripled over the last half-century, growing from 350 million in 1950 to 1 billion in 2000. According to the U.N. projections, India will add 515 million more people by 2050, in effect adding roughly twice the current U.S. population. Pakistan's numbers, which tripled over the last half-century, are now expected to more than double over the next 50 years, going from 156 million to 345 million in 2050. And Bangladesh is projected to add 83 million people during this time, going from 129 million to 212 million. The subcontinent, already the hungriest region on Earth, is thus expected to add another 787 million people by mid-century.[4]

No single factor bears so directly on the prospect of eradicating hunger in this region as population growth. When a farm passes from one generation to the next, it is typically subdivided among the children. With the second generation of rapid population growth and associated land fragmentation now unfolding, farms are shrinking to the point where they can no longer adequately support the people living on them.

Between 1970 and 1990, the number of farms in India with less than 2 hectares (5 acres) of land increased from 49 million to 82 million. Assuming that this trend has continued since then, India may now have 90 million or more families with farms of less than 2 hectares. If each family has six members, then 540 million people—over half India's population—are trapped in a precarious balance with their land.[5]

Whether measuring changes in farm size or in grainland per person, the results of continuing rapid population growth are the same. Pakistan's projected growth from 156 million today to 345 million by 2050 will shrink its grainland per person from 0.08 hectares at present to 0.03 hectares, an area scarcely the size of a tennis court. African countries, with the world's fastest population growth, are facing a similar reduction.

*   *   *

Further complicating efforts to expand food production are water shortages. Of the nearly 3 billion people to be added to world pop-

---

4. United Nations, *World Population Prospects: The 1998 Revision* (New York: December 1998).
5. R.K. Pachauri and P.V. Sridharan, eds., *Looking Back to Think Ahead* (abridged version), GREEN India 2047 Project (New Delhi: Tata Energy Research Institute, 1998), 7.

ulation in the next 50 years, almost all will be added in countries already facing water shortages, such as India, Pakistan, and many countries in Africa. In India, water tables are falling in large areas as the demands of the current population exceed the sustainable yield of aquifers. For many countries facing water scarcity, trying to eradicate hunger while population continues to grow rapidly is like trying to walk up a down escalator.[6]

* * *

Water shortages are forcing grain imports upward in many countries. North Africa and the Middle East is now the world's fastest growing grain import market. In 1999, Iran eclipsed Japan, which until recently was the world's leading importer of wheat. And Egypt, another water-short country, has also edged ahead of Japan.[7]

Many developing countries that are facing acute land and water scarcity will rely on industrialization and labor-intensive industrial exports to finance needed food imports. This brings a need to expand production in exporting countries so they can cover the import needs of the growing number of grain-deficit countries. Over the last half-century, grain-importing countries, now the overwhelming majority, have become dangerously dependent on the United States for nearly half of their grain imports.

This concentration of dependence applies to each of the big three grains—wheat, rice, and corn. Just five countries—the United States, Canada, France, Australia, and Argentina—account for 88 percent of the world's wheat exports. Thailand, Viet Nam, the United States, and China account for 68 percent of all rice exports. For corn, the concentration is even greater, with the United States alone accounting for 78 percent and Argentina for 12 percent.[8]

With more extreme climate events in prospect if temperatures continue rising, this dependence on a few exporting countries leaves importers vulnerable to the vagaries of weather. If the United States were to experience a summer of severe heat and drought in its agricultural heartland like the summer of 1988, when grain production dropped below domestic consumption for the first time in history, chaos would reign in world grain markets simply because the near-record reserves that cushioned the huge U.S. crop shortfall that year no longer exist.[9]

6. Population data from United Nations, op. cit. note 4; Sandra Postel, *Pillar of Sand* (New York: W. W. Norton & Company, 1999), 73–74.
7. USDA, *Grain: World Markets and Trade* (Washington, DC: October 2000), 6.
8. Ibid, 6, 11,19.
9. Grain production and consumption data from U.S. Department of Agriculture (USDA), *Production, Supply and Distribution*, electronic database, Washington, DC, updated September 2000.

The risk for the scores of low-income, grain-importing countries is that prices could rise dramatically, impoverishing more people in a shorter period of time than any event in history. The resulting rise in hunger would be concentrated in the cities of the Third World.

Raising Cropland Productivity

In a world where there is little new land to plow, raising the productivity of existing cropland is the key to feeding the 80 million people added each year.

* * *

With the rise in land productivity slowing, continuing rapid population growth makes eradicating rural hunger much more difficult, if not impossible. Perhaps the single most important thing India can do to enhance its future food security is to accelerate the shift to smaller families. This would enable it to move to the low-level U.N. population projection instead of the medium-level one, thereby adding only 216 million people instead of 515 million in the next 50 years.

Eradicating hunger in Africa, which has the world's lowest crop yields, is an even more daunting challenge. Africa has the fastest population growth of any region and a largely semiarid climate, which limits the potential for irrigation and fertilizer use. It has not had a Green Revolution for the same reason that Australia has not: it is too dry to use much fertilizer, the key to raising yields. And now a new variable—the HIV epidemic—is decimating the adult population in sub-Saharan Africa, reducing the number of able-bodied people who can work in the fields.

* * *

Realizing the genetic potential of the new seeds depends on removing any nutrient or moisture constraints of soils. Fertilizers are designed to remove the limits imposed by nutrient deficiencies. * * *

Where fertilizer use is excessive, nutrient runoff into rivers and oceans can lead to algal blooms that then use up all available oxygen in the water as the algae decompose, creating dead zones with no sea life. Nutrient runoff from the U.S. Mississippi basin creates a dead zone each year about the size of New Jersey in the Gulf of Mexico. Food output on land is expanding in part at the expense of that from the oceans.[1]

As world fertilizer use climbed from 14 million tons in 1950 to 134 million tons in 2000, it began in some countries to press against

1. Carol Kaesuk Yoon, "A 'Dead Zone' Grows in the Gulf of Mexico," *New York Times*, 20 January 1998.

the physiological limits of plants to absorb nutrients. In response, the use of fertilizer has leveled off in the United States, Western Europe, and Japan, and now possibly China as well. In these countries, applying additional nutrients has little effect on production. Some parts of the world, such as the Indian subcontinent and Latin America, can still profitably use additional fertilizer. But for the world as a whole, the ninefold growth in the use of fertilizer—the engine that helped triple the world grain harvest during the last 50 years—is now history.[2]

* * *

Biotechnology is often cited as a potential source of higher yields, but although biotechnologists have been engineering new plant varieties for two decades, they have yet to produce a single variety of wheat, rice, or corn that can dramatically raise yields. The reason is that conventional plant breeders have already done most of the things they could think of to raise grain yields. One area where biotechnology might prove useful is in the development of more drought-tolerant crop varieties. Perhaps the largest question hanging over the future of biotechnology is the lack of knowledge about the possible environmental and human health effects of using genetically modified crops on a large scale over the long term.

* * *

Raising Water Productivity

Over the last half-century, world irrigated area tripled, climbing from 90 million hectares in 1950 to an estimated 270 million in 2000. Most of the growth occurred from 1950 to 1978, when irrigated area expanded faster than population and boosted irrigated land per person from 0.037 hectares to 0.047 hectares, an increase of one fourth. Since 1978, however, the growth in irrigated area has slowed, falling behind that of population and shrinking irrigated area per person by 8 percent in 2000.[3]

During the next half-century, the combination of aquifer depletion and the diversion of irrigation water to nonfarm uses may bring the historical growth in irrigation area to an end. If so, the world will be facing a steady shrinkage in the irrigated area per person as long as

2. Fertilizer usage numbers based on series from FAO, *Fertilizer Yearbook* (Rome: various years), and on K.G. Soh and K.F. Isherwood, "Short Term Prospects for World Agriculture and Fertilizer Use," International Fertilizer Industry Association Meeting, 30 November-3 December 1999.

3. Worldwatch estimate based on FAO, *1948–1985 World Crop and Livestock Statistics* (Rome: 1987), and from FAO, *FAOSTAT Statistics Database*, <apps.fao.org> updated 5 April 2000, and on USDA, *Agricultural Resources and Environmental Indicators* (Washington, DC: 1996–97).

population continues to grow. This in turn could translate into falling food production per person.

In many countries, the competition for water between the countryside and cities is intensifying. As countries industrialize, water use in industry climbs, often at the expense of agriculture. * * *

Farmers everywhere face an uphill battle in the competition for water since the economics of water use do not favor agriculture. In China, for example, a thousand tons of water can be used in agriculture to produce one ton of wheat worth perhaps $200 or it can be used to expand industrial output by $14,000. Wherever economic growth and the creation of jobs are a central preoccupation of political leaders, scarce water will likely go to industry. * * *

In addition, key food-producing countries that are overpumping, such as China, India, the United States, and Mexico, will lose irrigation water from aquifer depletion. Once the rising demand for water surpasses the sustainable yield of an aquifer, the gap between demand and sustainable yield widens each year. As it does so, the drop in the water table also increases each year. In this situation, food production becomes progressively more dependent on the aquifer's depletion. When it is depleted, pumping is necessarily reduced to the amount of annual recharge. The resulting precipitous drop in food production could lead to rising food prices and political instability.

* * *

Eliminating hunger in this new century requires an effort that goes far beyond agriculture. Stabilizing population is as essential as it is difficult. If rapid population growth continues in many developing countries, it will lead to further land fragmentation of holdings, as well as to hydrological poverty on a scale that is now difficult to imagine. Literally hundreds of millions of people will not have enough water to meet their most basic needs, including food production.

Addressing this challenge requires an educational effort on two fronts. The first links various family sizes, say two-child and four-child families, to population projections and then relates these to the availability of land, water, and other basic resources. Without this information, individuals may not understand the urgency of shifting to smaller families. In addition, if policymakers lack this information, they will not be able to make responsible decisions on population and related policies, such as investment in family planning services.

The second front is the educational level of women. As female educational levels rise, fertility falls. As women's education rises, the nutrition of their children improves, even if incomes do not rise, apparently because more education brings a better understanding of nutrition. We should be educating young women in developing countries as though future progress depends on it, because indeed it may.[4]

The numbers used in discussing future population growth in this chapter are the U.N. medium projections, those that have world population going from 6 billion at present to nearly 9 billion by 2050. There is also a high projection, which has human numbers approaching 11 billion by 2050, and a low projection, which has population peaking at 7.5 billion in 2040 and then declining.

This low number assumes that the entire world will quickly move to replacement-level fertility of two children per couple. This is not only achievable, but it may be the only humane population option, simply because if the world does not shift quickly to smaller families, the spreading land and water scarcity that is already translating into increasing hunger and mortality in some countries could reach many more.

Many of the key decisions to achieve this lower figure have to be made by national governments, but unless world leaders—the Secretary-General of the United Nations, the President of the World Bank, and the President of the United States—urge governments and couples everywhere to adopt a goal of two surviving children per couple, hunger will not likely be eradicated, or even greatly reduced. The issue today is not whether individual couples can afford more than two children, but whether Earth can afford couples having more than two children.

*   *   *

4. Education of women as correlated to fertility from Lester R. Brown, Gary Gardner, and Brian Halweil, *Beyond Malthus* (New York: W. W. Norton & Company, 1999), 131; the role of education of women in regards to child nutrition from Lisa C. Smith and Lawrence Haddad, *Explaining Child Malnutrition in Developing Countries: A Cross-Country Analysis*, Food Consumption and Nutrition Division Discussion Paper No. 60 (Washington, DC: IFPRI, April 1999), 16–17.

C. Population and Water Supplies in the Twenty-First Century

SANDRA POSTEL

Last Oasis (1997)†

* * *

Demand for water, like that for many resources, has been growing exponentially. If world water demand continues to grow faster than population (as it has since 1950), say at 2 percent a year, it will double in 35 years. Given that water demand tripled between 1950 and 1990, a doubling over the next 35 years seems quite possible. Meanwhile, it is getting harder to expand the accessible supply. The construction of dams—which capture runoff and thus bring more water under human control—has slowed markedly over the last couple of decades as the public, governments, and financial backers have begun to pay more attention to the high economic, social, and environmental costs of dams. Whereas nearly 1,000 large dams began operation each year from the fifties through the mid-seventies, the number dropped to about 260 during the early nineties.[1] Even if conditions become more favorable to dam construction, it seems unlikely that new reservoirs built over the next 30–35 years will increase accessible runoff by more than 10 percent.

For several decades, the desalting of seawater has held out the promise of limitless supplies of fresh water, yet this source remains a minor contributor to the global supply picture. Global desalination capacity is now half again as large as the 1990 capacity, but it still

† Sandra Postel (b. 1956) is director of the Global Water Policy Project. The text is from her *Last Oasis: Facing Water Scarcity* (New York, 1997). Reprinted by permission of W. W. Norton & Company.
1. Patrick McCully, *Silenced Rivers: The Ecology and Politics of Large Dams* (London: Zed Books, 1996).

accounts for less than 0.2 percent of world water use.[2] After three decades of intensive research and development, removing salt from seawater remains energy-intensive and expensive. The world's water situation would no doubt be very different today if as much money and effort had gone into improving water efficiency as has gone into desalination. Although desalination will continue to provide drinking water to water-poor countries that can afford it, its contribution to the global supply picture is likely to remain small for the foreseeable future.

It may be hard to believe that water limits are drawing closer, for we hold in our minds an image of earth as a strikingly blue planet—a world of water spinning in space—thanks in part to the beautiful photographs taken by astronauts. But this picture creates a false sense of security, because we can tap only a tiny fraction of this water wealth, and that small share must sustain not only our growing population but millions of other species. Limits to our use of fresh water for the things we need—clean water to drink, food to eat, material sufficiency, and a healthy environment—are on the horizon. The best way to avoid costly shortages lies in reducing our water demand through conservation, efficiency, and better management. Meanwhile, as we struggle through the shift from a world of plenty to one of scarcity, we face some serious challenges—to food security, ecosystem health, and social and political stability.

Water for Food

Growing the food needed for a nutritious but low-meat diet for one person for a year takes about 1,100 cubic meters (nearly 291,000 gallons) of water.[3] In humid climates, rainfall delivers virtually all this needed moisture to the soil. But in less humid regions and in those with distinct wet and dry seasons, a portion of the needed moisture must be supplied by irrigation. If 40 percent of the water required to produce an acceptable diet for the 2.4 billion people expected to be added to the planet over the next 30 years has to come from irrigation, agricultural water supplies would have to expand by more than 1,750 cubic kilometers per year—equivalent to roughly 20 Nile Rivers, or to 97 Colorado Rivers.

It is not at all clear where that water could come from on a sustainable basis. * * * Per capita irrigated area, for example, has continued to decline, having fallen 7 percent from its 1979 peak as

2. Desalination capacity from Pat Burke, Secretary General, International Desalination Association, Topsfield, Mass., private communication, August 1, 1996.
3. Based on Wulf Klohn and Hans Wolter, "Perspectives of Food Security and Water Development," unpublished paper.

population growth outpaced the spread of irrigation.[4] As much as 2 million hectares of irrigated land—an area a bit larger than Kuwait and equal to nearly 1 percent of world irrigated area—comes out of production each year because of waterlogging and salinization of soils.[5] With additional irrigated land being lost to urbanization, David Seckler, Director General of the International Irrigation Management Institute, concludes that "the net growth of irrigated area in the world has probably become *negative*."[6]

Groundwater overpumping—another unsustainable practice—continues to plague future food production in some of the world's most important crop-producing regions, including the U.S. High Plains, California's Central Valley, the north China plain, and portions of India. In India's Punjab, for example, where a highly productive rice-wheat cropping pattern has turned the region into the nation's breadbasket, water tables are falling 20 centimeters annually over two thirds of the state. According to researchers at Punjab Agricultural University, "questions are now being asked as to what extent rice cultivation should be permitted in the irrigated Indo-Gangetic Plains, and how to sustain the productivity of the region without losing the battle on the water front."[7]

Agriculture is also losing some of its existing water supplies to cities as population growth and urbanization push up urban water demands. Worldwide, the number of urban dwellers is expected to double, to 5 billion, by 2025.[8] Pressure to shift water from farms to cities is thus bound to intensify—as is already happening in China, the western United States, and other water-short areas.

Casting a disturbing shadow over all these trends is the fact that limited water supplies combined with population growth appear to be eliminating the option of food self-sufficiency in more and more countries. At runoff levels below 1,700 cubic meters per person, food self-sufficiency is often highly problematic, if not impossible. Of the 28 countries in Africa and the Middle East that are at or below this benchmark, 19 already import at least 20 percent of their grain. As populations grow, more countries will join the water-stressed list, and those already on the list will acquire more people. Thus, dependence on grain imports is likely to deepen and spread. By 2025,

4. Gary Gardner, "Irrigated Area Dips Slightly," in Lester R. Brown, Christopher Flavin, and Hal Kane, *Vital Signs 1996* (New York: W. W. Norton & Company, 1996).
5. Dina L. Umali, *Irrigation-Induced Salinity* (Washington, D.C.: World Bank, 1993).
6. David Seckler, *The New Era of Water Resources Management: From 'Dry' to 'Wet' Water Savings* (Washington, D.C.: Consultative Group on International Agricultural Research, 1996).
7. International Rice Research Institute, *Water: A Looming Crisis* (Manila: 1995).
8. Gershon Feder and Andrew Keck, "Increasing Competition for Land and Water Resources: A Global Perspective," paper prepared for World Bank, Washington, D.C., March 1995.

Africa and the Middle East alone will have more than 1.3 billion people living in water-stressed countries, up from 380 million today. In Asia, India will join the list by 2025, and China will only narrowly miss doing so by then.[9]

All told, as many as 3.6 billion people could be living in countries where water supplies are too limited for food self-sufficiency. This raises some important questions. How much grain will these countries collectively need to import? Who will supply that grain, and at what price? Will importing countries, particularly those in Africa, be able to pay that price? With more than 1 billion people living in acute poverty and some 840 million people lacking sufficient food even in today's world of 5.8 billion, avoiding these issues could have severe repercussions in a world of 8 billion.[1]

An all-out effort to raise the water productivity of the global crop base—both irrigated and rain-fed—is urgently needed.

*   *   *

In the quest for better living standards and economic gain, modern society has come to view water only as a resource that is there for the taking, rather than a living system that drives the workings of a natural world we depend on. Harmonizing human needs with those of a healthy environment will require new ways of using and managing water. And it will require adjusting our production and consumption patterns so as to remain within ecological limits.

In each major area of water use—agriculture, industry, and cities—demands have risen markedly since 1950. At that time, both population and material consumption began a steep climb, driving water use rapidly upward. By and large, those pressures continue today, as worldwide needs for food, industrial products, and household services expand.

Agriculture claims the lion's share of all the water taken from rivers, lakes, and aquifers, accounting for an estimated 65 percent of global water use. As opportunities to extend cropland area have dwindled, augmenting food production has come to depend more on coaxing higher yields from existing farmland, which often requires irrigation. Over the course of this century, as the number of people to feed swelled from 1.6 billion to more than 5.4 billion, agriculture's water use increased fivefold. The really rapid rise began around mid-century, when water development entered its heyday, and continued

9. Africa runoff figures from FAO, *Irrigation in Africa in Figures* (Rome: 1995); other runoff figures from World Resources Institute, *World Resources 1994–95* (New York: Oxford University Press, 1994); population figures from Population Reference Bureau, *1995 World Population Data Sheet* (Washington, D.C.: 1995); net grain imports from U.S. Department of Agriculture, Economic Research Service, "Production, Supply, and Distribution," electronic database, Washington, D.C., updated February 1996.
1. UNDP, *Human Development Report 1996*; FAO, *Food for All*.

as the Green Revolution—involving fertilizers and pesticides, high-yielding seeds, and irrigation—took hold and spread.

Industries make the second largest claim on the world's water bodies, accounting for a fourth of global water use. Generating electricity in thermal power plants (nuclear and fossil fuel) takes copious amounts of water, as does making the paper, steel, plastics, and other materials we use every day. Spurred by droughts and strict pollution control requirements, industries in the richer countries have shown that they can reduce their water use dramatically by recycling and reusing their supplies. Yet these technologies remain greatly underused, particularly in the developing world, where industry's water use is now rising rapidly.

Water deliveries to households, schools, businesses, and other municipal activities account for less than a tenth of global water use today. Nonetheless, meeting these needs is no easy task. Drinking water must be treated to a high level of quality and supplied with a high degree of reliability, which makes it expensive. As cities expand, planners reach out to capture ever more distant and costly sources. Tapwater in many homes in Los Angeles, for instance, originates hundreds of kilometers away in northern California or the Colorado River basin. By the end of this decade, some 22 cities worldwide will have populations of 10 million or more, and 18 of them will be in the Third World. Serving these dense population centers will in many cases take more water, capital, and energy than is available or affordable.

Already today, there remains a large unmet demand for household water. Nearly one out of every three people in the developing world—some 1.2 billion people in all—do not have access to a safe and reliable supply for their daily needs. Often they resort to shallow wells or stagnant pools that are easily contaminated with human and animal waste. As a result, waterborne diseases account for an estimated 80 percent of all illnesses in developing countries. And women and children walk several kilometers each day just to collect enough water for drinking, cooking, and cleaning, a drudgery that saps time and energy from more productive activities.

Added up, total human demands for water—including agriculture, industries, and cities—still seem comfortably below the amount nature makes available each year. But this, too, is illusory. Much rainwater runs off in floods, falls in places too remote for us to capture it, or is needed to support the myriad other species and ecosystems with which we share the planet, and on which we depend.

Moreover, in many places, pollution is rapidly diminishing the usable supply. Each liter of polluted wastewater contaminates many additional liters in the water body that receives it. In Poland, for example, the share of river water of highest quality for drinking has dropped from 32 percent to less than 5 percent during the last two decades. Some three quarters of that nation's river water is now too contaminated even for industrial use. Similar situations increasingly can be found in developing countries, where unchecked pollution poses a mounting threat during industrialization.

Although water is part of a global system, how it is used and managed locally and regionally is what really counts. Unlike oil, wheat, and most other important commodities, water is needed in quantities too large to make it practical to transport long distances. No global water crisis is likely to shake the world the way the energy crisis of the seventies did. But with key crop-producing regions and numerous metropolitan areas showing signs of water scarcity and depletion, global food supplies and economic health are in jeopardy. Moreover, global warming from the buildup of greenhouse gases could greatly complicate regional water problems by shifting the patterns of rainfall and runoff that agriculture and urban water systems are geared to.

Without question, water development has been a key to raising living standards, and it needs to be extended to the one fifth of humanity who have largely missed out on its benefits. But in our rush for economic growth, food sufficiency, and material well-being we have repeatedly ignored nature's limits—depleting underground aquifers, deforesting watersheds, and diminishing streamflows to ecologically damaging levels.

Achieving water balance will not be easy. The policies, laws, and practices that shape water use today rarely promote all three basic tenets of sustainable resource use—efficiency, equity, and ecological integrity. Even a casual glimpse around the world shows water allocation and use to be in a chaotic state. While farmers in California's Central Valley were spreading copious amounts of inexpensive irrigation water on cotton and rice, Los Angeles was draining the streams feeding fragile Mono Lake to fill swimming pools and wash cars. Sugarcane growers in the Indian state of Maharashtra take 50 percent of available irrigation supplies even though they occupy only 10 percent of the cropland. And from the Everglades to the Aral Sea, aquatic habitats unravel from the siphoning off and pollution of rivers and streams.

Taking heed of water's limits, and learning to live within them, amounts to a major transformation in our relationship to fresh water. Historically, we have approached nature's water systems with a frontier philosophy, manipulating the water cycle to whatever degree engineering know-how would permit. Now, instead of continuously reaching out for more, we must begin to look within—within our regions, our communities, our homes, and ourselves—for ways to meet our needs while respecting water's life-sustaining functions.

Doing more with less is the first and easiest step along the path toward water security. By using water more efficiently, we in effect create a new source of supply. Each liter conserved can help meet new water demands without damming another stretch of river or depleting more groundwater. With technologies and methods available today, farmers could cut their water needs by 10–50 percent, industries by 40–90 percent, and cities by a third with no sacrifice of economic output or quality of life. Most investments in water efficiency, recycling, reuse, and conservation yield more usable water per dollar than investments in conventional water supply projects do. But they will not materialize until policies, laws, and institutions begin to foster such measures rather than hinder them.

New technologies and better policies have much to offer toward the goal of achieving a secure water future, but they will take us only so far. They alone cannot avert conflicts and shortages where populations are expanding faster than efficiency measures can release new supplies. Any hope for balancing the water budgets of most Middle Eastern countries, for instance, rests as much on lowering birth rates as it does on modernizing irrigation systems. And in many water-short African countries, slowing population growth appears to be the only way of meeting minimal per capita needs in the near future.

*   *   *

D. Population and Energy Supplies in the Twenty-First Century

DAVID PIMENTEL AND MARCIA PIMENTEL

Food, Energy, and Society (1996)†

Tough questions about conservation of natural resources, development of alternative energy resources, desired standards of living, types of diet, and optimum populations size must be answered. All require decisive action.

The foremost question is how humans will be able to provide a nutritionally adequate diet for a world population expected to be more than 6.1 billion by 2000 and 12 billion by about 2040.

Food security for all is dependent on and interrelated with many factors within the vast human social and ecological system. Fundamentally, it depends upon human population numbers and the standard of living those humans desire. Environmental resources such as arable land, water, climate, and fossil energy for fertilizers and irrigation influence the outcome. The food supply is also affected by crop losses to pests, availability of labor, environmental pollution, and the health and lifestyle of the people. Distribution systems and the social organization of families and countries play a role in the solution.

* * *

Rapid growth in the world population coincided with the exponential growth in the use of fossil fuels. Some of this energy has been used to promote public health, control disease, and increase food production for the ever-growing world population. The control of

† David Pimental (b. 1925) is professor of ecology and agricultural science at Cornell University. Marcia Pimentel is senior lecturer in the Division of Nutritional Sciences at Cornell University. The text is from their *Food, Energy, and Society* (Niwot, Colo., 1996). Reprinted by permission of the University Press of Colorado.

typhoid disease, for example, was achieved by improving water puri-
fication, which required large energy expenditures.[1] The program for
eradicating malaria-carrying mosquitoes required the application of
DDT and other insecticides. Producing these insecticides used substantial quantities of energy.[2]

*   *   *

Energy Needs in Food Production

In past decades humans did not have to concern themselves about
fossil fuel supplies, because relatively inexpensive and ample supplies were available. Such will not be the case in the twenty-first
century. An estimated 17 percent of the fossil energy consumed in
the United States is used in the food production system. This 17
percent may seem neither large nor important when considered as
a portion of the total U.S. energy expenditure, but compared to that
of other nations (especially developing countries) it is extremely
large. It amounts to more than twice the total per capita fossil use
in Asia and about 4 times that in Africa.

The following analysis may help clarify the relationships of fossil
fuel supplies to production of food supplies. The total energy used
annually in the United States for food production, processing, distribution, and preparation is about 1600 liters of oil per capita per
year. Using U.S. agricultural technology to feed the present world
population of 6 billion, a high protein/calorie diet for 1 year would
require the equivalent of 9000×10^9 liters of fuel annually.

Another way to understand the dependency of food production on
fossil energy is to calculate how long it would take to deplete the
known world reserve of petroleum if a high protein/calorie diet, produced using U.S. agricultural technologies, were fed to the entire
world population. The known world oil reserves have been estimated
to be 87×10^{12} liters[3] so if we assume that 75 percent of raw oil can
be converted to fuel[4] this would provide a usable reserve of 66×10^{12} liters of oil. Assuming that oil were the only source of energy
for food production and that all known oil reserves were used solely
for food production, the reserves would last a mere 7.3 years from
today. This estimate is based on a hypothetical stabilized population
of 5.5 billion. The reality is that each day an additional quarter million new mouths must be fed.

How then can food supply and energy expenditures be balanced

1. Audy, J. R., *Public Health and Medical Sciences in the Pacific—a Forty-Year Review*. (Hon-
olulu: Pacific Science Congress, 10th, University Press, 1964).
2. Ibid.
3. Matare, H.F., *Energy: Fact and Future* (Boca Raton, FL: CRC Press, 1989).
4. Jiler, H., *Commodity Yearbook* (New York: Commodity Research Bureau, 1972).

against a growing world population? Even tripling the food supply in the next 40 years would just about meet the basic food needs of the 11 billion people who will inhabit the earth at that time. Doing so would require about a 10-fold increase in the total quantity of energy expended in food production. The large energy input per increment increase in food is needed to overcome the incremental decline in crop yields caused by erosion and pest damage.

One practical way to increase food supplies with minimal increase in fossil energy inputs is for the world population as a whole to consume more plant foods. This diet modification would reduce energy expenditures and increase food supplies, because less food suitable for human consumption would be fed to livestock. With livestock, roughly 20 calories of increased energy are needed to obtain 1 calorie of food.

*　　*　　*

Worldwide, more than 10 million ha of agricultural land are abandoned annually because of serious soil degradation. During the past 40 years, about 30 percent of total world arable land has been abandoned because it was no longer productive. Loss of arable land is increasing because poor farmers worldwide have to burn crop residues and dung as fuel because firewood supplies are declining and fossil fuels are much too costly. It is expected that 750 million ha of cropland will be abandoned by 2050 because of severe degradation. This is extremely bad news; about half of the current arable land now in cultivation will be unsuitable for food production by the middle of the twenty-first century.

Wind and water erosion seriously reduce the productivity of land. In the United States, the rate of soil erosion is estimated at 13 tons/ha annually. The United States has already abandoned an estimated 100 million ha. At least one-third of the topsoil has been eroded from U.S. cropland during more than a century of farming. Iowa, which has some of the best soils in the United States, reportedly has lost half its topsoil after little more than 100 years of farming.[5]

So far, the reduced productivity of U.S. cropland due to erosion has been offset by increased use of fertilizers, irrigation, and pesticides. The estimate is that about 50 liters of oil equivalents per hectare are expended each year to offset cropland degradation. In developing countries, the rate of soil loss is more than twice that of the U.S., an estimated 30 to 40 tons/ha/yr.[6] Therefore, based on

5. Risser, J., "A Renewed Threat of Soil Erosion: It's Worse Than the Dust Bowl," *Smithsonian*, 11: 120–122, 126–130.

6. Pimentel, D. et al, "Soil Erosion and Agricultural Productivity," in D. Pimentel, ed., *World Soil Erosion and Conservation* (Cambridge, UK: Cambridge Univ. Pr., 1993).

what we presently know, both the amount of arable land available for crop production and the amounts of extra energy needed to put poor land into production are serious constraints on expansion of crop production.

*   *   *

The Future

There is no single cause of the growing shortages of food, land, water, and energy or pollution of the environment, nor are there simple solutions. When all the world's resources and assets must be divided among an increasing number of people, each one has a smaller share, until there are insufficient amounts to go around.

At this point it is relevant to reconsider the biological law Malthus proposed: "First, that food is necessary to the existence of man. Secondly, that the passion between the sexes is necessary and will remain nearly in its present state. . . . Assuming then my postula are granted, I say that the power of population is definitely greater than the power of the earth to produce sustenance for man." Malthus may not have been thinking about this aspect, but it is true that food production increases linearly, whereas the human population increases geometrically. Therefore, there is no biophysical way for food production to increase and stay with the growth of the human population. Even if population increase were not geometric, there are limits to the earth's carrying capacity.

Perhaps Bertrand Russell best expressed the biological law related to population growth when he wrote: "Every living thing is a sort of imperialist seeking to transform as much as possible of its environment into itself and its seed." This law suggests that the human population will increase until food or some other basic need limits its survival and growth.

Although science and technology will help alleviate some of the future shortages, they cannot solve all the problems the world faces today. Science has been unable to solve many of the world's problems during the past 50 years, and with fewer resources that must be shared with more people we have no reason to expect that biophysical limits can be overcome. For example, more, larger, and faster fishing vessels have not increased fish production; on the contrary, it is declining. Likewise, water flowing in the Colorado River now ceases to reach the Sea of Cortes. There is no technology that can double the flow of the Colorado and/or increase rainfall.

We remain optimists, for we see some signs that people are beginning to understand that resources are not unlimited and that a balance must be achieved between the basic needs of the human population and environmental resources, many of which are finite. This is the time to take action.

Above all else humans must control their numbers. This task is probably the most difficult one facing all of us today. If birth rates are to decline on a massive scale, parents must understand that having fewer children is in their own and their children's interest. This understanding can be achieved only if the direct costs of having children are increased and if socially acceptable substitutes for large families are developed. Within each country and each ecological system, difficult social changes must be encouraged in conjunction with policies that augment food supplies and improve health, education, and lifestyle.

What humans choose to do in the coming two decades will determine the kind of world the next generations will live in. Ultimately, it is up to each individual to reduce his or her reproductive rate. Clearly, if humans do not control their numbers, nature will do so through poverty, disease, and starvation.

E. Population and the Environment in the Twenty-First Century

PAUL R. EHRLICH AND ANNE H. EHRLICH

How Anti-Environmental Rhetoric Threatens Our Future (1996)†

The time has come to write a book about efforts being made to minimize the seriousness of environmental problems. We call these
attempts the "brownlash" because they help to fuel a backlash
against "green" policies. The brownlash has been generated by a
diverse group of individuals and organizations, doubtless often with
differing motives and backgrounds. We classify them as brownlash-
ers by what they say, not by who they are. With strong and appealing
messages, they have successfully sowed seeds of doubt among jour-
nalists, policy makers, and the public at large about the reality and
importance of such phenomena as overpopulation, global climate
change, ozone depletion, and losses of biodiversity.

* * *

Yet at the same time that brownlash activities are intensifying, the
conclusions and predictions of concerned environmental scientists
are being increasingly substantiated as more data are gathered and
computer and analytic models are refined.[1] Indeed, scientists from

---

† Paul R. Ehrlich (b. 1932) is Bing Professor of population studies at Stanford University.
  Anne H. Ehrlich (b. 1933) is associate director of the Center for Conservation Biology at
  Stanford University. The text is from their *Betrayal of Science and Reason: How Anti-
  Environmental Rhetoric Threatens Our Future* (Washington, D.C., 1996). Reprinted by
  permission of Island Press.
1. Growing support in the scientific community can be seen in recent documents such as
   the *Sustainable Biosphere Initiative* of the Ecological Society of America; the *Global
   Biodiversity Assessment* of the United Nations Environment Programme, generated by
   hundreds of scientists; and *Systematics Agenda 2000*, produced by a consortium of societies dealing with biodiversity. All these illustrate a growing involvement among biologists.
   More and more, professional organizations like the American Institute of Biological Sci-

disciplines as diverse as physics, chemistry, geology, and molecular biology, including many Nobel laureates, now support the conclusions of their colleagues in environmental science, as do most scientific academies around the world.

Despite the evidence and deepening consensus among scientists, humanity seems to be engaged in a remarkable episode of folly. Folly—pursuing policies injurious to self-interest while being advised against them—is nothing new; it has plagued governments since their inception. What has changed through the ages is not the lack of wisdom in politics but rather the price to be paid for that lack. Despite a vastly enhanced understanding of our planet's life-support systems, humanity is continually assaulting them—degrading and destroying within a few generations the ecosystems that provide the very basis of civilization. All the world's nations are pursuing this course despite knowledge of its consequences being available and despite the warnings of many of the world's most distinguished scientists. And that folly is being encouraged and promoted by the individuals and organizations whose efforts we refer to collectively as the brownlash.

* * *

The world food situation has been a favorite arena for brownlash writers and spokespeople who deny, often vehemently, that a growing population might someday run into absolute food shortages. The essence of their argument takes two forms: population growth is not a problem and (for some of them) is even virtually an unmitigated blessing and food production can be increased more or less forever without constraint. * * *

Let's take a look at some of the brownlash claims about population and food. Here and throughout the rest of this book, we summarize or directly quote brownlash statements, then present what we believe to be the consensus or majority view of environmental scientists. We begin with one of the most extreme brownlash claims.

> "We now have in our hands—in our libraries, really—the technology to feed, clothe, and supply energy to an ever-growing population for the next 7 billion years." (Julian Simon, 1994)[2]

---

ences and the Ecological Society of America have become active where science and society meet and interact. The Society for Conservation Biology and the International Society for Ecological Economics were both founded in the mid-1980s specifically to deal with aspects of the human predicament. They are now among the world's fastest-growing scientific societies.

2. N. Myers and J. Simon, 1994, *Scarcity or Abundance: A Debate on the Environment*, W. W. Norton & Company, New York, p. 65. That this is not a typo is attested to by Simon's repeating of the statement in the introduction to a volume he edited (1995, *The State of Humanity*, Blackwell, Oxford, p. 26) and adding "Even if no new knowledge were ever

Does Julian Simon really mean to suggest the world's population can continue to grow for billions of years at the rate it was growing when he wrote that statement? The world population was growing in 1994 at the rate of about 1.6 percent per year, which corresponds to a doubling time of about 43 years.[3] A bit of arithmetic reveals that such a population growth rate could not persist even for hundreds of years, let alone millions of years.[4] To suggest that an "ever-growing" population can persist for billions of years is, of course, ridiculous.

*   *   *

"There is no overpopulation today."

This is a popular theme with many brownlash writers.[5] To understand how fallacious this statement is requires recognizing that overpopulation can be reached very quickly by exponentially growing populations in situations of seeming abundance. There is overpopulation when organisms (people in this case) become so numerous that they degrade the ability of the environment to support their kind of animal in the future. The number of people Earth can support *in the long term* (without degrading the environment)—given existing socioeconomic systems, consumption patterns, and technological capabilities—is called the *human carrying capacity* of the planet at that time.[6] And carrying capacity can be exceeded without causing immediate effects obvious to the untutored observer. "Overshoots" commonly occur in nature with all kinds of organisms. A population has an "outbreak," grows far beyond its carrying capacity, consumes its resources (for animals, usually food), and "crashes" to a size far below the previous carrying capacity.

*   *   *

invented . . . we would be able to go on increasing our population *forever* while improving our standard of living" (our emphasis).

3. The mathematically inclined can easily show that the doubling time for an entity growing at X percent per year (when X is less than 5 percent) is roughly equal to $70/X$ years. Hence the doubling time corresponding to a growth rate of 1.6 percent per year is $70/1.6 = 43$ years.

4. Even 200 years of growth at the 1994 rate produces preposterous numbers. The human population in 2194 would consist of about two dozen individuals for everyone alive in 1994—137 billion people—a number that even the vast majority of technological optimists would agree would be unlikely to be supportable.

5. See, e.g., J. Bast, P. Hill, and R. Rue, 1994, *Ecosanity: A Common-sense Guide to Environmentalism*, Madison Books, Lanham, MD, p. 231: ". . . predictions of a 'population explosion' and eventual resource depletion were wrong because they were based on past trends." See also Myers and Simon, 1994, and other works by Simon.

6. G. Daily and P. Ehrlich, 1992, Population, sustainability, and Earth's carrying capacity, *BioScience* 42:761–771.

Overshoots can occur in human populations, too.[7] Humanity has already overshot Earth's carrying capacity by a simple measure: no nation is supporting its present population on *income*—that is, the sustainable flow of renewable resources. Instead, key "renewable" resources, the natural *capital* of humanity, are being used so rapidly that they have become effectively non-renewable.[8] *Homo sapiens* is collectively acting like a person who happily writes ever larger checks without considering what's happening to the balance of the account.[9]

Warning signs that the human enterprise is nearing the end of exponential growth include declines in the amount or availability of good farmland,[1] soil,[2] fresh water,[3] and biodiversity,[4] all of which are crucial elements of natural capital essential for sustaining humanity and especially for sustaining agricultural production.[5] A more fundamental but indirect indicator of how close humanity is to its limits is that it is already consuming, co-opting, or destroying some 40

7. W. Catton, 1980, *Overshoot: The Ecological Basis of Revolutionary Change*, University of Illinois Press, Urbana.

8. P. Ehrlich and A. Ehrlich, 1990, *The Population Explosion*, Simon and Schuster, New York. See chapter 2 and the references cited there.

9. For a fine overview of some of the critical trends, see R. Naylor, 1996, Energy and resource constraints on intensive agricultural production, *Annual Review of Energy*, in press; and N. Myers, 1995, *Ultimate Security: The Environmental Basis of Political Stability*, W. W. Norton & Company, New York.

1. See, e.g., H. Colby, F. Crook, and S.-E. Webb, 1992, Agricultural statistics of the People's Republic of China, 1949–1990, *Statistical Bulletin* no. 844, U.S. Department of Agriculture, Washington, DC; M. Imhoff et al., 1986, Monsoon flood boundary delineation and damage assessment using space-borne imaging radar and Landsat data, *Photogrammatic Engineering and Remote Sensing* 53:405–413. For an overview, see pp. 171–180 of P. Ehrlich, A. Ehrlich, and G. Daily, *The Stork and the Plow: The Equity Answer to the Human Dilemma* (New York: Grosset/Putnam, 1995).

2. For an overview, see chapter 6 of Ehrlich, Ehrlich, and Daily, 1995.

3. See, e.g., P. Gleick (ed.), 1993, *Water in Crisis*, Oxford University Press, New York; M. Reisner, 1986, *Cadillac Desert*, Viking, New York; S. Postel, 1990, *Water for Agriculture: Facing the Limits*, Worldwatch paper no. 93, Worldwatch Institute, Washington, DC; S. Postel, G. Daily, and P. Ehrlich, 1996, Human appropriation of renewable fresh water, *Science* 271:785–788.

4. P. Ehrlich, A. Ehrlich, and J. Holdren, 1977, *Ecoscience: Population, Resources, Environment*, W. H. Freeman, San Francisco, chapters 3, 4, 6, and 11; N. Myers, 1979, *The Sinking Ark*, Pergamon Press, New York; P. Ehrlich and A. Ehrlich, 1981, *Extinction: The Causes and Consequences of the Disappearance of Species*, Random House, New York; E. Wilson (ed.), 1988, *Biodiversity*, National Academy Press, Washington, DC; P. Ehrlich and E. Wilson, 1991, Biodiversity studies: Science and policy, *Science* 253:758–762; E. Wilson, 1992, *The Diversity of Life*, Harvard University Press, Cambridge, MA; J. Lawton and R. May (eds.), 1995, *Extinction Rates*, Oxford University Press, Oxford; S. Pimm, G. Russell, J. Gittleman, T. Brooks, 1995, The future of biodiversity, *Science* 269:347–350; E. Hoyt, 1988, *Conserving the Wild Relatives of Crops*, International Union for the Conservation of Nature, Gland and Rome; C. Fowler and P. Mooney, 1990, *Shattering: Food, Politics, and the Loss of Genetic Diversity*, University of Arizona Press, Tucson.

5. See, e.g., L. Oldeman, V. Van Engelen, and J. Pulles, 1990. The extent of human-induced soil degradation, annex 5 of L. Oldeman, R. Hakkeling, and W. Sombroek, *World Map of the Status of Human-Induced Soil Degradation: An Explanatory Note* (rev. 2nd ed.), International Soil Reference and Information Centre (ISRIC), Wageningen, Netherlands; R. Repetto, 1994, *The "Second India" Revisited: Population, Poverty, and Environmental Stress over Two Decades*, World Resources Institute, Washington, DC; G. Daily, 1995, Restoring value to the world's degraded lands, *Science* 269:350–354; National Research Council, Committee on the Role of Alternative Farming Methods in Modern Production Agriculture, Board on Agriculture, 1989, *Alternative Agriculture*, National Academy Press, Washington, DC.

percent of the terrestrial food supply of all animals (not just human beings).[6]

* * *

> One needn't worry about population growth in the United States, because it's still nowhere near as densely populated as the Netherlands.[7]

The idea that the number of people per square mile is a key determinant of population pressure is as widespread and persistent as it is wrong—Paul and physicist John Holdren (now at the Kennedy School of Government at Harvard) long ago named it the "Netherlands fallacy."[8] * * *

Our response is perfectly straightforward. First, the key issue in judging overpopulation is not how many people can fit in any given space but whether the population's requirements for food, water, other resources, and ecosystem services can be met on a sustainable basis. Most of the "empty" land in the United States either grows the food essential to the well-being of Americans and much of the world (as in Iowa) or supplies us with forestry products (northern Maine), or, lacking water, good soil, and a suitable climate (as in much of Nevada), it is land that cannot directly contribute much to the support of civilization.

The key point here is that the Netherlands, Bermuda, and Monaco (and Singapore, Hong Kong, São Paulo, Mexico City, Tokyo, London, and New York) *can be crowded with people only because the rest of the world is not.* The Netherlands, for example, imports large amounts of food[9] and extracts from other parts of the world much of the energy and virtually all the materials it requires. It uses an estimated seventeen times more land for food and energy than exists within its borders.[1]

* * *

6. P. Vitousek, P. Ehrlich, A. Ehrlich, and P. Matson, 1986, Human appropriation of the products of photosynthesis. *BioScience* 36:368–373.
7. M. Forbes, 1989, Fact and comment II, *Forbes*, 20 March.
8. P. Ehrlich and J. Holdren, 1971, Impact of population growth, *Science* 171:1212–1217; see also P. Ehrlich and A. Ehrlich, 1972, *Population, Resources, Environment: Issues in Human Ecology* (2nd ed.), W. H. Freeman, San Francisco, p. 257.
9. In 1989–1991, the Netherlands had average net imports of more than 3 million metric tons of cereals and 800,000 metric tons of pulses (peas and beans, including soybeans) (World Resources Institute 1994, *World Resources 1994–95*, Oxford University Press, New York).
1. M. Wackernagel, 1993, *How Big Is Our Ecological Footprint? A Handbook for Estimating a Community's Carrying Capacity*, discussion draft, Task Force on Planning Healthy and Sustainable Communities, University of British Columbia, Department of Family Practice, Mather Building, 5804 Fairview Avenue, Vancouver, B.C., Canada V6T 1Z3, 15 July. The Netherlands' "ecological footprint" or "appropriated carrying capacity" is defined as "the aggregate land (and water) area in various categories required by the people in a region (a) to provide continuously all the resources they presently consume, and (b) to

"Those who are concerned about world hunger are simply wrong."[2]

* * *

The principal problem, of course, is not acute famines; it is chronic undernutrition of huge numbers of extremely poor people. Overall, since *The Population Bomb* was published [1968], roughly 8 to 10 million people (mostly young children) have died each year from hunger and hunger-related diseases, according to studies by the World Bank and other international agencies.[3] And such numbers may well be underestimates. First of all, governments don't like to admit they can't feed their people; and second, starvation compromises the immune system, so often the proximate cause of death—the final blow—is not starvation per se but disease.[4]

Today some 700 to 800 million people, perhaps even as many as a billion, don't get enough food to support normal daily activities.[5] Even if the actual number of hungry people were only half as high, it would still indicate a level of human suffering that doesn't match the rosy views of the brownlash. * * *

---

absorb continuously all the waste they presently discharge, using current technology" (p. 10).

2. See, e.g., R. Bailey, 1993; J. Simon, 1995, Betting on the Future, Australian Broadcasting Company (ABC) television, 30 November.
3. In 1980, there were about 36 million deaths in developing nations, about 16 million of them among children under age five (World Bank, 1993, *World Development Report 1993: Investing in Health*, Oxford University Press, Oxford). The estimate assumes that since 1968 about half of the infant-child deaths were from hunger or hunger-related diseases (see the discussion in World Bank, 1993, ch. 4, especially pp. 75–79 for the current situation, which is an improvement over previous decades). See also World Health Organization, 1995, *The World Health Report 1995; Bridging the Gaps*, World Health Organization, Geneva; and *International Health News*, September 1987, which estimated that over 14 million children were dying annually of hunger and hunger-related disease.
4. See, e.g., W. Beisel, 1984, Nutrition, infection, specific immune responses, and nonspecific host defenses: A complex interaction, in R. Watson (ed.), *Nutrition, Disease Resistance, and Immune Function*, Marcel Dekker, New York, pp. 21–30; G. Harrison and J. Waterlow (eds.), 1990, *Diet and Disease in Traditional Developing Societies*, Cambridge University Press, Cambridge; P. Ellner and H. Neu, 1992, *Understanding Infectious Disease*, Mosby—Year Book, St. Louis, MO.
5. Estimates of the number of chronically malnourished people range from about half a billion (United Nations, 1993, *Report on the World Social Situation 1993*, United Nations, New York, chapter 2; World Food Council, 1992, *The Global State of Hunger and Malnutrition*, WFC/12, World Food Council, New York) to more than a billion (United Nations Children's Fund, 1992, *State of the World's Children 1992*, United Nations, New York; and World Bank estimates cited in R. Kates and V. Haarmann, 1992, Where the poor live: Are the assumptions correct?, *Environment* 34 (4): 5–11, 25–28). The Food and Agriculture Organization of the United Nations (FAO) estimated that 786 million people in developing regions were undernourished in 1988–1990 (Food and Agriculture Organization, 1992, *The State of Food and Agriculture, 1992*, Food and Agriculture Organization, Rome); for a more conservative estimate of hunger in one area, see P. Svedberg, 1991, Undernutrition in sub-Saharan Africa: A critical assessment of the evidence, in J. Dreze and A. Sen (eds.), *The Political Economy of Hunger*, vol. 3, *Endemic Hunger*, Oxford University Press, Oxford, pp. 155–193.

"Feeding the world's population is a problem of distribution, not supply.[6] "Famine is a thing of the past for most of the world's people."[7]

These are two of the most common assertions about food supplies made by the brownlash. There is some truth to the first statement. If there were no maldistribution, if everyone shared equally, and if no grain were fed to animals, all of humanity could be adequately nourished today.[8] Unfortunately, such claims are irrelevant. Although people in developed countries could eat lower on the food chain, it is as unrealistic to think we will all suddenly become vegetarian saints as it is to think we will suddenly trade in our cars for bicycles or go to bed at sunset to save energy.

Overpopulation and carrying capacity are calculated on the basis of animals—and people—as they are, not as we might wish them to be. Human carrying capacity is the *long-term* ability of an area to support human beings. When people are living on natural capital rather than what might be called "natural interest"—sustainable resource flows based on natural capital—then, by definition, carrying capacity is exceeded and the area is overpopulated. The circumstance of overpopulation sometimes can be remedied by changing patterns of behavior without changing the numbers of people—for instance, by adopting vegetarian diets or better soil husbandry practices. Overpopulation exists whenever people trying to produce food allow soil to erode faster than new soil can be generated, or drain aquifers faster than they can be recharged, or exterminate populations and species that are working parts of the ecosystems that support agriculture and fisheries faster than recolonization and speciation can reestablish them. Today overpopulation prevails worldwide.

*   *   *

6. Many writers on the food problem have made this assertion in one form or another; some examples include F. Lappé and J. Collins, 1977, *Food First*, Houghton Mifflin, Boston; M. Swaminathan and S. Sinha (eds.), 1986, *Global Aspects of Food Production*, Tycooly International, Riverton, NJ; R. Lee, W. Arthur, A. Kelley, G. Rodgers, and T. Srinavasan, 1988, *Population, Food, and Rural Development*, Clarendon Press, Oxford; and G. Norton and J. Alwang, 1993, *Introduction to the Economics of Agricultural Development*, McGraw-Hill, New York. These writers focus strongly on the poverty and underdevelopment of rural areas and sometimes on the exploitation of the rural poor by the rich, factors that are important in explaining hunger. But they usually discount the roles of population growth and environmental deterioration in generating the problems and hindering solutions.

7. D. Avery, 1995. Saving the planet with pesticides. In Bailey (ed.), *The True State of the Planet*. Free Press, New York, p. 51.

8. R. Chen (ed.), 1990, *The Hunger Report: 1990*, The Alan Shawn Feinstein World Hunger Program, Brown University, Providence RI; M. Alberti, D. Layton, G. Daily, and P. Ehrlich, 1997, in preparation.

"There is no need to worry about any population-related problem. The human mind is the 'ultimate resource,' and growing populations will always be able to solve their resource problems. We need more people in order to have more geniuses; it would be immoral to keep them from being born."[9]

How typical of the brownlash to define away population problems as self-solving while arguing that limiting the number of people alive at any given time—something virtually all societies have tried to do to one degree or another[1]—is immoral! As Julian Simon put it, "What business do I have trying to help arrange it that fewer human beings will be born, each one of whom might be a Mozart or a Michelangelo or an Einstein—or simply a joy to his or her family or community, and a person who will enjoy life?"[2] The obvious response might be: What business does anyone have trying to help arrange it that more human beings will be born, each one of whom might be a Judas, an Attila the Hun, or a Hitler—or simply a burden to his or her family and community and a person who will live a life that is nasty, brutish and short?

*   *   *

There is no evidence that larger numbers of human beings translates into more talented or more humane individuals. Of course, there is a certain threshold—a community of 50 souls cannot have 100 geniuses. But arguably, Athens with perhaps 50,000 people in the year 425 B.C., had more geniuses than does San Francisco today, with fifteen times the number of citizens.

*   *   *

Whatever the causal relations, contrary to Julian Simon's expectations, as California's population has soared, its quality of life and intellectual potential have fallen. A state school system that ranked as one of the best in the nation now ranks thirty-eighth in expenditures per child and essentially ties with Utah for having the largest classes.[3] The University of California, Berkeley, has lost much of the financial support it needs to remain one of the world's best institutions of higher education, a development that may negatively influence California's economy and quality of life for generations.

9. See, e.g., J. Simon, 1981, *The Ultimate Resource*, Princeton University Press, Princeton, NJ, p. 347.
1. A. Carr-Saunders, 1922, *The Population Problem: A Study in Human Evolution*, Oxford University Press, London; J. Neel, 1970, Lessons from "primitive" people, *Science* 170: 816–817; Ehrlich, Ehrlich, and Daily, 1995, chapter 2.
2. Simon, 1981, p. 10.
3. Yvonne Burtness, Palo Alto School System, personal communication, 3 January 1996. The decline has continued in recent years. In 1992–1993, California was the thirty-sixth state in expenditures per child; it dropped to thirty-eighth by 1994–1995.

*   *   *

The point is that virtually all human individuals have enormous potential, and as soon as there are hundreds or thousands of them together, the appearance of genius of one sort or another is almost assured. Once there are tens of millions, the success of a society cannot be seriously constrained by a lack of brains, only by the environments in which those brains must develop and operate. Put another way, it's very hard to become the next Mozart if one is starving to death on the outskirts of Port-au-Prince! Having more people today is not the solution for generating more geniuses. Creating environments in which the inherent talents of people now disadvantaged—by race or gender discrimination, poverty, malnutrition, or whatever—can be fully expressed is. Indeed, there is every reason to believe that having *fewer* people would make it easier to create those environments. Thus Simon seems to have the genius-population relationship exactly backward: smaller, smoothly-functioning, nurturing societies are far more apt to give rise to geniuses than are large, debt-ridden, disintegrating, and inequitable societies.

If human resources are not necessarily increased by population growth, supplies of other resources—non-living and living—certainly are not enlarged by the explosion of human numbers.

*   *   *

A quick review of some compelling statistics reveals how wrong—and indeed how threatening to humanity's future—the brownlash can be. The roughly fivefold increase in the number of human beings over the past century and a half is the most dramatic terrestrial event since the retreat of ice-age glaciers thousands of years ago. That explosion of human numbers has been combined with about a fourfold increase in consumption per person and the adoption of a wide array of technologies that needlessly damage the environment.

The result has been something like a twentyfold escalation since 1850 of the pressure humanity places on its environment—an unprecedented assault on natural ecosystems. The symptoms of this assault, all clearly linked to overpopulation, include the following:

1. Land degradation, with Earth having already lost some of the potential value of more than 40 percent of its land surface;
2. Deforestation, with about a third of the original forest cover having been removed without replacement since the invention of agriculture and much of the remaining forest highly modified and disrupted;
3. Ecosystem toxification, with thousands of synthetic chemi-

cals being poured into the environment and disturbing signs emerging that many of them interfere with ecosystem functioning, human developmental processes, and human resistance to disease;

4. Loss of biological diversity, with populations and species, which are working parts of our life-support systems, being exterminated at rates unprecedented since the mass extinction 65 million years ago that finished off the dinosaurs;

5. Depletion of Earth's vital ozone shield, which may be corrected by the Montreal Protocol but which still must be considered a potential threat;

6. The prospect of rapid climate change threatening agricultural productivity, causing coastal flooding, and altering the epidemiological environment, made more credible by the news that 1995 was the warmest year on record and the consensus of the scientific community that global warming has arrived;

7. Crop and fisheries production already lagging behind population growth, with little prospect of a new "green revolution" to produce increases in agricultural yields that soon may be desperately needed; and

8. Deterioration of the human epidemiological environment, with causal connections to all of the above, which threatens humankind with great epidemics, the potential seriousness of which is only hinted at by AIDS, recent outbreaks of the Ebola virus, and rapid proliferation of antibiotic-resistant strains of bacteria.

*   *   *

F. Population and Social Dynamics in the Twenty-First Century

BINGHAM KENNEDY JR.

Environmental Scarcity and the Outbreak of Conflict (2001)†

How can environmental problems contribute to civil unrest and violence? The connection is a complicated one, involving several steps and processes. The research led by Thomas Homer-Dixon at the University of Toronto has focused on how environmental scarcity leads to certain destabilizing social effects that make violence more likely.

Environmental scarcity refers to the declining availability of renewable natural resources such as freshwater or soil. There are three basic ways in which such scarcity can arise:

- **Demand-induced scarcity:** Population growth or increasing consumption levels decrease the amount of limited natural resources available to each individual. The population of sub-Saharan Africa, for example, has increased from 177 million in 1950 to 657 million in 2000, shrinking the amount of land and freshwater available to the average person. In the case of Rwanda, demographic pressures created extreme environmental scarcity that played a role in the 1994 genocide.

- **Supply-induced scarcity:** Environmental degradation decreases the overall amount of a limited natural resource, decreasing the amount available to each individual. In western China, overgrazing in portions of the Qinghai-Tibet Plateau

† Bingham Kennedy Jr. (b. 1968) is former associate editor at the Population Reference Bureau. The text is from "Environmental Scarcity and the Outbreak of Conflict," from www.prb.org, January, 2001. Reprinted by permission of the Population Reference Bureau.

has combined with drought to degrade precious topsoil over the past several years. Chinese scientists estimate that 900 square miles of land in the region degrade into desert each year. As a result, herders and farmers have found it increasingly difficult to earn a living in the area.

- **Structural scarcity:** Unequal access to natural resources in a given society makes them scarce for large segments of the population. In South Africa, the system of apartheid provided whites with 87 percent of the land, while blacks (almost 75 percent of the country's population) lived within restricted areas that accounted for only 13 percent of the land. Resources were also inequitably distributed within the restricted areas, as local elites controlled access to productive agriculture and grazing land.

In some cases, different sources of environmental scarcity may interact, exacerbating the problem:

- **Resource capture:** When a resource becomes relatively scarce—say, because of population growth—it often becomes more valuable. This increase in value may motivate powerful groups within society to take greater control of the resource, making it scarcer still. In this way, the demand-induced scarcity that accompanies an increase in population may lead to an increase in structural scarcity following efforts to monopolize the resource.
- **Ecological marginalization:** When vital resources such as fertile land become scarce due to population growth and unequal access, impoverished people often move into ecologically-sensitive areas such as hillsides, tropical rain forests, and areas at risk of desertification. The rising population in these areas, combined with unsustainable land use practices, leads to environmental degradation and further scarcity.

The Philippines is one of many countries in which ecological marginalization has occurred. High rates of population growth—over 2 percent per year—have made cropland relatively scarce in the fertile lowlands, forcing many farmers to move into the less productive uplands. This migration was also encouraged by the fact that the land ownership in the lowlands was concentrated in the hands of a few elite landholders. As the lowland-to-upland migration proceeded, rising cultivation in the ecologically fragile uplands has led to erosion and ecological degradation, further shrinking the supply of available cropland.

These various forms of environmental scarcity can lead to a number of potentially destabilizing social effects, specifically:

- lower agricultural production
- economic stagnation or decline
- migrations from areas of resource scarcity to areas of perceived opportunity
- weakened governing institutions.

While the specific process varies from case to case, Pakistan's experience over the past two decades is illustrative. Rapid population growth, environmental degradation, and inefficient practices led to increasing scarcity of both cropland and water by the early 1990s. This scarcity, along with the spread of agricultural technologies that favored large landholders, helped concentrate valuable land in the hands of the country's economic and military elite (i.e., resource capture). As a result, while agricultural production and the national economy continued to grow, the benefits of this growth were not enjoyed equitably and income inequality has increased. Impoverished rural residents have flooded into cities looking for work, along with refugees from Afghanistan and returning workers from overseas. The influx of migrants overwhelmed municipal services in cities like Karachi, where population growth rates exceeded six percent in the mid-1990s. Squatter settlements were housing an estimated 41 percent of Karachi's population in the early 1990s, and frequent shortages water and electricity aggravated tensions between these and more established communities in the city.

Disruptive social effects such as these, in turn, can lead to violence under certain conditions. If group tensions in society are high, migration and relative deprivation can be a particularly volatile mix. In Pakistan, ethnic conflict became a serious urban problem as the influx of migrants altered the ethnic balance in the cities. The result has been long-running but diffuse urban violence that has simmered since the mid-1980s. The murder rate in Karachi, for example, more than doubled between 1990 and 1994, and attacks on municipal offices—particularly the electricity and water utilities—became common.

In sum, the connection between environmental scarcity and civil violence is indirect but important. Environmental scarcity is never the sole cause of conflict, but it is often an aggravating or contributing factor. Future efforts at conflict prevention and resolution should take the role that environmental scarcity plays into account, and appropriate interventions to prevent demand-, supply-, and structurally-induced scarcity should be pursued.

LESTER R. BROWN

The Emergence of Demographic Fatigue (1999)†

* * * Until the middle of [the twentieth] century, no country had experienced the sustained 3-percent growth that has been posted in scores of developing countries since then. Now with several decades of rapid population growth behind us, we can begin to see some of the effects of such growth. It comes as no surprise that governments in many countries that have experienced rapid growth for nearly two generations are showing signs of demographic fatigue. Worn down by the struggle to deal with the consequences of rapid population growth, they are unable to respond to new threats, such as AIDS, aquifer depletion, and the flooding that can follow deforestation.

Problems routinely managed in industrial societies are becoming full-scale humanitarian crises in many developing ones. As a result, some developing countries with rapidly growing populations that were until recently headed for a doubling of their populations are now looking at population stability, or even population decline—not because of falling birth rates, but because of rapidly rising death rates. This reversal in the death rate trend marks a tragic new development in world demography. In the absence of a concerted effort by national governments and the international community to quickly shift to smaller families, events in many countries could spiral out of control, leading to spreading political instability and economic decline.

To help assess the likelihood that the increases projected by the United Nations will actually occur, we turn to the concept of the demographic transition, formulated by Princeton demographer Frank Notestein in 1945. Among other things, its three stages help explain widely disparate population growth rates. In the first stage, which prevails in preindustrial societies, birth rates and death rates are both high, essentially offsetting each other and leading to little or no population growth. As countries begin to modernize, however, death rates fall and countries enter stage two, where death rates are low while birth rates remain high. At this point, population growth typically reaches 3 percent a year. Countries cannot remain in this stage long.[1]

† Lester R. Brown (b. 1934) is president of the Earth Policy Institute. The text is from his *Beyond Malthus: Nineteen Dimensions of the Population Challenge* (New York, 1999). Reprinted by permission of W. W. Norton & Company.
1. Frank Notestein, "Population—The Long View," in F. M. Schulz, ed., *Food for the World* (University of Chicago Press: 1945); Warren Thompson, "Population," *American Journal of Sociology*, vol. 34, no. 6 (1929).

As modernization continues, birth rates fall and countries enter the third and final stage of the demographic transition, when birth rates and death rates again balance, but at low levels. At this point, population size stabilizes.

*   *   *

The question now facing the world is whether the 160 or so countries that are still in stage two, with continuing population growth, can make it into stage three by quickly reducing births. Over the next half-century, most countries where population growth is still substantial seem likely to break out of stage two, achieving the demographic stability of stage three. In these nations, the combination of falling fertility, rising incomes, and rising educational levels will lead to population stabilization within the foreseeable future. Economic and social gains and the decline in fertility will reinforce each other.

This can be seen most clearly in the developing countries of East Asia, such as South Korea and Taiwan, where successful early efforts to reduce fertility set the stage for the diversion of capital from rearing large numbers of children to investment in modernization and the overall improvement of living conditions. As the number of children per couple declined, so too did dependency ratios—the proportion of the nonworking dependent population, primarily children, to the working-age population—easing the financial burden of supporting these dependents. The freeing of funds allowed increased savings rates and investment, leading ultimately to enhanced productivity, strong economic growth, and rising incomes. The resulting improvements in living standards then reinforced the trend to smaller families.[2]

Countries that are already pressing against the limits of land and water resources and that are faced with a projected doubling or tripling of their population may face falling living standards that will further reinforce the prevailing high fertility. This reinforcing mechanism, referred to by demographers as the demographic trap, could keep living standards at the subsistence level, and eventually lead to rising mortality as the land and water resource base deteriorates, driving countries back into stage one.

Nations in stage two where population is still growing rapidly will thus either shift quickly to smaller families and advance to stage three or eventually fall back into stage one of the demographic transition when their economic and social systems break down under mounting population pressure. One or the other of the two self-reinforcing cycles will take over. There are no other options. Among the many countries at risk of falling back into stage one if they do

2. Rodolfo A. Bulatao, *The Value of Family Planning Programs in Developing Countries* (Santa Monica, CA: RAND, 1998).

not quickly check their population growth are Afghanistan, Egypt, Ethiopia, Ghana, Haiti, Honduras, India, Myanmar, Nigeria, Pakistan, the Sudan, Tanzania, and Yemen.

Governments of countries that have been in stage two for several decades are typically worn down and drained of financial resources by the consequences of rapid population growth, in effect suffering from demographic fatigue. This includes trying to educate ever growing numbers of children reaching school age, creating jobs for the swelling numbers of young people entering the job market, and dealing with the various environmental problems associated with rapid population growth, such as deforestation, increased flooding, soil erosion, and aquifer depletion.

With leadership and fiscal resources stretched thin in trying to cope with so many pressures at once, governments are often unable to respond effectively to emerging threats such as water shortages or food shortages. This is perhaps most evident in the inability of many governments to cope with new diseases, such as AIDS, or the resurgence of more traditional ones, such as malaria or tuberculosis.

If these threats are not dealt with, they can force countries back into stage one. For several African countries with high HIV infection levels, this is no longer a hypothetical prospect. Although industrial nations have been able to control the spread of the disease, holding infection levels under 1 percent of their populations, governments in many developing countries—already overwhelmed by the pressures just described—have not been able to do so.

＊   ＊   ＊

There is no recent historical example for an infectious disease threatening to take so many lives as the HIV epidemic. To find a precedent for such a potentially devastating loss of life from an infectious disease, we have to go back to the decimation of New World Indian communities by the introduction of smallpox in the sixteenth century or to the bubonic plague that claimed roughly a fourth of Europe's population during the fourteenth century. The HIV epidemic should be seen for what it is—an epidemic of epic proportions that, if not checked soon, could claim more lives during the early part of the twenty-first century than World War II did during the twentieth century.[3]

Another situation that could easily become unmanageable is life-

3. The HIV/AIDS pandemic also differs substantially from past plagues in the disease gestation period. While the Black Death, smallpox, and influenza all had short gestations typical of global plagues, with victims succumbing within days or weeks of infection, HIV/AIDS has an unusually long gestation. Adults typically die within 5–10 years of HIV infection, though costly antiretroviral therapies can extend lifespans; children generally die within 6 months to 2 years of infection. The lengthened gestation leads to a slow-steady growth pattern, rather than a boom-bust, as with other plagues, complicating responsive public health measures and making the disease particularly insidious.

threatening shortages of food due to either land or water shortages or both. For example, Pakistan and Nigeria face an impossible challenge in trying to feed their future populations as their cropland per person promises to shrink below the survival level. The projected growth for Pakistan to 345 million by 2050 will reduce its grainland per person from 0.08 hectares at present to 0.03 hectares, roughly the strip between the 10-yard markers on a football field. Nigeria's projected growth will reduce its grainland per person from the currently inadequate 0.15 hectares to 0.07 hectares.[4]

As India's population approaches the 1 billion mark and as it faces the addition of another 500 million people by 2050, it must deal with steep cutbacks in irrigation water. David Seckler, head of the International Water Management Institute in Sri Lanka, the world's premier water research body, observes in a new study that "the extraction of water from aquifers in India exceeds recharge by a factor of 2 or more. Thus almost everywhere in India, fresh-water aquifers are being pulled down by 1–3 meters per year."[5]

Seckler goes on to speculate that as aquifers are depleted, the resulting cutbacks in irrigation could reduce India's harvest by 25 percent. In a country where food supply and demand are precariously balanced and where 18 million people are added to the population each year, the cutbacks in irrigation that are in prospect could drop food supplies below the survival level, creating a national food emergency.[6]

*　*　*

The issues discussed here raise several complex questions. For example, what is the psychological effect on a society that loses a substantial share of its adult population in a matter of years? What happens when aquifer depletion starts shrinking the food supply in countries with fast-growing populations? Will governments that have permitted AIDS to decimate their populations or that have allowed aquifers to be depleted lose their legitimacy and be voted out or overthrown? No one knows the answer to these questions because continuing population growth and the problems it eventually generates are taking the world into uncharted territory.

As demographic fatigue sets in and the inability of governments to deal effectively with the consequences of rapid population growth becomes more evident, the resulting social stresses are likely to exacerbate conflicts among differing religious, ethnic, tribal, or geographic groups within societies. Among these are differences

4. From U.S. Department of Agriculture (USDA), *Production, Supply, and Distribution*, electronic database, Washington, DC, updated December 1998, note 3.
5. David Seckler, David Molden, and Randolph Barker, "Water Scarcity in the Twenty-First Century" (Colombo, Sri Lanka: International Water Management Institute, 27 July 1998).
6. Ibid.

between Hindus and Moslems in India; Yorubas, Ibos, and Hausas in Nigeria; Arabs and Israelis in the Middle East; Hutus and Tutsis in Rwanda and Burundi; and many others. Aside from enormous social costs, these spreading conflicts could drive countless millions across national borders as they seek safety, putting pressure on industrial countries to admit them as political refugees.

As pressures on the Earth's resources build, they may also lead to international conflicts over shared water resources, oceanic fisheries, or other scarce resources. Nowhere is the potential conflict over scarce water more stark than among the three principal countries of the Nile River valley—Egypt, the Sudan, and Ethiopia. In Egypt, where it rarely rains, agriculture is almost wholly dependent on water from the Nile. Egypt now gets the lion's share of the Nile's water, but its current population of 66 million is projected to reach 115 million by 2050, thus greatly boosting the demand for grain, even without any gains in per capita consumption.

The Sudan, whose population is projected to double from 29 million today to 59 million by 2050, also depends heavily on the Nile. The population of Ethiopia, the country that controls 85 percent of the headwaters of the Nile, is projected to expand from 58 million to 169 million. With little Nile water now reaching the Mediterranean, if either of the two upstream countries, Sudan or Ethiopia, use more water, Egypt will get less.[7]

After the political situation stabilized in Ethiopia, national attention turned to economic development and the government built 200 small dams. Although these are collectively taking only 500 million cubic meters of water out of the Nile's total flow of 85 billion cubic meters, the government plans to use much more of the Nile's water as it expands power generation and irrigation in the effort to lift its people out of poverty.[8]

With gross national product per person in Ethiopia averaging only $100 per year compared with $1,080 in Egypt, it is difficult to argue that the former should not use more of the Nile's water. As the collective population of these three countries expands by 190 million, going from 153 million at present to 343 million in 2050, it is simply outstripping the local supply of water. Although it is only one of the many potential conflicts that could be triggered as population pressures mount, this one—involving both Muslims and Christians—could destabilize the entire Middle East.

The adverse effects of population growth will affect citizens in seemingly far removed nations, such as the United States or Germany, as globalization increasingly defines national economies and domestic welfare. As economist Herman Daly observes, whereas in

7. Sandra Postel, *Pillar of Sand* (New York; W. W. Norton & Commpany, 1999).
8. Ibid.

the past surplus labor in one nation had the effect of driving down wages only in that nation, "global economic integration will be the means by which the consequences of overpopulation in the Third World are generalized to the globe as a whole." Large infusions into Brazil's or India's work force that may lower wages in those nations mean large infusions into the global work force with potentially similar consequences.[9]

As the recent Asian economic downturn further demonstrates, "localized instability" is becoming an anachronistic concept. The consequences of social unrest in one nation, whether resulting from a currency crisis or an environmental crisis, can quickly cross national boundaries. Several nations, including the United States, now recognize world population growth as a national security issue with economic, environmental, and military consequences. As the U.S. Department of State Strategic Plan, issued in September 1997, explains, "Stabilizing population growth is vital to U.S. interests. . . . Not only will early stabilization of the world's population promote environmentally sustainable economic development in other countries, but it will benefit the U.S. by improving trade opportunities and mitigating future global crises."[1]

As we look to the future, the challenge for world leaders is to help countries maximize the prospects for breaking out of stage two of the demographic transition and moving into stage three before demographic fatigue takes over and nature brutally forces them back into stage one.

In a world where both grain output and fish catch per person are falling, a strong case can be made on humanitarian grounds for an all-out effort to stabilize world population. There is nothing inevitable about a projected mid-century population of 8.9 billion. We can choose to move to the lower trajectory of the three U.N. projection scenarios, which has world population stabilizing at 7.3 billion by 2050. This would reduce the number to be added by 2050 from 2.8 billion to a more manageable 1.3 billion.[2]

What is needed, to use a basketball term, is a full-court press—an all-out effort to lower fertility, particularly in high-fertility countries, before demographic fatigue takes over, leading to higher mortality and forcing countries back into stage one of the demographic transition. We see two parts to this effort: national carrying capacity assessments to help governments and the public at large to better

9. Herman E. Daly, "Population and Economic Globalization," *Organization & Environment*, December 1998.
1. Craig Lasher, "U.S. Population Policy Since the Cairo Conference," *Environmental Change and Security Project Report*, The Woodrow Wilson Center, spring 1998.
2. Population trajectories from United Nations, *World Population Prospects: The 1998 Revision* (New York: December 1998).

understand the urgency of stabilizing population, and national population programs that bring population growth rates under control by emphasizing the empowerment of women, strengthening health care, and promoting family planning.

Two hundred years ago, Thomas Malthus advanced humanity's understanding of carrying capacity through his insights into the population-food supply relationship. Today, our understanding of carrying capacity encompasses many of the dimensions discussed in this book, and the tools used are far more sophisticated. Malthus would be astonished at the variables used in today's analyses of carrying capacity with regard to food.

We know, for example, what every country's crop-land area is and roughly what it will be a half-century from now. Current hydrological data give us a good sense of how much water will be available for each country in 2050, assuming no major changes in climate. And we know that annual increases in yields—the engine of growth in world food production over the past 50 years—will likely continue to slow, as crop yields in more countries push up against physiological limits.[3]

With this information, governments can calculate their population carrying capacity for food, and assess their population policy in light of the results. And they can do similar analyses of their country's need for materials, energy, waste absorption, and other dimensions of carrying capacity.

*   *   *

Given the limits to the carrying capacity of each country's natural resources, every government now needs a carefully articulated and adequately supported population policy, one that takes into account the country's carrying capacity at whatever consumption level citizens decide on. As Harvard biologist Edward O. Wilson observes in his landmark book *The Diversity of Life,* "Every nation has an economic policy and a foreign policy. The time has come to speak more openly of a population policy. By this I mean not just the capping of growth when the population hits the wall, as in China and India, but a policy based on a rational solution of this problem; what, in the judgment of its informed citizenry, is the optimal population?"[4]

Once the urgency of the population challenge becomes apparent to governments and citizens, population programs—the second part of the equation—form the backbone of a national population policy

3. Thomas R. Sinclair, "Limits to Crop Yield?" in American Society of Agronomy, Crop Science Society of America, and Soil Science Society of America, *Physiology and Determination of Crop Yield* (Madison, WI: 1994).
4. Edward O. Wilson, *The Diversity of Life* (New York: W.W. Norton & Company, 1993).

by offering the means to reduce fertility rates and stabilize population.

*   *   *

We live in a demographically divided world—one where some countries have reached or are approaching the stability of stage three of the demographic transition and one where rising mortality is forcing other countries back into stage one. Despite this sharpening contrast, our world is more environmentally integrated and more economically interdependent than ever before. In this integrated world, there are no longer "their problems" and "our problems." Only our problems.

G. Some Contemporary Critics of Malthusianism

FRANCES MOORE LAPPÉ, JOSEPH COLLINS, AND PETER ROSSET

Beyond the Myths of Hunger (1998)†

* * * In all of our educational efforts during the past twenty-five years, no question has been more common than Do too many people cause hunger? We've answered no, but in the eyes of some this is tantamount to irresponsibly dismissing population growth as a problem.

We do not take lightly the prospect of human numbers so dominating the planet that other forms of life are squeezed out, that all wilderness is subdued for human use, and that the mere struggle to feed and warm ourselves keeps us from more satisfying pursuits.

The question of population is so vital that we can't afford to be the least bit fuzzy in our thinking. So here we will focus on the three most critical questions this myth poses. Is the human population of the world growing "out of control"? Are population density and population growth the cause of hunger? And what is the nature of the link, if any, between slowing population growth and ending hunger?

* * *

It has become clear that human fertility and population growth rates are dropping rapidly around the world. In the early 1950s, when we began to hear echoes of Thomas Malthus in warnings of an impending population explosion, the global total fertility rate (the number of children per woman) was five, more than double the

† Frances Morre Lappé (b. 1944) is president of the Center for Living Democracy. Joseph Collins (b. 1945), is a cofounder of the Institute for Food and Development Policy. Peter Rosset (b. 1955), is codirector of Food First/The Institute for Food and Development Policy. The text is from their *World Hunger: 12 Myths* (New York, 1998). Reprinted by permission of Grove Press.

replacement rate of 2.1 (the number that gives a stable population size over time).[1] By the late 1970s the total fertility rate had fallen to four, and by the mid-1990s it was 2.8 and dropping.

*   *   *

There is abundant evidence that the human population-growth rate is slowing and will eventually stop. It is hardly out of control. Populations will continue to grow rapidly for several decades before leveling off in many third world countries, but that does not, in and of itself, mean that population density or growth causes hunger in our world, an issue we address in the following section.

Does "Overpopulation" Cause Hunger?

Our second question can now be restated as: Do too many people *already* cause hunger? If that were the case, then reducing population density might indeed alleviate hunger. But for one factor to cause another, the two must consistently occur together. Population density and hunger do not.

Hunger is not caused by too many people sharing the land. In the Central America and Caribbean region, for example, Trinidad and Tobago show the lowest percentage of stunted children under five and Guatemala the highest (almost twelve times greater); yet Trinidad and Tobago's cropland per person—a key indicator of human population density—is less than half that of Guatemala's.[2]

*   *   *

But what about population growth? Is there not an obvious correlation between rapid population growth and hunger? Without doubt, most hungry people live in Asia, Africa, and Latin America, where populations have grown fastest in recent decades. This association of hunger and rapid population growth certainly suggests a relationship between the two. But what we want to probe is the nature of that link. Does rapid population growth cause hunger, or do they occur together because they are both consequences of similar social realities?

In 1989 Cornell University sociologists Frederick Buttel and

1. Unless indicated otherwise, all population growth and fertility figures in this chapter come from *World Population Prospects: The 1996 Revision*, the conservative and most widely accepted set of population data and projections, produced periodically by the highly regarded Population Division of the Department for Economic and Social Information and Policy Analysis, United Nations, New York. The projections produced by the division are known popularly as the "UN Projections."
2. 1990 hectares-per-capita values are: Trinidad and Tobago 0.09, Guatemala 0.20 (World Resources Institute, *World Resources 1922–93* [New York: Oxford University Press, 1992], table 18.2). 1987 prevalence-of-stunted-children values are: Trinidad 5.0, Guatemala 57.9 (Food and Agricultural Organization, *The Sixth World Food Survey* [Rome: FAO, 1996], table 8; appendix 2).

Laura Raynolds published a careful study of population growth, food consumption, and other variables in ninety-three third world countries.[3] Their statistical analysis found no evidence that rapid population growth causes hunger. What they did find was that the populations of poorer countries, and those countries where the poorest 20 percent of the population earned a smaller percentage of a nation's total income, had less to eat. In other words, poverty and inequality cause hunger.

*   *   *

No one should discount the consequences of high population density, including the difficulties it can add to the already great challenge of development. While in some African countries low population density has been an obstacle to sustainable agricultural development, in many countries much higher population densities would make more difficult the tasks of social and economic restructuring necessary to eliminate hunger. But if it is eliminating hunger that we are after, then we should attack poverty, inequality, and powerlessness head on. That is especially true as they are the root causes of high fertility and rapid population growth. Improving living standards and lessening inequality, including providing education for women, have proven to be the best ways to lower fertility.

The Challenge Ahead

In this brief chapter, we've outlined what we believe are the critical points too often muddled in discussions of population:

- Fertility and population-growth rates are declining worldwide.
- Population density nowhere explains today's widespread hunger.
- Rapid population growth is not the root cause of hunger but is—like hunger—a consequence of social inequities that deprive the poor majority, especially poor women, of the security and economic opportunity necessary for them to choose fewer children.
- To bring the human population into balance with economic resources and the environment, societies must address the extreme maldistribution of access to resources—land, jobs, food, education, and health care. That is our real challenge.
- Family planning cannot by itself reduce population growth, though it can speed a decline. Family planning can best con-

---

3. Frederick H. Buttel and Laura T. Raynolds, "Population Growth, Agrarian Structure, Food Production, and Food Distribution in the Third World," in *Food and Natural Resources*, ed. David Pimentel and Carl W. Hall (New York: Academy Press, 1989), 325–361.

tribute to the transition when it is but one part of comprehensive changes in health care that expand human freedom and opportunity rather than control behavior.

We believe that precisely because population growth is such a critical problem, we cannot waste time with approaches that do not work. We must unflinchingly face the evidence telling us that the fate of the world hinges on the fate of today's poor majorities. Only as their well-being improves can we attack hunger and assure that fertility decline is sustainable.

To attack high birth rates without attacking the causes of poverty and the disproportionate powerlessness of people is fruitless. It is a tragic diversion our small planet can ill afford.

*   *   *

Some approaches to world hunger elicit our guilt (that we have so much) or our fear (that they will take it from us). Others imply impossible tradeoffs. Do we protect the environment or grow needed food? Do we seek a just or an efficient food system? Do we choose freedom or the elimination of hunger?

But our search for the roots of hunger has led us to a number of positive principles that neither place our deeply held values in conflict nor pit our interests against those of the hungry. We offer the following principles as working hypotheses, not to be carved in stone but to be tested through experience:

- Since hunger results from human choices, not inexorable natural forces, the goal of ending hunger is obtainable. It is no more utopian than the goal of abolishing slavery was, not all that long ago.
- While slowing population growth in itself cannot end hunger, the very changes necessary to end hunger—the democratization of economic life, especially the empowerment of women—are key to reducing birth rates so that the human population can come into balance with the rest of the natural world.
- Ending hunger does not necessitate destroying our environment. On the contrary, it requires protecting it by using agricultural methods that are both ecologically sustainable and within the reach of the poor.
- Greater fairness does not undercut the production of needed food. The only path to increased production that can end hunger is to devise food systems in which those who do the work have a greater say and reap a greater reward.
- We need not fear the advance of the poor in the third world. Their increased well-being can enhance our own.

These and other liberating principles point to possibilities for narrowing the unfortunate rifts we sometimes observe among those concerned about the environment, population growth, and world hunger.

* * *

ERIC B. ROSS

The Malthus Factor (1998)†

* * *

The view that poverty is "natural" has a long history. But what Malthus did for the first time was to purport to have discovered a "law of nature" which explained poverty as natural and inevitable.

* * *

Malthus and those who thought like him acted as if they believed that wholly different laws of nature applied to the rich and the poor. Poverty may have been the inevitable fate of most people, but it was certainly not theirs.

* * *

But what Malthus commended was a choice between the entirely impractical path of moral restraint and the crueller alternative represented by the operation of what he termed "the laws of nature."[1] The seeming paradox of his position is fairly easily resolved by appreciating that Malthusian theory never aimed to be the basis of a policy of fertility regulation. On the contrary, it not only suggested that the fertility of the poor was the main source of their poverty, but implied that it was actually best if that fertility was not significantly controlled by human intervention, because that would reduce poverty and with it the chief stimulus for the poor to seek work.

* * *

While he is famous for arguing that poverty was the result of "the natural tendency of the labouring classes of society to increase beyond the demand for their labour, or the means of adequate support",[2] he also viewed population growth and competition among

† Eric B. Ross is an anthropologist at the Institute of Social Studies. The text is from his *The Malthus Factor: Population, Poverty and Politics in Capitalist Development* (London, 1998). Reprinted by permission of Zed Books.
1. Thomas Malthus, *A Summary View of the Principle of Population* (London, 1830), p. 41
2. Ibid., p. 74.

workers as "a necessary stimulus to industry". As I have suggested, he had no intention of removing such pressures, but only of reducing the material obligation of the rich to mitigate the human misery caused by chronic or periodic unemployment. Such an obligation was, in his view, fundamentally incompatible with the ultimate rights of private property.[3] So it was that his so-called law of population acquitted the property-owning class of any such accountability, by arguing that poverty was the "natural" product of the fertility of the poor, rather than of the social or economic system. The solution therefore was a matter of individual, not systemic, responsibility.

*   *   *

His principle of population was meant to hold the struggle for a better world for the majority in check. Even if the poor wanted, at least, to address the question of how to exert some control over their fertility—not because this would resolve every economic or social problem, but because it might contribute to their aspirations to participate more fully in the determination of their own fate—Malthus again counselled against any expectation that human effort could be effective. "It is to the laws of nature, therefore," he wrote in 1830, "and not to the conduct and institutions of man, that we are to attribute the necessity of a strong check on the natural increase of population."[4]

It is hardly surprising that Malthus had no wish to advocate effective human means of limiting population. If the reproduction of the poor was necessary for the production of wealth and if poverty was necessary to make the poor work cheaply, the pressure of population on the means of subsistence was, as Marx and Engels argued, part of the fundamental and necessary dynamic of capitalist economy. That remains true today, and it has made Malthusianism an equally necessary element of mystification in the dynamic of capitalist ideology. It has ensured that, while Malthus is remembered chiefly as the originator of a theoretical perspective which has left us with an unremitting anxiety about "over-population", his greatest achievement, in fact, was to devise such an enduring argument for the prevention of social and economic change.

While such an argument has impressed intellectuals and proven useful for policy-makers, it has never managed to constrain the aspirations and the dreams of the poor. That would not have escaped Malthus's attention, especially when the Swing uprisings of 1830 reached the county of Hertford where Haileybury is situated. As such events, locally or magnified on a larger scale, from the French Revolution to the peasant revolutions of the twentieth century, from the

3. Ibid., p. 73.
4. Ibid., p. 41.

Russian Revolution through the decades of the Cold War, have frightened the rich and privileged, for whom "over-population" has always simply been a short-hand for "the majority", they have ensured that Malthusianism would be continually revived and revised in the defence of the changing strategic interests of capital.

As an ideological framework which naturalised poverty, which sought to reconcile the contradiction between hunger and abundance by attributing poverty and starvation to personal inadequacy and excess fertility, contested the philosophical premises of socialism and defended the private property system for over a century, the Malthusian vision acquired a firm place in the ideology of capitalism. With the inclusion of "birth control" in its practical armoury, it has proven to be a perspective which, in its compelling simplicity and practical application, could give the cover of legitimacy to Western interests, as expressed in their development theories and strategies (such as the Green Revolution), in a world defined by those interests as engaged in a fundamental struggle between systems based on private or collective ownership, capital or labour. Among the many explanations of poverty—genetic, cultural, environmental, etc.—which depend for their credibility on a superficial and opportunistic reading of history, none ever has managed to achieve the effect of the Malthusian argument because, in presenting over-population as the root cause of most human ills, it could always threaten us with such apocalyptic scenarios that reasoned debate about alternative explanations has been consistently overwhelmed. The fear of pending famine has systematically distracted attention from the fact that it is not the reproductive habits of the poor, but the contradictions and motives of capitalist development—of the morbid inequalities upon which the productive potential of such a system is based—that are the principal source of most of the misuse or waste of the world's human and material resources.

As we shall see, Malthusianism has been employed, not only to justify policies designed to resist criticism of such development, but also to contain the potential for the revolutionary transformation of capitalist economy throughout (but not only within) the developing world. From Ireland in the early nineteenth century to India, Guatemala and the Philippines in the mid-twentieth, it has rationalised development policies—above all, the advance of commercial agriculture—which have led to the gradual displacement of peasant cultivators. The aim of the present work is to explore how and why this has happened; to question the validity of the Malthusian vision of the necessity of inequality, of a world deemed incapable of progressive change; and to challenge the economic and political agenda of those who have gainfully employed that vision. In so doing, it seeks to reaffirm the priority of the hopes of the many over the privileges of the few.

JULIAN L. SIMON

The Ultimate Resource (1996)†

Preview of the Book

Here follow some of the main conclusions of the book. * * *

Food. Contrary to popular impression, food production per capita has been increasing for the half-century since World War II, the only decades for which we have acceptable data. We also know that famine has progressively diminished for at least the past century. Average height has increased in developed countries in recent centuries, a sign that people are eating better. And there is compelling reason to believe that human nutrition will continue to improve into the indefinite future, even with continued population growth.

Land. Agricultural land is not a fixed resource. Rather, the amount of agricultural land has been increasing substantially, and it is likely to continue to increase where needed. Paradoxically, in the countries that are best supplied with food, such as the United States, the quantity of land under cultivation has been *decreasing* because it is more economical to raise larger yields on less land than to increase the total amount of farmland. For this reason, among others, the amount of land used for forests, recreation, and wildlife has been increasing rapidly in the United States—hard to believe, but substantiated beyond a doubt.

Natural resources. Hold your hat—our supplies of natural resources are not finite in any economic sense. Nor does past experience give reason to expect natural resources to become more scarce. Rather, if history is any guide, natural resources will progressively become less costly, hence less scarce, and will constitute a smaller proportion of our expenses in future years. Population growth is likely to have a long-run beneficial impact on the natural-resource situation.

Energy. Grab your hat again—the long-run future of our energy supply is at least as bright as that of other natural resources, though government intervention can temporarily boost prices from time to time. Finiteness is no problem here either. And the long-run impact

---

† Julian L. Simon (1932–1998) was a professor of business administration at the University of Maryland. The text is from his *The Ultimate Resource 2* (Princeton, N.J., 1996). Reprinted by permission of Princeton University Press.

of additional people is likely to speed the development of cheap energy supplies that are almost inexhaustible.

Pollution. This set of issues is as complicated as you wish to make it. But even many ecologists, as well as most economists, agree that population growth is not the villain in the creation and reduction of pollution. And the key trend is that life expectancy, which is the best overall index of the pollution level, has improved markedly as the world's population has grown. This reflects the enormous decline during the past couple of centuries in the most important pollutions—diseases borne by air and water.

The standard of living. In the short run, additional children imply additional costs, though the costs to persons other than the children's parents are relatively small. In the longer run, however, per capita income is likely to be higher with a growing population than with a stationary one, both in more-developed and less-developed countries. Whether you wish to pay the present costs for the future benefits depends on how you weigh the future relative to the present; this is a value judgment.

Human fertility. The contention that poor and uneducated people breed without constraint is demonstrably wrong, even for the poorest and most "primitive" societies. Well-off people who believe that the poor do not weigh the consequences of having more children are simply arrogant, or ignorant, or both.

Future population growth. Population forecasts are published with confidence and fanfare. Yet the record of even the official forecasts made by U.S. government agencies and by the UN is little (if any) better than that of the most naive predictions.

For example, experts in the 1930s foresaw the U.S. population declining, perhaps to as little as 100 million people well before the turn of the century. In 1989, the U.S. Census Bureau forecast that U.S. population would peak at 302 million in 2038 and then decline. Just three years later, the Census Bureau forecast 383 million in 2050 with no peaking in sight. The science of demographic forecasting clearly has not yet reached perfection.

Present trends suggest that even though total population for the world is increasing, the density of population on most of the world's surface will decrease. This is already happening in the developed countries. Although the total populations of developed countries increased from 1950 to 1990, the rate of urbanization was sufficiently great that population density on *most* of their land areas (say,

97 percent of the land area of the United States) has been decreasing. As the poor countries become richer, they will surely experience the same trends, leaving most of the world's surface progressively less populated, astonishing as this may seem.

Immigration. The migration of people from poor to rich countries is as close to an everybody-wins government policy as can be. Countries in North America and Western Europe thereby advance just about all their national goals—higher productivity, a higher standard of living, and an easing of the heavy social burdens caused by growing proportions of aged dependents. And of course the immigrants benefit. Even the sending countries benefit on balance from the remittances that immigrants send back, and from improved ties between the countries. Amazingly, immigration does not even increase native unemployment measurably, even among low-income groups. * * *

Pathological effects of population density. Many worry that mental health is worse in more densely populated areas. This idea was reinforced by research on animal populations. But this putative drawback of population growth has been falsified by psychological studies of humans.

Similar "common sense" convinces many people—including the powers-that-be in the CIA—that population growth increases the likelihood of wars. The data show otherwise.

World population policy. The first edition documented that tens of millions of U.S. taxpayers' dollars are being used to tell the governments and people of other countries that they ought to reduce their fertility. The long-time head of the Population Branch of the U.S. State Department Agency for International Development (AID)— for many years the single most important U.S. population official— publicly said that the United States should act to reduce fertility worldwide *for the country's own economic self-interest.* And a secret policy assessment issued by the National Security Council in 1974— finally declassified in 1989, but with many pages still blacked out— specifies population-control activities for U.S. governmental agents to carry out in various countries, especially Africa; this includes twisting the arms of foreign governments in a variety of ways to ensure "cooperation." But economic data and analyses do not justify this policy. Furthermore, might not such acts be an unwarranted (and resented) interference in the internal affairs of other countries?

Domestic population activities. The first edition also documented that other millions of public dollars go to private organizations in the population lobby whose directors believe that, for environmental and related reasons, fewer Americans should be born. With these funds they propagandize the rest of us to believe—and act—in ways consistent with the views of such organizations as the Population Crisis Committee, the Population Reference Bureau, the Worldwatch Institute, and the Association for Voluntary Sterilization.

Still other tens of millions of U.S. tax dollars target the fertility of the poor in the United States. The explicit justification for this policy (given by the head of Planned Parenthood's Alan Guttmacher Institute) is that it will keep additional poor people off the welfare rolls. Even if this were proven—which it has not been, so far as I know—is this policy in the spirit or tradition of America? Furthermore, there is statistical proof that the public birth control clinics, which were first opened in large numbers in the poorer southern states, were positioned to reduce fertility among blacks.

Involuntary sterilization. Also shown in the first edition: Tax monies are used to involuntarily sterilize poor people (often black) without medical justification. As a result of the eugenics movement, which has been intertwined with the population-control movement for decades, there were (when last I checked) laws in thirty states providing for the involuntary sterilization of the mentally defective. These laws have led to many perfectly normal poor women being sterilized without their knowledge, after being told that their operations were other sorts of minor surgery.

In the chapters to come, you will find evidence documenting these and many other surprising statements about resources, population, environment, and their interconnections. You will also find a foundation of economic theory that makes sense of the surprising facts.

* * *

POPE PAUL VI

Humanae Vitae (1968)†

* * *

2. The changes which have taken place are in fact noteworthy and of varied kind. In the first place, there is the rapid demographic development. Fear is shown by many that world population is growing more rapidly than the available resources, with growing distress

---

† Pope Paul VI (1897–1978) became pope in 1963. The text is from the papal encyclical *Humanae Vitae* (July 25, 1968).

to many families and developing countries, so that the temptation for authorities to counter this danger with radical measures is great.

* * *

10. * * * conjugal love requires in husband and wife an awareness of their mission of "responsible parenthood," which today is rightly much insisted upon, and which also must be exactly understood. Consequently it is to be considered under different aspects which are legitimate and connected with one another.

In relation to the biological processes, responsible parenthood means the knowledge and respect of their functions; human intellect discovers in the power of giving life biological laws which are part of the human person.[1]

In relation to the tendencies of instinct or passion, responsible parenthood means that necessary dominion which reason and will must exercise over them.

In relation to physical, economic, psychological and social conditions, responsible parenthood is exercised, either by the deliberate and generous decision to raise a numerous family, or by the decision, made for grave motives and with due respect for the moral law, to avoid for the time being, or even for an indeterminate period, a new birth.

* * *

14. In conformity with these landmarks in the human and Christian vision of marriage, we must once again declare that the direct interruption of the generative process already begun, and, above all, directly willed and procured abortion, even if for therapeutic reasons, are to be absolutely excluded as licit means of regulating birth.[2]

Equally to be excluded, as the teaching authority of the church has frequently declared, is direct sterilization, whether perpetual or temporary, whether of the man or of the woman.

15. Similarly excluded is every action which, either in anticipation of the conjugal act or in its accomplishment, or in the development of its natural consequences, proposes, whether as an end or as a means, to render procreation impossible.[3]

* * *

1. Cf. St. Thomas, "Summa Theologia," 1–11, Q. 94, art. 2.
2. Cf. Catechismus Romanus Concilii Tridentini, Part II, Ch. VIII; Pius XI, Encyc. "Casti Connubi," in A.A.S. XXII (1930), pp. 562–64; Pius XII, Discorai e Radiomessaggi, VI (1944), pp. 191–92; A.A.S. XLIII (1951), pp. 842–43; pp. 857–59; John XXIII, Encyc. "Pacem in Terris," Apr. II, 1963, in A.A.S. LV (1963), pp. 259–60; "Gaudium et Spes," No. 51.
3. Cf. Catechismus Romanus Concilii tridentini, Part II, Ch. VIII; Pius XII, A.A.S. XLIII (1951), p. 843; A.A.S. L (1958), pp. 734–35; John XXIII, Encyc. "Mater et Magistra," in A.A.S. LIII (1961), p. 447.

23. To rulers, who are those principally responsible for the common good, and who can do so much to safeguard moral customs, we say: Do not allow the morality of your peoples to be degraded; do not permit that by legal means practices contrary to the natural and divine law be introduced into that fundamental cell, the family.[4]

*   *   *

Given at Rome, from St. Peter's, this twenty-fifth day of July, feast of St. James the Apostle, in the year nineteen hundred and sixty-eight, the sixth of our pontificate.

---

4. At the United Nations General Assembly in 1965, Pope Paul VI, addressing the delegates of hunger-plagued nations, denounced population limitation and called for more babies to join in the "banquet of life." [*Editor*]

H. Rethinking Endless Population Growth

JOEL E. COHEN

How Many People Can the Earth Support? (1995)†

* * *

Though the future is hazy, much that is very clear can be known about the present. First, the size and speed of growth of the human population today have no precedent in all the Earth's history before the last half of the twentieth century. Human numbers currently exceed 5.7 billion [in 1995] and increase by roughly an additional 90 million people per year. Second, the resources of every kind (physical, chemical and biological; technological, institutional and cultural; economic, political and behavioral) available to people are finite today both in their present capacity and in their possible speed of expansion. Today's rapid relative and absolute increase in population stretches the productive, absorptive and recuperative capacities of the Earth as humans are now able to manage those capacities. It also stretches human capacities for technological and social invention, adaptation and compassion.

The unprecedented growth in human numbers and in human power to alter the Earth requires, and will require, unprecedented human agility in adapting to environmental, economic and social problems, sometimes all at once. The Earth's human population has entered and rapidly moves deeper into a poorly charted zone where limits on human population size or well-being have been anticipated and may be encountered. Slower population growth, along with many other improvements in human institutions and behaviors, would make it easier for people to retain control of their fate and to turn their attention from the numbers to the qualities of humankind.

These themes have consequences for action. Stopping a heavy

† Joel E. Cohen (b. 1944) is head of the Laboratory of Populations at Rockefeller University. The text is from his *How Many People Can the Earth Support?* (New York, 1995). Reprinted by permission of W. W. Norton & Company.

truck and turning a large ocean liner both take time. Stopping population growth in noncoercive ways takes decades under the best of circumstances. Ordinary people—including professionals and politicians—still have time to end population growth voluntarily and gradually by means that they find acceptable. Doing so will require the support of the best available leadership and institutions of politics, economics and technology to avoid physical, chemical and biological constraints beyond human control. Migration can ameliorate or exacerbate local problems, but at the global level, if birth rates do not fall, death rates must rise.

If most people would prefer a decline in birth rates to a rise in death rates, then they should take actions to support a decline in fertility[1] while time remains to realize that choice. In choosing how to encourage a global decline in fertility, people should be mindful of a major lesson of the twentieth century: tyranny by governments does not work in the long run. The focus of action should be to create conditions in which people voluntarily regulate their fertility to levels low enough not to require a rise in death rates. Though there is much more to learn about the best ways to do this, certain clearly useful options are already in hand.

* * *

Estimating how many people the Earth can support requires more than demographic arithmetic. Like calculating one plus one, it involves both natural constraints that humans cannot change and do not fully understand, and human choices that are yet to be made by this and by future generations. Therefore the question "How many people can the Earth support?" has no single numerical answer, now or ever. Because the Earth's human carrying capacity is constrained by facts of nature, human choices about the Earth's human carrying capacity are not entirely free, and may have consequences that are not entirely predictable. Because of the important roles of human choices, natural constraints and uncertainty, estimates of human carrying capacity cannot aspire to be more than *conditional* and *probable* estimates: *if* future choices are thus-and-so, *then* the human carrying capacity is *likely to be* so-and-so.

No sharp line separates human choices and natural constraints. For example, technology obeys the laws of physics, chemistry and biology, but humans choose how, and how much, to invest in creating and applying technology. Hence the technology that people use

---

1. I use *fertility* to refer to the actual number of children born, and *fecundity* to refer to the biological potentiality for bearing children. Thus, well-fed, disease-free, educated women may have high fecundity (high biological capacity to have children) and low fertility (few actual children). A population cannot combine low fecundity and high fertility. The words "fecundity" and "fertility" are used differently in different fields of science. My usage is standard in demography.

depends jointly on human choices and natural constraints. In another example, how the human body responds to chemicals is a natural constraint on health, but individual choices (about food, smoking, alcohol and other drugs) and social and economic decisions (about the use of lead in gasoline and paints, about the production and disposal of radioactive wastes) determine the extent to which human bodies are exposed to chemicals.

The fuzzy zone between choices and constraints shifts as time passes. Changes in knowledge can reveal constraints that had not been recognized previously, and can also make possible new choices.

Further, a choice open to rich people may be a constraint for poor people. People from rich countries who become infected with malaria, tuberculosis or trachoma generally choose to get the infection specifically diagnosed, treated and cured. People in poor countries may be unable to make the same choice because they cannot afford to pay for prevention, diagnosis or treatment. A rich landowner may choose to leave forest uncut and cropland idle; a subsistence farmer with small holdings may not enjoy the luxury of choosing.

This chapter presents some questions of human choice that make the question "How many people can the Earth support?" more precise:

1. How many at what average level of material well-being?
2. How many with what distribution of material well-being?
3. How many with what technology?
4. How many with what domestic and international political institutions?
5. How many with what domestic and international economic arrangements?
6. How many with what domestic and international demographic arrangements?
7. How many in what physical, chemical and biological environments?
8. How many with what variability or stability?
9. How many with what risk or robustness?
10. How many for how long?
11. How many with what values, tastes and fashions?

* * *

The human carrying capacity of the Earth will obviously depend on the typical material level at which people choose to live. Material well-being includes food (people choose variety and palatability, beyond the constraints imposed by physiological requirements); fiber (people choose cotton, wool or synthetic fibers for clothing; wood pulp or rag for paper); water (tap water or Perrier or the nearest river or mudhole for drinking, washing, cooking and watering your lawn if you have one); housing (Auschwitz barracks with two men to a plank, or Thomas Jefferson's Monticello); manufactured goods; waste removal (for human, agricultural and industrial wastes); natural hazard protection (against floods, storms, volcanoes and earthquakes); health (prevention, cure and care); and the entire range of amenities such as education, travel, social groups, solitude, the arts, religion and communion with nature.

*   *   *

The human population of the Earth now travels in the zone where a substantial fraction of scholars have estimated upper limits on human population size. These estimates are no better than present understanding of humankind's cultural, economic and environmental choices and constraints. Nevertheless, the possibility must be considered seriously that the number of people on the Earth has reached, or will reach within half a century, the maximum number the Earth can support in modes of life that we and our children and their children will choose to want.

*   *   *

Proposals for dealing with population problems confront an intellectual and ideological minefield. While plausible, well-intentioned suggestions for mitigating population problems abound, no one knows exactly what will work across the whole range of population problems, or will work most efficiently in a given situation. Since generally accepted conclusions about what works in which circumstances are scarce, almost all proposed actions are motivated by some explicit or implicit ideology.

Suggestions for ameliorating population problems fall into three main groups: those intended to amplify human productive capacities, given the number and expectations of people to be served (the "bigger pie" school); those intended to reduce the number and expectations of people to be served, given human abilities to find well-being (the "fewer forks" school); and those intended to change the terms under which people interact, whatever the technology or population (the "better manners" school). The enthusiasts of one school often neglect and suspect suggestions from the others.

The "bigger pie" school calls for new industrial, agricultural and civil technology of all types for both developed and developing countries. One enthusiast of technology, Jesse H. Ausubel, of the Program for the Human Environment at Rockefeller University, wrote: "The only way to meet the challenge of the multiplication of needs is to substantially enhance the contributions of science and technology to development and to enhance the cooperation between the science-rich and the science-poor."[2]

The "fewer forks" school calls for family-planning programs, for more effective and more acceptable contraceptives and sometimes for vegetarian diets (to reduce demand for animal feeds). Some proponents of the "fewer forks" school view technology as responsible for many adverse human impacts on the environment. Some argue, at the opposite extreme from Ausubel, that "the only way" to save the natural systems that support human life is to decrease human population growth rates, human numbers or human levels of consumption.

The "better manners" school calls for freer markets[3] or socialism (depending on taste), the breakup of large countries or the institution of world government or new forms of shared governance for sovereign states (depending on taste), democratic institutions, improved public policies, less corruption and the full life-cycle costing of business products. If poverty is the problem, the "better manners" school would propose to help poor people obtain increased access to credit, land, public infrastructure, education and health. In this approach, "a family planning program that emphasizes health services to the poor may be more easily justified on the grounds that it directly redistributes health resources to the poor than on the grounds that lower fertility may decrease poverty."[4]

*   *   *

The United Nations Fund for Population Activities (UNFPA) is foremost, though not alone, among the U.N. agencies that attempt to affect population growth. Other agencies with related responsibilities include the World Health Organization (with responsibilities for reproductive health and sexually transmitted diseases), the Food and Agricultural Organization, the U.N. Development Program, the U.N. Environmental Program, the U.N. Children's Fund (UNICEF) and the U.N Educational, Scientific and Cultural Organization (which has sponsored studies of the Earth's human carrying capacity).

The UNFPA's 1993 *Population Issues: Briefing Kit* highlighted the agency's major concerns in ten chapters of two pages each. These

2. Ausubel, Jesse H., "2020 Vision," *The Sciences* (New York Academy of Science), 33, no. 6 (Nov.–Dec., 1993), 17.

3. E.g., Carlson, Elwood, and Bernstam, "Population and Resources under the Socialist Economic System. In *Resources, Environment, and Population: Present Knowledge, Future Options*, ed. Kingsley Davis and Mikhail S. Bernstem, New York: Oxford University Press, 1990,

4. Dennis A. Ahlburg in Cassen, Robert, et al., *Population and Development: Old Debates, New Conclusions*, New Brunswick, NJ, Transaction Publishers, 1994.

concerns were rapid population growth; the special burdens of developing countries ("Continued rapid growth in developing countries has brought human numbers into collision with the resources to sustain them"); more adequate financing for population programs; family planning as a human right; comprehensive national population policies embracing family planning, demographic research, data collection, the wants of children and the elderly, urbanization, migration, education and communication; "gender equality: a country's best investment," to be achieved through equal educational opportunities for girls and boys, men and women; the degradation of air, land, water and biota "from ever-increasing numbers of people, ever-increasing demands for resources and ever-increasing pollution"; urbanization and migration; information, education and communication adapted to local cultures; and population data.

*   *   *

Questions

An end to long-term average population growth is inevitable, very probably within the twenty-first century. Questions under debate are: just how soon and by what means and at whose expense? Here are eight issues that remain to be resolved.

1. How will the bill for family planning and other population activities be distributed between the developing countries (who now pay perhaps 80 percent) and the rich countries?
2. Who will spend the money, and how? How will the available monies be allocated between governments and nongovernmental organizations? How much will go for family planning and how much for allied programs like reproductive health?
3. How will environmental goals be balanced against economic goals? For example, if reducing poverty requires increased industrial and agricultural production in developing countries, can the increases in production be achieved at acceptable environmental costs?
4. How will cultural change be balanced against cultural continuity? In some cultural settings, the goal of empowering women directly contradicts the goal of maintaining "full respect for the various religious and ethical values and cultural backgrounds." Both goals were often repeated in the final document of the 1994 International Conference on Population and Development. Women achieved the vote in the United States only in 1920 and only after considerable struggle. Asking for equality for women now asks some cul-

tures to make far greater change in far less time. I fully support such demands, but they should be made with a clear and sympathetic understanding that they require profound cultural change.

5. How will the often-asserted right of couples and individuals to control their fertility be reconciled with national demographic goals if the way couples and individuals exercise that right happens not to bring about the demographic goals?

6. How will national sovereignty be reconciled with world or regional environmental and demographic goals? This question arises in the control of migration, reproduction and all economic activities that involve the global commons of atmosphere, oceans and international water bodies, and the management of the plant and animal populations that inhabit them.

7. How will the desire and moral obligation to alleviate poverty and suffering as rapidly as possible be reconciled with the use of local scarcities as an efficient market signal?

8. In efforts to protect the physical, chemical and biological environments provided by this finite sphere, how will rapid population growth and economic development in poor countries be balanced against high consumption per person in the rich countries?

*   *   *

I now suggest ways of improving some population problems. These suggestions concern the infrastructure for solving population problems; they are not solutions in themselves. The approaches I propose do not depend on complete knowledge of the past, present or future. I offer them in addition to, and not instead of, the suggestions offered by others. * * *

The four suggestions I will offer here are: to develop institutions that balance the goals of efficiency and equality; to improve the accounting of social well-being, materials and the consequences of actions; to integrate thinking about populations with thinking about economies, environments and cultures; and to create a better understanding of mutual aid, emphasizing the benefits that the well-off derive from helping the poor live better lives.

Institutions to Reconcile Efficiency and Equality

In developing countries, as elsewhere, investments that help the poor directly (egalitarian investments) may differ from investments that yield the largest growth in aggregate economic output (efficient or utilitarian investments). The choice between enhancing the well-being of the poor directly and maximizing aggregate output illustrates the practical conflict between egalitarianism and utilitarianism. Social and political institutions could mediate this conflict by assuring the poor a share of the increase in output that would result from more efficient (utilitarian) investments. For such arrangements to succeed domestically or internationally, the wealthier regions must understand and concede that they have a stake in the well-being of the poorer regions and must justify the trust that the poorer regions would be required to place in them.

* * *

Accounting

Accounting should recognize and correctly assign positive or negative values to more of the effects of current economic and noneconomic activities, especially the effects on the stocks and flows of physical, chemical, biological and human resources.[5] If economic actors bore the full costs of economic activities, including costs that are now evaded as externalities, environmental damage might be greatly reduced. Much more knowledge is available to define the full effects of present activities than is used, but still more knowledge is required.

* * *

Better accounting could improve the management of hazardous wastes.[6] Toxic chemicals could be tracked from production to disposition with the same care that a dollar in sales is tracked from receipt to expenditure. For example, chemicals are sometimes legally dumped on land bought or rented for that purpose. Better understanding of the fate of such chemicals in the soil and subsurface aquifers would clarify the long-term impact of such dumping both on the natural environment and on humans who may settle on the land later or who may use the groundwater. If there are adverse effects, as were reported in Love Canal, near Niagara Falls, New York, and in Times Beach, Missouri, the costs of such effects should be counted as part of the costs of making, using and disposing of hazardous chemicals. A careful accounting of where toxic chemicals come from could stimulate companies to reduce the production of those chemicals in the first place, rather than try to dispose of them after they are created.

5. Repetto, Robert, et al., *Wasting Assets: Natural Resources in the National Income Accounts*, Washington, DC, 1989; Smith, V. Kerry, *Valuing Natural Assets: The Economics of Natural Resource Damage Assessment*, Washington, DC, 1993.
6. Gore, Al, *Earth in the Balance; Ecology and the Human Spirit*, New York, 1992, pp. 305–307.

Better accounting could make the use of natural resources such as water and soil more rational. The Ogallala aquifer, which lies under more than 40 million hectares in seven states[7] in the center of the United States, supplies water to vast fields of wheat and other important crops. That water is being extracted from underground reserves faster than it is being replenished by percolating groundwater. The aquifer is reported to be more than half depleted beneath almost a million hectares in Kansas, Texas and New Mexico.[8] When the wheat grown with mined water and the beef fed on grain grown with mined water are sold at home or abroad, the price takes no account of the likely replacement cost of the water. Thus when the wheat and beef are sold, water is given away. At the same time, to prevent surplus crops from depressing prices, the U.S. government pays farmers not to cultivate rain-fed cropland. The cost of replenishing the Ogallala aquifer or finding alternative sources of fresh water or going without the services the Ogallala aquifer might have provided will be borne by future Americans, who may not benefit from the current profits or consumption of wheat and beef. Future generations are subsidizing some people in the present generation.

Better accounting, based on better understanding, could make the conservation of soil more rational. The difficulty is to compare the future income earned when soil is conserved today with the future income forgone when soil is eroded today.[9] Farmers who pay the cost of regenerating the soil concurrently as their cultivation erodes it may be a short-term disadvantage in competing with other farmers who mine the soil. But farmers who conserve soil contribute to the long-term productivity of the land. Their contribution may be imperfectly reflected in the market price of well-conserved land. Better accounting could reflect more of the value of conserving soil.

Much better accounting is needed for human behavior and its consequences. Some behavior that is economically profitable has bad consequences that are not charged to the actors. Such behavior is currently rewarded more than is economically or socially rational.

For example, successful producers and advertisers of tobacco are not charged for the effects of tobacco on health. "Why should they be?" you might ask. "After all, nobody charges makers of ice cream and candy for tooth decay." True, but ice cream and candy are not addictive in the same way as tobacco, and the consumer has a fairly full picture of the consequences of use. At the opposite extreme, many societies do penalize makers, purveyors and sometimes users of addictive drugs. If there were an economic justification for penal-

7. Ibid., pp. 313–314.
8. Mauldin, W. Parker and Ross, John A., "Family Planning Programs: Efforts and Results," *Studies in Family Planning*, 22, no. 6 (1991), 350–367.
9. Bongaarts, John, "Population Policy Options in the Developing World," *Science*, 263 (11 Feb.), 774.

izing them, it would probably be that drug dealers should bear more of the externalities of addictive drugs, which impose large costs on both users and non-users. Pushing tobacco falls on a spectrum between pushing hard drugs and pushing ice cream. Better accounting could make clearer where on that spectrum the tobacco industry lies and what its real costs are.

* * *

Research on Population, Culture, Economics and Environment

To understand present population problems, to examine the possible paths by which the human population growth rate will drop to or below zero and to make more credible concepts and estimates of the Earth's human carrying capacity, scientists must learn more of the four-way interactions of population, the environment, economy and culture. It is useless to imagine that population interacts with the environment while economics and culture have no effect and are unaffected; and equally useless to pretend that population growth interacts with economic development independently of the environment and culture. Populations, the environment, economics and culture all interact *jointly*. Think of a string quartet: the combined effect exceeds that of any single player or pair or trio of players.

Population, environment, economy and culture should be interpreted broadly. Population includes size, growth rate and age structure (how many young people want schooling? how many old people want pensions?), health (are people free of parasites? are they well fed? are they in good mental health?), spatial distribution (are people in cities or rural areas? near or far from fresh water?) and migration (are people moving from poor countries to other poor countries or to rich countries?). The environment includes soil, fresh water, salt water, air, all nonhuman living creatures and the Earth's stage of soils, rocks, mountains, rivers, plains, oceans, volcanoes, earthquakes, meteorites and solar flares. The economy includes all the human and material arrangements for the production and exchange of goods and services to satisfy people's wants. Culture includes values (what do people want? what do people think is right?), technology (what knowledge and artifacts, including machines, do people inherit and create?) and social and political institutions (how do people interact in satisfying their wants?). The boundaries are fuzzy: for example, law and technology belong both to culture and to the economy.

Any proposed description or solution of a population problem that does not include all four of population, environment, economy and culture is incomplete. In any partial description or solution, the omitted aspects are explicitly or implicitly assumed to remain constant. A partial description or solution is vulnerable to failure when one, or more, of the omitted aspects changes.

*   *   *

Improving the Art of Living

A beautiful quotation from the 1848 *Principles of Political Economy* of the British philosopher John Stuart Mill commends a change of values. You may not agree with all of it. But every part is worthy of serious consideration and, if not assent, serious argument. For perspective, it is useful to know that, at the next censuses after Mill wrote, the combined population of England, Wales and Scotland in 1851 was 21 million; the population of the United States in 1850 was 23 million. The world's population in 1848 was just over one billion, less than one-fifth of its present size.

> There is room in the world, no doubt, and even in old countries, for a great increase of population, supposing the arts of life to go on improving, and capital to increase. But even if innocuous, I confess I see very little reason for desiring it. The density of population necessary to enable mankind to obtain, in the greatest degree, all the advantages both of cooperation and of social intercourse, has, in all the most populous countries, been attained. A population may be too crowded, though all be amply supplied with food and raiment. It is not good for man to be kept perforce at all times in the presence of his species. A world from which solitude is extirpated, is a very poor ideal. Solitude, in the sense of being often alone, is essential to any depth of meditation or of character; and solitude in the presence of natural beauty and grandeur, is the cradle of thoughts and aspirations which are not only good for the individual, but which society could ill do without. Nor is there much satisfaction in contemplating the world with nothing left to the spontaneous activity of nature; with every rood of land brought into cultivation, which is capable of growing food for human beings; every flowery waste or natural pasture ploughed up, all quadrupeds or birds which are not domesticated for man's use exterminated as his rivals for food, every hedgerow or superfluous tree rooted out, and scarcely a place left where a wild shrub or flower could grow without being eradicated as a weed in the name of improved agriculture. If the earth must lose that great portion of its pleasantness which it owes to things that the unlimited increase of wealth and population would extirpate from it, for the mere purpose of enabling it to support a larger but not a better or a happier population, I sincerely hope, for the sake of

posterity, that they will content to be stationary, long before necessity compels them to it.

It is scarcely necessary to remark that a stationary condition of capital and population implies no stationary state of human improvement. There would be as much scope as ever for all kinds of mental culture, and moral and social progress; as much room for improving the Art of Living, and much more likelihood of its being improved, when minds ceased to be engrossed by the art of getting on. Even the industrial arts might be as earnestly and as successfully cultivated, with this sole difference, that instead of serving no purpose but the increase of wealth, industrial improvements would produce their legitimate effect, that of abridging labour. . . . Only when, in addition to just institutions, the increase of mankind shall be under the deliberate guidance of judicious foresight, can the conquests made from the powers of nature by the intellect and energy of scientific discoverers, become the common property of the species, and the means of improving and elevating the universal lot.[1]

GARRETT HARDIN

Nobody Ever Dies of Overpopulation (1993)†

Poverty, Disasters, and the Population Crunch

On 4 February 1976, at 3:05 A.M., an earthquake struck Guatemala, killing 22,778 and injuring 76,504, according to the accepted statistics. * * *

A detailed study of a village of 1,577 Indians was revealing.[1] The greatest mortality was suffered by people who lived in adobe *casitas* ("little houses") roofed with heavy wooden timbers. More than 85 percent of the population was so housed. People in shacks made of cornstalks or mud-chinked slats fared much better. (Expensive reinforced concrete homes were best, but there were few of these in this village.)

The cost of adobe homes is low in money but high in "sweat equity" for those who do their own work. Cornstalks and slats are cheaper in both money and labor. Because of these differences, mor-

---

1. Mill, John Stuart, *Principles of Political Economy with Some of Their Applications to Social Philosophy* (1848), Book IV, Chapter VI.

† Garrett Hardin (b. 1915) is professor emeritus of human ecology at the University of California at Santa Barbara. The text is from his *Living within Limits* (New York and Oxford, 1993). Reprinted by permission of Oxford University Press.

1. Roger Glass, et al., "Earthquake Injuries Related to Housing in a Guatemalan Village" *Science* 197 (1977): 638–43.

tality in the village, and throughout most of Guatemala, was complexly correlated with socioeconomic status.

So what should we say killed those 22,778 Guatemalans? The earthquake? But most of them would have survived had they lived in reinforced concrete houses. Since concrete costs money, should we attribute the deaths to poverty? But the poorest people of all, living in cornstock or slat shacks, survived best. Why didn't more people live in the simple abodes? Because increasing population had nearly exhausted the resources of the biotic environment—photosynthetic products like trees and cornstocks. Should we then attribute the earthquake deaths to overpopulation? No newspaper, no radio broadcast, and no television show did so. An unspoken taboo decrees that *no one ever dies of overpopulation*.[2]

*   *   *

Focusing on the Furnishings of the Mind

Birth control is not population control. Improvements in the technology of birth control will make population control easier, but perfect methods of birth control are not enough. How much these methods are used is determined by the furnishings of the mind.

The ideas that are necessary for population control are easily accessible to the ordinary mind. They are widely known, but people are not as acutely aware of them as they must be if population control is ever to be achieved. If talented teachers can find striking ways of fitting the following generalizations into primary and secondary education, the advance of population control will be greatly furthered.

Exponential growth: This is just a fancy term for growth by compound interest in which people understand from their banking experience. Most economic literature fails however to emphasize the following important point: no positive rate of exponential growth of a population can safely be regarded as "small." A bank that offered only 1 percent interest on deposits would be ridiculed, but in a population 1 percent growth per year is so very, very great that it was not achieved worldwide until the year 1950. (More important: such a rate cannot long be maintained.)

Our world is finite: Television space operas, like the fairy tales they displaced, leave children with expectations of limitless worlds. We need to disillusion children. They need to grow up feeling in their bones that they cannot escape earth's problems by fleeing to the stars.

2. Garrett Hardin, "Nobody Ever Dies of Overpopulation," *Science* 171 (1971): 527. This has been slightly shortened for the box on pages 262–63. What was then the East Bengal region of Pakistan has since become Bangladesh.

There will never be a perpetual motion machine: Time after time a proposed method of escape from limits turns out to be a fraudulent but cleverly disguised perpetual motion machine. Students need to be trained to detect such fraud.

Diseconomies of scale are the rule: Whatever may be the relative frequencies of economies and diseconomies of scale, human beings naturally recognize and exploit the economies first. Increasingly, society is left with diseconomies. As a result, in ever more instances, more (of almost anything) is worse. This expectation contradicts the "bigger is better" philosophy of the recent past.

Carrying capacity is measured in terms of (number of people) multiplied by (the physical quality of life): The maximum number of people can be supported only if the per capita share of physical wealth (energy, space, food, luxuries) is kept to the minimum. (Of course some aspects of the "quality of life" call for little or no substantive expenditures: friendliness, for example.)

Population size is demostatically controlled: It takes negative feedback to keep the potential of exponential growth from destroying a population. A community has a choice of negative feedbacks; but if it refuses to choose, nature will step in with the painful negative feedbacks of famine, disease and social chaos.

Zero population growth is the NORM *for every population*: Ignoring minor fluctuations, more than 99 percent of the existence of every species is passed in an essentially ZPG condition. The rapid growth of the human population during the past two centuries is very exceptional. It must soon come to an end. The experience will probably never be repeated.

ZPG *can be exciting*: The conservation rules of science apply to matter and energy, the joint product of which can be neither destroyed nor created. Conservation does *not* rule "information," which can be either destroyed or created. Economic growth and population growth must finally come to a halt: but there is no perceivable limit to progress in the arts—including the art of living together!

Without the control of immigration, no country can succeed in controlling its population size: The Marxist philosophy, "From each according to his ability, to each according to his needs," defines an unmanaged commons, which ends in ruin.

One of the most reliable things in the world is human unreliability: It is for this reason that complex technologies with tremendous potential for harm (such as nuclear reactors) must probably be abandoned.

So long as demand increases exponentially, solving a material shortage is impossible: People are repeatedly surprised when building more roads merely makes traffic jams worse. They are also surprised when giving food to a starving population today increases the number of the starving in future years.

Every "shortage" of supply is equally a "longage" of demand: Focusing on shortages encourages greed (and makes a favored few people rich). Focusing on longages encourages temperance in making demands. The problem of balancing supply and demand is not in the stars, and the solution is not in technology: it is in our heads.

Every complex function is subject to spontaneous decay and loss of the sort that physicists call "entropy": Knowledge is one of the most valuable complex functions, and the evidence of its entropic degeneration are everywhere. Some 2,500 years ago the Greeks inscribed this advice on the temple at Delphi: *Nothing in excess.* Somewhat later Epicurus said, "If you live according to nature you will never be poor; if you live according to opinion you will never be rich."

In 1971 the U.S. Council of Economic Advisors, apparently ignorant of both classical literature and modern science, solemnly proclaimed that, "If it is agreed that economic output is a good thing it follows by definition that there is not enough of it." The advisors wisely started their statement with an "if," but it looks like they forgot the "if" before they reached the conclusion of the sentence. The council evidently believed that wealth is not subject to the ancient doctrine that "There can be too much of a good thing."

Probably every one of these economists had a Ph.D. degree. Yet a well-educated teenager could have set them straight. Food is a good thing, but it is all too easy to have too much of it. The fat-soluble vitamins are good things, but he who eats a generous slab of polar bear liver dies of the excess. Oxygen is a good thing; but breathe 100 percent oxygen for a few hours and you're dead.

Ours is a society that finds it difficult to keep a firm hold on the concept of temperance. When the Women's Christian Temperance Union was formed to reduce the drinking of alcohol the word "temperance" was soon corrupted to mean total abstinence. Prohibition laws polarized much of society into heavy drinkers and teetotalers. Discussions of population control risk a similar polarization. Already a pronatalist has condemned the idea of population control by entitling a book *The War Against Population,* a title that implies that only a thorough misanthrope could hope that the human population might be less than the maximum possible—that is to say, the most miserable possible.

Pure pronatalism and pure misanthropy are both suicidal in their thrust. With population, as with most goods in life, a golden mean is to be sought. An understanding of numbers and ratios is essential, but the level of mathematical ability required is within reach of most of humankind.

The preceding italicized principles represent so many pieces of mental furniture that must be installed in the minds of men and women if nature is to be kept from controlling population by her own more brutal means. The resistance to positioning this furniture in the minds of citizens is very great among many interested parties. All advertisers will fight against the change, as will those who believe in science fiction, as well as all people who are "conservative" in the sense of wanting to conserve the present social and political arrangements forever. Opposition will also be expressed by some Marxists, some Christians, some idealistic atheists, some capitalists, some socialists and some ethnofugalists. Radical changes are called for in universal education. These will be supported by ecological conservatives, whose aim is to preserve as much wealth as possible for our children and grandchildren. The educational challenge is formidable.

Temperance must be the guiding ideal. There is no all-powerful world government to achieve universal population control; and there is no reason to expect one to develop. Population control must be coextensive with sovereignty. The existence of many sovereignties calls for the parochial control of population. Here and there throughout the world one sees hints that temperance in balancing population size and the quality of life is being achieved. Let us hope that ours is one of the countries that manages to find—and accept—effective means of controlling its population.

Nobody Ever Dies of Overpopulation.

I was in Calcutta when the cyclone struck East Bengal in November 1970. Early dispatches spoke of 15,000 dead, but the estimates rapidly escalated to 2,000,000 and then dropped back to 500,000. A nice round number: it will do as well as any, for we will never know. The nameless ones who died, "unimportant" people far beyond the fringes of the social power structure, left no trace of their existence. Pakistani parents repaired the population loss in just 40 days; and the world turned its attention to other matters.

What killed those unfortunate people? The cyclone, newspapers said. But one can just as logically say that overpopulation killed them. The Gangetic delta is barely above sea level. Every year several thousand people are killed in quite ordinary storms. If Pakistan were not overcrowded, no sane man would bring his family to such a place. Ecologically speaking, a delta belongs to the river and the sea; man obtrudes there at his peril.

Were we to identify overpopulation as the cause of a half-million deaths, we would threaten ourselves with a question to which we do not know the answer: *How can we control population without recourse to repugnant measures?* Fearfully we close our minds to an inventory of possibilities. Instead, we say that a cyclone caused the deaths, thus relieving ourselves of responsibility for this and future catastrophes. "Fate" is *so* comforting.

What will we say when the power shuts down some fine summer on our eastern seaboard and several thousand people die of heat prostration? Will we blame the weather? Or the power companies for not building enough generators? Or the econuts for insisting on pollution controls?

One thing is certain: we won't blame the deaths on overpopulation. No one ever dies of overpopulation. It is unthinkable.

"Nobody Ever Dies of Overpopulation," 1971.

RODOLFO A. BULATAO

The Value of Family Planning Programs in Developing Countries (1998)†

High Fertility and Unmet Need

The world's population is still growing. Although fertility has fallen worldwide from about five children per couple to about three since 1960, annual population growth in the 1990s is still approximately 80 million people, equivalent to adding a country the size of Germany to the world's population each year. Most of this growth is occurring in developing nations, where fertility rates remain high. * * *

High fertility and rapid population growth can pose problems for developing nations. They can deny opportunities for socioeconomic development; contribute to high levels of infant mortality; and strain public resources for health, education, and other vital services.

In addition, high fertility runs counter to the preferences expressed by millions of couples in developing countries, who actually want to have smaller families. Motivated by practical concerns about finances, health, and their families' futures, millions around the world would prefer to have fewer children than they are actually having.

† Rodolfo A. Bulatao (b. 1944) is an independent consultant in Silver Spring, Maryland. The text is from his *The Value of Family Planning Programs in Developing Countries* (Santa Monica, Calif, 1998). Reprinted by permission of RAND. (The summary was drafted by David Adamson, senior research communicator, with other members of the staff of the RAND Population Matters project.)

This gap between preferences and fertility springs from what demographers label the "unmet need for contraception." This concept refers to the needs of women who want no more children but do not practice contraception. Survey research indicates that unmet need affects an estimated 10 to 40 percent of married women of reproductive age in developing countries. Levels of unmet need are high in high-fertility countries, such as Malawi (36 percent), and can also be sizable in more developed regions, such as Latin America, where they range from 12 to 29 percent. For all developing countries, the total number of women with unmet need is estimated at 150 million.

Benefits of Family Planning

Family planning programs help developing countries address these issues. They help to moderate high fertility, fill the unmet need for contraception, and reduce the number of unwanted pregnancies. At their most elemental, family planning programs are organized efforts to provide contraception—ranging from temporary methods, such as oral contraceptives and condoms, to sterilization—and related reproductive health services. Since the first national programs in developing countries were established in the late 1950s, family planning has been associated with notable increases in the use of contraception in the developing world. This has been true across an astonishing range of cultural, political, and socioeconomic environments.

Family planning has been successful in filling unmet need by helping women in developing countries overcome obstacles to the use of contraception. The two barriers women most commonly cite are (1) lack of knowledge about contraceptive methods and availability and (2) concern about health effects. By increasing access to contraception and promoting wider knowledge about proper use and low health risks, family planning programs have helped address these barriers as well as others, such as the supply and cost of contraceptives. Reducing unmet need can also help to reduce the number of unplanned and unwanted pregnancies. Since they are more likely to end in abortion, these pregnancies increase health risks for mothers when the abortions are unsafe. Unplanned children may have other negative impacts: Families with unwanted children tend to invest less in each child's education.

*　*　*

Increased use of contraception has been instrumental in reducing fertility rates since the mid-1960s from about six children per couple in developing countries to about three during this interval. Statistical analysis indicates that family planning programs have been responsible for as much as 40 percent of this decline.

Lower fertility from increased use of contraception has in turn been associated with a range of benefits for developing countries. At the macroeconomic level, reduced fertility has helped create favorable conditions for socioeconomic development in some countries. A prime example of this connection has been the so-called "Asian Economic Miracle." From 1960 to 1990, the five fastest-growing economies in the world were in East Asia: South Korea, Singapore, Hong Kong, Taiwan, and Japan. Two other Southeast Asian nations, Indonesia and Thailand, were not far behind. During this 30-year span, women in East Asia reduced their childbearing from an average of six children or more to two or fewer in the span of a single generation. This reduction in fertility contributed to East Asia's remarkable socioeconomic development.

One way in which lower fertility can help promote socioeconomic development is by reducing the proportion of dependent children in the population. A lower ratio of children to adults can create what demographers call a "demographic bonus": With fewer children, families can save more or invest more money per child in, for example, education or health care. Furthermore, a smaller proportion of children means that a greater percentage of the population is in the working ages. The impressive rise in East Asian savings and investment rates since the late 1960s can be explained in part by the equally impressive decline in youth dependency burdens.

* * *

In addition to moderating fertility, family planning can yield other benefits, including improved health for women and children and a greater degree of freedom for women. The clearest health benefit for women is reduced risk of maternal death. Death in childbirth is almost 20 times as likely for each birth in developing countries as in developed countries. Having many successive pregnancies puts mothers at even greater risk. For example, at the total fertility rate in sub-Saharan Africa of 5.6 children, the average woman has a 1 in 18 lifetime risk of dying in childbirth. Reducing fertility by half would also reduce this risk by about half. Also, lower fertility, especially at younger and older ages, and greater spacing between births reduces the risk of infant and child mortality.

Reduced dependency burdens can also improve educational performance. Countries can send more children to school and invest more per child, thus improving the quality of the future labor force. * * *

Additional opportunities created by lower fertility include reduced pressures on public funds and a grace period for dealing with environmental pressures and for managing typically limited resources, such as water.

Program Costs and the Role of Donor Support

Expenditures on family planning across all developing countries are approximately US$10 billion annually. Most of this amount is paid by national governments or individual households. Equivalent to around US$1-2 per person per year, this is not large by many standards.

Governments typically cover the bulk of family planning expenditures in developing countries.

* * *

International donors play an especially prominent role in helping programs get started and later helping them expand. Typically, donor involvement decreases over time as programs mature and recipient nations become more self-sufficient in funding and operating them.

Donor commitments have fluctuated in recent years. They increased substantially, to US$1.37 billion, the year following the 1994 International Conference on Population and Development held in Cairo (as they did after the previous world conference in 1984). However, these comparisons are complicated by the expanded mandate from the Cairo conference to tackle reproductive health. Excluding funding for reproductive health, donor commitments actually fell from 1994 to 1995 by 7 percent in real terms. Even counting reproductive health funding, larger increases will be needed to meet the Cairo conference goal of donor support for a third of the cost of population and reproductive health programs by 2000.

The primary donor countries are the United States, Japan, and the other member nations of the Organisation for Economic Co-Operation and Development. Historically, the United States has been the largest contributor to population programs around the world and the most significant provider of technical assistance. However, there are signs that the United States has started to relinquish its role as world leader. The U.S. share of contributions diminished in the late 1980s and has not recovered to previous levels. In fact, U.S. population assistance fell 20 percent from fiscal 1995 to fiscal 1996 and fell a further 10 percent to fiscal 1997. The effect of these declines is uncertain. It is unclear whether other donor nations are willing or able to make up the shortfall.

The Challenges Ahead

Despite their history of success, family planning programs still have much to accomplish. Programs face challenges in improving service, dealing with sexually transmitted diseases, including HIV/AIDS, and ensuring broader attention to women's reproductive health needs, as urged by the Cairo conference. One specific challenge will be serving the needs of the huge cohort of young women just coming to child-bearing age. The group aged 15 to 24 will total 900 million by the turn of the century.

*　*　*

Dealing with these issues will involve building on the past success of family planning programs and strengthening current efforts with continuing support from donor nations and the international community.

MARK W. NOWAK

Why Population Policy Matters to America (1998)†

Although the United States is generally thought of as a leader in social policy, when it comes to demographic policy the U.S. is well behind much of the rest of the world. In 1993, for example, each of 116 countries—about 60% of all nations—had developed and imple-mented a population policy of some kind.[1] * * * The United States—a signatory to most population documents encouraging the creation of national population policies—is one of the few countries that sup-ports the creation of population policies in principle, but currently is making no effort to develop its own such policy.

Why is this so? The simple answer is that most policy makers in the United States consider explicit demographic decision-making anathema to the democratic process. "It is not up to the government to tell people how many children they can have," reason these leg-islators. "Childbearing is a deeply personal matter that should be left entirely to the individuals involved."

The irony here is that by refusing to engage in demographic deci-

† Mark W. Nowak (b. 1965) is an environmental writer and former executive director of Population-Environment Balance. The text is from his *Our Demographic Future: Why Population Policy Matters to America* (Washington, D.C., 1998). Reprinted by permission of Negative Population Growth, Inc.

1. United Nations, *Global Population Policy Database, 1993*, (New York: Department for Economic and Social Information and Policy Analysis, Population Division, 1995), p. 197.

sion making, policy makers do not escape the task of setting demographic policy—they merely give up the opportunity to set *explicit* policy. Policy makers still make *implicit* demographic decisions every day—some with enormous consequences—the majority of which occur without the slightest demographic scrutiny.

Consider that during a typical session Congress might make laws or establish initiatives on family planning and birth control, sex education, teen pregnancy, reproductive rights, immigration, housing, welfare, marriage and taxation. Collectively these issues have a measurable impact on both the childbearing decisions of Americans as well as the demographic trajectory of the nation. But, since few of the policies are explicitly designed to effect a demographic change (one exception would be the recent changes in welfare law intended to reduce out-of-wedlock childbearing), our political system continues to behave as if demographic decisions can be made, should be made, and are made exclusively by individuals without any influence from government policy.

※   ※   ※

[President Nixon argued] in 1969 that continued growth could only lead to negative consequences: "Look ahead to the end of this century," he said. "There are 200 million Americans now. By the end of the century there will be 300 million. Where are those 100 million going to be? You can't pour them into New York, into Los Angeles, into Chicago and the rest and choke those cities to death with smog and crime and all of the rest that comes with overpopulation."[2]

But, in fact, that is exactly what we have done and just as our legislators were concerned, our communities and our environment have paid the price.

Our Communities

As population growth in our cities has increased, so have congestion, crime and competition for housing. As a result, Americans have taken to the suburbs to find cheaper housing and to regain open space and solitude. Between 1970 and 1990 the nation's central cities grew by only 12 million while the suburbs increased in size by 41 million.[3] One of the costs of this shift has been longer commute times with no attendant decrease in congestion.

2. Richard M. Nixon, "Remarks at the 50th Anniversary Meeting of the American Farm Bureau Federation (December 8, 1969)," *Public Papers of the Presidents*, No. 480, (Washington, DC: Office of the Federal Register, National Archives, 1970), p. 1002.
3. U.S. Bureau of Transportation Statistics, *Transportation Statistics Annual Report 1996*, Washington, DC, 1996, p. 8.

* * *

Our Environment

ENERGY

Just as President Johnson's administration predicted, as our population has increased in size, so has our demand for energy. Since 1970, the U.S. population has grown by about 31%[4] while total energy demand has increased by about 36%.[5] For the most part, the United States has met this increased demand through increased domestic production of coal, natural gas, petroleum, nuclear power and, to a much smaller extent, renewable energies.

Starting about 25 years ago, however, domestic production of petroleum began to decline, causing petroleum imports to inch up. Since 1970, annual imports of crude oil have more than quadrupled and imports now supply more of our annual oil budget than does domestic supply.[6] Declining domestic petroleum production means that we face a less certain energy future regarding a fuel that we depend upon for more than one-third of our annual energy needs.[7]

FARMLAND LOSS

In a recent study of farmland loss, the American Farmland Trust found that urban sprawl in the United States was responsible for the destruction of more than 4 million acres of prime or unique farmland between 1982 and 1992, or about 400,000 acres lost every year.[8] When erosion and other factors are considered, total farmland loss is close to one million acres annually.[9]

Urban sprawl consumes the best farmland because most cities were built where prime agricultural resources were abundant. As the boundaries of our urban areas expand, the surrounding farmland is paved over. Consider that Texas lost more high quality farmland to development than any other state between 1982 and 1992, account-

---

4. U.S. Bureau of the Census, Population Division release PPL-57, "United States Population Estimates, by Age, Sex, Race, and Hispanic Origin 1990 to 1996"; U.S. Bureau of the Census, *Current Population Reports*, P25-1045.
5. Energy Information Administration, *Annual Energy Review 1995*, Washington, DC, 1996, p. 9.
6. *Annual Energy Review 1995*, pp. 143, 145.
7. *Annual Energy Review 1995*, p. 9.
8. A. Ann Sorenson, Richard P. Greene and Karen Russ; American Farmland Trust, *Farming on the Edge* (Center for Agriculture in the Environment, Northern Illinois University), Washington, DC: 1997, Table 7 (via http://farm.fic.niu.edu/foe2/).
9. *Farming on the Edge*, p. 18.

ing for 11.5% of the total loss in the United States.[1] During this same period, the three largest cities in Texas—Houston, Dallas and San Antonio—grew by 20%, 33% and 22%, respectively, expanding their boundaries. This rapid rate of growth—two and three times higher than the national growth rate of 10%—explains Texas' massive farmland loss during the period.[2]

BIODIVERSITY

Preserving biological diversity is fundamental to maintaining a healthy environment. Species and ecosystems are interdependent so that the loss of just one species—depending upon its role in the environment—can generate enormous ecological consequences and environmental impact.

Unfortunately, rather than preserving biodiversity in the United States, human population growth and activities are threatening it. The intensification of modern agriculture, degradation of water quality in critical aquatic habitats and contamination of the environment with toxic substances have all played a role, but the primary cause of biodiversity loss in the United States is habitat loss and fragmentation resulting from growth-driven development.[3] The U.S. coastal regions, which are particularly biologically rich, have also been particularly vulnerable to development.

*   *   *

Obstacles to Stopping Growth Remain Formidable

Looking back is certainly instructive, but the policy implications of doing so are limited: we can't turn the clock back to 1970 in order to follow a different demographic path. We can, however, look to the future and enact policies today that will enable us to achieve an optimum population size tomorrow.

In doing so, however, we need to be aware that some of the policies that would be required would generate substantial resistance from policy makers, just as they did during the 1970s.

Certainly access to abortion and contraception are issues that continue to divide Congress today, and their inclusion in any demographic policy would likely generate significant opposition. Immigration rates today are more than double what they were in the

1. *Farming on the Edge*, III. Major Findings.
2. U.S. Bureau of the Census, *Statistical Abstract of the United States: 1996* (116th ed), Washington, DC 1996, Tables 28, 43.
3. The variety of causes of habitat loss are referred to throughout *Our Living Resources*, (Washington, DC: U.S. Department of the Interior, National Biological Service, 1995).

1970s, so more substantial reductions in immigration would be necessary today to achieve population stabilization, and an even more acrimonious fight would ensue over such a proposal.

Challenging Pro-Growth Attitudes Fundamental

But perhaps the greatest opposition to the creation of a national population policy will not be in response to specific policy proposals, but simply to the idea that growth is something that must be controlled. For two centuries we have fostered pro-growth attitudes, and these views have become central to our understanding of progress.

Businesses measure success through growth, and thus the business community heralds reports that the U.S. population has increased: more people mean more customers. Religious communities generally favor growth, perceiving large families as blessings. The political community adores growth because enlarged districts bring the possibility of additional votes and re-election. Growth also means increased political power: growing states may gain political representatives; shrinking states will surely lose them.

Grassroots Activists and Public Opinion Receptive to Change

Although opposition to the creation of a national population policy will be substantial, we cannot afford to back away from difficult choices simply because they are difficult. * * *

The good news is that some U.S. communities may already be questioning our pro-growth policies. The same cities that herald their higher-than-average growth rates are implementing initiatives to fight suburban sprawl. Communities that embrace growth are looking for relief from traffic, school overcrowding and a declining urban quality of life. Pro-growth communities want to know how they can permanently protect their open space and water, and coastal communities are looking to reverse declines in their fisheries.

Even more encouraging, direct measures of public opinion reveal that Americans show a growing preference for small family size in the United States. According to the General Social Survey, the percentage of Americans who prefer two-child families has increased from 41% in 1972 to 55% in 1994, with declines in the percentage of Americans who prefer substantially larger families.[4]

4. Davis, James A., and Tom W. Smith. *General Social Surveys*, 1972–1994: Cumulative File (Computer File), Chicago, IL: National Opinion Research Center, 1994 (Producer). Computer-assisted Survey Methods Program (CSM) at the University of California, Berkeley (distributor).

An Optimum and Sustainable Population—
More Needed Than Ever

The desire of Americans to ameliorate the consequences of growth combined with evidence that communities are looking for sustainable solutions to over-development and urban sprawl indicates that the United States may be ready once again to pursue a much-needed domestic population policy.

The first step would be to adopt as an explicit target, the goal of reducing the U.S. population to a sustainable and optimum size of not more than 150 million people.

*   *   *

This population size would be sufficient to provide all the goods and services needed by U.S. residents while improving quality of life and substantially reducing our impact on the environment. To achieve this demographic goal, two conditions would need to be satisfied:

First, enact an all-inclusive cap on immigration of 100,000 a year. Since immigration will be the largest contributor to future U.S. population growth, this is a critical first step in shifting the country to a sustainable demographic path. Reducing immigration will also reduce overall U.S. fertility, since first-generation immigrants tend to have larger-than-average families.

*   *   *

Incentives to Achieve a Voluntary and Temporary Reduction in
Fertility to below Replacement Level

Reducing our population size and stabilizing it at not more than 150 million would require that U.S. total fertility be maintained at below replacement level, but only for several decades. A gradual decline in fertility to no lower than 1.5 children per woman, followed by a slow increase back to replacement level (2.1), would be ideal in terms of achieving a "soft path" to an optimum population. * * *

A variety of options are available to help achieve this goal without inappropriately involving the government in individuals' childbearing decisions.

First, the United States could increase its support for contraceptive research and access. Every year, nearly six million women in the United States become pregnant, and nearly 50% of these pregnancies are unintended.[5] Eighty-five percent of teen pregnancies are unintended,[6] and births to teens account for nearly 13% of all births.[7] Simply addressing these issues would result in a substantial decline in fertility. In addition, the United States could abandon incentives for increased childbearing by, for example, restructuring the dependency tax deduction.

*   *   *

An Optimum Population Is Still Achievable

The good news is that about two-thirds of current U.S. biologic growth (net natural increase, births minus deaths) is due to population momentum from the baby boom. That is, pre-1970 fertility which we can do little about—the large majority of women from this generation have already completed their families or are reaching the end of their child bearing years. *   *   *

Were the United States to immediately enact an all-inclusive cap on immigration at 100,000 a year and provide incentives to voluntarily and gradually reduce fertility to sub-replacement levels, we could see U.S. population growth stop by 2050. Once growth stops, the U.S. would then begin a very gradual transition to a smaller, sustainable population.

*   *   *

5. *Contraception Counts: State-by-State Information*, (New York: The Alan Guttmacher Institute, 1998).

6. Alan Guttmacher Institute, tabulations of data from the 1988 National Maternal and Infant Healthy Survey, 1993; Henshaw, S. K., "Abortion Trends in 1987 and 1988: Age and Race," *Family Planning Perspectives*, 24:85–86, 1992, Table 1, p. 86 in *Sex and America's Teenagers*. The Alan Guttmacher Institute. New York: Alan Guttmacher Institute, 1994.

7. *Statistical Abstract of the United States: 1996*, Table 91.

274

J. KENNETH SMAIL

Remembering Malthus: A Preliminary Argument for a Significant Reduction in Global Human Numbers (2002)†

> It remains to inquire whether this power can be checked, and its effects kept equal to the means of subsistence, without vice or misery.
>
> —Malthus

It has become increasingly apparent over the past several decades that there is a growing tension between two seemingly irreconcilable trends. On one hand, moderate-to-conservative demographic projections indicate that global human numbers will almost certainly reach 9 billion (or more) by the mid-to-late 21st century. On the other, prudent and increasingly reliable scientific estimates suggest that the Earth's long-term sustainable carrying capacity (at what might be defined as an "adequate to comfortable" standard of living) may not be much greater than 2–3 billion.

As a consequence of this modern-day "Malthusian dilemma," it seems reasonable to suggest that it is now time—indeed, past time—to think boldly about the midrange future, and to consider alternatives that go *beyond* merely slowing the growth, or even the stabilization, of global human numbers. In this brief hortatory essay, I shall argue that it has now become necessary for the human species to develop and implement, as quickly as possible, a well-conceived, clearly articulated, broadly equitable, and internationally coordinated program designed to bring about a *very significant reduction* in global human numbers over the next two or more centuries. In simple quantitative terms, this effort will likely require a global population "shrinkage" of at least two-thirds to three-fourths, from a mid-21st century peak of 9-plus billion to a future (early 23rd century) population optimum in the 2–3 billion range. Obviously, a numerical change of this magnitude (whether brought about by conscious design or forces beyond human control) will require a major reorientation of human thought, values, expectations, and lifestyle(s). Unfortunately, there is no guarantee that such a program will be successful. Moreover, if humanity fails in this effort, it seems likely that nature's even harsher realities will almost certainly be imposed.

† J. Kenneth Smail (b. 1938) is professor of anthropology at Kenyon College. The text is from his "Remembering Malthus: A Preliminary Argument for a Significant Reduction in Global Human Numbers," *American Journal of Physical Anthropology* 118 (2002), 292–97. Reprinted by permission of the *American Journal of Physical Anthropology*.

In order better to appreciate the scope and ramifications of what is still a partly hidden crisis, perhaps the greatest ecological/evolutionary hurdle that our species has yet encountered, the body of this essay will call attention to a reasonably well-documented data set consisting of 10 "inescapable realities" that must not only be fully understood but soon confronted. The first five of these broad-based empirical observations focus on various demographic projections and concerns, while the latter five pertain to the finite ecological (and other) limitations inherent in any discussion of global carrying capacity.

Five Fundamental Demographic Observations

First, during the century just completed, world population grew from somewhere around 1.6 billion in 1900 to slightly more than 6 billion in the year 2000, an almost fourfold increase in but 100 years. This is an unprecedented numerical expansion. Throughout human history, global population growth measured over similar 100-year intervals has been virtually nonexistent or, at most, modestly incremental; the rate of increase has only become markedly more pronounced within the last few hundred years (becoming exponential in appearance if not in reality). To illustrate this on a more easily comprehensible scale, human population growth during the 1990s alone amounted to 0.9 billion, an astonishing increase (of nearly 20%) in but a single decade. Just by itself, this 10-year increase is equivalent to the entire global population in the late 18th century (during Malthus' lifetime), and is approximately triple the estimated world population (ca. 300 million) at the height of the Roman Empire. It is a chastening thought that even moderate-to-conservative demographic projections suggest that a comparable rate of increase, approaching 0.8 billion per decade, will continue well into this century. This means that the current global total of 6.2 billion (in the year 2002) could easily reach 9 billion or more by mid-21st century, an increase of 50% in only two generations.

Second, even if a fully effective program of zero population growth (ZPG) were to be implemented immediately, by limiting human fertility to what demographers term the *replacement rate* (roughly 2.1 children per female in the developed world, and slightly higher elsewhere), the global population would nevertheless continue its rapid rate of expansion. In fact, demographers estimate that it would take at least 2–3 generations (50–75 years) at ZPG fertility levels just to reach a point of population stability, unfortunately at numbers considerably higher than those at present. This powerful *population momentum* results from the fact that an unusually high proportion (nearly one-third) of the current world population is under the age of 15 and has not yet reproduced. Even more broad-based *population profiles* may be found throughout the developing world, where the under-15 age cohort often exceeds 40% and where birth rates have remained high even as mortality rates have fallen. While there is clear evidence that fertility rates have been declining over the past several decades, not only in the developed world but also in various parts of the less-developed world, it is important to recognize that the current composite fertility rate for the less-developed world (excluding China) is still nearly double (ca. 3.7) that needed for ZPG.

Third, in addition to fertility levels, it is essential to understand that population growth is also significantly affected by changes in mortality rates. In fact, demographic transition theory suggests that the earlier stages of rapid population expansion are typically fueled more by significant reductions in death rates (i.e., decreased childhood mortality and/or enhanced adult longevity) than by changes in birth rates. Nor does recent empirical data suggest that average human life expectancy has reached anywhere near its theoretical upper limit, in either the developing or developed worlds. Consequently, unless there appears a deadly pandemic, a devastating world war, or a massive breakdown in public health (or a combination of all three), it is obvious that ongoing global gains in human longevity will continue to make a major contribution to world population expansion over the next half-century, regardless of whatever progress might be made in reducing fertility.

A further consequence of this continuing trend is the fact that most national populations will inevitably get "older," with mean ages in the 35–40-year range and perhaps as many as 20–25% of their members over age 60, as both mortality and fertility rates decline and human numbers (hopefully) reach stable levels. Not surprisingly, each of these aging populations will develop its own unique set of problems to resolve, not the least of which might be understandable—but in the longer term almost certainly misguided—"pronatalist" efforts to increase the size and overall economic productivity of younger age cohorts by encouraging higher fertility (and perhaps enhanced immigration).

Fourth, it is important to recognize that the quantitative scale, geographic scope, escalating pace, and functional interconnectedness of these impending demographic changes are of such a magnitude that there are few if any historical precedents to guide us. All previous examples of significant human population expansion—and subsequent (occasionally rapid) decline—have been primarily local or, at most, regional phenomena. At the present time, given the current global rate of increase of some 225,000 people per day (more than 9,000 per hour), it is ludicrous to speak of there being any significant empty spaces left on Earth to colonize, certainly when compared with but a century ago. And it is even more ridiculous to suggest that "off Earth" (extraterrestrial) migration will somehow be sufficient to siphon away excess human numbers, in either the near or the more distant future.

*   *   *

Fifth, given the data and observations presented thus far, it becomes increasingly apparent that the time span available for implementing an effective program of population "regulation" may be quite limited, with a window of opportunity (even in the more optimistic scenarios) that may not extend much beyond the middle of the 21st century. Other projections are rather more pessimistic, allowing no more than another 15–20 years for taking effective remedial action. In any event, while future population trends are notoriously difficult to predict with precision (dependent as they are on a broad range of factors), even low-to-moderate demographic projections for the year 2050 (a little more than two generations from now) are in the 8–9 billion range.

Several observations might help to bring these demographic estimates, and the above-mentioned "limited" time span, into somewhat better perspective: 1) the year 2050 is now closer to the present than the year 1950; 2) an infant born in 2002 will be only 48 years old in the year 2050; and 3) a young person entering the job market in the early 21st century will just have reached retirement age by the year 2050. By any reasonable standard of comparison, this is hardly the remote future. These observations also make it quite clear that it is primarily *those already born*—ourselves, our children, and our grandchildren—who will have to confront the overwhelming impact of an additional 3 billion people within the next half century.

Five Matters Pertaining to Global Carrying Capacity

Sixth, it is extremely important to come to terms with the fact that the Earth's long-term sustainable carrying capacity, in terms of resources broadly defined, is indeed finite, despite the continuing use of economic models predicated on seemingly unlimited growth, and notwithstanding the high probability of continued scientific/technological progress. Some further terminological clarification may be useful. "Long-term" is most reasonably defined on the order of several hundred years at least (in human terms, a minimum of 8–10 lifetimes). It emphatically does *not* mean the 5–15-year horizon typical of much economic forecasting or political prognostication. Over this much longer time span, it thus becomes much more appropriate (perhaps even essential to civilization's survival) to define a sustainable human population size in terms of *optimums* rather than maximums. In other words, *what "could" be supported in the short term is not necessarily what "should" be humanity's goal over the longer term.*

As far as resources are concerned, whether these be characterized as renewable or nonrenewable, it is becoming increasingly apparent that the era of inexpensive energy (derived from fossil fuels), adequate food supplies (whether plant or animal), readily available or easily extractable raw materials (from wood to minerals), plentiful fresh water, and readily accessible "open space" is rapidly coming to a close, almost certainly within the next half-century. In addition, the consequences of future scientific/technological advances (whether in terms of energy production, technological efficiency, agricultural productivity, or creation of alternative materials) are much more likely to be *incremental* than revolutionary, notwithstanding frequent and grandiose claims for the latter.

Seventh, it is becoming increasingly apparent that rhetoric about "sustainable growth" is at best a continuing exercise in economic self-deception and at worst a politically pernicious oxymoron. Almost certainly, working toward some sort of *steady-state sustainability* is much more realistic scientifically, (probably) more attainable economically, and (perhaps) more prudent politically. Assertions that the Earth might be able to support a population of 10, 15, or even 20 billion people for an indefinite period of time at a standard of living superior to the present are not only cruelly misleading but almost certainly false. Rather, extrapolations from the work of a growing number of ecologists, demographers, and numerous others, including even a few prescient economists, suggest the distinct possibility that *the Earth's true (optimal) carrying capacity—defined simply as humans in long-term adaptive balance with their ecological setting, resource bases, and each other—may already have been exceeded by a factor of two or more.*

To the best of my knowledge, there is no clear-cut or well-documented evidence that effectively contradicts this sobering—perhaps even frightening—assessment. Consequently, since at some point in the not-too-distant future the negative ramifications and ecological damage stemming from the mutually reinforcing effects of excessive human reproduction and overconsumption of resources could well become irreversible, and because there is only one Earth with which to experiment, it is undoubtedly better for our species to err on the side of prudence, exercising wherever possible a cautious and careful stewardship.

At the very least, economic analyses (and future projections based on these analyses) should not be formulated without taking the *Earth's finite physical and ecological limitations* into account. It should by now be obvious that continued economic growth (surely the dominant political mantra of the 20th and early 21st centuries) has had significant social and ecological consequences, many of which have been negative. And it should further be obvious that the (often hidden) "external costs" of today's economic activity, costs not only of production but also of consumption, pollution, conservation, and irretrievable loss (unavoidable "wastage"), must be fully factored in. After all, these "externalities" are costs borrowed from what some have termed finite natural capital, the profligate use and continued degradation of which will surely have a considerable effect on the quality of life in future generations. Put simply, in the real world of physical limits and biological constraints, in contrast to the theoretical world of monetary analysis, neither nature nor the future can be "discounted."

Eighth, only about 20% of the current world population (ca. 1.2 billion people) could be said to have a *"generally adequate"* standard of living, defined here as a level of affluence roughly approximately that of the so-called "developed" world (e.g., Western Europe, Japan, North America, Australia). The other 80% (ca. 5.0 billion), including most of the inhabitants of what have been termed the "developing nations," live in conditions ranging from mild deprivation to severe deficiency. Despite well-intentioned efforts to the contrary, there is little evidence that this imbalance is going to decrease in any significant way, and a strong likelihood that it may get worse, particularly in view of the fact that more than 90% of all future population expansion is projected to occur in these less-developed regions of the world.

In fact, there is growing concern that when this burgeoning population growth in the developing world is combined with excessive or wasteful per capita energy and resource consumption in much of the developed world, widespread environmental deterioration (systemic breakdown) in a number of the Earth's more heavily stressed ecosystems will become increasingly likely. This is especially worrisome in regions already beset by short-sighted or counterproductive economic policies, chronic political instability, and growing social unrest, particularly when one considers that nearly all nations in the less-developed world currently have an understandable desire (not surprisingly expressed as a fundamental right) to increase their standard of living (per capita energy and resource consumption) to something approximating "first world" levels.

Ninth, to follow up on the point just made, the total impact of human numbers on the global environment is often described as the product of three basic multipliers: 1) population size; 2) per capita energy and resource consumption (level of affluence); and 3) technological efficiency in the production, utilization, and conservation of such energy and resources. This relationship is usually expressed by some variant of the now well-known I = PCT equation: Impact = Population × Consumption × Technology. This simple formula enables one to demonstrate much more clearly the quantitative scope of humanity's dilemma over the next 100 years, particularly if the following projections are anywhere near accurate: 1) that human population could almost double over the next century, from our current 6.2 billion to perhaps 10–11 billion; 2) that per capita global energy and resource demand could easily grow four-, six-, or even eightfold during the same period, particularly if the less-developed nations are successful in their current efforts to significantly improve their citizens' standard of living to something approaching developed-world norms; and 3) that various new technologies applied to reducing current energy and resource inefficiencies might be successful in reducing per capita consumption by as much as 50–75%, in both the developed and developing worlds.

Given these more-or-less reasonable estimates, and factoring them together as per the above formula, the conclusion seems inescapable that the human species' "total impact" on the Earth's already stressed ecosystem(s) could easily *quadruple* (or more) by the mid/late 21st century. This impact could in fact be *much greater* if current (and future) efforts at energy and resource conservation turn out to be less successful than hoped for, or if (as seems likely) the mathematical relationship between these several multipliers is something more than simply linear. Consider, for example the following scenario provided by Myers:

> Per capita consumption worldwide has increased by 3% per year during the past quarter century, so it is reasonable to suppose that people in the future will want it to increase by at least 2% per year (provided it can be sustainable). Per capita consumption would then double in 35 years, quadruple in 70 years and increase eight-fold by 2100 . . . Were global population to reach 11 billion people by 2100, total consumption would [then] expand 15 times—an amount surely unsustainable given available stocks of nonrenewable natural resources and given the Earth's limited capacity to absorb pollution among other forms of waste. Even a low-variant projection for global population, 6.0 billion by 2100 (albeit after a mid-century peak of 8.0 billion), would leave consumption soaring 8.4 times.[1]

It is therefore very important to keep a close watch—for harbingers of future trends and/or problems—on current events in the growing group of nations now experiencing rapid economic development, with particular attention being given to ongoing changes in

1. Myers N. 1997. The population/environment predicament: even more urgent than supposed. Politics Life Sci 16:211–213.

India and China, two states whose combined size represents nearly half the population of the less-developed world.

Tenth, and finally, there are two additional considerations (matters not usually factored into the I = PCT equation) that must also be taken into account in any attempt to coordinate appropriate responses to the rapidly increasing global environmental impact described in points 6–9 above. First, given current and likely ongoing scientific uncertainties about environmental limits and ecosystem resilience, not to mention the potential dangers of irreversible damage if such limits are stretched too far (i.e., a permanently reduced carrying capacity), it is extremely important to design into any future planning an adequate safety factor (or a sufficient margin for error). In other words, any attempt at "guided social engineering" on the massive scale that will likely be necessary over the next century will require at least as much attention to safety margins, internal coordination, and systems redundancy as may be found in other major engineering accomplishments—from designing airplanes to building the Channel Tunnel to landing astronauts on the moon.

In addition, such planning must consider yet another seemingly intractable problem. Because the human species not only shares the Earth—but has also coevolved—with literally millions of other life forms, the closely related issues of *wilderness conservation* and *biodiversity preservation* must also be taken fully into account, on several different levels (pragmatic, aesthetic, and moral). In simplest terms, it has now become a matter of critical importance to ask some very basic questions about what proportion of the Earth's surface the human species has the right to exploit or transform, or conversely, how much of the Earth's surface should be reserved for the protection and preservation of all other life forms. As many have argued, often in eloquent terms, our species will likely be more successful in confronting and resolving these questions (not to mention the other complex problems that are now crowding in upon us) if we can collectively come to regard ourselves more as the Earth's long-term stewards than its absolute masters.

To sum up, if the above "inescapable realities" have indeed been correctly described, it is obvious that empirically justifiable, broadly equitable, and realistically attainable population goals will have to be established in the very near future. It is also obvious that these goals will have to address (and in some fashion resolve) a powerful internal conflict: how to create and sustain an adequate standard of living for all the worlds' peoples, minimizing as much as possible the growing inequities between rich and poor, while simultaneously neither over-stressing nor exceeding the Earth's longer-term carrying capacity. *I submit that these goals cannot be reached, or this conflict resolved, unless and until world population is dramatically reduced—*

to somewhere around two to three billion—within the next two centuries.

*   *   *

Quite frankly, I hope my hypothesis is wrong and that various demographic optimists are correct in their recent claims that not only will human numbers begin to show a "natural" stabilization and subsequent decline somewhat sooner than expected, but also that enhanced efficiencies in energy and resource production, consumption, and conservation will allow for considerably larger carrying capacities (i.e., higher population optimums) than we currently imagine. But this optimism is warranted only by corroborative data, i.e., only if the above-mentioned "irreconcilable numbers" show unmistakable evidence of coming into much closer congruence.

Perhaps it is time to suggest that the burden of proof on these matters, so long shouldered by so-called "neo-Malthusian pessimists," be increasingly shifted to the "cornucopian optimists." In other words, for those who might be inclined to minimize (or summarily reject) the hypothesis put forth here, the *scientific* burden of proof should be quite clear: *What is the evidence that the Earth can withstand, without irreparable damage, another two or more centuries during which global human numbers and per capita consumption greatly exceed the Earth's optimal (sustainable) carrying capacity?*

Closing Thoughts

I very much hope that this brief and somewhat speculative essay has helped to clarify an important if often underappreciated point: that ongoing population growth has a significant influence on, or connection with, nearly every other issue that humanity currently faces. I hope it is also obvious that this influence is both reciprocal and mutually reinforcing, resulting in numerous and interconnected positive feedback (or deviation amplifying) systems and subsystems. It may therefore be entirely appropriate to characterize rapid and continuing population expansion as the primary (or underlying) cause of many, if not most, of our species' growing political, economic, social, environmental, and moral difficulties. Put most simply, until demonstrated otherwise, I would argue that *unchecked or "insufficiently restrained" population growth should be considered the single most important feature in a complex (and synergistic) ecological, biocultural, and sociopolitical landscape.* More than two centuries after the publication of *An Essay on the Principle of Population,* it is surely worth remembering that—except perhaps for not fully anticipating the subsequent human capacity to overcome (at least temporarily) certain "checks" on population expansion—the Reverend

Thomas Malthus' analysis of the "constantly operating check on population [emerging] from the difficulty of subsistence" may have been right on target!

More than half a century ago, at the dawn of the nuclear age, Albert Einstein suggested that we shall require a new manner of thinking, if mankind is to survive. Even though the aptly named "population explosion" is neither as instantaneous nor as spectacular as its nuclear counterpart, the ultimate consequences may be just as real (and potentially just as devastating) as the so-called "nuclear winter" scenarios promulgated in the early 1980s. That there will be a large-scale reduction in human numbers over the next two or three centuries appears to be inevitable. The primary issue seems to be whether this process will be under conscious human control and (hopefully) relatively benign, or whether it will turn out to be essentially chaotic and (perhaps) utterly catastrophic. Clearly, we must begin our "new manner of thinking" about this critically important global issue now, so that Einstein's prescient and very legitimate concerns about human (and civilization's) survival into the 21st century and beyond may be addressed as rapidly, as fully, and as humanely as possible.

* * *

ROBERT ENGELMAN, BRIAN HALWEIL, AND DANIELLE NIERENBERG

Rethinking Population, Improving Lives (2002)†

The Politics of Population

After the Earth Summit, the Cairo conference, and the Beijing conference on women, the community of nations knows why and how to slow world population growth. And this work is moving forward. The global fertility rate has fallen almost by half in just 40 years. Yet the promise of reproductive health for all and equality for women remains unfulfilled. As a result, so does the vision of a world moving swiftly toward a population peak based on intended childbearing.

At the ICPD in Cairo in 1994, governments agreed to spend $17 billion a year (in 1993 dollars) by 2000 to achieve universal

† Robert Engelman (b. 1951) is vice president for research at Population Action International. Brian Halweil (b. 1975) is a research associate at the Worldwatch Institute. Danielle Nierenberg (b. 1973) is a staff researcher at the Worldwatch Institute. The text is from their *State of the World 2002* (New York, 2002). Reprinted by permission of W. W. Norton & Company.

access to basic reproductive health services for all by 2015. This was to include $10.2 billion for family planning services, $5 billion for maternal health and care at delivery, and $1.3 billion for prevention of HIV/AIDS and other sexually transmitted diseases. Since Cairo, the emerging deadliness of the HIV/AIDS pandemic has framed it almost as a separate health issue in international dialogue, with agreement that much more will need to be spent than the ICPD envisioned. But so far there is no consensus on just how much money will be needed in the effort to contain HIV/AIDS, what it will buy, and who will pay for it.

Of the original Cairo sum for family planning and other reproductive health needs, wealthy nations pledged to cover one third of the cost, with the developing world agreeing to pay the remainder. In 1998, the most recent year with comprehensive data, wealthy nations contributed less than 40 percent of their Cairo commitment. By contrast, developing nations have been spending close to 70 percent of their committed levels. (This proportion is somewhat distorted, however, by high spending in China, India, and Indonesia, with much lower spending in sub-Saharan Africa).[1]

The U.S. contribution to Cairo spending levels has been the most disappointing. The nation with the world's largest economy should be spending, according to calculations by Population Action International, $1.9 billion annually on family planning and related health programs in developing countries. The current U.S. contribution, however, is $500 million for reproductive health programs, as appropriated for fiscal year 2001, including $450 million for family planning and ancillary services and $50 million specifically for maternal health. Abortion-related restrictions—the "global gag rule" reinstated by the Bush administration—complicate the allocation of these funds.

*   *   *

Historically, the world's major religions have erected some of the most formidable barriers to increased availability of family planning services and reproductive health care in general. Some Catholic, Islamic, and other religious leaders continue to preach abstinence as the only effective and moral means of controlling births. Nonetheless, from Iran to Italy, nations in which religion plays a major role have made great progress in widening access to family planning and reproductive health care and improving the status of women.[2]

1. Commitments at Cairo from Programme of Action of the International Conference on Population and Development; developing-country spending from UNFPA, *Financial Resource Flows for Population Activities in 1998* (New York: 1999), p. i; 40 percent from Shanti R. Conly and Shyami de Silva, *Paying Their Fair Share? Donor Countries and International Population Assistance* (Washington, DC: PAI, 1998), p. 4.
2. Religious opposition to contraception from Oscar Harkavy, *Curbing Population Growth:*

Many religious leaders are coming to realize that there is no inherent conflict between family planning and religion, and that in fact lack of reproductive rights represents a grave social injustice. In Iran, Islamic clerics have even issued *fatwas*, or religious edicts, approving family planning methods—from oral contraceptives and condoms to sterilization. This approval, along with the integration of family planning services with primary health care, the provision of free contraceptives, and the strengthening of men's role in reproductive health, resulted in the total fertility rate in Iran dropping from 5.6 children in 1985 to 2.8 children in 2000—among the most precipitous declines in family size in the modern demographic transition.[3]

The influence of religious leaders tends to occur at the level of policymakers—undermining agreements on population and reproductive health, for example, and discouraging government health programs that include effective access to a range of contraceptives. At the household level, in contrast, women and men make the choices that affect their daily lives. In the privacy of their bedrooms, many see contraception not as a sin or a sign of lack of faith, but as an important part of loving, committed relationships.

Where religion continues to hamper efforts to give people greater control over their reproductive lives, the world's religious leaders may need to reconcile their actions with their humanitarian ideals. For instance, Bishop Kevin Dowling recently risked his career when he introduced a proposal at the Southern African Catholic Bishops conference in support of condom use as part of the wider effort to stop the spread of HIV in his region—home to the highest HIV infection rates in the world. Although the proposal was rejected, and the Church remains aggressively opposed to condom use, Bishop Dowling's efforts give some sense of the leadership that will be needed if religions are to work with others in the fight against HIV/AIDS and other public health problems related to reproduction.[4]

The gap between the opinions of church leaders and church members on reproductive issues mirrors a wider chasm between elected officials and their constituencies. According to a recent Gallup poll, for example, over 75 percent of Mexicans believe in a woman's right to choose abortion. Yet Mexico's politicians oppose reforms allowing women and couples greater access to safe abortion procedures. Conservative U.S. politicians, too, would like to see *Roe v. Wade*, the 1973 Supreme Court decision legalizing abortion in the United States, overturned. And they continue to stymie efforts to fund inter-

An Insider's Perspective on the Population Movement (New York: Plenum Press, 1995), pp. 93, 95, 163.
3. Farzaneh Foudi, "Iran's Approach to Family Planning," *Population Today*, July/August 1999, p. 4.
4. "Church Active in Care for Those with AIDS," *Catholic News Service*, 9 July 2001.

national family planning programs, even though opinion polls show that the vast majority of Americans support both a woman's right to control her own fertility and U.S. efforts in this area overseas.[5]

From some political and religious organizations, yet another misconception clouds discussion and muzzles debate—the idea that providing choices about pregnancy and childbearing is synonymous with the promotion of abortion. In the United States, a consistent effort by a small number of groups and politicians to promote this point of view has politicized what was once a bipartisan effort to guarantee worldwide access to contraception, and it has created a web of restrictions on U.S. spending to support international family planning. Ironically, demographic research confirms what logic tells us: wider provision of good family planning services reduces the numbers of abortions that would otherwise occur. When researchers looked at two similar areas of rural Bangladesh, one with good family planning services and the other without, they found that abortion rates had increased over the past two decades in the one with poor family planning services but had held steady at low rates in the area with good services.[6]

Just as important as spending levels are the political attitudes that shape and expand population policies and reproductive health programs around the world. In the spirit of Cairo, countries in Africa, Asia, and Latin America are rethinking population policies and programs and looking to the Programme of Action for guidance on new directions related to overall health and development. Progress is uneven, of course. The governor of the Indian state of Andhra Pradesh, for example, publicly urges the parents of large families to "immediately go" for state-sponsored sterilizations. And China's central government resists the key principle of reproductive freedom of choice by continuing to insist that most Chinese couples limit their families to a single child. Nonetheless, the government has at least acknowledged the importance of the principles agreed to at Cairo. And India's federal government is abandoning its decades-long history of targets and quotas for family planning and its reliance on sterilization rather than the contraceptives that are more appropriate for tens of millions of couples.[7]

5. Marta Lamas, "Standing Fast in Mexico: Protecting Women's Rights in a Hostile Climate," *NACLA Report on the Americas*, March/April 2001, p. 40; David M. Adamson et al., *How Americans View World Population Issues: A Survey of Public Opinion* (Santa Monica, CA: RAND, 2000), pp. 40, 41, 51, 52.
6. Mizanur Rahman, Julie DaVanzo, and Abdur Razzaque, "Do Better Family Planning Services Reduce Abortion in Bangladesh?" *Lancet*, 29 September 2001, pp. 1051–56.
7. Karen Hardee et al., *Post-Cairo Reproductive Health Policies and Programs: A Comparative Study of Eight Countries*, Policy Papers No. 2 (Washington: The Futures Group International, September 1998); Celia W. Dugger, "Relying on Hard and Soft Sells, India Pushes for Sterilization," *New York Times*, 22 June 2001; China from Sophia Woodman, "Draft Law Fails to Address Real Population Issues," *South China Morning Post*, 9 July 2001; India from Rami Chhabra, "Saying Goodbye to Targets," *People & the Planet*,

The overall movement among national governments in developing countries is clearly away from bureaucratic population "control" and toward supporting the choices of couples and individuals to have children, when desired, in good health.

Correcting Gender Myopia

In the long view of where population policy is heading, the most daunting issues include not only religious obstacles or public division over abortion rights, but also the social and psychological shifts that will occur as women approach equal status with men. The more we learn about the interconnections between population growth, fertility, timing of pregnancy, and reproductive health, the more we see their links to ingrained attitudes about the relative roles and power between females and males.

As long as girls and women are envisioned as less able than boys and men to navigate human experience and decide for themselves how to live, population policy will always be imperfect. When girls go to secondary school free of fear of violence and sexual coercion and when women approach economic, social, and political parity with men, they have fewer children and give birth later on average than their mothers did—and, assuming good access to health and family planning services, fertility almost invariably reaches replacement level or lower. That slows the growth of population.

Yet this centrality of women to population's future also introduces discomfort, implying that interest in slowing population growth can turn women into instruments for some "larger" purpose, or into commodities to be counted and valued for the results of their reproductive decisions and actions. Those who work to slow the growth of population and those who work for women's parity with men sometimes are the same people, aiming at many of the same interim objectives: access to comprehensive and integrated reproductive health care, ending the gender gap in education and in economic opportunities, eliminating violence against women. The fact is that certain changes are essential for women themselves—simply from a perspective of fairness and equal rights for all humans—while simultaneously contributing to broader improvements in population trends and in human and environmental welfare.

The pervasiveness of violence against women around the world—verbal, physical, sexual, or economic—stands as the strongest indict-

vol. 6, no. 1 (1997), pp. 14–15, from Leela Visaria, Shireen Jejeebhoy, and Tom Merrick, "From Family Planning to Reproductive Health: Challenges Facing India," *International Family Planning Perspectives*, vol. 25 supplement (1999), pp. S44–49, and from Michael A. Koenig, Gillian H. C. Foo, and Ketan Joshi, "Quality of Care Within the Indian National Family Welfare Programme: A Review of Recent Evidence," *Studies in Family Planning*, March 2000, p. 13.

ment against current relations between the sexes.[8] As many as half of all women have experienced domestic violence, according to the World Health Organization.

*   *   *

Used as a weapon, sexual violence in all its forms—coerced sex, rape, incest—inhibits women's ability to control their own reproductive health. Ending this violence will be first and foremost its own reward. The supplemental benefit for positive demographic change comes from the simple fact that women can scarcely be free to decide for themselves when and with whom to become parents if they cannot even control the security of their persons.

Gender-related violence, however, is simply the most direct form of discrimination against women. Economies and societies generally undervalue women's work, from the household to the farm, the factory, and the office. Women typically work longer hours than men—nurturing children, caring for elders, maintaining homes, farming, and hauling wood and water home from distant sources. This labor is largely invisible to economists and policymakers, but by some estimates it amounts to a third of the world's economic production.[9]

*   *   *

With the emergence of strong women's NGOs in the decade since Cairo, it seems likely that full political participation by women in national politics may become the last and most important frontier in achieving the gender equity needed for truly sustainable societies. Women remain underrepresented at all levels of government in almost all countries. * * *

Evidence from Sweden, South Africa, India, and other nations shows that when more women hold political office, issues important to women and their families rise in priority and are acted on by those in power. Over the past decade, the Swedish government—where women currently hold almost 43 percent of the seats in Parliament and 82 percent of the cabinet ministries—has passed expansive equal opportunity and child care leave acts. And in South Africa,

8. WHO, *Violence Against Women* (Geneva: 1996); Lori Heise, Mary Ellsberg, and Megan Gottemoeller, "Ending Violence Against Women," *Population Reports*, December 1999, p. 5. Box 6–3 from the following: UNICEF, "Domestic Violence Against Women and Girls," *Innocenti Digest*, May 2000, p. 6; Celia W. Dugger, "Modern Asia's Anomaly: The Girls Who Don't Get Born," *New York Times*, 6 May 2001; UNICEF, *Innocenti Digest*, May 2000, p. 3; WHO, "Female Genital Mutilation," fact sheet no. 241 (Geneva: June 2000); UNFPA, *The State of World Population 2000* (New York: 2000), p. 29; Molly Moore, "In Turkey, Honor Killing' Follows Families to Cities," *Washington Post*, 8 August 2001; Suzan Fraser, "Suicides of Women Rising in Traditional Southeast Turkey," *Washington Post*, 9 November 2000; UNFPA, op. cit., p. 38.
9. World Bank, *Engendering Development: Through Gender Equality in Rights, Resources, and Voice* (New York: Oxford University Press, 2001), pp. 152–54; one third share from UNFPA, op. cit. note 8, p. 38.

which established a quota for women candidates to parliament in 2000, women hold 119 of the 399 seats in the National Assembly and 8 of the 29 cabinet positions. These female politicians have played a key role in lobbying for the Choice of Termination of Pregnancy Act and the Domestic Violence Act and in establishing governmental institutions that promote gender equality.[1]

Despite such progress and the evidence of its benefits, gender myopia continues to cloud the vision needed by development agencies, international lenders, and governments. From agriculture to trade liberalization to health care reforms, policy decisions affect women in quite distinct ways. If their specific concerns are not made part of the policy process, the results can be disastrous.

* * *

As the growing concerns about population aging and decline in some countries illustrate, it is increasingly possible that world population growth will end within the next 50 years. By the end of this century, there may be few countries whose populations are still growing. For the sake of the environment and healthy human relations, we should encourage this historic process, resisting the urge to try to roll back population aging in some countries by stoking continued population growth. We can work, as well, to make sure that the inevitable end to that growth is driven by intended reductions in births, not by increases in deaths.

If we succeed, history will note that world population growth ended not because governments commanded it to do so, but because the free decisions of women and men made that end inevitable. And the population peak will arrive as one momentous ripple from an equally momentous drop of a stone in a pond—the stone by which women at last gain their full rights, choices, and standing as equal members of the human family.

1. WEDO, "Fact Sheet 2: Women Making a Difference," at <www.wedo.org/fact_sheet_2.htm>, viewed 18 July 2001; Inter-Parliamentary Union (IPU), "Women in National Parliaments," at <www.ipu.org/wmn-e/world.htm>, updated 12 October 2001.

I. THREE SIGNIFICANT POSTSCRIPTS

World Scientists' Warning to Humanity (1993)†

Introduction

Human beings and the natural world are on a collision course. Human activities inflict harsh and often irreversible damage on the environment and on critical resources. If not checked, many of our current practices put at serious risk the future that we wish for human society and the plant and animal kingdoms, and may so alter the living world that it will be unable to sustain life in the manner that we know. Fundamental changes are urgent if we are to avoid the collision our present course will bring about.

The Environment

The environment is suffering critical stress:

THE ATMOSPHERE

Stratospheric ozone depletion threatens us with enhanced ultraviolet radiation at the earth's surface, which can be damaging or lethal to many life forms. Air pollution near ground level, and acid precipitation, are already causing widespread injury to humans, forests, and crops.

WATER RESOURCES

Heedless exploitation of depletable groundwater supplies endangers food production and other essential human systems. Heavy demands on the world's surface waters have resulted in serious shortages in some 80 countries, containing 40 percent of the world's population. Pollution of rivers, lakes, and groundwater further limits the supply.

† The text is from *Population Summit of the World's Scientific Academies* (Washington, D.C., 1993). Reprinted by permission of the National Academy of Sciences.

OCEANS

Destructive pressure on the oceans is severe, particularly in the coastal regions, which produce most of the world's food fish. The total marine catch is now at or above the estimated maximum sustainable yield. Some fisheries have already shown signs of collapse. Rivers carrying heavy burdens of eroded soil into the seas also carry industrial, municipal, agricultural, and livestock waste—some of it toxic.

SOIL

Loss of soil productivity, which is causing extensive land abandonment, is a widespread by-product of current practices in agriculture and animal husbandry. Since 1945, 11 percent of the earth's vegetated surface has been degraded—an area larger than India and China combined—and per capita food production in many parts of the world is decreasing.

FORESTS

Tropical rain forests, as well as tropical and temperate dry forests, are being destroyed rapidly. At present rates, some critical forest types will be gone in a few years, and most of the tropical rain forest will be gone before the end of the next century. With them will go large numbers of plant and animal species.

LIVING SPECIES

The irreversible loss of species, which by 2100 may reach one-third of all species now living, is especially serious. We are losing the potential they hold for providing medicinal and other benefits, and the contribution that genetic diversity of life forms gives to the robustness of the world's biological systems and to the astonishing beauty of the earth itself.

Much of this damage is irreversible on a scale of centuries or permanent. Other processes appear to pose additional threats. Increasing levels of gases in the atmosphere from human activities, including carbon dioxide released from fossil fuel burning and from deforestation, may alter climate on a global scale. Predictions of global warming are still uncertain—with projected effects ranging from tolerable to very severe—but the potential risks are very great.

Our massive tampering with the world's interdependent web of life—coupled with the environmental damage inflicted by deforestation, species loss, and climate change—could trigger widespread adverse effects, including unpredictable collapses of critical biological systems whose interactions and dynamics we only imperfectly understand.

Uncertainty over the extent of these effects cannot excuse complacency or delay in facing the threats.

Population

The earth is finite. Its ability to absorb wastes and destructive effluent is finite. Its ability to provide food and energy is finite. Its ability to provide for growing numbers of people is finite. And we are fast approaching many of the earth's limits. Current economic practices that damage the environment, in both developed and underdeveloped nations, cannot be continued without the risk that vital global systems will be damaged beyond repair.

Pressures resulting from unrestrained population growth put demands on the natural world that can overwhelm any efforts to achieve a sustainable future. If we are to halt the destruction of our environment, we must accept limits to that growth. A World Bank estimate indicates that world population will not stabilize at less than 12.4 billion, while the United Nations concludes that the eventual total could reach 14 billion, a near tripling of today's 5.4 billion. But, even at this moment, one person in five lives in absolute poverty without enough to eat, and one in ten suffers serious malnutrition.

No more than one or a few decades remain before the chance to avert the threats we now confront will be lost and the prospects for humanity immeasurably diminished.

Warning

We the undersigned, senior members of the world's scientific community, hereby warn all humanity of what lies ahead. A great change in our stewardship of the earth and the life on it is required if vast human misery is to be avoided and our global home on this planet is not to be irretrievably mutilated.

What We Must Do

Five inextricably linked areas must be addressed simultaneously:

1. We must bring environmentally damaging activities under control to restore and protect the integrity of the earth's systems we depend on. We must, for example, move away from fossil fuels to more benign, inexhaustible energy sources to cut greenhouse gas emissions and the pollution of our air and water. Priority must be given to the development of

energy sources matched to Third World needs—small-scale and relatively easy to implement.

We must halt deforestation, injury to and loss of agricultural land, and the loss of terrestrial and marine plant and animal species.

2. We must manage resources crucial to human welfare more effectively. We must give high priority to efficient use of energy, water, and other materials, including expansion of conservation and recycling.

3. We must stabilize population. This will be possible only if all nations recognize that it requires improved social and economic conditions, and the adoption of effective, voluntary family planning.

4. We must reduce and eventually eliminate poverty.

5. We must ensure sexual equality, and guarantee women control over their own reproductive decisions.

The developed nations are the largest polluters in the world today. They must greatly reduce their overconsumption if we are to reduce pressures on resources and the global environment. The developed nations have the obligation to provide aid and support to developing nations, because only the developed nations have the financial resources and the technical skills for these tasks.

Action on this recognition is not altruism, but enlightened self-interest: whether industrialized or not, we all have but one lifeboat. No nation can escape from injury when global biological systems are damaged. No nation can escape from conflicts over increasingly scarce resources. In addition, environmental and economic instabilities will cause mass migrations with incalculable consequences for developed and undeveloped nations alike.

Developing nations must realize that environmental damage is one of the gravest threats they face and that attempts to blunt it will be overwhelmed if their populations go unchecked. The greatest peril is to become trapped in spirals of environmental decline, poverty, and unrest, leading to social, economic, and environmental collapse.

Success in this global endeavor will require a great reduction in violence and war. Resources now devoted to the preparation and conduct of war—amounting to over $1 trillion annually—will be badly needed in the new tasks and should be diverted to the new challenges.

A new ethic is required—a new attitude toward discharging our responsibility for caring for ourselves and for the earth. We must recognize the earth's limited capacity to provide for us. We must recognize its fragility. We must no longer allow it to be ravaged. This ethic must motivate a great movement, convincing reluctant leaders and reluctant governments and reluctant peoples themselves to effect the needed changes. The scientists issuing this warning hope that our message will reach and affect people everywhere. We need the help of many.

We require the help of the world community of scientists—natural, social, economic, political;

We require the help of the world's business and industrial leaders;

We require the help of the world's religious leaders; and

We require the help of the world's peoples.

We call on all to join us in this task.

The following is an abridged list of signatories of the Warning. Over 1,670 scientists, including 104 Nobel laureates—a majority of the living recipients of the Prize in the sciences—have signed it so far. These men and women represent 71 countries, including all of the 19 largest economic powers, all of the 12 most populous nations, 12 countries in Africa, 14 in Asia, 19 in Europe, and 12 in Latin America.[1]

Walter Alvarez, Geologist, National Academy of Sciences, USA

Philip Anderson, Nobel laureate, Physics; USA

Christian Anfinsen, Nobel laureate, Chemistry; USA

Werner Arber, Nobel laureate, Medicine; Switzerland

Michael Atiyah, Mathematician; President, Royal Society; Great Britain

Mary Ellen Avery, Pediatrician, National Medal of Science, USA

Julius Axelrod, Nobel laureate, Medicine; USA

Howard Bachrach, Biochemist, National Medal of Science, USA

John Backus, Computer Scientist, National Medal of Science, USA

David Baltimore, Nobel laureate, Medicine; USA

David Bates, Physicist, Royal Irish Academy, Ireland

Georg Bednorz, Nobel laureate, Physics; Switzerland

Baruj Benacerraf, Nobel laureate, Medicine; USA

Sune Bergstrom, Nobel laureate, Medicine; Sweden

Hans Bethe, Nobel laureate, Physics; USA

Konrad Bloch, Nobel laureate, Medicine; USA

Nicholaas Bloembergen, Nobel laureate, Physics; USA

Bert Bolin, Meteorologist, Tyler Prize, Sweden

Norman Borlaug, Agricultural Scientist; Nobel laureate, Peace; USA & México

1. From Paul R. Ehrlich and Anne M. Ehrlich, *Betrayal of Science and Reason* (Washington, D.C., 1996).

E. Margaret Burbidge, Astronomer, National Medal of Science, USA

Adolph Butenandt, Nobel laureate, Chemistry; Former President, Max Planck Institute; Germany

Ennio Candotti, Physicist; President, Brazilian Society for the Advancement of Science; Brazil

Georges Charpak, Nobel laureate, Physics; France

Paul Crutzen, Chemist, Tyler Prize, Germany

Jean Dausset, Nobel laureate, Medicine; France

Margaret Davis, Ecologist, National Academy of Sciences, USA

Gerard Debreu, Nobel laureate, Economics; USA

Paul-Yves Denis, Geographer, Academy of Sciences, Canada

Thomas Eisner, Biologist, Tyler Prize, USA

Mohammed T. El-Ashry, Environmental scientist, Third World Academy, Egypt & USA

Mahdi Elmandjra, Economist; Vice President, African Academy of Sciences; Morocco

Richard Ernst, Nobel laureate, Chemistry; Switzerland

Dagfinn Follesdal, President, Norwegian Academy of Science, Norway

Otto Frankel, Geneticist, Australian Academy of Sciences, Australia

Konstantin V. Frolov, Engineer; Vice President, Russian Academy of Sciences; Russia

Kenichi Fukui, Nobel laureate, Chemistry; Japan

Robert Gallo, Research scientist, Lasker Award, USA

Murray Gell-Mann, Nobel laureate, Physics; USA

Donald Glaser, Nobel laureate, Physics; USA

Sheldon Glashow, Nobel laureate, Physics; USA

Marvin Goldberger, Physicist; Former President, California Institute of Technology, USA

Stephen Jay Gould, Paleontologist, Author, Harvard University, USA

Stephen Hawking, Mathematician, Wolf Prize in Physics, Great Britain

Dudley Herschbach, Nobel Prize, Chemistry; USA

Dorothy Crowfoot Hodgkin, Nobel laureate, Chemistry; Great Britain

Roald Hoffman, Nobel laureate, Chemistry; USA

Nick Holonyak, Electrical Engineer, National Medal of Science, USA

Sarah Hrdy, Anthropologist, National Academy of Sciences, USA

Kun Huang, Physicist, Chinese Academy of Sciences, China

Hiroshi Inose, Electrical Engineer; Vice President, Engineering Academy; Japan

François Jacob, Nobel laureate, Medicine; France

Carl-Olof Jacobson, Zoologist; Secretary-General, Royal Academy of Sciences; Sweden

Daniel Janzen, Biologist, Crafoord Prize, USA

Harold Johnston, Chemist, Tyler Prize; USA

Robert Kates, Geographer, National Medal of Science, USA

Frederick I. B. Kayanja, Vice-Chancellor, Mbarara University, Third World Academy, Uganda

Henry Kendall, Nobel laureate, Physics; Chairman, Union of Concerned Scientists; USA

Gurdev Khush, Agronomist, International Rice Institute, Indian National Science Academy, India & The Philippines

Klaus von Klitzing, Nobel laureate, Physics; Germany

Aaron Klug, Nobel laureate, Chemistry; Great Britain

E. F. Knipling, Agricultural Researcher, National Medal of Science, USA

Walter Kohn, Physicist, National Medal of Science, USA

Torvard Laurent, Physiological chemist; President, Royal Academy of Sciences Sweden

Leon Lederman, Nobel laureate, Physics; Chairman, American Association for the Advancement of Science; USA

Wassily Leontief, Nobel laureate, Economics; USA

Luna Leopold, Geologist, National Medal of Science, USA

Rita Levi-Montalcini, Nobel laureate, Medicine; USA & Italy

William Lipscomb, Nobel laureate, Physics; USA

Jane Lubchenco, Zoologist; President-Elect, Ecological Society of America

Lynn Margulis, Biologist, National Academy of Sciences, USA

George Martine, Institute for Study of Society, Population, & Nature; Brazil

Ernst Mayr, Zoologist, National Medal of Science, USA

Digby McLaren, Past President, Royal Society of Canada; Canada

James Meade, Nobel laureate, Economics; Great Britain

Jerrold Meinwald, Chemistry, Tyler Prize, USA

M. G. K. Menon, Physicist; President, International Council of Scientific Unions; India

Gennady Mesiatz, Physicist; Vice President, Russian Academy of Sciences; Russia

César Milstein, Nobel laureate, Medicine; Argentina & Great Britain

Franco Modigliani, Nobel laureate, Economics; USA

Walter Munk, Geophysicist, National Medal of Science, USA

Lawrence Mysak, Meteorologist; Vice President, Academy of Science, Royal Society of Canada; Canada

James Neel, Geneticist, National Medal of Science, USA

Louis Néel, Nobel laureate, Physics; France

Howard Odum, Ecologist, Crafoord Prize, USA

Yuri Ossipyan, Physicist; Vice President, Russian Academy of Sciences; Russia

Autar Singh Paintal, Physiologist; Former President, Indian National Science Academy; India

Mary Lou Pardue, Biologist, National Academy of Sciences, USA

Linus Pauling, Nobel laureate, Chemistry & Peace; USA

Roger Penrose, Mathematician, Wolf Prize in Physics, Great Britain

John Polanyi, Nobel laureate, Chemistry; Canada

George Porter, Nobel laureate, Chemistry; Great Britain

Ilya Prigogine, Nobel laureate, Chemistry; Belgium

Edward Purcell, Nobel laureate, Physics; USA

G. N. Ramachandran, Mathematician, Institute of Science, India

Peter Raven, Director, Missouri Botanical Garden; National Academy of Sciences, USA

Tadeus Reichstein, Nobel laureate, Medicine; Switzerland

Gustavo Rivas Mijares, Engineer; Former President, Academy of Sciences, Venezuela

Wendell Roelofs, Entomologist, National Medal of Science, USA

Miriam Rothschild, Biologist, Royal Society, Great Britain

Sherwood Rowland, Chemist; Past President, American Association for the Advancement of Science; USA

Carlo Rubbia, Nobel laureate, Physics; Italy & Switzerland

Albert Sabin, Virologist, National Medal of Science, USA

Carl Sagan, Astrophysicist & Author, USA

Roald Sagdeev, Physicist, Russian & Pontifical Academies, Russia & USA

Abdus Salam, Nobel laureate, Physics; President, Third World Academy of Sciences; Pakistan & Italy

José Sarukhan, Biologist, Third World Academy, México

Richard Schultes, Botanist, Tyler Prize, USA

Glenn Seaborg, Nobel laureate, Physics; USA

Roger Sperry, Nobel laureate, Medicine; USA

Ledyard Stebbins, Geneticist, National Medal of Science, USA

Janos Szentgothai, Former President, Hungarian Academy of Sciences; Hungary

Jan Tinbergen, Nobel laureate, Economics; The Netherlands

James Tobin, Nobel laureate, Economics; USA

Susumu Tonegawa, Nobel laureate, Medicine; Japan & USA

James Van Allen, Physicist, Crafoord Prize, USA

Harold Varmus, Nobel laureate, Medicine; USA

George Wald, Nobel laureate, Medicine; USA

Gerald Wasserburg, Geophysicist, Crafoord Prize, USA

James Watson, Nobel laureate, Medicine; USA

Victor Weisskopf, Wolf Prize in Physics, USA

Fred Whipple, Astronomer, National Academy of Sciences, USA

Torsten Wiesel, Nobel laureate, Medicine; USA

Geoffrey Wilkinson, Nobel laureate, Chemistry; Great Britain

Edward O. Wilson, Biologist, Crafoord Prize, USA

Solly Zuckerman, Zoologist, Royal Society, Great Britain

Statement on Population Stabilization by World Leaders (1985/1995)†

Humankind has many challenges: to obtain a lasting peace between nations, to preserve the quality of the environment; to conserve natural resources at a sustainable level; to advance the economic and social progress of the less developed nations; to assure basic human rights and at the same time accept responsibility for the planet Earth and future generations of children; and to stabilize population growth.

† This statement, originally written by Robert W. Gillespie, president of Population Communication, was presented, with the assistance of Hal Burdett and Werner Fornos of the Population Institute, to Rafael Salas, Secretary General of UNFPA, at the 1984 United Nations Conference on Population in Mexico City. In 1985 the statement was presented by Prime Minister Rajiv Gandhi of India, with forty signatories, to the United Nations Secretary General, Javier Perez de Cuellar, in collaboration with the Global Committee of Parliamentarians on Population and Development. In 1995, President Suharto of Indonesia presented the statement to the United Nations Secretary General, Boutros Boutros-Ghali.

Degradation of the world's environment, income inequality, and the potential for conflict exist today because of rapid population growth, among other factors. If this unprecedented population growth continue, future generations of children will not have adequate food, housing, health services, education, earth resources, and employment opportunities.

We believe that the time has come now to recognize the worldwide necessity to achieve population stabilization and for each country to adopt the necessary policies and programs to do so, consistent with its own culture and aspirations. To enhance the integrity of the individual and the quality of life for all, we believe that all nations should participate in setting goals and programs for population stabilization. Measures for this purpose should be voluntary and should maintain individual human rights and beliefs.

We urge national leaders to take an active personal role in promoting effective policies and programs. Emphasis should be given to improving the status of women, respecting human rights and beliefs, and achieving the active participation of women in formulating policies and programs. Attention should be given to realistic goals and timetables and developing appropriate economic and social policies.

Recognizing that early population stabilization is in the interest of all nations, we earnestly hope that leaders around the world will share our views and join with us in this great undertaking for the well-being and happiness of people everywhere.

The Statement has been signed by the heads of government of the following countries:

Austria	Grenada	Liberia
Bangladesh	Guinea-Bissau	Libya
Barbados	Guyana	Macedonia
Bhutan	Haiti	Malawi
Botswana	Iceland	Malaysia
Cape Verde	India	Maldives
China, People's	Indonesia	Malta
Republic of	Israel	Mauritius
Colombia	Jamaica	Moldova
Cyprus	Japan	Morocco
Dominica	Jordan	Myanmar
Dominican Republic	Kenya	Namibia
Egypt	Korea, DPR	Nepal
Fiji	Korea,	Nigeria
Gambia	Republic of	Pakistan
Ghana	Laos	Palau

Panama
Peru
Philippines
Romania
Rwanda
Saint Kitts and Nevis
Saint Lucia
Saint Vincent and
    the Grenadines
São Tomé and Prin-
    cipe

Senegal
Seychelles
Singapore
Slovak Republic
South Africa
Sri Lanka
Sudan
Suriname
Swaziland
Tanzania
Thailand

Tonga, Kingdom of
Trinidad and Tobago
Tunisia
Turkey
Uganda
United Arab Emir-
    ates
Uzbekistan
Vanuatu
Zimbabwe

Priority Statement on Population (1991)†

"Among the most important issues affecting the world's future is the rapid growth of human population. Together, the increase in population and in resource consumption are basic causes of human suffering and environmental degradation and must become major priorities for national and international action.

"Because of its pervasive and detrimental impact on global ecological systems, population growth threatens to overwhelm any possible gains made in improving human conditions. Failure to curb the rate of world population growth will magnify the deterioration of the Earth's environment and natural resources and undermine economic and social progress. A humane, sustainable future depends on recognizing the common ground between population and the environment.

"Current national and international efforts to address the world's rapidly expanding population are not sufficient. A new commitment to population programs which enhance human rights and conditions is urgently needed. The United States and all nations of the world must make an effective response to the issue of population growth a leading priority for this decade."

---

† This statement evolved from cooperative efforts by various environmental and population organizations in 1991 as part of the preparations for the International Conference on Population and Development in Cairo, 1994.

Signatories as of September 5, 1991

African Wildlife Foundation

American Association of Zoological Parks and Aquariums

The American Fisheries Society

The American Humane Association

American Institute of Biological Sciences

American Wildlands

Dr. Betsy Ancker-Johnson, *Vice President, Environmental Activities, Staff, General Motors Corporation**

Nancy Anderson, *Director, New England Environmental Network**

P. W. Anderson, *Nobel Prize for Physics 1977**

Aspen Airport Business Center Foundation

Aspen Center for Environment Studies

Dr. Albert A. Bartlett, *Professor Emeritus of Physics, University of Colorado at Boulder**

Edwin L. Bierman MD, *Professor of Medicine, University of Washington**

Mary Lynne Bird, *Director, American Geographical Society**

Dr. Stephanie J. Bird, *President, Association for Women in Science**

Nicolaas Bloembergen, *Harvard University, Nobel Prize for Physics 1981**

Norman E. Borlaug, *Nobel Peace Prize 1970**

Lester R. Brown, *President Worldwatch Institute**

The Bulitt Foundation

Rodger W. Bybee, *Associate Director, Biological Sciences Curriculum Study**

Californians for Population Stabilization

Carrying Capacity Network

Center for Immigration Studies

Center for Population Options

Centre for Development and Population Activities

Ralph J. Cicerone, *Geosciences Department, School of Physical Sciences, University of California at Irvine**

Michael Clark, *President, Friends of the Earth**

Philander Claxton, *The World Population Society**

Conservation Council for Hawaii

Conservation International

Dr. Stanley J. Cristol, *National Academy of Sciences, Professor of Chemistry, University of Colorado at Boulder**

Herman E. Daly, *Economist, Environment Department, World Bank**

Wayne H. Davis, *Professor, School of Biological Sciences, University of Kentucky**

Agnes Denes, *Executive Committee, Global Forum**

Robert A. Duce, *Dean of the Graduate School of Oceanography, University of Rhode Island**

EarthKind, USA

Educational Foundation of America

Dr. Paul R. Ehrlich, *Professor of Population Biology, Stanford University**

Dr. Gertrude B. Elion, *Scientist Emeritus—Burroughs Wellcome Company, Nobel Laureate in Medicine**

Environmental Defense Fund

John W. Farquhar, *Stanford Center for Research in Disease Prevention**

Ann Farris, *President, Global Art and Business**

The Federation for American Immigration Reform

Dr. John Firor, *National Center for Atmospheric Research**

Florida Wildlife Federation

George T. Frampton, Jr., *President, The Wilderness Society**

Fund for the Feminist Majority

Chris Glenny, *President, New Hampshire Wildlife Federation**

Otis L. Graham, Jr., *Professor of History, University of California at Santa Barbara**

Ambassador Marshall Green

LaDonna Harris, *President, Americans for Indian Opportunity Association**

Helen Mayer Harrison, *Professor of Visual Arts, University of California at San Diego**

E. Richard Hart, *Executive Director, Institute of the North American West**

Denis Hayes, *President, Green Seal**

Donald S. Heintzelman, *President, Wildlife Information Center, Inc.**

Hazel Henderson, *Author and economic futurist**

Ernest M. Henley, *Professor of Physics; Director, Institute for Nuclear Theory, University of Washington**

Tina Hobson, *Executive Director, Renew America**

Carroll Ann Hodges, *U.S. Geological Survey**

John P. Holdren, *Professor of Energy and Resources, University of California at Berkeley**

Howard L. Hosick, *Professor of Genetics, Washington State University**

John A. Hoyt, *President, The Humane Society of the United States*

Institute for Alternative Agriculture

Interfaith Council for the Protection of Animals and Nature

Island Foundation

Gomer E. Jones, *President National Institute for Urban Wildlife**

Dr. Jerome Karle, *Naval Research Laboratory, Nobel Prize for Chemistry 1985**

Daniel R. Katz, *Executive Director, Rainforest Alliance**

Donald Kennedy, *President Emeritus, Stanford University**

Jan Konigsberg, *Executive Director, Alaska Conservation Foundation**

David Kramer, *President, Environmental Literacy Group**

Gerald P. Kruth, *Board member, Rachel Carson Homestead**

John F. Kullberg, *President, The American Society for the Prevention of Cruelty to Animals**

Steven C. Kussmann, *Chairman, Alliance for Environmental Education**

John H. Larsen, Jr., *Electron Microscopy Center, Washington State University**

The Lazar Foundation

Leon M. Lederman, *Professor of Physics, University of Chicago**

Donald R. Leah, *President, Global Tomorrow Coalition**

Lighthawk, the Environmental Airforce

L. Hunter Lovins, *President, Rocky Mountain Institute**

Jim Maddy, *Executive Director, League of Conservation Voters**

Lynn Margulis, *Professor of Botany, University of Massachusetts, Amherst**

Milenko Matanovic, *Director, Pomegranate Foundation**

Jean Mayer, *President Tufts University**

Ian L. McHarg, *Professor, University of Pennsylvania, National Medal of Art 1990**

Joseph D. McInerney, *President, National Association of Biology Teachers**

Charles W. McNeil, *Professor of Zoology, Washington State University**

Thomas W. Merrick, *President, Population Reference Bureau**

Ministry for Population Concerns

William J. Nagle, *President, Nagle and Associates**

National Audubon Society

National Council of Jewish Women

National Energy Associates, Inc.

National Science Teachers Association

National Wildlife Federation

Natural Resources Defense Council

Negative Population Growth

New England Biolabs Foundation

William A. Nitze, *President, The Alliance to Save Energy**

Oregon Wildlife Federation

Richard L. Ottinger, *Professor of Law, Pace University Law School, Former member of Congress**

Robert W. Parry, *Distinguished Professor of Chemistry, University of Utah**

Patagonia

Pathfinder International

Dr. Linus Pauling, *Linus Pauling Institute of Science and Medicine, Nobel Prize for Chemistry 1954, Nobel Peace Prize 1962**

People for the Ethical Treatment of Animals

Russell W. Peterson, *President Emeritus, National Audubon Society**

Planned Parenthood Federation of America

Fred O. Pinkham, *The David and Lucile Packard Foundation**

Population Communication

David O. Poindexter, *President, Population Communications International**

The Population Council

Population Crisis Committee

Population-Environment Balance

The Population Institute

Barbara Y.E. Pyle, *Vice President, Environmental Policy, Turner Broadcasting Systems**

Rainforest Action Network

Peter H. Raven, *Director, Missouri Botanical Garden**

J. Wayne Reitz, *President Emeritus, University of Florida**

Burton Richter, *Stanford Linear Accelerator Center, Nobel Prize for Physics 1976**

Martin J. Rosen, *President, Trust for Public Land**

Roger W. Sant, *Chairman, The AES Corporation**

Charles C. Savitt, *President, Center for Resource Economics/Island Press**

John C. Sawhill, *President, The Nature Conservancy**

Paul O. Schroeder, *Professor of Zoology, Washington State University**

David Seals, *Sovereignty Organizing Committee, Lakota Nation**

Maurice M. Shapiro, *Professor of Physics, University of Maryland, Naval Research Lab for Cosmic Physics**

Sierra Club

Dr. Robert Singer, *Coolidge Center for Environmental Leadership**

James Gustave Speth, *President, World Resources Institute**

Ann C. Stephens, *Vice President, Compton Foundation**

Christine Stevens, *President, Animal Welfare Institute**

Sunnen Foundation

Switzer Foundation

Elizabeth Thorndike, *President, Center for Environmental Information**

20/20 Vision National Project

Abigail Van Buren, *Nationally syndicated columnist**

Vermont Natural Resources Council

Konrad Von Moltke, *Professor of Environmental Studies, Dartmouth College**

Frank Weeden Foundation

Dr. David O. Wiebers, *Chair of the Scientific Advisory Council, The Humane Society of the United States**

Wildlife Conservation International

Wildlife Management Institute

The Wildlife Society

Richard Wilke, *Past President, North American Association for Environmental Education**

Dr. Grant R. Wilkinson, *Professor of Pharmacology, Vanderbilt University**

Dr. Edward O. Wilson, *Harvard University, Medal of Science 1976, Pulitzer Prize 1979, 1991**

Dael Wolfle, *Professor Emeritus, University of Washington**

Henry C. Wolking, *Professor of Music, University of Utah**

World Federalist Association

The World Population Society

World Wildlife Fund

The Wray Charitable Trust

Molly Yard, *President, National Organization for Women**

Marvin Zelen, *Harvard School of Public Health**

Zero Population Growth

Organizations/honors listed for identification purposes only

Selected Readings

• indicates works excerpted in this Norton Critical Edition

Malthus' Life and Works

Bonar, James. *Malthus and His Work*. London, 1886.
James, Patricia D., ed. *Population Malthus, His Life and Times*. London: Routledge & Kegan Paul, 1979.
Peterson, William. *Malthus*. Cambridge, Mass.: Harvard University Press, 1979.
Turner, Michael, ed. *Malthus and His Time*. New York: St. Martin's Press, 1986.
Winch, Donald, ed. *Malthus*. Cambridge, UK: Cambridge University Press, 1987.
———, ed. *An Essay on the Principle of Population*. 2nd ed. Cambridge UK: Cambridge University Press, 1987.
Wrigley, Anthony, and David Souden, eds. *The Works of Thomas Robert Malthus*. London: Pickering and Chatto, 1986.
A number of Web sites are devoted to Malthus, Malthusianism, and population studies.

Part IV. Malthus in the Twenty-First Century

A. Population Growth in the Twenty-First Century

• Brown, Lester R., Gary Garner, and Brian Halweil. *Beyond Malthus: Nineteen Dimensions of the Population Challenge*. New York: W. W. Norton & Company, 1999.
• Catton, William R. Jr. *Overshoot: The Ecological Basis for Revolutionary Change*. Urbana and Chicago: University of Illinois Press, 1982.
• Ehrlich, Paul R., and Anne H. Ehrlich. *The Population Explosion*. New York: Simon & Schuster, 1990.
Population Reference Bureau. *World Population Data Sheet*. Washington, D.C.: issued annually.
Schofield, Roger, and David Coleman, eds. *Population Theory: Forward from Malthus*. Oxford, UK: Blackwell, 1986.
United Nations. *Population and Environmental Change: The State of World Population 2001*. New York: United Nations, 2001.

B. Population and Food Supplies in the Twenty-First Century

Brown, Lester R. *The Agricultural Link: How Environmental Deterioration Could Disrupt Economic Progress*. Washington, D.C.: Worldwatch Institute, 1997.
———. *Who Will Feed China?* New York: W. W. Norton & Company, 1995.
Feder, Gershon, and Andrew Keck. *Increasing Competition for Land and Water Resources: A Global Perspective*. Washington, D.C.: World Bank, 1995.
Food and Agriculture Organization. *The State of World Fisheries and Aquaculture, 1996*. Rome: Food and Agriculture Organization, 1997.
• Gardner, Gary. *Shrinking Fields: Cropland Loss in a World of Eight Billion*. Washington, D.C.: Worldwatch Institute, 1996.

308   SELECTED READINGS

International Food Policy Research Institute. *Fourth Report on the World Nutrition Situation*. Geneva: International Food Policy Research Institute, 1999.
Sen, Amartya, and Jean Dreze. *Hunger and Public Action*. Oxford, UK: Clarendon Press, 1989.

C. Population and Water Supplies in the Twenty-First-Century

Abramovitz, Janet N. *Imperiled Waters, Impoverished Future: The Decline of Freshwater Ecosystems*. Washington, D.C.: Worldwatch Institute, 1996.
Barbash, Jack E., and Elizabeth A. Resek. *Pesticides in Ground Water*. Chelsea, Mich.: Ann Arbor Press, 1996.
Barzilay, Joseph I., Winkler G. Weinberg, and J. William Eley. *The Water We Drink*. New Brunswick, N.J.: Ruters University Press, 1999.
Gardner-Outlaw, Thomas, and Robert Engelman. *Sustaining Water, Easing Scarcity (A Second Update)*. Washington, D.C.: Population Action International, 1997.
Gleick, Peter H. *The World's Water 2000–2001*. Washington, D.C.: Island Press, 1998.
• Postel, Sandra L. *Last Oasis: Facing Water Scarcity*. New York: W. W. Norton & Company, 1997.
———. *A Pillar of Sand*. New York: W. W. Norton & Company, 1999.
Rosegrant, Mark. *Water Resources in the Twenty-First Century: Challenges and Implications for Action*. Washington, D.C.: International Food Policy Research Institute, 1997.
Seckler, David, et al. *Water Scarcity in the Twenty-first Century*. Colombo, Sri Lanka: International Water Management Institute, July 27, 1998.

D. Population and Energy Supplies in the Twenty-first Century

Brown, Kathryn S. "Bright Future—Or Brief Flare—For Renewable Energy?" *Science*, July 30, 1999.
Casten, Thomas R. *Turning Off the Heat: Why America Must Double Energy Efficiency to Save Money and Reduce Global Warming*. Amherst, N.Y.: Prometheus Books, 1998.
Dunn, Seth. "Decarbonizing the Energy Economy." In Lester R. Brown, Christopher Flavin, and Hilary French, eds. *State of the World 2001*. New York: W. W. Norton & Company, 2001, pp. 83–102.
———. *Hydrogen Futures: Toward a Sustainable Energy System*. Washington, D.C.: Worldwatch Institute, 2001.
Engelman, Robert et al. *People in the Balance: Population and Natural Resources at the Turn of the Millennium*. Washington, D.C.: Population Action International, 2000.
"The Future of Fuel Cells" (special issue). *Scientific American* (1999).
• Pimentel, David, and Marcia Pimentel, eds. *Food, Energy and Society*. Niwot, Colo.: University Press of Colorado, 1996.

E. Population and the Environment in the Twenty-first Century

Bryant, Dirk, Daniel Nielsen, and Laura Tangley. *The Last Frontier: Forests, Ecosystems and Economics on the Edge*. Washington, D.C.: World Resources Institute Institute, 1997.
Durning, Alan. *How Much Is Enough?* New York: W. W. Norton & Company, 1992.
Ehrlich, Paul R., and Anne H. Ehrlich. *Betrayal of Science and Reason*. Washington, D.C.: Island Press, 1996.
Hansen, James, et al. "Global Warming in the Twenty-First Century: An Alternative Scenario." *Proceedings of the National Academy of Sciences*, 16 June 2000, 1–6.
National Academy of Sciences. *Population Summit of the World's Scientific Academies*. Washington, D.C.: National Academy of Sciences, 1993.
Pimentel, David. "Skeptical of the Skeptical Environmentalist." *Skeptic*, 9 (2002), 90–94.
Wackernagel, Mathis, and William Rees. *Our Ecological Footprint*. Philadelphia: New Society Publishers, 1996.
Wigley, Tom M. L. *The Science of Climate Change: Global and U.S. Perspectives*. Arlington Va.: Pew Center on Global Climate Change, June 29, 1999.
Wilson, Edward O. *The Diversity of Life*. New York: W. W. Norton & Company, 1992.
Worldwatch Institute. *State of the World* and *Vital Signs*. New York: W. W. Norton & Company, published annually.

F. Population and Social Dynamics in the Twenty-first Century

• Brown, Lester. "The Emergence of Demographic Fatigue." In Lester R. Brown, Gary Gardner, and Brian Halweil, eds., *Beyond Malthus: Nineteen Dimensions of the Population Challenge*. New York: W. W. Norton & Company, 1999, pp. 111–137.

Homer-Dixon, Thomas, and Valerie Percival. "The Project on Environment, Population, and Security." In *Environmental Scarcity and Violent Conflict: Briefing Book*. Washington, D.C.: American Association for the Advancement of Science, 1996, pp. 6–10.

International Labour Organization. *Jobs for Africa: A Policy Framework for an Employment-Intensive Growth Strategy*. Geneva: 1997.

International Labour Organization. *World Employment 1996/97*. Geneva: 1997.

Klare, Michael T., and Daniel C. Thomas, eds. *World Security: Challenges for a New Century*. New York: St. Martin's Press, 1994.

Mandel, Robert. *Conflict Over the World's Resources*. New York: Greenwood Press, 1988.

Nowak, Mark W. *Our Demographic Future: Why Population Policy Matters to America*. Washington, D.C.: Negative Population Growth, 1998.

Pimentel, David, et al. "Ecology of Increasing Disease: Population Growth and Environmental Degradation," *Bioscience* (1998), 1–24.

G. Some Contemporary Critics of Malthusianism

Esterlin, Richard. *Growth Triumphant*. Ann Arbor: University of Michigan Press, 1996.

Kasun, Jaqueline. *The War Against Population*. San Francisco: Ignatius Press, 1988.

• Lappé, Frances Moore, Joseph Collins, and Peter Rosset. *World Hunger: 12 Myths*. New York: Grove Press, 1998.

Lomborg, Bjorn. *The Skeptical Environmentalist*. Cambridge, UK: Cambridge University Press, 2001.

• Ross, Eric B. *The Malthus Factor*. London and New York: Zed Books, 1998.

Sen, Amartya. *Development as Freedom*. New York: Anchor Books, 1999.

• Simon, Julian. *The Ultimate Resource 2*. Princeton, N.J.: Princeton University Press, 1996.

H. Rethinking Endless Population Growth

• Bulatao, Rodolfo A. *The Value of Family Planning Programs in Developing Countries*. Santa Monica, Calif.: RAND, 1998.

• Cohen, Joel E. *How Many People Can the Earth Support?* New York: W. W. Norton & Company, 1995.

Ehrlich, Paul. *Human Natures*. Washington, D.C.: Island Press, 2000.

• Engelman, Robert, Brian Halweil, and Danielle Nierenberg. "Rethinking Population, Improving Lives." *State of the World 2002*. New York: W. W. Norton & Company, 2002.

Grant, Lindsey. *Too Many People: The Case for Reversing Growth*. Santa Ana, Calif. Seven Locks Press, 2000.

• Hardin, Garrett. *Living within Limits*. New York: Oxford University Press, 1993.

Rohe, John. *A Bicentennial Malthusian Essay: Conservation, Population and the Indifference to Limits*. Traverse City, Mich.: Rhodes & Easton, 1997.

• Smail, J. Kenneth. "Remembering Malthus: A Preliminary Argument for a Significant Reduction in Global Human Numbers." *American Journal of Physical Anthropology* 118 (2002), 292–97.

Index

316 INDEX

　　tary on, 137–61; in twenty-
　　first century, *see* twenty-first
　　century, Malthus in
Population Bomb (Ehrlich), 216
"Population Challenge, The"
　　(Brown), 168–73
population control, 209; birth
　　control, *see* birth control; by
　　"moral restraint," xx; Roman
　　Catholic Church and, xxxi
population growth, xiii, xvi, xxvii,
　　xxix–xxx, xxxi, 168–73, 215,
　　233–34, 235, 241–42, 293;
　　eradicating hunger and, 190–
　　95; rethinking endless, 247–
　　58; in the twenty-first
　　century, xxv, xxxiii, 163–84;
　　zero, 260, 275
Population Issues: Briefing Kit
　　(UNFPA), 251–52
Portugal, 44
Postel, Sandra, 197–203
poverty, xxviii–xxix, 7, 127–28,
　　190, 237–38
Price, Dr. Richard, 44*n*, 46–47,
　　49, 50, 66, 108–9, 109–11
Principles of Political Economy
　　(Mill), xxiii, 148–53, 257–58
"Priority Statement on Popula-
　　tion" (1991), 301–5
Progress and Poverty (George),
　　xxiv

Quito, 43–44

rationality, 84–88
Raynolds, Laura, 235
"Remembering Malthus: A Pre-
　　liminary Argument for a Sig-
　　nificant Reduction in Global
　　Human Numbers" (Smail),
　　274–83
"Rethinking Endless Population
　　Growth," xxviii–xxix

"Rethinking Population, Improv-
　　ing Lives," 283–89
Ricardo, David, xiii–xiv, xxii, xxiii
Roman Catholic Church, xxxi,
　　243–45, 284
Ross, Eric B., 237–39
Rosset, Peter, 233–37
Rousseau, Jean Jacques, xiii, xiv
Russell, Bertrand, 208
Russia, 30, 49
Russian Revolution, 239
Rwanda, 221

Seckler, David, 199, 227
Senior, Nassau W., xviii*n*, xxii,
　　xxiii, 140–43
Shaw, George Bernard, 158–61
Shelley, Percy Bysshe, xxv
Short, Dr., 49–50
*Shrinking Fields: Cropland Loss
　　in a World of Eight Billion*
　　(Field), 185–88
Silent Explosion, The (Apple-
　　man), xxix
Silent Spring (Carson), xxi
Simon, Julian, 212–13, 218, 219,
　　240–43
Singapore, 265
*Sketch for a Historical Picture of
　　the Progress of the Human
　　Mind* (Condorcet), 8*n*, 55–
　　59
Smail, J. Kenneth, 274–83
Smith, Adam, xv, xvi, 6–8, 18,
　　32, 44, 53, 93, 94, 99–105,
　　106, 108
social dynamics in the twenty-
　　first century, xxvi–xxvii, 221–
　　32
Solomon, 121
"Some Contemporary Critics of
　　Malthusianism," xxvii
South Africa, 222, 288–89
South Korea, 225, 265
space ship, emigration by, 182–83